# THE GENTLE REVOLUTION

WITHDRAWN

ALSO WRITTEN, PRODUCED OR
CO-AUTHORED BY HELENA CORNELIUS

## BOOKS
*Everyone Can Win* (Simon & Schuster)
*Conflict Resolution Trainers' Manual: 12 Skills* (Conflict Resolution Network)
*Conflict Resolution Trainers' Manual: 8 Sessions* (Conflict Resolution Network)
*Mediation Training for Teenagers: A Trainer's Manual* (Conflict Resolution Network)
*Conflict Kit* (Conflict Resolution Network)
*CR School Community Inservice Manual* (Conflict Resolution Network)

## RESOURCES
*The Resolution of Conflict*, audio tape series (Australian Broadcasting Commission)
*CR Essentials Training*, video (Conflict Resolution Network)
*Negotiation and Mediation Training*, video (Conflict Resolution Network)
*Conflict Resolution Key Concepts*, video (Conflict Resolution Network)
*Conflict Resolution Skills Workshop*, video (Conflict Resolution Network)
*Active Listening with a Child*, video (Conflict Resolution Network)

# THE GENTLE REVOLUTION

## Men and women at work—
## what goes wrong and how to fix it

### HELENA CORNELIUS
#### CONFLICT RESOLUTION NETWORK

SIMON & SCHUSTER

AUSTRALIA

THE GENTLE REVOLUTION

First published in Australia in 1998 by
Simon & Schuster Australia
20 Barcoo Street, East Roseville  NSW 2069

A Viacom Company
Sydney  New York  London  Toronto  Tokyo  Singapore

© Helena Cornelius 1998
Cartoons © John Bates 1998

All rights reserved. No part of this publication may be
reproduced, stored in a retrieval system, or transmitted,
in any form or by any means, electronic, mechanical,
photocopying, recording or otherwise, without the prior
permission of the publisher in writing.

National Library of Australia
Cataloguing-in-Publication data

Cornelius, Helena.
    The gentle revolution : men and women at work — what goes
    wrong and how to fix it.

    Bibliography.
    Includes index.
    ISBN 0 7318 0571 2.

    1. Communication — Sex differences. 2. Sex role in the work
    environment. 3. Conflict management. 4. Men — Employment.
    5. Women — Employment. I. Title.

302.35

Cover design: Anna Soo, Joseph Loewy
Original cover illustration: Evert Ploeg; adapted by Joseph Loewy
Cartoons: John Bates
Internal design: Siobhan O'Connor
Typset in 10/13 pt Sabon
Printed in Singapore by South Wind Production(s) Pte Ltd

# CONTENTS

# PREFACE

Men and women argue, more than is necessary, about the wrong things and often at cross-purposes.

> I am seven years old. It's late and I'm in bed. My head is under the sheets. Tears are on my cheeks. The door to my bedroom is closed. Its translucent brown glass offers no protection from the raised voices of my parents arguing in their bedroom down the hall. My father is yelling. My mother clips her words and sounds coldly precise. They work together, partners in a fashion business. They are quarrelling about whether to take a half-page or a full-page ad in the Sunday newspaper.

Or were they? Perhaps the argument was really about money, or about power, or about whether or not they loved each other. About whether, as a man, he had a right to expect his wife to give in. About whether she, equally committed in time and risk, should have equal say in important decisions. What I sensed, but as a child couldn't possibly have explained, was that there was a heck of a lot going on underneath this disagreement over an apparently trivial topic.

Conflicts between men and women often trigger underlying agendas. Rarely are these truly understood or adequately addressed. My purpose in writing *The Gentle Revolution* is to peel back some of the layers of cross-gender conflict and, considering both the surface and the underlying issues, look at what it takes to improve mutual respect, cooperation and resolution. Much is relevant from what I have already gleaned from twelve years of writing, teaching, consulting and managing for the Conflict Resolution Network. But the topic of gender conflicts stretches me, and I hope you, too, to develop new understandings and techniques.

Researching this book has been a period of intense inquiry. I've listened to the problems from both men's and women's perspectives. All of my friends and the many people I've met while researching this book have been enormously generous with their time, chatting into my tape recorder, telling their stories, heartaches and triumphs, offering their views on the emerging nature of gender-based conflicts today. The examples I've used here are based on real experiences and real issues, but to protect anonymity I've altered the descriptions of organisations and people. My heartfelt thanks also go to the more than 500 people who responded to my questionnaires on gender-related attitudes and values. The results of these surveys have guided many of the comments I make.

While I've confined myself here to the arena of the workplace, I believe the principles apply in families and friendships, too. This book is written for both women and men. I care enormously about the inequalities of opportunity and discrimination many women face. But my sympathy is equally with many men who are left angry, mystified, misunderstood or hurt by conflicts with the opposite sex. I wish my father — he died eighteen years ago — could have read it. He was a magnificent human being who won most of his battles (except with my mother), but he really was a lousy arguer. He'd demolish his opposition, leaving many who crossed him quivering wrecks. Then he'd go into the kitchen and overeat. Conflicts that don't end well tend to have that sort of effect. Some of us drink too much, smoke, use drugs, take it out on our nearest and dearest or, at best go shopping! May this book provide you with the extra skills to hang on in there, fight fair, work it out and build relationships rather than destroy them.

## LANGUAGE

We probably cannot make one definitive statement about 'all men' or 'all women'. So I aim to talk only of trends and create a model with enough flexibility to include the many exceptions — hence so many 'probablys', 'oftens' and 'mights' in the text. If ever I have left one out to make a point more forcefully, please read one between the lines.

I have made a distinction not always apparent in common usage. In this book, the adjectives *female* and *male* denote sex type, and *feminine* and *masculine* refer to psychological qualities which might reside in either sex. In order not to limit discussion, I often indicate the person by the *value* that is motivating them at the time, to avoid naming a specific *gender*. For instance, an *equaliser* will often, but not always, be a woman. A *status-watcher* will often, but not always, be a man.

My comments are relevant to the cross-*value* conflict. This is often, but not always, a cross-*gender* conflict.

When I use terms such as *equaliser* and *status-watcher*, I am not regarding them as permanent descriptions of the person. They are temporary roles we may move into and out of, depending on how broad the range of circumstances is in which the value is significant to us.

## STEREOTYPING

I've trodden as carefully as I can in the minefield of stereotypes. However, there are bound to be a few explosions in the text waiting for you to discover. They're inevitable in any book on gender issues. We each carry inside us our own norms for men and women, even though we ourselves probably don't completely fit our norm for our own sex. Yet consciously or unconsciously, we will often mould our own behaviour to fit our version of an accepted sex-role stereotype. We know people are 'norming' when they say things like: 'That's just like a man', or 'Women shouldn't be like that'. There's not much point saying we shouldn't norm or stereotype. We do it. It's how we make sense of our world and form yardsticks for judging our own and other people's behaviour, even though those judgments are often the source of tension and conflict.

Gender stereotypes are artificial generalisations, but each of us creates a personal set of them nonetheless. In part, we build them from our own unique experiences, but we also absorb them through the shared culture of the society in which we find ourselves.

# PART I
## INTRODUCTION

# 1 WHAT IS THE GENTLE REVOLUTION?

## PREVIEW

▶ The quest for wholeness

▶ The struggle

▶ Undervaluing the feminine

▶ Nature versus nurture — reflections on the great debate

## THE QUEST FOR WHOLENESS

While each of us has, I believe, locked within us the seeds of both the masculine and feminine principles, the feminine principle has been dormant in most men through many centuries of patriarchal dominance. But now a societal shift is under way. Individually and collectively we are reassessing feminine qualities and their role in the modern workplace. This reappraisal is the gentle revolution. Men need permission from their culture to honour the gifts of the feminine quite as desperately as women do.

What will be the benefits of this gentle revolution?

▶ Better relationships between men and women.
▶ Workplaces empowered with a richer mix of skills and strengths.
▶ The freedom for both men and women to draw on their true selves and to express that in their daily lives.

One side of our nature balances the other. Deep fulfilment comes from drawing forth unexplored aspects of ourselves to create that balance and to unfold the whole of who we really are.

Patriarchal society and its traditional requirement that men be chief provider for the family have placed crippling demands on both men and women to develop only one side of themselves. As women free their masculine side through participation at work, men can free their feminine side. Indeed, the two processes must go hand in hand.

Men are just beginning to wage their half of the revolution. Freeing men's feminine side is still dangerous and costly. Their difficulties in making this transition prolong first, their own entrapment in a confining gender role and second, their underestimation of women's contributions in the workplace.

Workplaces are challenging the modern woman to draw on her masculine side — her focus on goals, initiative and participation in hierarchies. Her potential benefit is empowerment. However, a woman's quest for wholeness through work demands that her workplace honours not only her emerging masculine nature but also her feminine, otherwise she may ultimately face despair and self-alienation.

Good managers work in remarkably similar ways regardless of their gender. If they truly understand the integration they themselves have achieved, they will foster its development in others also, creating a climate of respect for the gifts from both the masculine and the feminine.

Societal shifts are slow and often painful. Individuals live them out in their daily conflicts. The gentle revolution makes for turbulent times in which both men and women have work to do.

## THE STRUGGLE

Many women regard workplaces as alien territory. The excitement and glamour of trying to make it in a man's world have worn off. Promised opportunities have not eventuated. A disturbingly large number of apparently successful women want out. Here is Libby's story:

> I took months thinking about it, but on Monday I woke up and just knew I'd decided. I handed in my letter of resignation.
>
> 'Why?' was all my boss said when he read it.
>
> 'I've had enough, Bill. To get to the top round here you've got to tread on other people. I just can't stand it any more,' I said.

*Many women regard the*
*workplace as alien territory*

'Had an argument with the latest beau?' he asked.

'No, Bill. I didn't.' I get so tired of this sort of put down. 'I'm dead serious. Success in this company is about control. Whoever has the control has the power.'

Bill didn't say anything to that. I think he was a bit stunned. I'm one of his top executives. But I don't think he sees what's going on. I tried again.

'This isn't a snap decision. It's about goals, Bill, life goals. I want to take my hands off the wheel — not manipulate, not manoeuvre, not ingratiate. I've had enough of it for one lifetime.'

Bill just looked at me over the top of his reading glasses.

'Bill, I need to run my life with integrity, and I can't do that around here,' I said.

*He looks exhausted,* I remember thinking. *He looks like I feel.* Fundamentally, he's a really decent guy. They all are if you get them alone.

At first Libby had loved the challenge, proving herself, playing up there with the big boys. But she'd always have to watch her back, or she'd be brushed aside in meetings that counted, or find her ideas ignored unless she fought for them tooth and nail. She had tried to play by her perception of their rules. Yet others manoeuvred in ways she would never contemplate and landed promotions she felt they didn't deserve. The power politicking that seemed so necessary was just not her. Her gentle revolution, her struggle to contribute the gifts of the feminine in a masculine workplace system had worn her out. She was repeatedly defeated in gender conflicts. She'd failed to consolidate respect for her contributions. She couldn't change the corporate culture.

As a result, Libby's organisation has lost a first-rate employee. She plans to start her own private consultancy. She's got the know-how to succeed. It's an answer that many women executives are choosing when their gentle revolution fails to take hold.

Sally is a 28-year-old journalist who writes for a small specialist newspaper. She's in the midst of the struggle. She says:

> I can't stand the constant battles to get my ideas into print. My perspectives aren't appreciated.

Talent is not Sally's problem. I think she's an excellent journalist. I've read her work. Her problem is the culture of her workplace. To Sally, it seems the world of journalism runs on relentless opposition and hierarchical power. It is highly relevant to her that all the senior managers on the newspaper are men.

Sally is hanging in there — just. She believes change is best effected by working within the system. If she is not to lose heart, she needs to understand the causes of her gender-linked conflicts. She needs to know her own stumbling blocks and how to step over them. To win, she needs skills that suit her egalitarian style.

## UNDERVALUING THE FEMININE

Women are by no means the only campaigners in the gentle revolution. I sat at a dinner party chatting about the feedback I was getting from women such as Libby and Sally. Jonathan itched to comment:

Don't think the patriarchal system works for us either. It's soul destroying trying to be the macho, go-get-it male that the culture demands. My biggest difficulties are not with my women colleagues, but with other men. [Much head-nodding from the two other men at the table. They were listening closely.]

Our office is smallish, only twelve of us. We make computer graphics for the video industry. Joe's our head honcho. He called us four senior guys into his office for a meeting. We're computer artists. We could all work freelance or get another job anywhere, but we choose to work together so we can jointly pay for the infrastructure we need in the marketplace. In our company, the administration work happens to be done by women.

Joe wanted the meeting to discuss the rerouting of initial client contacts. As a job came in, it would first go through Joe. Well, Joe's very busy. Sometimes he doesn't attend to client call-backs fast enough.

'Let's have Marge field the calls and get them off to one of you immediately. Then, if you're not the right person, you pass it on,' he said.

'This could cause a problem with the commission system and the time logging,' I said.

'You want us to go on just as we are?' Joe sounded sarcastic. He can be like that.

'No, Joe, I'm definitely not saying that. I just think we should discuss it with everyone first,' I said.

'You're a wimp, Jonathan. Being a boss means you just tell people what they have to do. What's to discuss?'

'I'd rather talk to Marge and Carol first before we decide. I reckon it needs a new recording system,' I said.

'Got to ask Mum if it's okay, do you?' I shut up. I can't get round Joe when he gets into one of his macho moods.

In this commercial art company, participative practices don't exist. Joe's a forceful character. If he says you're a wimp if you consult, you'll stop consulting pretty fast. Jonathan needs more skills to handle this sort of bullying. Though Libby's workplace paid lip service to participation, it was more an invitation to do battle than to participate. *Give us your idea and we'll shoot it down in flames.* Hardly an effective way to nurture creative spirit!

Libby is keen to develop a more constructive mix of competition and cooperation when she is in charge of her own consultancy. Sally's organisation issues demoralising unexplained vetos on her suggestions. Sally doesn't know how to engage support.

Conflict resolution skills are essential for men and women engaged in the gentle revolution. However, alone they are not enough. These three organisations are out of balance. There are many more like them. Participative decision-making, nurturing ideas and people, valuing all members of the work team are missing ingredients. These organisations have failed to develop and respect feminine-style process and have failed to value the people who could best deliver it.

It's not a conscious or sinister plot to keep women 'in their place'. The men in these organisations are not women haters, but neither are they women valuers. Many would not dare to be. They'd be misunderstood and sidelined. In undervaluing feminine preferences, communication styles and skills, we under-utilise the human resources of both men and women. The resistance to men balanced in both their masculine and feminine qualities is still entrenched. Jonathan expressed it like this:

*In undervaluing feminine preferences, communication styles and skills, we under-utilise the human resources of both men and women.*

> I guess I have a very feminine perspective in some respects. I've been rubbished if I worry about how our employees are going to feel about receiving directives with no chance to contribute their own ideas. What that means is they're really asking me to disconnect from a part of myself that's alive and well and wants to be acknowledged. It is very hard to be authentic in that situation.

Of course, even in highly patriarchal workplaces, some women do break through the glass ceiling — that invisible barrier which prevents women rising to the top of organisational hierarchies. But to do so, many have taken on the qualities of the stereotyped male and appear disconnected from their feminine side. Many control with a dominating operating style. It's obvious to us that some aberration has occurred when we see women like this. The tragedy is that when we see men behaving this way, we regard it as normal. It's not normal. It's no more in balance for a man than it is for a woman. The solution to such dilemmas used to be simple. Men were supposed to develop the masculine principle and women the feminine. But this was at a huge cost to women, which they no longer tolerate, and at a huge cost to men, which they are only just beginning to articulate. We are ready for new solutions. I believe we'll find them in people achieving their full potential from the dynamic balance of both masculine and feminine within.

Women are in search of workplace situations where they can be authentic and act from the whole of their natural selves. Men, too, in rethinking the sole provider role and the relentless pressure of money-defined success, are searching for less rigidly defined gender roles and the freedom to be authentic.

## NATURE VERSUS NURTURE –
## REFLECTIONS ON THE GREAT DEBATE

The gentle revolution is under way. Its promise is authenticity and wholeness. Many of our conflicts, and not just those between men and women, are part of the struggle for a new equilibrium of traditionally masculine and traditionally feminine perspectives.

Can we really free ourselves from constraining gender roles? As we consider this, we are thrown squarely into the nature–nurture debate. Elizabeth Grosz puts the dilemma like this:

> Sex role theories must either assume a natural/biological/evolutionary explanation, an explanation in terms of the species; or see the individual as the result of 'conditioning' or 'learning' imprinting.[1]

Let's score this debate as we look at both sides of the argument.

*Both men and women can learn to make a sponge cake or drive a forklift truck.*

Both men and women can learn to make a sponge cake or drive a forklift truck. Yet we identify making the sponge cake as a more likely task for a woman and driving the forklift truck as a more likely task for a man. How fundamental are biological differences in the development of these expectations? Margaret Mead in *Sex and Temperament* showed that despite biological differences there are very different ways in which men and women in isolated, primitive societies divide up male and female tasks.[2] In some societies, for instance, men take a more sedentary role and women a more active one.

*Score: Nurture — 1*

In 1976, Dorothy Dinnerstein wrote that the core fact to be dealt with was the 'predominantly female responsibility for the early care and education of neonatally, immature, slow-growing, intelligent young'.[3]

*Score: Nature — 1*

Or maybe not! Many young men today reject this role division.

> Richard, a new father, was furious that he was treated as an outsider in an early childhood parenting class. Literature distributed in the class which exhorted mothers to let their male partners be involved in nappy-changing and feeding irritated him, because he didn't just want to *dabble* in parenting his young baby. He wanted equal responsibility.

We are moving towards greater individual freedom of expression than ever before. As women move into and stay in the workforce and men respond by taking on more household and child-nurturing tasks, we are blurring the sharp distinctions between men's and women's roles. While we respond to the culture of society, we also influence it.

*Score: Nurture — 1*

However, many a mother will attest to definite differences in the behaviour of male and female children. Here is my own experience.

> I've had three children — two girls and then a boy. Toys my husband and I provided our girls with included not only dolls and dolls' houses, but also trucks, soccer balls and battery-operated cars. We had the theory of balancing feminine and masculine covered, or so we thought. In reality, however, our daughters always reached for the dolls and the dolls' houses, while as soon as our son could crawl, he located the dusty trucks and cars under the bed, at the bottom of the toy box or rusting in the sandpit. The girls' cast-offs were his treasures. Our son indicated his preferred 'masculine' toys from the moment he had enough mobility to express that choice.

*Score: Nature — 1*

For the first six weeks of life of an embryo, there are no discernible distinctions between male and female brains. It has been said that structurally the brain is the same in the foetuses of both sexes and that we all start life with a female brain. It is the release of male hormones, androgens, triggered by the genetic programming in a male baby which, from about the sixth week, begins to change the growth pattern of a male embryo's brain.

*Score: Nature — 1*

By adulthood, some physiological differences in male and female brains are objectively observable. They have shown up in biopsies. For instance, the corpus callosum, the connecting pathway between the left and right hemispheres, has been found to be more substantial in women than in men.[4]

Psychological differences can also be measured in tests of some abilities and preferences. Men tend to perform better on mathematical problems demanding analytic thinking. Women tend to do somewhat better in tests which require responsiveness to sensory information. Statistically, slightly more men than women prefer to operate from their logical, reasoning side and slightly more women than men prefer to operate from feeling, intuitive, relational perspectives. The average score differences between men and women on some aptitude tests are as great as 25 per cent.[5]

*Score: Nature — 1*

Usually, however, the problem in generalising about differences is that the overlap in scores is so great. The picture is not straightforward. Equivalent education for boys and girls is rapidly minimising differences in aptitude and abilities. Interest, conscious learning, environmental influences and even fluctuations in hormonal levels alter our expertise. Even at a purely biological level we are very similar and capable of the most extraordinary adaptations to our environment. A baby suckling on a man's nipple has been known to produce lactation!

*Score: Nurture — 1*

Physiology and culture interact dynamically. Modern brain surgery techniques combined with high-powered microscopes are unravelling the mysteries of learning. As we learn something new in response to life's challenges or the pursuit of our goals, the neurones in our brain forge new pathways.[6] Structural changes are constantly occurring within our brain. This process continues throughout life. We're beginning to discover just how fluid is the interaction between nature and culture.

Only 150 years ago, slavery was acceptable, work relationships were structured on severe hierarchical lines, and women were subordinate to men and denied equal power and status in public. The dominance–submission pattern so strongly evident in many species of animal has also been very much a part of human culture. However, while these genetic patterns tell us about our propensities, we must also consider our ability to adapt. Other possibilities also reside in our genetic makeup.

*The dominance–submission pattern so strongly evident in many species of animal has also been very much a part of human culture.*

Societal demands, education and habit can impact on the individual, causing psychological and, we now suspect, corresponding physiological change. The flexibility available to us gives us opportunities for resolving conflicts between the sexes in new and expansive ways.

Carl Sagan and Ann Druyan in *Shadows of Forgotten Ancestors* write:

> Many ancient voices speak within us. We are capable of muting some, once they no longer serve our best interests, and amplifying others as our need for them increases. This is cause for hope.[7]

*Final score: Undecided*
*Awaiting further evidence*

▼▼▼

As society changes, we are seeing more scope for movement in gender roles and expertise than in any other period of history. Now *feminine* and *masculine* as terms are just loose net bags for temporary storage of concepts. We are constantly reassessing what we'll keep and what we'll throw out of these bags.

Can we break free of genetic patterns and cultural rigidities evolved thousands of years ago to ensure our species' survival in conditions very different from those we face today? The gentle revolution is in the process of proving we can.

# SUMMARY

► Workplaces challenge the modern woman to draw on her masculine side — her goal focus, initiative and participation in hierarchies. The potential benefit is empowerment.

► Women's quest for wholeness through work demands that their workplaces honour not only their emerging masculine nature, but also their feminine, otherwise they are ultimately bound for despair and self-alienation.

► Most workplaces perpetuate the suppression of some parts of ourselves and an overemphasis on others. The more extreme this is, the more alienated we feel as we are forced to act out society-defined roles.

► Workplaces that undervalue feminine preferences, communication styles and skills, under-utilise the human resources of both men and women.

► The gentle revolution rebalances and re-evaluates feminine qualities to stand alongside masculine ones.

► Both men and women are increasingly rejecting traditional gender roles.

► We are beginning to appreciate the dynamic inter-action between nature and nurture, and the vast potential for development that lies within each one of us.

# 2  THE VALUES– GENDER LINK

The twentieth century has released women to the workforce. Women, in general, enter the twenty-first century in better health, with more energy and more time freed from domestic chores than at any previous point in history. The numbers of foetal, infant and child deaths have plummeted. Modern contraception enables planned pregnancies. Technology has lightened the load of housework. Workplace work is no longer seen as an episode in a woman's life. In fact, child-rearing and full-time homemaking are more likely to be seen as the short episode and work as the stable pattern.

As a result, our concepts of masculine and feminine roles and qualities are shifting. The edges are blurring. The crossover increases yearly. It's a revolution alright. Is it already complete or is the merging of roles still in progress? In my early interviews for this book, I often asked: 'Do you think men and women behave the same?'

I asked this question of both men and women. 'No way', 'You're joking' were the answers time after time. However, when I asked people to be precise about these differences, they became vague.

The next step in my inquiry was a survey to capture some of these differences statistically. With the help of a market researcher, my research assistant and I designed and sent out a questionnaire to around 200 men and women.[8] By our deadline, more than 140 people had replied. We were staggered with the response rate. People are either very interested in the topic or feel very guilty if you give them a stamped envelope and they don't use it! Detailed analysis of some results is contained in Appendix 1 (see the number references in square brackets below).

## SURVEY RESULTS AND
## THE QUESTIONS IT RAISES

The survey summaries lay before us like scattered pieces of a jigsaw. We had also amassed hundreds of pages of notes on gender differences. 'What does it all *mean*?' we asked each other. At first, the huge variety of problems men and women encounter with each other seemed to defy classification, but we began to group some ideas.

▶ *Men and women disagree about the way women approach work.* Nine out of ten women think the two sexes approach their work differently, yet only seven out of ten men are of the same opinion.[9] Are women more aware of real differences or are they hypersensitive to slight nuances? Women are going into a male-defined workplace: they're likely to be more aware of differences. Perhaps past socialisation or political correctness has scared some men out of talking or even thinking about differences they might observe. [1]

▶ *Women feel they are often undervalued in the workplace.* Eight out of ten women experience a glass ceiling blocking their chances of promotion. Only five out of ten men observe this. Nine out of ten women notice that they have to do better than men to receive adequate recognition. Seven out of ten men indicate they are aware of this. The inequity undoubtedly causes conflict. The gentle revolution, the equal valuing of the feminine alongside the masculine, is certainly not complete. [2, 3]

▶ *Many women believe they are paid less than they're worth.*
Nine out of ten women believe they undervalue themselves
when asking for a raise. What does this say about women's self-
confidence? Or is it that asking for more money puts a strain on
their sense of fairness and equality? Only four out of ten men
agree that women undervalue themselves. Does this mean that
men often place a lower value on women's contributions than
men's? Women still earn less than men, on average.[10]      [4]

▶ *While being respected is very important for both sexes, it seems
to be particularly important for men.* Seven out of ten men
regard it as more important than being liked. Six out of ten
women believe it is more important to be liked than respected.
Status seemed to have a significantly higher priority for men
than friendship. Women are less concerned with status. Six out
of ten women won't do what their boss asks if they disagree
with it. Significantly more men say that they will follow orders
even if they disagree.                              [5, 6, 7]

▶ *Women will frequently alter their behaviour around men, in
order to try to please them.* Eight out of ten women report
this. In follow-up interviews, a number of women describe how
they let men lead the conversation, 'as they usually want to
anyway'.                                                    [8]

▶ *Women often dislike giving orders.* Eight out of ten women would
rather reach agreement than instruct. However, almost half of
the men feel they are often told what to do by women!      [9]

▶ *More women than men seem to prefer agreement-oriented
conversations.* Six out of ten women prefer compromise to
argument, but only four out of ten men prefer compromise.
Seven out of ten women believe they are more likely than men
to work on ensuring problems don't arise.              [10, 11]

▶ *For many men the link between achievement and self-worth
seems very close.* Establishing worth is an important part of a
man's communication process. Most of the women surveyed
believe men like to talk about their achievements more than

women do. The large majority of men agree. One of our interviewees, a woman, suggested: 'This is one of the ways men are competitive in conversation. They like to top each other. They compete about who's best.' Seven out of ten men dislike others boasting. In follow-up interviews, some report that in order to put the other person back in their place, men will often outdo the boast with one of their own.          [12, 13]

▶ *Men usually put their jobs before their families.* The majority of men and women surveyed agree on this. It seems that men are more goal- than feeling-focused. Most people surveyed believe women usually put their families before their jobs.[11] Women express their focus on nurturing and intimacy most easily in personal relationships. Women's emotional life appears to be very important to them.          [14, 15]

▶ *Women are more likely than men to be affected by unresolved conflict.* While both men and women find it stressful to work with someone they dislike, more women find it highly stressful to do so.          [16]

▶ *For men, the other person's feelings often have a lower priority than the task at hand.* Men often don't take time out to praise others. Two-thirds of the women surveyed believe they receive more praise from other women than from men. Here's the rub, however. Few men in our sample believe that they receive more praise from women than from men. Are a lot of men ignoring the praise they receive from women? Do men value other men's praise far more? Or are women praising other women and not men? Do highly task-focused men look as though they don't need praise?          [17]

▶ *Women appear to be more alert to the mutual interdependence of a work team.* Women are somewhat more focused on other people than men seem to be. The results indicating that women tend to praise more and attend more often to potential problems before they blow up supports this. It's relevant to note, however, that men did not perceive these qualities in women.          [11, 17]

▶ *Men tend to be more independent.* Close to half of both men and women believed men preferred working independently.     [18]

▶ *Men seem to have a greater desire for and/or ability to achieve autonomy regarding family finances.* In our sample, the majority of men were the main financial provider of their household compared with only half of the women.     [19]

Gradually, the raw data began to take form. I continued listening to people recounting workplace clashes with their opposite sex. Slowly I began to see that there were a limited number of major concepts under which most of these conflicts could be classified. Differences in underlying values emerged repeatedly from my notes. They offered clues to the apparent intractability of many gender conflicts. Values clashes are notorious for defying solution.

---

**I now believe that most arguments that people assume have a 'gender' component are rooted in apparently incompatible values.**

The purpose of the rest of this book is to explain how these differences in values contribute to conflict and to offer some win/win solutions. In the midst of this revolution in gender roles and behaviours it becomes increasingly important for us to:

▶ notice;

▶ name, at least for ourselves; and

▶ become skilled at resolving the values issues underlying the substance of many problems men and women face in working together.

---

## WHAT ARE VALUES?

The *World Book Dictionary* defines *values* as 'the established ideals of life, objects, customs, ways of acting, and the like that the members of a given society regard as desirable'. The *Shorter Oxford English Dictionary* adds an extra dimension to our usage:

'That which is worthy of esteem for its own sake; that which has intrinsic worth.' This definition casts some light on why values cause so many conflicts. People often disagree on *what* value has the most intrinsic worth in a situation.

Values are our rules for the road. They determine what behaviours and paradigms we regard as acceptable. They colour our perceptions of morality, beauty, justice, sound practice and fair play. They underlie our decision-making about goals as well as our methods of achieving them. Values determine mind-set, offer a consistency of behaviour over time and govern the 'how' as well as the 'what' of behaviour. They are the mechanism behind the clock face, the workings of what we loosely call 'personality'.

The degree of our commitment to a value indicates how core to our personality it is, and gives some indication of how flexible or inflexible we are, and hence how hard it will be to find a meeting ground in a conflict situation.

Dr Greg Tillet believes we express values as:

▶ preferences;

▶ opinions;

▶ beliefs; and

▶ principles.[12]

This list follows our increasing commitment to the value we hold and indicates how deeply it resides in the core of our personality. (See **Figure 1: Common values terminology**, p. 19.)

People hold some values consciously, such as being for or against abortion, or for or against gun control. But often people take their values for granted. These unconscious values emerge only when the person reflects on why they choose to act in a particular way, perhaps in response to being questioned. These unconscious viewpoints are often expressed in very personal terms. Don't expect a handy label.

For example, Al was often very irritated at office brainstorming sessions and sometimes refused to attend. 'Waste of time! Garbage in, garbage out!' was his personal explanation of his problem. Only when questioned more deeply did he begin to consider other issues that were contributing to his reaction. What then emerged

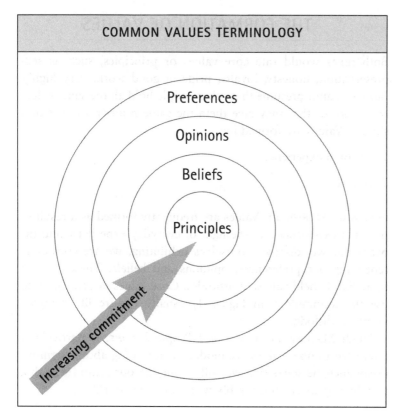

Figure 1: Common values terminology

was that the slow progress made in brainstorming sessions blocked his need to plan future directions quickly and independently. He was extremely frustrated by the wait for team consensus.

## THE FORMATION OF VALUES

Both sexes would rate core values or principles, such as self-preservation, honesty, loyalty, pride in good work, very highly. But we cannot presume that other people hold all the same values as we do, or that they give them the same priority, or that they should. Values are formed by:

1. personal experience

2. culture

PERSONAL EXPERIENCE: Values are frequently formed as a result of personal experiences. In the light of everyday experience and the behaviour we 'discover' ourselves exhibiting, we are constantly redefining our preferences, opinions and beliefs. These are our more lightly held values or attitudes. Core values or principles (to use the terminology in Figure 1) usually require life-changing events to dislodge.

Hugh Mackay, in *Why Don't People Listen?*, is particularly interested in how values are modified. In writing about cognitive dissonance, he states that we will '... modify our attitudes so that they line up more comfortably with our behaviour'.[13]

CULTURE: Children learn values, openly or by implication, from others who hold that value; for example, in the family or at school. As we have seen, men and women have usually grown up in and continue to be affected by different subcultures. These subcultures influence our values and the order of importance they hold for us. Certainly there is a large overlap. Men's and women's lives are different, but not *that* different.

## GENDER VALUES QUIZ

Enough theory! Let's get personal. Can we tease out some of your own values? You might like to take a few moments to rate yourself on a number of behaviours that frequently feed back into values and often line up with gender differences.

# Gender values quiz

Circle the number that most closely represents the answer that best applies in your workplace.

| | Statement | 0 Never | 1 Very rarely | 2 Rarely | 3 Some-times | 4 Quite often | 5 Often | 6 Always |
|---|---|---|---|---|---|---|---|---|
| 1 | When introduced to someone at work, I think it is important to indicate your level of experience. | 0 | 1 | 2 | 3 | 4 | 5 | 6 |
| 2 | I enjoy being competitive with others in work-related projects. | 0 | 1 | 2 | 3 | 4 | 5 | 6 |
| 3 | I prevent interruptions when I'm busy. | 0 | 1 | 2 | 3 | 4 | 5 | 6 |
| 4 | I prefer the responsibility of working alone on a task rather than as part of a team. | 0 | 1 | 2 | 3 | 4 | 5 | 6 |
| 5 | I am uncomfortable when I have to give a direct order. | 0 | 1 | 2 | 3 | 4 | 5 | 6 |
| 6 | I actively focus on restoring harmony when there's been a conflict. | 0 | 1 | 2 | 3 | 4 | 5 | 6 |
| 7 | If I have a major personal problem, I prefer to talk it over with colleagues. | 0 | 1 | 2 | 3 | 4 | 5 | 6 |
| 8 | I prefer to discuss work problems with others rather than solve them alone. | 0 | 1 | 2 | 3 | 4 | 5 | 6 |
| 9 | I'm unconcerned if someone at work doesn't like me, as long as I have their respect. | 0 | 1 | 2 | 3 | 4 | 5 | 6 |
| 10 | I like being motivated by chal-lenges where you must prove you're better than someone else. | 0 | 1 | 2 | 3 | 4 | 5 | 6 |

| | Statement | 0 Never | 1 Very rarely | 2 Rarely | 3 Some-times | 4 Quite often | 5 Often | 6 Always |
|---|---|---|---|---|---|---|---|---|
| 11 | When chatting, I prefer to talk about things and activities rather than personal matters. | 0 | 1 | 2 | 3 | 4 | 5 | 6 |
| 12 | If I'm confused, I try to work it out myself rather than ask for help or advice. | 0 | 1 | 2 | 3 | 4 | 5 | 6 |
| 13 | If I disagree with an explicit order, I debate it or find a way to get around it. | 0 | 1 | 2 | 3 | 4 | 5 | 6 |
| 14 | Unresolved conflict makes me very uncomfortable. | 0 | 1 | 2 | 3 | 4 | 5 | 6 |
| 15 | If someone appears to be upset, I'll find an opportunity to let them talk about it with me. | 0 | 1 | 2 | 3 | 4 | 5 | 6 |
| 16 | If I come across new information, I go out of my way to share it with my colleagues. | 0 | 1 | 2 | 3 | 4 | 5 | 6 |
| 17 | I like it if my work status is higher than that of others around me. | 0 | 1 | 2 | 3 | 4 | 5 | 6 |
| 18 | I enjoy challenging someone's point of view and seeing if I can win. | 0 | 1 | 2 | 3 | 4 | 5 | 6 |
| 19 | I get annoyed with people who let their emotions interfere with their effectiveness. | 0 | 1 | 2 | 3 | 4 | 5 | 6 |
| 20 | When I know what needs to be done, I find that consultation in the workplace isn't worth the time it takes. | 0 | 1 | 2 | 3 | 4 | 5 | 6 |

| | Statement | 0<br>Never | 1<br>Very<br>rarely | 2<br>Rarely | 3<br>Some-<br>times | 4<br>Quite<br>often | 5<br>Often | 6<br>Always |
|---|---|---|---|---|---|---|---|---|
| 21 | If I've got to discipline someone at work, I start or finish with an apology. | 0 | 1 | 2 | 3 | 4 | 5 | 6 |
| 22 | I would rather compromise than create an argument | 0 | 1 | 2 | 3 | 4 | 5 | 6 |
| 23 | I rely on gut feeling more than logic when making difficult decisions. | 0 | 1 | 2 | 3 | 4 | 5 | 6 |
| 24 | I would be hurt if a close colleague spoke against a project of mine when other important people are present. | 0 | 1 | 2 | 3 | 4 | 5 | 6 |

© Copyright Helena Cornelius, *The Gentle Revolution* (Simon & Schuster, Australia, 1998).
For further information contact: The Conflict Resolution Network, PO Box 1016,
Chatswood NSW 2057, Australia. Tel.: +61 (0)2 9419 8500. Fax: +61 (0)2 9413 1148.
This quiz may be reproduced for non-commercial use if this credit appears.

## GENDER VALUES QUIZ: SCORE SHEET

Now insert your score for each statement beside the question number. You will end up with a score for the following eight values.

### FEMININE STYLE

| Equality | |
|---|---|
| Q.5 | |
| Q.13 | |
| Q.21 | |
| Subtotal 1 | |

| Agreement | |
|---|---|
| Q.6 | |
| Q.14 | |
| Q.22 | |
| Subtotal 2 | |

| Feeling | |
|---|---|
| Q.7 | |
| Q.15 | |
| Q.23 | |
| Subtotal 3 | |

| Interdependence | |
|---|---|
| Q.8 | |
| Q.16 | |
| Q.24 | |
| Subtotal 4 | |

Grand total
Feminine values
(Add subtotals 1, 2, 3 & 4)

### MASCULINE STYLE

| Status | |
|---|---|
| Q.1 | |
| Q.9 | |
| Q.17 | |
| Subtotal 5 | |

| Competition | |
|---|---|
| Q.2 | |
| Q.10 | |
| Q.18 | |
| Subtotal 6 | |

| Actions and objects | |
|---|---|
| Q.3 | |
| Q.11 | |
| Q.19 | |
| Subtotal 7 | |

| Autonomy | |
|---|---|
| Q.4 | |
| Q.12 | |
| Q.20 | |
| Subtotal 8 | |

Grand total
Masculine values
(Add subtotals 5, 6, 7 & 8)

© Copyright Helena Cornelius, *The Gentle Revolution* (Simon & Schuster, Australia, 1998).
For further information contact: The Conflict Resolution Network, PO Box 1016,
Chatswood NSW 2057, Australia. Tel.: +61 (0)2 9419 8500. Fax: +61 (0)2 9413 1148.
**This gender values quiz and score sheet may be reproduced for non-commercial use if this credit appears.**

## Interpreting your results

The values in the left column of the gender values quiz score sheet represent a more feminine style and those in the right column a more masculine style.

▶ Compare your grand total scores. Were your scores higher on masculine or on feminine values? Do you think that is an accurate assessment of where you stand?

▶ Did you score about the same on both grand totals? Would you say that you are fairly evenly balanced in masculine and feminine values?

▶ Is there a large discrepancy between your two grand total scores? It may indicate that you don't fit one style (masculine or feminine) very well. Would you agree with this? Does this explain any conflicts in which you've been involved?

▶ A subtotal of more than eleven probably indicates this value is rather important to you. Is this true?

▶ A mix of some high scores on both masculine and feminine values could point to some internal conflicts. Do your scores help you to identify any? For example, if you have high scores on both 'status' and 'interdependence', you may sometimes be anxious about how to get adequate respect from people with whom you also want warm human interaction.

*SOME POINTS TO THINK ABOUT:*

▶ Please keep in mind that we are not talking about sexuality here, but differences in perceived styles.

▶ Don't be surprised or concerned if as a woman you score highly on a number of masculine values or as a man you score highly on a number of feminine ones. However, if you sometimes feel out of step with your same-sexed peers or with expectations from the opposite sex, perhaps your scores offer some explanation.

▶ You may have noticed that the values are arranged in pairs. For example, the feminine style of 'equality' corresponds with the masculine style of 'status', and so on. While your scores may align with your own sex's style across a number of the pairs, it is very likely you do not fit the style for your sex across all pairs of values. In reality, almost no one has a completely feminine or masculine style. These styles are stereotypes that live inside our heads. It is very important to note this.

© Copyright Helena Cornelius, *The Gentle Revolution* (Simon & Schuster, Australia, 1998).
For further information contact: The Conflict Resolution Network, PO Box 1016,
Chatswood NSW 2057, Australia. Tel.: +61 (0)2 9419 8500. Fax: +61 (0)2 9413 1148.
This page may be reproduced for non-commercial use if this credit appears.

If you are able to persuade others to answer the quiz or you are working through this book in a group, you could hold some very interesting discussions on how well you and others fit and diverge from the stereotypes and why that might be so.

## DIFFERING PERSPECTIVES

*The stereotypes live inside our heads. Rarely do they match external reality completely.*

If you have completed the quiz, you will have had an experiential preview of the eight values around which gender-related problems most frequently occur.

These gender-linked values cluster in pairs, apparently opposing each other, creating conflicts that are difficult to resolve because they arise from very different perspectives. Conflicts are often surface manifestations of differences in deeply held beliefs about how the world works.

The perspectives measured in the quiz aim to cover four key areas: use of power, interacting style, focus of attention and comfort zone. While both men and women are likely to hold the same values in these areas, there is often a difference in the *priority* they will give a value. We frequently simplify decision-making by using only the value with the highest priority as our guide.

There is enough consistency in these different priorities to influence our stereotypes — our own internal norming process — of what we call *feminine* and what we call *masculine*.

| FEMININE–MASCULINE MATRIX | | |
|---|---|---|
| PERSPECTIVES | FEMININE STEREOTYPE | MASCULINE STEREOTYPE |
| Use of power: | Equality | Status |
| Interacting style: | Agreement | Competition |
| Focus of attention: | Feeling | Actions and objects |
| Comfort zone: | Interdependence | Autonomy |

*Figure 2: Feminine–masculine matrix*

In the process of arriving at these eight gender-linked values, I grouped and regrouped my survey, interview and literature research many times. I believe these eight values crystallise what men and women are most frequently arguing about in the workplace. Although I present them to you as hypotheses rather than fact, I do not stand alone in unscrambling masculine and feminine values in this way. Appendix 2 outlines some related research that corroborates my interpretations.

In times of conflict, these values may express as opposite polarities. The polarisation is emphasised with the following acronyms:

| VALUES AS POLARITIES | |
|---|---|
| FEMININE STEREOTYPE | MASCULINE STEREOTYPE |
| **S**ame<br>*(Equality)* | **D**ifferent<br>*(Status)* |
| **I**nclusive<br>*(Agreement)* | **E**xclusive<br>*(Competition)* |
| **F**eeling<br>*(Focus on feeling)* | **A**ction<br>*(Focus on actions & objects)* |
| **T**ogether<br>*(Interdependence)* | **L**one<br>*(Autonomy)* |

*Figure 3: Values as polarities*

This SIFT–DEAL model is useful as a simplified explanation of common gender-based conflicts. A word of caution, however! The values are *not* mutually exclusive. Your scores on the previous quiz probably proved this. The eight values can also be considered as related dimensions (see **Figure 4: Values as dimensions**, page 29). When not pressured, most people will fall somewhere close to centre, holding both values in each pair, though in their own individual mix.[14]

However, I believe that when a particular value is called into question during a conflict, people tend to polarise and move to

opposing extremities — their conflict corner. At these times, particularly when they are in opposition to someone of the opposite sex, many men may align more closely with values from the stereotypically masculine style, women with values from the stereotypically feminine style.

If we move to our conflict corner, a polarised extreme, we are liable to play out the conflict as a win/lose game. Whoever shouts louder or has the greater power or manipulates best, wins. On the day it can seem great, but winning when the other person is losing sows the seeds for resurrection of the conflict. In the workplace, resurrections are just as dangerous as they are in a politically unstable government. They can cost us a repeat order, a promotion, or our job. They can isolate us from our peers and poison cooperative effort. Long-term solutions that won't backfire or break down will usually require us to acknowledge and accommodate other people's values as well as our own. Each of the eight gender-linked values is inherently valid in itself, and has much to contribute to workplace success. Each value needs due consideration and respect. *This is the essence of the win/win approach to conflict resolution.* I'm deeply committed to this approach to gender conflicts because I believe that masculine and feminine perspectives together create solutions that are whole, balanced and therefore viable in the long term.

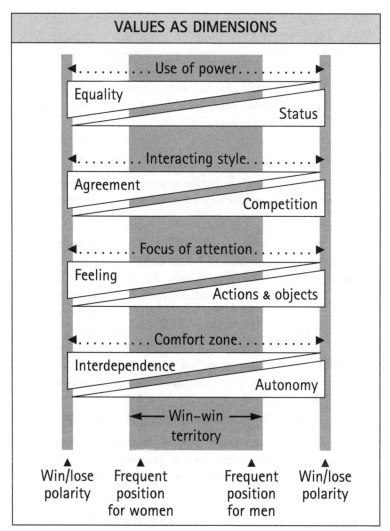

Figure 4: Values as dimensions

## DANGERS OF STEREOTYPING

We do form opinions of men in general and women in general. We base them on frequently observed behaviour. They help our sifting, sorting and re-evaluation process. Roger Fisher and Scott Brown, in *Getting Together*, say:

> We organise ideas into mental images and theories to help us interpret events and behaviour. It is essential to categorise and generalise. We cannot analyse every bit of information about everyone.[15]

But there are enormous individual differences. Almost no one sits right on the norm about everything they believe. What a boring world we'd live in if everyone did!

We must beware of thinking too much in stereotypes. It can blind us to real here-and-now contact. Fisher and Brown continue:

> Our tendency to prejudge can damage or preclude a working relationship when it determines whether, or how we interact with others.[16]

*Interpretations of masculine and feminine values can be dynamite if misused. But they can also be the building blocks for better relationships.*

Far from encouraging the *error of stereotyping* — using oversimplified and unvarying images of people — knowledge of this model can prevent it. We will not make assumptions simply because that person is male or female. We can use these concepts to assess more accurately the gender-related characteristics of a person we are dealing with. The model alerts us to gender stereotyping when we meet it in others. If others are presuming you, as a man or as a woman, will hold certain values or will behave in certain ways, you'll become skilled at gauging this and nipping misconceptions in the bud. Interpretations of masculine and feminine values can be dynamite if misused. But they can also be the building blocks for better relationships. We should note that:

▸ *We are looking at tendencies only.* A number of boys and girls will grow up with influences more common to their opposite sex. As adults, they are then likely to take on the values more usual in their opposite sex, even in conflict.

▸ *Circumstances direct which value is uppermost.* Circumstances may lead to a woman putting a traditionally masculine value ahead of the more feminine one she usually espouses. Circumstances may cause a man to be passionate about a traditionally feminine value such as equality, even when he is demanding respect for his status.

Getting to know a particular person's gender culture is valuable for conflict resolution, just as getting to know a Vietnamese or Arabic person's racial culture can be valuable, if it is very different from our own. But to overcome any tendency to prejudge from limited information, we need to take the advice offered by Blainey, Davis and Goodwill in *Valuing Diversity*: 'Each person is a culture.'[17]

*Each person is a culture.*

> Culture [involves] a number of factors. These include gender, age, profession, skills, birthplace, nationality, habits, hobbies, abilities, experiences, preferences as well as ethnicity, race and religion.
>
> When we take into account all the factors noted above we realise that within each person is a great deal of diversity... We each have our own traditions and at different stages of our lives might choose to identify with different aspects of ourselves.[18]

Gender-linked values will give us some clues to help us resolve conflict, but we're going to need to know much more about that person in particular. Most people in modern societies today have the freedom, if not necessarily the skills, to create their own individual and unique culture — as unique as a fingerprint or voiceprint. We master the influence of culture once we truly understand its impact.

▼▼▼▼

Research gives us some evidence that the eight values discussed are linked frequently to gender, but it certainly cannot tell us about how all men and women should be or what they could become. In our masculine stereotype we tend to group together the values of status, competition, actions-and-objects focus and autonomy. In our feminine stereotype, we're likely to include equality, agreement, feeling focus and interdependence. Yet I know, and I'm sure you do too, some men who put a greater focus on one or a number of values on the feminine list. I'll bet you also know some women who are very influenced by status, competition, actions-and-objects focus or autonomy.

While we base stereotypes on our intuitively assessed norms, these are constantly changing. What we might have perceived as a norm for men or women only ten years ago is probably not as clear-cut today. The objective of the gentle revolution is to balance the masculine and feminine within organisations and ultimately within each person. This process is fast-tracked when we handle cross-gender conflict successfully. To do so requires that both masculine and feminine values are validated and advanced.

*The objective of the gentle revolution is to balance the masculine and feminine within organisations and ultimately within each person.*

Decision-making based on the complexity of values this entails demands our emotional maturity. New solutions that meet both masculine and feminine priorities must emerge. When we get it right, it sure looks like wisdom!

## SUMMARY

> ▶ **Values** are expressed through preferences, opinions, beliefs and principles. They often underlie decision-making about goals and methods of achieving them.
> ▶ **Formation of values** is based on personal experience and culture.
> ▶ **Male and female differences:** While both men and women are likely to hold similar values, there is often a difference in the priority they will give a value.
> ▶ **Feminine priorities:** Women often tend to give a higher priority to equality, agreement, feeling and interdependence.
> ▶ **Masculine priorities:** Men often tend to give a higher priority to status, competition, actions and objects and autonomy.
> ▶ **Stereotypes live inside our heads.** They rarely match external reality completely.
> ▶ **The objective of the gentle revolution** is to balance the masculine and feminine within organisations and within each person.

## OVERVIEW OF VALUES

The following eight tables expand on each value in **Figure 2: Feminine–masculine matrix**, page 26. They summarise Parts II–V of this book and provide an overview for the key discussion areas that follow. Glance at them now to get your bearings. They'll become more meaningful as you read on. You may want to refer back to them as a quick reference.

# Perception of power

**Equality:** often a higher priority for women. Conforms to feminine stereotype.[19]

| Characteristics | Good intentions | Stumbling blocks | Common conflict triggers |
|---|---|---|---|
| Prefer to share power with others rather than use power over them<br><br>Create a level playing field<br><br>Want equality of opportunity<br><br>Measure with a yardstick of fairness<br><br>Tolerate different viewpoints<br><br>See everyone as basically the same<br><br>Consult<br><br>Seek power for the opportunity to self-actualise | Supporting the rights of friends and colleagues<br><br>Avoiding arousing others' jealousy<br><br>Using fairness as a yardstick for evaluating<br><br>Negotiating from a win/win perspective<br><br>Encouraging others' participation in decision-making | Being too modest<br><br>Taking offence at inequality<br><br>Continued resentment<br><br>Intolerance of high-fliers<br><br>Insubordination<br><br>Being indecisive | Others engage in power plays<br><br>Others demand blind obedience<br><br>Their skills and abilities are undervalued<br><br>A situation seems to be extremely unfair |

*Figure 5: Overview — equality*

**Status:** often a higher priority for men. Conforms to masculine stereotype.[20]

| Characteristics | Good intentions | Stumbling blocks | Common conflict triggers |
|---|---|---|---|
| Shoulder responsibility<br><br>Measure status by output, position, resources or strength<br><br>Test relationships to check their relative standing<br><br>Accept legitimate authority<br><br>Validate hierarchies<br><br>Observe power issues carefully<br><br>Regard people as basically different<br><br>Demand respect<br><br>Seek status as a yardstick for self-respect | Striving for self-improvement or self-reliance<br><br>Building self-respect<br><br>Creating a clear chain of command<br><br>Using a strategically sound approach<br><br>Supporting justice and law | Domination<br><br>Defensiveness and low self-esteem<br><br>Territory protection<br><br>Hunger for status symbols<br><br>Undervaluing others | They lose face<br><br>They are not shown due respect<br><br>Others are insubordinate<br><br>They are cast in subservient roles or relationships |

*Figure 6: Overview — status*

# Interacting style

**Agreement:** often a higher priority for women. Conforms to feminine stereotype.[21]

| Characteristics | Good intentions | Stumbling blocks | Common conflict triggers |
|---|---|---|---|
| Keep the peace<br><br>Emphasise similarities and common ground<br><br>Are urgent about concluding disagreements<br><br>Modify behaviour and suppress needs readily to fit in with others<br><br>Need harmonious teamwork for job satisfaction | Avoiding arguments where possible<br><br>Creating friendly work climates and bonded relationships<br><br>Responding to the needs of the team<br><br>Minimising conflict<br><br>Facilitating joint planning<br><br>Building trust | Arguments lost<br><br>People pleasing<br><br>Failure to achieve positive results from conflict<br><br>Stuck on sticky steps if not tough enough<br><br>Leadership expertise undervalued | Others use an adversarial style<br><br>Others refuse to address issues<br><br>Others won't give up entrenched issues<br><br>Others are in bad moods |

*Figure 7: Overview — agreement*

**Competition:** often a higher priority for men. Conforms to masculine stereotype.[22]

| Characteristics | Good intentions | Stumbling blocks | Common conflict triggers |
|---|---|---|---|
| Enjoy the challenge of competitive strategies<br><br>Value competition because it drives people forward and tests worth<br><br>Accept some aggression as part of the 'rough and tumble'<br><br>See interaction with others as inevitably competitive<br><br>Use and receive one-upmanship as a comfortable light-hearted way of relating | Thwarting a perceived attack<br><br>Pursuing a clear goal in the face of opposition<br><br>Responding to a challenge with plenty of energy<br><br>Proving they're intelligent, street-smart, a winner<br><br>Coming up with the best answer<br><br>Inviting relationship with playful teasing or baiting | Leadership style relies too heavily on warrior skills<br><br>Fear of being seen as an outsider to the pack<br><br>Alienation from others<br><br>Poor listening skills<br><br>Lack of support for those who could be potential threats | Their successes are not acknowledged<br><br>Others challenge their competitive style<br><br>There is no opportunity to prove themselves<br><br>They repeatedly fail when competing |

*Figure 8: Overview — competition*

# Focus of attention

**Feeling:** often a higher priority for women. Conforms to feminine stereotype.[23]

| Characteristics | Good intentions | Stumbling blocks | Common conflict triggers |
|---|---|---|---|
| Believe the feelings, and sometimes intuition or creativity, are what really matter | Considering other people's feelings | Extreme emotional reactions | People are not considered |
| Closely observe their emotions, creativity and intuition throughout the day | Supporting someone through a difficult time | Difficulty confronting others | Their emotions are ignored or not respected |
| Are relatively willing to disclose vulnerable feelings | Responding to anxiety, concern or injustice | Focus too open | Logic is used against them or others to manipulate or confuse |
| Believe workplace climates and processes should support employees | Communicating what really matters to them | Low resilience to other people's bad moods | Others offer advice, when they just want to be heard |
| Believe discussion of feeling cements a team | Building rapport | Stuck in resentment | |
| Use emotions as a guide to action | Working through emotions in order to move forward | | |
| Tolerate ambiguity and uncertainty relatively well | | | |
| See life as fundamentally an inner journey | | | |
| Try to extract emotional meanings from their experiences | | | |

*Figure 9: Overview — feeling*

## Focus of attention (continued)

**Actions and objects:** often a higher priority for men. Conforms to masculine stereotype.[24]

| Characteristics | Good intentions | Stumbling blocks | Common conflict triggers |
| --- | --- | --- | --- |
| Are happiest when they are doing something | Getting the job done | Task at the expense of people | Their judgment is questioned by others |
| Focus on the external world or the world of ideas | Moving forward quickly | Poor skills in the domain of feeling | Their action is blocked by others |
| Resist the expression of vulnerable emotions | Solving problems, taking responsibility | Contracted awareness under stress | Someone else's response is not well thought through |
| Focus almost exclusively on tasks and output when in the workplace | Dealing objectively with difficult situations | Snap decisions | Other people's emotions interfere with their effectiveness |
| Build rapport through the exchange of concrete information and conversations about acitivities and objects | Making conversation on non-emotional, non-threatening topics | Low tolerance for ambiguity | |
| Use logical thought to plan action | Avoiding being overwhelmed by emotions | Self-esteem achieved from what they do rather than who they are | |
| Are often willing to take risks | | | |
| Believe life is about mastery of objective facts and circumstances through action | | | |
| Aim for competence and want others to trust and respect their abilities | | | |

*Figure 10: Overview — actions and objects*

# Comfort zone

**Interdependence:** often a higher priority for women. Conforms to feminine stereotype.[25]

| Characteristics | Good intentions | Stumbling blocks | Common conflict triggers |
|---|---|---|---|
| Believe we don't get anywhere alone, nor do we have to | Planning with a team or wider system focus in mind | Too dependent on others | Others refuse to consult |
| See people as a resource for support, information and advice | Inviting interaction and support from others | Merged attachment to others inhibits personal power | The impact of an action on the whole team is not considered |
| Accept responsibility to care for others | Offering interaction and support to others | Alienated if others won't make real contact | Opportunities to interact with others are withdrawn or are not available |
| Place their own personal goals second to group goals | Trying to be patient with or tolerant of others | Creating 'them' and 'us' situations | Others don't take on or recognise a responsibility of care |
| Prefer a consultative approach | Self-revealing and open to others | Disadvantaged when negotiating | |
| Prefer collective group activity | Encouraging emotional closeness | Alienation from true self in bureaucratic workplaces | |
| Closely observe the patterns of interconnections between people | | | |
| Use their social context to define themselves | | | |

*Figure 11: Overview — interdependence*

## Comfort zone (continued)

**Autonomy:** often a higher priority for men. Conforms to masculine stereotype.[26]

| Characteristics | Good intentions | Stumbling blocks | Common conflict triggers |
|---|---|---|---|
| Aim to be an independent, powerful contributor to the organisation | Being self-reliant | Concern about invasion of autonomous areas | They are forced to depend on others *(eg. in group projects or because of infirmity)* |
| Like the freedom to make independent contributions | Avoiding being a burden on others | Resentment about taking orders or advice | Someone else who has responsibility does not use it well |
| Make tough decisions and see them through | Enjoying being different and individual | Inability to include others in decision-making processes | They have to accept orders or instructions |
| Prefer to have total responsibility for a task | Taking responsibility for leadership | Hidden dependence | How they work is too closely supervised |
| Form strong personal opinions | Responding to their own sense of timing | Inability to sustain contact | |
| Rise to leadership easily | Preventing themselves being diminished by another's opinion of them | | |
| Protect individual rights | | | |
| Value self-sufficiency and ego-strength, and expect others to act responsibly | | | |

*Figure 12: Overview — autonomy*

# PART II
# EQUALITY AND STATUS

## EIGHT COMMON CONFLICTS

*Equalisers' complaints:*
- ▶ 'They're wheeler-dealing power maniacs!'

- ▶ 'They just want yes men!'

- ▶ 'Why not me? I'm just as capable. Why can't they see that?'

- ▶ 'This is grossly unfair!'

*Status-watchers' complaints:*
- ▶ 'I'll show you! No way will you make me lose face.'

- ▶ 'How dare they speak disrespectfully to me!'

- ▶ 'I won't be disobeyed like that.'

- ▶ 'Make your own coffee. I'm not doing it.'

## Synopsis — where are we now?

Chapter 1 made the point that slowly, and sometimes painfully, we are beginning to shift workplace values towards the feminine. We reviewed how far changing culture is able to support this process, and whether biological differences predefine some limits.

In Chapter 2 we considered underlying differences in the priority given to a number of key values by many men and women, and their effects on our gender stereotypes. These are:

| PERSPECTIVES | FEMININE STEREOTYPE | MASCULINE STEREOTYPE |
|---|---|---|
| Use of power: | Equality | Status |
| Interacting style: | Agreement | Competition |
| Focus of attention: | Feeling | Actions and objects |
| Comfort zone: | Interdependence | Autonomy |

The arrows above indicate the discussion areas for the next three chapters.

While few people completely fit their own gender's stereotype, the distinctions pinpoint gender conflicts arising when men and women champion opposing values. We'll explore in detail equality and status, considering their differing use of power and the conflicts they generate.

# QUIZ

Circle the number in the column that best reflects your response to the following statements:

## Quiz 1

|  | RARELY | SOMETIMES | OFTEN |
|---|:---:|:---:|:---:|
| I prefer to work in a team, rather than be the leader. | 0 | 1 | 2 |
| I take action to oppose discrimination based on gender, race or age. | 0 | 1 | 2 |
| I am intolerant of arguments over privileges, such as company cars and exclusive lunch rooms. | 0 | 1 | 2 |
| I am uneasy when people seem to be putting me on a pedestal. | 0 | 1 | 2 |
| I judge a person more by how they treat others than by the position they hold in the workplace. | 0 | 1 | 2 |

Total:

+ =

## Quiz 2

|  | RARELY | SOMETIMES | OFTEN |
|---|:---:|:---:|:---:|
| I find it easy to issue firm orders to ensure a job is done efficiently. | 0 | 1 | 2 |
| I believe in respecting authority and not trying to challenge it. | 0 | 1 | 2 |
| I measure success in terms of position and salary more than creativity or usefulness. | 0 | 1 | 2 |
| I think it's better when one person takes charge, rather than everyone having their say. | 0 | 1 | 2 |
| People have to earn my respect. I don't give it out automatically. | 0 | 1 | 2 |

Total:

+ =

Add up your circled numbers for each quiz separately then compare the two scores.

If your score was higher in Quiz 1, you probably focus strongly on *equality*. If you scored higher in Quiz 2, you probably put more of a priority on *status*. If your scores were equal, you may swing between the two polarities, depending on the situation.

The next three chapters will tell you more about these qualities.

# 3 EQUALITY–STATUS: use of power

The first pair of values in the feminine–masculine matrix introduced in Chapter 2 is equality and status. In this chapter we'll compare their characteristics. The objective is to become more comfortable with the value that is not usually your own priority. We'll also consider how to locate the good intentions behind behaviour that might be disturbing to you. As equality and status play themselves out in the arena of power, we'll become familiar with how power is used and misused.

Chapter 4 is devoted to the stumbling blocks of those who have equality as a high priority, and Chapter 5 to the stumbling blocks associated with status. In both these chapters we consider stepping stones: possible solutions and conflict resolution skills.

By the end of Part II, you should have a better understanding of equality–status clashes and the improved skills to transform them into mutually successful encounters in the gentle revolution.

# CHARACTERISTICS: EQUALITY

The equality value is likely to influence behaviour and a range of related values in the workplace. I use the term *equalisers* to describe those people motivated by the value of equality at a particular time.[27] They are often, but not always, women. A number of characteristics cluster around the equality value. Equalisers:

▶ *Prefer to share power with others rather than use power over them.* There is no question about whether or not equalisers want power. Undoubtedly they do. Being powerless in the workplace is not an equal relationship. Equalisers are defined by their greater interest in jointly shared power rather than by total control. (Some, of course, will state they hold this value while their actions and language belie it.)

▶ *Create a level playing field.* Equalisers generally want a level playing field in the workplace. They are not against upward mobility in position and responsibility, but they are likely to resent privilege if it offers others an unfair advantage.

▶ *Want equality of opportunity.* Equalisers will frequently be strong supporters of equal employment opportunity and affirmative action programs. Not only might they demand that their own gender is not unfairly disadvantaged, they may also support moves against other common prejudices such as age, race and disability.

▶ *Measure with a yardstick of fairness.* Equalisers frequently judge what is right or wrong in a situation by what they regard as fair. 'That's not fair' is usually the complaint of an equaliser. (This is not always an objective assessment.)

▶ *Tolerate different viewpoints.* At their best, equalisers accept that not everyone will have the same perspective or come up with the same answers to a problem. They make allowance for this and will often have a wide acceptance of different styles.

▶ *See everyone as basically the same.* If they are totally consistent, an equaliser doesn't regard anyone as better or worse than anyone else. In truth, few of us are capable of this level of abdication from comparisons. Equalisers are likely to espouse the principle, even if they fall short in reality.

▶ *Consult.* Their emphasis on equality comes to the fore in team endeavours. A practising equaliser offers others (and expects to receive) equal rights to be heard, to contribute suggestions and to be acknowledged.

▶ *Seek power for the opportunity to self-actualise.* Equalisers' own use of power can present them with a serious moral challenge. Rather than seeking power for its own sake or for the increased status it brings, they are more likely to be motivated by the desire to grow.

## CHARACTERISTICS: STATUS

We should note that equalisers are also likely to enjoy their status, though they probably seek it less avidly than those who put a high priority on the status value.

Let's continue exploring the apparent split between equality and status by considering the cluster of characteristics common to *status-watchers*. I use this term to refer to people at the particular time they are motivated by the status value. They will often, but not always, be men. Status-watchers:

▶ *Shoulder responsibility.* Those using status wisely will be more concerned with the duties and responsibilities it involves, and the breadth of vision and information it demands, than with the trappings of power. Some, however, will be caught up in what they should get, rather than what they can give.

▶ *Measure status by output, position, resources or strength.* Status-watchers check their social and professional standing relative to others. In the workplace, their yardsticks are likely to include position attained in the organisational hierarchy, performance and, depending on the nature of the workplace, relative physical strength or intellectual prowess. Salary is often an important measure of status.

▶ *Test relationships to check their relative standing.* From time to time, a status-watcher may challenge others to prove themselves worthy of respect; for example, an intellectual debate or a physical challenge.

▶ *Accept legitimate authority.* If the status-watcher perceives a person worthy, they will usually offer loyalty and obedience to legitimate authority. They relax into their own rank, enjoying their known place in the scheme of things, the privileges it offers and the limits it imposes. Status, once accepted, brings social stability and simplifies relationships.

▶ *Validate hierarchies.* Status-watchers generally understand and respect the need for power structures. They see the necessity of chains of command to facilitate the flow of work.

▶ *Observe power issues carefully.* Status-watchers may watch power plays very closely, often noticing when power is being tested or applied. They tend to be alert to hidden agendas. They may understand the finer points of how power is used far more readily than equalisers, who are often unaware of power issues.

▶ *Regard people as basically different.* Status-watchers don't perceive all people as equal. Therefore respect — given and received — is particularly important. It isn't offered automatically. It must be earned through achievement or natural advantage. They expect the worthy to rise through the ranks.

▶ *Demand respect.* Status-watchers believe that status and power give them the right to demand respect from others.

▶ *Seek status as a yardstick for self-respect.* Status, as measured by external things such as job title and salary, often forms the backbone of status-watchers' self-respect. Thus they can be doubly devastated by retrenchment or a change of financial fortune. Not only must they deal with the fall in outer circumstances, their inner sense of self-worth may crumble as well. Opportunities to increase status through promotion, or by taking on additional responsibilities or challenging projects, are often keenly sought as concrete measures of self-worth.

# WHAT IS THE GOOD INTENTION?[28]

*Behind almost every action, no matter how inconvenient or hurtful it is to us, lies a good intention in the eyes of the doer.*

It's easy to misjudge people whose value systems are very different from our own, particularly if their actions impede our own needs or what we believe is for the best. Identifying a good intention will temper our negative judgment. Even if we don't directly mention our appreciation of other people's good intentions, our own identification of it will subtly affect the way we communicate with them and significantly improve the climate of negotiations. Behind almost every action, no matter how inconvenient or hurtful it is to us, lies a good intention in the eyes of the doer.

*We don't have to agree with the underlying value or motivation*, merely understand it so we can open up discussion. Good intentions don't excuse inappropriate behaviour for either the equaliser or the status-watcher. An equaliser who insists on consensus when an urgent answer is needed may be obstructive in the decision-making process. A status-watcher who willingly shoulders the responsibilities of the position may disempower others by refusing to delegate. Yet when we identify the other person's best intention, we offer ourselves a reality check. Of course, there may be some other pretty poor intentions, but refrain from angry confrontation until you find at least one positive (or acceptable) purpose for their behaviour. Good conflict resolution begins with respect for the other person and the values that they stand for.

While the range of people's good intentions is enormously broad, a number arise directly out of the equality value. Equalisers often adopt *rules for equitable relationship*. These include:

▶ supporting the rights of friends and colleagues;

▶ avoiding arousing others' jealousy;

▶ using fairness as a yardstick for evaluating;

▶ negotiating from a win/win perspective;

▶ encouraging others' participation in decision-making.

It is just as important for status-watchers to value and adopt these practices — and many do. They tone down the 'dog-eat-dog' mentality that can occur in an environment that is overly competitive. Equalisers are more likely to adopt the above principles automatically. For status-watchers, such principles are frequently hard won, and achieved later in life after much consideration. They may not arise spontaneously from a masculine gender culture with its emphasis on status as the key to success. On-the-job training programs such as Total Quality Management are particularly effective in building these rules for equitable relationships into workplace practices.

Good intentions of status-watchers may include:

▶ striving for self-improvement or self-reliance;

▶ building self-respect;

▶ creating a clear chain of command;

▶ using a strategically sound approach;

▶ supporting justice and law.

Of course, equalisers may also cherish these intentions, but for status-watchers they are likely to arise directly from their status value. So significant are these motivations to some status-watchers that they become *rules for personal conduct* in the workplace. They are very useful rules for a competitive environment, though someone who is unmoved by them can fail to respect them in others. We have every right to object to manoeuvres that, in the process of promoting personal needs, damage our own or others' interests. On the other hand, self-interest is not an unreasonable motivation, and it is one we can often support in another person.

*Self-interest is not an unreasonable motivation, and it is one we can often support in another person.*

Equalisers can counteract a common tendency to sell themselves short by including these rules for personal conduct with their own rules for equitable relationship. To develop our full potential, we each need a considered balance between the good intentions so natural to the equaliser and those that mould the status-watcher.

*EXERCISE*

Stop for a moment and think of someone you know, or know of, who you would classify as an equaliser. Think of a time when something they did annoyed you. Did they have a good intention that arose out of their equality value? Were there other 'good intentions' that motivated them as well?

| Equalisers'<br>good intentions | Probable<br>motivation<br>for ............. :<br>(name) |
|---|---|
| Supporting the rights of<br>friends and colleagues | |
| Avoiding arousing others' jealousy | |
| Using fairness as a yardstick for<br>evaluating | |
| Negotiating from a win/win<br>perspective | |
| Encouraging others' participation<br>in decision-making | |
| Other good intentions:<br><br>...................................................<br>...................................................<br>...................................................<br>...................................................<br>...................................................<br>................................................... | |

*Place crosses against relevant motivations*

*Figure 13: Equalisers' good intentions*

Now consider someone you know, or know of, who is strongly motivated by the status value. For a particular action, statement or decision you've judged harshly, consider at least one good intention that may have been a motivation. Choose from the list and add others that come to mind.

| Status-watchers' good intentions | Probable motivation for .............. : (name) |
|---|---|
| Striving for self-improvement or self-reliance | |
| Building self-respect | |
| Creating a clear chain of command | |
| Using a strategically sound approach | |
| Supporting justice and law | |
| Other good intentions: ........................................................... ........................................................... ........................................................... ........................................................... ........................................................... ........................................................... | |

*Place crosses against relevant motivations*

*Figure 14: Status-watchers' good intentions*

## CONFRONTING WHILE SUPPORTING GOOD INTENT

If you choose to reflect back to the other person your understanding of their good intentions, you can achieve two valuable results:

1. You focus their attention on the best in themselves;

2. You indicate that you do hold them in respect.

The climate in which you confront another person can be softened dramatically by a sincere and open acknowledgment of their good intent. (See **Figure 15: Confronting while supporting good intent**, page 50.)

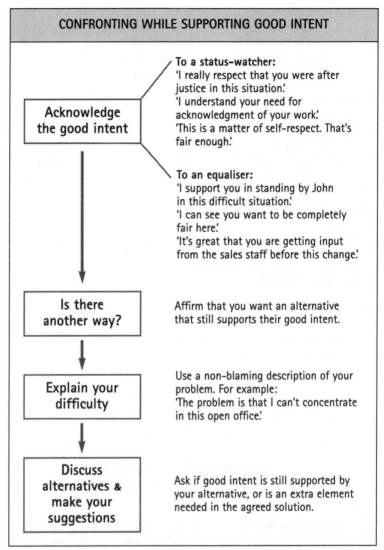

Figure 15: Confronting while supporting good intent

Confrontation is often far more effective when you begin by acknowledging the other person's good intent. When you show respect for the best in them, they are more likely to live up to the best in themselves. When you need change, affirming your ongoing support of the other person's good purpose helps to build bridges rather than burn them.

## DOMINANCE VERSUS POWER SHARING

A subtle but effective revolution is occurring in the workplace — the re-prioritising of traditionally masculine values, particularly *status* and *dominance*. The dominant male who has everyone around him trembling and bending to his will is increasingly viewed as having paranoid delusions of grandeur. While once he reigned supreme, today he's out of step — he's likely to be offered counselling, or even be retrenched in leadership changeovers.

Workplace values are becoming feminised. While once equality was well down on most men's lists, this is no longer so. Best practice in leadership now fosters traditionally feminine values. These values are the driving force behind consultative approaches to decision-making and negotiation procedures that emphasise mutual gain. This new focus on equality chips away at narrowly based hierarchies, broadening the base and flattening the apex. This helps a larger group of people undertake more satisfying and more responsible work.

*A revolution is taking place — the re-prioritising of traditionally masculine values.*

This process of feminisation evolves alongside women's increasing involvement in the workforce and their own demand (certainly not always delivered) for equal status. Women are pushing hard for work and political responsibilities that reflect their abilities, and to achieve this they are undoubtedly flexing their power muscles.

Men often feel threatened by these changes — not totally unreasonable in a new era in which roles are by no means finalised. Some men are very concerned about the shift in the male–female balance of power. With status being a high priority for many men, the rise of women to positions of responsibility can rock the traditional masculine paradigm of 'if I'm not on top, I'm a loser'. It is this underlying fear that keeps the glass ceiling intact.

Women are usually acutely aware of how their increasing power threatens their male domestic partners, but often fail to understand the mounting concern felt by male colleagues in the workplace: 'Where will they stop?'.

How valid is this concern? To get some inkling of where we are heading as a feminising society, we can consider a few examples from history. Some pre-industrialised societies provide a possible model. Ken Wilber, in *Sex, Ecology, Spirituality: The Spirit of Evolution*, considers the historical context of women's relative power. Citing the research of Janet Chafetz, he says:

> The most feminine societies (such as early hoe/horticultural societies) were not ones dominated by females, but ones where females shared public/productive power roughly 50–50 with men; whereas the most masculine societies (such as the plow/agrarian) were ones where men possessed virtually 100 percent of public/productive power (with women relegated to the private/reproductive sphere).[29]

In feminised societies of the past, women sought equality of leadership rather than dominance. Their ambitions are no more than this today and for the same age-old reasons. Says Janet Chafetz:

> Women's activities are either specialised in non-productive roles, which leads to inferior status, or divided between the two realms, which may afford them relatively equal status ... Why do women as a category never specialise solely in productive/public sector roles? ... a

*set of biological constants* helps to answer the question raised: the women carry babies in their bodies and lactate, which circumscribes their physical mobility.[30]

Certainly, the nature of women's commitment to family is changing. With household technology, fast food and institutional child care, the time demanded by family duties has decreased significantly. But fundamentally that commitment is just as relevant today. For many women it creates a self-imposed glass ceiling. They won't pursue top management positions because they don't choose to give work the dedicated attention that this level of leadership demands.

*Women's commitment to family often creates a self-imposed glass ceiling.*

Women-driven change in organisational policy is often aiming for equality, but in the process it is opening up choices for men, too. Workplace regulations are changing to accommodate the realities of family commitments. This aspect of the gentle revolution in the workplace is typified by new policy guidelines introduced at the New South Wales National Parks and Wildlife Service (NPWS). It has recently adopted a new and very much broader definition of family:

► a group of persons of common ancestry; or
► all persons living together in one household; or
► a primary social group consisting of parents and their offspring.

NPWS defines a dependent as:

► a partner, husband, wife, child, elderly parent or family member with a disability.[31]

The definition has important implications. It forms the backbone of an upgrade of employment conditions to provide time out to attend to sick family members or children who must be cared for. On the principle of equal rights for men and women, men in the Service have the same right as women to take time off for family commitments.

This is the reality of 'feminising' the workplace. It can work *for* men, not *against* them. However, those men who have chosen to limit their involvement at work in order to spend more time with their family have been looked down upon by less family-oriented men. They've had to endure criticism about 'their lack of commitment to the organisation'. As family responsibilities become enshrined in the guidelines of more organisations, men's as well as women's choices will broaden, and hopefully the right to those choices will come to be accepted by the majority of men. If we intend to achieve again a full employment economy—a job for all who want one—we may have to rethink the morality of overtime. It has a societal cost as well as a personal and family one.

While we are still very much in the midst of a sometimes turbulent transition, power sharing between men and women is becoming the new norm. Status-watching behaviours by men are becoming much more subtle. Women today seem to be complaining more frequently of nit-picking, passive resistance, covert action or opposition to an idea for no apparent reason. Overt standover tactics are rapidly being stamped out by legislation and social condemnation. Yet cross-gender differences are still at the heart of many male–female power struggles.

## WHAT PREDISPOSES WOMEN TO EQUALITY AND MEN TO STATUS?

A number of forces still predispose women more towards the value of equality and men more towards status. These include:

► differing views on power in relationships;

► a long history of suppressing women's self-esteem and self-actualisation needs.

Let's look at both these areas in some detail, bearing in mind that they interact with each other and cannot ultimately be treated in isolation.

### Differing views on power in relationship

*Ultimate power is our ability to fulfil our own needs and the needs of people we care about.*

Anthony Robbins describes ultimate power as our ability to fulfil our own needs and the needs of people we care about.[32] If we accept this definition, the development of power is a necessary step for achieving what we want in life. Important as it is, some people are hypersensitive to where they stand power-wise in relation to others. For these people, every interaction is a test of

| RESPONSE TO POWER RELATIONSHIPS | | |
|---|---|---|
| If their power position is: | EQUALISERS | STATUS–WATCHERS |
| One-up | Feel uncomfortable about it, if they notice it at all. If aware, they minimise status differences in small but significant ways (e.g. asking advice, praising). | Enjoy it! |
| One-down | Dislike it. Resentment gradually builds as self-esteem grows. They assert power with a variety of tactics until a sense of equality is achieved. | Hate it unless they're sure they are nevertheless respected. Their self-esteem is challenged. They often react immediately with a put-down. They look for proof of expertise. From time to time, status-watchers may challenge the legitimacy of the other person's right to higher status, over-turning it if possible. If unsuccessful, they temporarily accept lower status, while looking for opportunities to alter the one-down position. |
| Equal | Enjoy it! | If major positional superiority is out of reach, they may push towards the preferred one-up position in small but significant ways (e.g. controlling the flow of information). |

*Figure 16: Response to power relationships*

present power and an opportunity for its growth. They are constantly checking their status. Their sense of self-worth depends on being on top. This fixation on power can be extremely annoying to others. Though it is sometimes a woman who is hypersensitive to power issues, more usually it is a man.

Of course, all status-watchers aren't voracious power-seekers, nor are all equalisers unaware of power issues. Nevertheless, once equality-oriented people have achieved reasonable status in relation to another person, they are usually satisfied for the time being. Equalisers may not recognise that a criticism or instruction they have issued in innocence has challenged the power base in the relationship. They aren't motivated by power in their interactions, unless their current position is significantly challenged. Status-watchers, however, always have an eye on how their position compares with that of the other person. There is a distinct difference between the equaliser and the status-watcher's power push. (See **Figure 16: Response to power relationships**, page 55.)

Both the status-oriented and the equality-oriented person will seek to alter two out of three of the relative power positions — one-up, one-down, equal — in which they find themselves. We can see here the seeds of many power-related conflicts. How much energy we put into such conflicts depends on our core beliefs about how the world works.

As is obvious from the list below, the core beliefs that produce a high sensitivity to relative power are based on a far less benign world view. They are a response to a more demanding culture to perform. These core beliefs affect not only the value placed on status, but also use of competition, focus on actions and objects, and the need for autonomy. I believe that most people who are extreme in the priority they place on these values have had

| CORE BELIEFS OF THOSE WITH: | |
|---|---|
| LOW sensitivity to relative power | HIGH sensitivity to relative power |
| The world is fundamentally supportive of my needs. | If I don't look out for myself, no one else will. |
| Other people are generally well-meaning. | It's a dog-eat-dog world. |
| I'm as good as anybody else. | If I'm not on top, I'm a loser. |
| There's enough of most things to go round, and if there's not we share. | There's never enough for everyone, so I'd better grab what I can. |
| We're all basically the same. | We each have our place. |

*Figure 17: Core beliefs*

significant or repeated experiences in childhood where their efforts to ensure their needs were met were frustrated or made much more difficult. Such experiences include:

► aggression used repeatedly in interactions;

► autocratic discipline;

► power used over them to hold them back;

► victimisation by others who are physically stronger.

Boys more frequently grow up in a harsher subculture. This is likely to affect their core beliefs about struggle and power significantly. In most animal species it is the male that's generally more aggressive and that appears to be true for humans, too. Boys will often solve disputes with their fists. Boys who are bullies tend to use their superior physical strength to terrorise weaker boys. Steve Biddulph quotes research by Professor Ken Rigby, an expert on bullying. Rigby found that:

*A harsher culture affects boys' core beliefs about struggle and power.*

> ... one in five boys gets bullied at school at least once per week. A boy who has had a gentle and cooperative start in life at home may find that to be accepted he has to put on macho pretensions, act mean, disparage girls and even join in acts of bullying.[33]

A number of teachers informed me that they frequently found boys in their classes to be naughtier, more rebellious and more self-oriented than girls. Boys' behaviour may test the adults in charge of them to their limits, often resulting in cold and uncaring interactions. At worst, boys are cruelly abused in these exchanges. At best, most boys probably receive stricter demands and harsher discipline than girls.

Ongoing situations of threat and danger trigger rises in testosterone levels. This increases aggressiveness, which is its survival value, but it also perpetuates negative spirals of bullying and abuse. It is interesting to note that:

> Among sportsmen, testosterone levels are higher at the end of a match, or a season, than at the beginning.[34]

Until well into their teenage years, children play most frequently with others of the same sex, making for two very different gender

*Girls often suppress needs to retain friendship.*

cultures and life experiences. Girls usually grow up in a gentler environment. Young girls share fairly readily. Generally, amongst friends at least, they don't have to struggle too hard to ensure their needs are met. They more willingly suppress their needs in order to retain friendship. This is not to say that young girls can't be aggressive. They often are. I remember having to cut my daughters' fingernails very short when they were little, so they left no evidence on each other of the battles they got into. Usually, though, girls tend to be verbally rather than physically aggressive. They'll form 'in' groups and use the pressure of acceptance or rejection from these groups to mould others to their will. They may use malicious gossip to build and split alliances. Unpleasant as this aggression is, it's generally less disruptive to parents and teachers. Thus they are likely to treat girls in more kindly, more permissive ways. All these factors have an effect on girls' development of core beliefs about the amount and type of power necessary to ensure their needs are met. While many will learn the value of equality and sharing in this relatively benign subculture, they may also learn the effectiveness of manipulation and malicious gossip. Covert aggression may produce better results in girls' subculture than in boys'.

Though aggression differences between boys and girls may be genetically and hormonally encoded, there is an extra cultural component here as well. Serious aggression in girls often meets with more horror from parents and teachers. Very aggressive responses are likely to be firmly squashed. Girls receive significant negative reinforcement for power displays.

Aggressive responses in young boys are often tolerated with the attitude 'boys will be boys'. Society has many ways of encouraging boys' aggressive impulses. Competitive sports are a good example. There are many valuable lessons to be learnt on the sports field — the vital role of teamwork, working together for a common purpose, knowing your place in the scheme of things. However, sometimes far too much responsibility and pressure is placed on young shoulders. On those shoulders, boys often carry the hopes and dreams of parents who are desperate for them to excel. Boys are told they are defending the honour of the school and must win at all costs. Lessons from the sports field quickly generalise. Winning and the aggression it demands seem to be the way to get on in life. Boys' more demanding gender culture may direct men towards a world view where:

▶ status relative to others must be carefully monitored so that you don't slip back as others around you struggle forwards; and

▶ aggression and force imply 'you're a real man'.

Those who don't hold these views are likely to develop lower self-esteem and a sense they aren't leadership material. They are left believing they are not the movers and shakers in this world. Indeed, in the male-dominated society of the past, they weren't. However, the requirements of leadership are changing. Feminine qualities of consultation, emphasis on process as well as result, and genuine concern for the wellbeing of employees are now being valued as aspects of enlightened leadership.

This is another feature of the gentle revolution. But have our less aggressive, less status-conscious men discovered their leadership potential for these new times? It might take another generation or two to change traditional masculine mindsets, which will require some significant shifts in our social education of boys.

Girls' gender culture more frequently generates in women a set of core beliefs supporting a limited sensitivity to and desire for power and status. They don't need to be as alert to power issues to ensure their *everyday* needs are met. However, that culture also needs fine-tuning for the gentle revolution.

## A long history of suppressing women's self-esteem and self-actualisation needs

Male-dominated cultures of the past have recognised and supported men's need to achieve status in the workplace and in public affairs, but have discriminated against women achieving in these areas. The shadows of this history remain:

▶ Some men still regard women as second-class citizens, just because they are women.

▶ In undervaluing their own family responsibilities, men often undervalue women who must assume dual roles as employee and caretaker.

Insofar as male domination is still intact, this situation is an ongoing battle for women. Few women have been able to achieve their potential in the public arena, precisely because they are not oriented to engage in the power struggles men use to jockey for status. Preferring not to play by those rules, many women have therefore chosen more subtle and behind-the-scenes methods of exercising power and status.

*Many men build self-esteem on their achievement in the workplace.*

Many men build self-esteem almost exclusively on their achievement in the workplace. By the same token, men have strongly discouraged women's status and the building of self-esteem in their domains. Most women in male-dominated societies have had this door closed to them. Historically, women have built self-esteem on beauty, helpfulness and a pleasant disposition. Even their sense of their own intelligence has been suppressed by inequality of education opportunities, and men's distaste for marriage partners who were smarter than they were. This thinking is still not uncommon. Reputation, prestige, status, fame and glory were, and often still are, out of the question for most women, unless they can somehow avoid the dominant masculine culture in work and public affairs.

*Women are struggling to fulfil self-esteem needs.*

Psychologist Abraham Maslow places the need for self-actualisation, the realisation of our potential, at the apex of our hierarchy of needs.[35] Most women in the past could not even begin to contemplate what this might mean, let alone achieve it. Total absorption in domestic affairs gave limited scope to self-actualisation. Maslow believed, and women's experience supports, that self-actualisation needs can only be addressed after physiological needs, safety, belongingness, love and self-esteem are attended to (see **Figure 18: Maslow's hierarchy of needs**, page 61). Women's limited power and less persistent demand for status often leaves them caught and struggling at the self-esteem level of need fulfilment.

Certainly, expressing one's potential as a parent and home-maker can be immensely satisfying, and for many women it has been and will continue to be sufficient. However, large numbers of women, particularly as education standards for women improve and domestic chores reduce, are desperate to achieve their potential outside of the home. Many men are equally desperate to find the time for their fulfilment as parents. The traditional gender stereotypes fail both men and women in different ways.

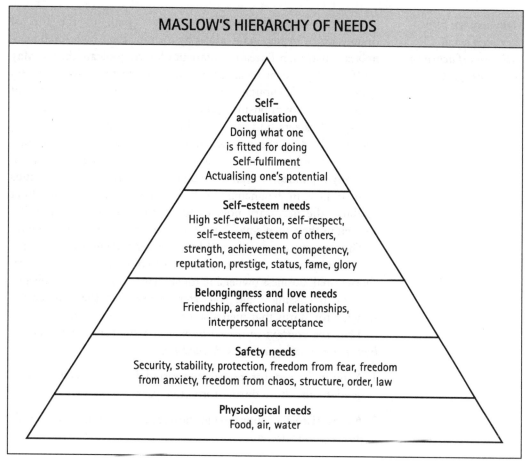

Figure 18: Maslow's hierarchy of needs[36]

Women's power issues in the workplace today often centre on their right to have work that uses their skills and abilities, that is fulfilling, and that offers opportunities for appropriate promotion. This is particularly difficult for women with a strong commitment to family. Patriarchal workplace policies demand a choice between either:

▶ a low-status position that allows women to manage their family duties; or

▶ fulfilling, challenging, responsible work.

*Many women form their own small businesses if deprived of a career path.*

Many women deprived of a career path to the top of organisations bypass male power by forming their own small businesses. Australian Bureau of Statistics figures indicate that in May 1995, 32.4 per cent of all people working in their own business were women.[37] Though they are likely to enjoy the status of directing their own business, their primary purpose is probably to satisfy self-esteem and self-actualisation needs, often while being very involved in the process of parenting. Of course, boosting income while homemaking responsibly is another significant goal.

Many organisations fail to recognise the extraordinary demands women face in balancing work and family duties, and don't establish the necessary policies for it to occur successfully. Yet women in their own small businesses are proving that they can do it. They structure in the flexible hours, relief and childcare arrangements necessary for their dual areas of commitment. Many men choose small business ownership for similar reasons. It is an effective way of bypassing male role stereotypes and the unrelenting struggle for status that men also can find very wearing.

*Thus the context in which women are predisposed to place a high priority on equality is defined by:*

1. A limited need for power supported by a relatively benign gender subculture during formative years.

2. A long history of suppressing status and self-actualisation needs in the public arena.

*The context in which men are predisposed to place a high priority on status is defined by:*

1. A high sensitivity to relative power supported by a relatively aggressive gender subculture.

2. Male domination — with self-esteem and self-actualisation needs expressed by proving themselves better than others in the workplace and public arenas.

Lest we imply that men are wrong for holding these values, let's be clear about the underlying social purpose. The masculine gender value of competition for status is to protect and support the homemaker and children. Those men in touch with this purpose feel insecure and irresponsible if they fail to compete successfully for status. Many have had to put up with terrible work conditions as 'bread winners' and the mental strain that goes with this role.

## SPOTTING THE UNDERLYING VALUES

Do you notice underlying values or are you just swept along?

The underlying value — equality or status — will influence decision-making and sensitivities in a wide variety of situations. These priorities aren't easily altered, so we'd do well to recognise and accommodate them instead.

*Listen to people's language.* It often tells us about the values they are using. Notice when you hear words such as those listed in **Figure 65: Language driven by equality and status values** (Appendix 3, page 403) and listen to the subtext of implied concepts in the other person's conversation.

*People's language often tells us about the values they are using.*

Here's a summary of a phone conversation I had recently. I've italicised some of the status and equality clue words that reverberated throughout.

A representative for a group of hospital staff, mainly women, phoned the Conflict Resolution Network. We chatted. She thought her group probably needed some sort of team-building workshop. They had serious morale problems to deal with. She described for me the *hierarchical structure* of operating theatres where *control* and the issuing of orders and instant *obedience* were necessary for efficient operating practice. The doctors and surgeons (mainly men) have superior *status* by virtue of position and education.

'We know they have to be in charge, but we wish they had more of a *win/win* approach. Surely, we deserve a *fairer* deal?' she said.

'You want it to be more *even-handed*?' I asked.

Her next comment betrayed her group's deep hurt and anger. 'Sometimes doctors treat us like dirt. Some of the men, in particular, act like we're their slaves.' Although very dissatisfied, they kept their conflicts hidden. Status-holders in their hospital system had the power to deal with troublemakers summarily. 'Do I call it *"equal rights"*?' queried my caller.

'What would it look like if you had it?' I asked.

'Well', she said, 'the other day we had a new woman surgeon on duty. We had a car crash patient in theatre. When the operation was over, it needed a big clean-up — there was lots of blood around. This woman surgeon just pitched in and started helping. "You don't have to do that, you know," I said to her. "I do know," she replied, "but I'm already dirty so I might as well help." She wasn't *setting herself up as higher* than us. How could we encourage more of that sort of attitude from the men?'

Not an easy one, I thought. Time pressures in the hospital system must make status issues worse. 'I'm really not saying that they should help clean up', she said, 'but we need something to change their attitude. They think we won't look up to them if they treat us like *equals*, but in fact we'd *respect* them much more.'

Her group was quietly desperate and feeling totally unheard. The senior hospital staff of doctors and administrators weren't tuned in to equality language and values. The nurses and orderlies were just as dedicated to goals of efficiency and patients' wellbeing. They believed they were entitled to a team relationship. They accepted their lower positional status, but didn't believe it required the type of work atmosphere they presently endured. This group didn't really need structural changes. They wanted changes in day-to-day communication and attitudes.

The language and concepts this woman used in trying to define the problem, pointed clearly to her group's thirst for recognition beyond relative status.

*Delivering a sense of equality within a hierarchy is the new challenge.*

Many organisations today face the difficulty of delivering a sense of equality within a hierarchical structure. The hospital group, for example, wanted low cost, deliverable changes such as:

▶ valuing consultation as part of major decision-making;

▶ treating others with respect;

▶ acknowledging people as individuals in daily interactions.

These attitudes are the oil in the works, providing a sense of equality within hierarchical structures. As more women join the workforce, and as they grow more confident in the values they have to offer, many organisations are beginning to change. Those that don't change face diminishing morale and declining efficiency as workplace cultures feminise. Sally Helgesen, author of *The Female Advantage*, in a chapter aptly entitled 'The End of the Warrior Age', states:

> Feminine principles [of human connection and interdependence] are entering the public realm because *we can no longer afford* to restrict them to the private domestic sphere, nor allow a public culture obsessed with Warrior values [autonomy, competition and control] to control human destiny if we are to survive.[38]

It would be very wrong to think that status-watchers don't include equality as a value at all. But when interacting in organisations they may focus first on status and position, and be slower to recognise that within positional power structures lie other possibilities for relating with others.

## HOW POWER IS EXERCISED

Many people feel powerless to bring about the changes necessary in their organisations and in the way they are treated. What tools are at our disposal? Usually, we'll draw on one or a number of interpersonal *power bases*. The five primary ones are:

1. valued relationship;

2. position;

3. expertise;

4. reward/punishment; and

5. persuasiveness.

Each of these is widely used in the workplace. Each can be a legitimate tool of influence.

1 ► The *valued relationship power base* relies on people doing what we want because otherwise they risk our displeasure and our emotional withdrawal. Equalisers tend to use this power base extensively. While it is a legitimate form of influence, it can also be used for manipulation. It will give some leverage over another person, but is most effective when used to command respect and

*Equalisers often use valued relationships as their power base.*

fair play. It works best by minimising coercive power, rather than competing with it.

Networking, an important leverage source in the workplace, is another example of the valued relationship power base. Keeping in contact, jovial conversing, building friendship, exchanging favours and diplomatic negotiating with win/win outcomes are all important skills for the person who uses their connections as a power source.

> Elizabeth, a journalist, was putting together a radio magazine program on a well-known political leader who had died that week. It was due to air the next day. When she presented it to her editor he was disappointed: 'It's too negative. What about that speech he gave on unemployment a couple of months ago?' Her own station only archived for a month. She rang a fellow journalist whose station kept an excellent library. After their usual banter, she asked if he could check whether his library had the speech she needed. Ten minutes later, he rang back. 'Send over a courier. They're copying the tape for me right now.' Within the hour she had the amended program on her editor's desk. He was impressed. Effective networking helped Elizabeth look good on the job. She knew this source of her power relied on favour-for-favour trades and warm human contact. She scribbled herself a note to pass on to her fellow journalist a book she'd just read that she thought he might rather enjoy.

We use valued relationships in conflict situations, too. It can provide the 'muscle' we need to help us change the other person's mind. It can be used quite manipulatively when we go silent, look disappointed, drop playful interchanges, frown, snap, make a sarcastic comment, or nag when we're not getting what we want. Not infrequently a woman's way! Such tactics can be as coercive as more overt uses of power, sometimes even more so as it can be very difficult to initiate frank discussion when the relationship is at stake. Men can feel very disempowered if they don't know how to play the same game. Using valued relationships as a power base can be effective and will often lead the other person to make a compromise.

Many women say they prefer to sidestep power issues altogether. They believe they're not involved in power struggles, yet unconsciously they rely heavily on the value to others of their continued good will. Sometimes this base works very well for them. At others, it fails miserably to support their goals, and its overuse can alienate rather than endear.

I interviewed Thomas, who shares an office with Claire. He reports:

> Claire ducks outside for a cigarette several times a day and just expects me to handle her phone while she's gone. It drives me mad. She just presumes that, because I'm always polite to her, I'll cover for her. I'm fed up!
>
> *[Thomas badly needs to make a clear statement on how it is for him in order to deal effectively with this issue.[39]]*

2 ► The *position power base* rests on others respecting our authority and our right to have things go our way because of our superior place in the hierarchy. Status-watchers will often rely heavily on this power base. So do many equalisers, but sometimes they don't recognise that. Does your position as manager or parent, for example, subtly influence others' compliance even when you're not actually laying down the law?

*Status-watchers tend to use position as their power base.*

To use position with integrity is to have the overall good of the whole organisation as well as each individual at heart. Ideally, the higher position provides a wider view from which to make such assessments. Position is misused when other people's best interests are not taken into account. It may simplify decision-making for the time being, but it sows the seeds for conflict, even revolution, when those who've been repeatedly disadvantaged grow powerful enough to assert themselves.

3 ► The *expertise power base* depends on the knowledge and skills of the person using it. During interviews for this book, a number of women complained to me that, to get anywhere in their organisations, they had to be *more* skilled and *better* informed than their male peers. Bias against them often denied them access to the workplace training programs that were being offered to their male co-workers. Women more frequently have to educate themselves out of hours at their own expense. While expertise alone may be enough for promotion and respect, sometimes you need an awful lot of it to counter discrimination. Nine out of ten

women responding to my original survey had formed the same opinion.[40]

*Greater positional power puts greater rewards and punishments at your disposal.*

4 ► The *reward/punishment power base* is one of the most widely used by both sexes. Rewards may be *open*, with a clear cause–effect relationship between compliance and reward; for example, praise, a pay rise or a bonus. Rewards can be just as powerful an incentive for compliance when they are *covert*; that is, there is no immediate relationship between the reward and agreement. Examples include an implied obligation — 'He owes me one' — and the ability to offer more interesting work at some future date. Overt punishments might include demoting someone, bypassing them for promotion in a salary review, or criticising them in front of their peers. Covert punishments might include 'misfiling' someone's promotion application or speaking negatively about them to their superiors in private. Those in a higher position in the organisation have more punishments and rewards at their fingertips. But the office boy who delivers someone's mail late or feeds them an interesting piece of gossip, and the secretary who 'loses' an important phone message or orders in someone's favourite felt-tipped pens can also punish or reward from the bottom of the hierarchy.

5 ► The *persuasiveness power base* arises from being trusted and respected. We respect others for a wide number of reasons, which can include:

► *integrity*

► *commonsense*

Mercifully, these are two qualities equally distributed between both sexes. Other factors that impact on persuasiveness often favour men.

► *The ability to sell an idea well.* Although women are often more verbally skilled than men,[41] in the workplace their reticence about speaking up, particularly in meetings or with superiors, can work against them.

► *Charisma.* Men, by virtue of larger size, often appear more charismatic in the workplace and in political life. Someone suggested to me that male executives tend to be taller than average. It seemed an oddball hypothesis, yet my own observations in a large bank where I was working seemed to confirm it. All the senior executives were men and all but one were taller than average.

Charisma also relies on being at ease with a superior stance, an unbalanced relationship that can make equality-minded women very uncomfortable and one which some women will go to great lengths to minimise. They are often less persuasive with others as a result. A necessary but not sufficient condition for charisma is a strong sense of self-worth and self-confidence.

All the power bases can be used as a platform from which to push for what we want and to persuade others to do it our way. The bases we'll in fact choose, however, are coloured by our underlying priorities for equality or status.[42]

## POWER TACTICS

The five power bases are our interpersonal *sources* of power. Our power tactics are the *methods* by which we apply the pressure of those sources. Most methods of exercising power aren't good or bad in themselves. It is the purpose to which the methods are put that determines their social acceptability.

People have many different reactions to their own power. Some feel tainted by it, particularly if they themselves have been victims of its misuse in the past. Some are scared of their own potential and the possibility of using power unwisely. Some avoid it, being unwilling to pay the price of responsibility that goes with power. Distinguishing between *manipulation* and *influence* can clarify our thinking (see **Figure 19: Manipulation or influence**, page 70.)[43]

Both men and women sometimes use very underhanded, annoying tactics to keep another person in their place, reduce their power, maintain a preferred status quo, or push through an unpopular idea. You can, of course, be manipulated 'for your own good', but you will feel disempowered from the decision-making process. While many tactics can be used to influence with integrity, they can also be highly manipulative. In choosing your

*Influence* involves the other person in the decision-making process.

| MANIPULATION OR INFLUENCE | |
| --- | --- |
| Manipulation | Influence |
| ► People feel tricked. | ► People feel persuaded. |
| ► Outcomes favour the manipulator, often at the expense of another. | ► Outcomes favour others as well as the influencer. |
| ► Input from others is discouraged. | ► Input from others is encouraged and valued. |
| ► Biased information is supplied. | ► More balanced information is supplied. |
| ► Needs and concerns of others are less frequently considered. | ► Needs and concerns of others are more frequently considered. |
| ► Tends to stunt relationships. | ► Tends to build relationships. |
| ► Less commitment from others to make the solution work. | ► Greater commitment from others to make the solution work. |

*Figure 19: Manipulation or influence*

*Manipulation disempowers the other person from the decision-making process.*

own tactics, consider whether the manoeuvre respects the rights of the parties to the transaction. When people feel tricked or stood over, chances are that someone has used a power tactic manipulatively. The ones most prone to misuse by both sexes include:

► interrupting;

► being overcritical;

► behaving righteously;

► rebelling;

► withholding information;

► backstabbing;

► refusing to discuss the issue.

People tend to get very righteous about the tactics they personally wouldn't use. In Figure 20 below, which list annoys you more?

*Equalisers and status-watchers often use different power tactics.*

| MANIPULATIVE POWER TACTICS | |
|---|---|
| Used more by equalisers | Used more by status–watchers |
| Bitching | Putting others down |
| Being sick | Threatening with physical size |
| Behaving stubbornly | Playing win/lose |
| Being apologetic | Sabotaging |
| Being overhelpful | Giving advice |
| Sulking | Being aggressive, shouting, hitting |
| Crying | Dismissing by logical argument |
| Collecting allies | Pulling rank |
| Withdrawing | Excluding others from decision-making |

*Figure 20: Manipulative power tactics*

*INTERPRETING FIGURE 20: MANIPULATIVE POWER TACTICS*

► Sometimes the use of one or more of the above tactics is justified, or even necessary, and can be used for influence rather than manipulation.

► While some behaviours, such as shouting or crying, begin as knee-jerk reactions to the conflict, it's very easy for them to become manipulative devices. They are far more prone to misuse than methods such as clear 'I' statements and open access to information.[44]

► We are only looking at trends. Each list in the figure above isn't exclusively used by one sex, or only by people with high priority on the value which heads it.

*Relative power affects our choice of power tactics.*

▶ Relative power affects our choice of power tactics. When the person — male or female — feels they are the more powerful party, they are more likely to use behaviours from the right-hand list. If they feel they would be likely to lose in a showdown, they are more likely to choose tactics from the left-hand list.

When a manipulative power tactic is used against you, try not to be overly hurt, overwhelmed or vindictive. If you can recognise and accept the underlying value driving the tactic you can often take it in your stride and redirect the conversation towards positive solutions.[45]

# SUMMARY

*CHARACTERISTICS*

| EQUALISERS | STATUS-WATCHERS |
| --- | --- |
| Prefer to share power with others rather than use power over them | Shoulder responsibility |
| Create a level playing field | Measure status by output, position, resources or strength |
| Want equality of opportunity | Test relationships to check their relative standing |
| Measure with a yardstick of fairness | |
| Tolerate different viewpoints | Accept legitimate authority |
| See everyone as basically the same | Validate hierarchies |
| Consult | Observe power issues carefully |
| Seek power for the opportunity to self-actualise | Regard people as basically different |
| | Demand respect |
| | Seek status as a yardstick for self-respect |

*GOOD INTENTIONS*

| EQUALISERS | STATUS-WATCHERS |
| --- | --- |
| Supporting the rights of friends and colleagues | Striving for self-improvement or self-reliance |
| Avoiding arousing others' jealousy | Building self-respect |
| Using fairness as a yardstick for evaluating | Creating a clear chain of command |
| Negotiating from a win/win perspective | Using a strategically sound approach |
| Encouraging others participation in decision-making | Supporting justice and law |

*POWER BASES*

| EQUALISERS OFTEN CHOOSE: | STATUS-WATCHERS OFTEN CHOOSE: |
| --- | --- |
| ► valued relationship | ► position |
| ► expertise | ► reward/punishment |
| ► verbal persuasiveness in one-on-one situations | ► persuasiveness in meetings using verbal skills and charisma |

**Delivering a sense of equality within a hierarchical structure**
*Influence rather than manipulate*

► value consultation in major decision-making
► treat others with respect
► acknowledge people as individuals in daily interactions

*When a tactic you dislike is used on you, redirect the conversation towards the positive.*

# 4 EQUALITY: stumbling blocks & stepping stones

## PREVIEW

*STUMBLING BLOCK*

1 ▶ Being too modest

2 ▶ Taking offence at inequality

3 ▶ Continued resentment

4 ▶ Intolerance of high-fliers

5 ▶ Insubordination

6 ▶ Being indecisive

So far I've painted a fairly rosy picture of the equality value, but to put it into perspective we need to consider its downside. Equality has a number of potential stumbling blocks. In this chapter we examine these obstacles and the insights and skills needed to avoid them. Usually it's women who place the higher priority on equality. Usually it's women who succumb to its pitfalls.

*Will I react or respond?*

Values such as equality often reside below consciousness, but that doesn't mean they're inactive. In any moment, they can trigger reactions in us which may or may not be functional in the situation. At times we'll need to choose a more considered response. We sharpen our conflict resolution expertise when we ask ourselves: 'Will I react or respond?'

> **React:** To behave impulsively. To act out of conditioning (habit), whether or not that action is appropriate. To be swept away by emotion.
> **Respond:** To behave thoughtfully. To act out of freedom, tailoring action to the circumstances. Emotions guide but do not rule.

There are women who always react to men who call them 'dear', 'sweetheart' or 'love' with a sharp reply. They react globally and non-specifically. Of course, a woman has every right to object to being patronised, but her instant negative reaction can widen the gulf between her and the man. This is not helpful, for example, when they really need to work cooperatively on a common project. Most men don't perceive themselves as condescending when they use these phrases, but they may well become so after being ticked off. Sometimes women can handle the problem most effectively by *educating* rather than *correcting*. A simple explanation that such terms are not appropriate to the workplace is often sufficient.

The question *Will I react or respond?* is very relevant to the equaliser who is about to succumb to habitual blaming patterns. It's also a good question for the person who is dealing with someone caught up in reaction. To follow their reaction with your reaction is tempting, but it only compounds the problem. In the example above, the man who has just been ticked off might *react* with 'bloody feminist!' or *respond* with an apology and a mental note to address this woman carefully, in ways that she registers as recognising her equality.

In many conflicts, the best antidote is to hold our first reaction in check and plan a considered response.

## STUMBLING BLOCK 1: BEING TOO MODEST

Modesty, or humility, is seen as a virtue in both men and women, but was particularly encouraged in women living in patriarchal societies where the accolades of public recognition were handed out to men. Women were rewarded for developing modest behaviour into a high art. It made them more 'feminine' in the eyes of both men and other women. With the participation of women in the modern workplace, feminine modesty about achievements is no longer always a productive strategy. Modesty might still be an equaliser's conditioned reaction when it comes to discussion of personal achievements, but it may cause unforeseen problems.

### Hiding achievements

**'It's nothing, really.'**

*Modesty is not always good strategy.*

Equalisers may be very alert to and uncomfortable with situations in which they are envied by others. Acutely sensitive to unequal power relationships, some will underplay their achievements to avoid alienation from less successful friends and workmates.

> Sarah was a stockbroker. She'd recently been commissioned to present a weekly radio program on the share market for small investors, an area in which she specialised. She told very few workmates about it. While privately delighted, she was embarrassed by her success, believing her colleagues might feel alienated. Of course, word spread anyway. Sarah reacted to their new deference by putting herself down about other areas of her workplace performance, her stress levels, her private life, her weight, almost anything, to re-balance the 'I am not better than you' relationship.

Sarah's reactions were based on a fear of alienation, because her radio program had suddenly increased her status in the industry. Of course, some women don't let others know about their achievements owing to a natural reticence — a preference for privacy. But more exuberant equalisers may also keep workplace milestones to themselves because they share Sarah's concerns. They only discuss successes amongst close friends who recognise that they are *sharing the excitement* they feel, not trying to raise their own status in the other person's eyes. Sometimes they'll swing erratically between pride and modesty. If they get carried away and share their excitement with those other than their close friends — people who might put them on a pedestal or think badly of them for boasting — they can be tormented by guilt.

*Equalisers' boasts are more about sharing the excitement than building status.*

*STEPPING STONES*

Delight in our successes is healthy self-actualising. Over-inflation of ego is different, but can be easily confused with self-actualising. Modesty will always have its place. If we don't want to irritate others, we need to practise self-disclosure about achievements with discretion. However, sometimes it's important to sing your own song, to blow your own trumpet. If your achievements are unknown, you may not be given the respect you deserve. Your ideas may not be taken seriously and opportunities for promotion may unfairly pass you by. There are times when potential envy and fear of boasting are valid considerations, but don't react with modesty if it really doesn't serve sound business strategy.

## Playing down your position

**'I'm nothing special. They call everyone a manager around here.'**

Inappropriate modesty may also be a trap when equality-focused managers play down their position because they are embarrassed by the authority they wield and the one-up position it creates. Perhaps they fear it will diminish their connection with other people. While enjoying the responsibility, the scope of activity and the influence the position brings, they try to combine it with equal status relationships with others. Sometimes this is a difficult but worthwhile challenge. Sometimes they can take it too far.

*Reticence about status can be misinterpreted.*

> One chief executive loathes wearing a name tag that states his position when he is attending public conferences. His reticence goes further. At a coffee break during a conference, he introduced himself, saying: 'I work with ETW.' He never clearly told the woman that he is the chief executive officer of ETW, and she certainly wouldn't have picked it up from his name tag, which he'd put in his pocket. His conversation with her was brief. She quickly moved on and spent the rest of the break chatting to some of his colleagues. He found out from them later that she and he held very similar positions in their respective companies. He would have enjoyed comparing notes with her.

There's appropriate modesty and then there's appropriate disclosure. This particular executive is missing out on some excellent opportunities for networking by allowing modesty to rule in this situation. If other people are using the more masculine, here-are-my-credentials approach, he is immediately undervalued.

> Sharon runs a property management company. Though the buildings she manages are large and impressive, her staffing is lean. Often at the end of the day she answers her own telephone. One day, a client wanting to rent space in one of the properties on her books rang her. The client assumed that the person answering the phone couldn't

possibly be the senior executive and spoke to Sharon in a very demeaning way. Sharon found it very difficult to insert a clear indication of her executive role into the conversation.

*(Was the client a man? No. It was a woman who had fallen into the gender trap of assuming that because Sharon answered the phone and because she's a woman, she was the secretary. Needless to say, Sharon didn't place this client very high on her list of suitable tenants.)*

### STEPPING STONES

Some people will presume that if you don't announce your position, it must be because it isn't a senior one. Even though it makes you uncomfortable, sometimes a clear statement of your status is needed. It's far better to do this than to become resentful because your status isn't being recognised when you need it to be.

## Socialising with subordinates

**'I'm just one of the guys.'**

Many equalisers don't insist on outward signposts of authority. They build intimacy on openness about their own foibles and flaws. They mix socially with people at all levels of the organisation. A traditional status-watcher can become concerned when they see equalisers being too friendly with people lower than them in the chain of command.

Lauren was recently appointed as department director. As part of the new job, she had some major restructuring to enforce. In her view, the way to build good working relationships is to socialise with colleagues outside working hours. She was horrified when her husband warned her that if she wanted to be respected, she shouldn't play tennis (a favourite sport of hers) with a group of lower level employees. He was most concerned that she would undermine her authority when she issued instructions in the work environment, particularly when dealing with men.

Lauren had always based her workplace interactions on equality. She built relationships with subordinates and enlisted their support using her power base of valued relationships.[46] In truth, she was never very conscious about why her methods so far had been successful. She hadn't considered the possibility that she might undermine her ability to perform in her new role by continuing to build off-the-job friendships with subordinates. She'd presumed they would automatically respect the status and authority that came with her new position.

Many people who are promoted find they become alienated from colleagues who were once close friends. There are a number of causes of this:

► Time pressures from their new appointment may place greater limits on social contact.

► Envy from less successful friends.

► The promotion itself says 'this person is better', and relationships based on equality are shaken.

► Sometimes the previous relationship has been built on 'isn't it awful here' conversations. Sharing irritations about management may no longer be politic.

Many people find the path to the top a lonely one. Lauren was trying hard not to let this happen to her, but some of the issues listed above were relevant.

*STEPPING STONES*

Socialising with subordinates may work well for those who are able to use the power base of valued relationships effectively. It can be an excellent form of networking. However, this approach may need to be combined with practices that indicate you expect to have the power of your position taken seriously; for example, by adopting a less chatty, more formal style when 'on duty'. Without a comfortable acceptance of the different perspectives offered by equality and status, Lauren could easily have rubbished her husband's advice. After consideration, Lauren chose her own way. She set up her tennis games, but, aware now of the potential problem, she bought a new wardrobe of 'power dressing' clothes to help with her executive image when on the job. At work she acted authoritatively, shouldering decisions when they were needed, consulting where it was wise. Her new workmates soon learnt to accept her off-duty/on-duty switches.

*Friends in the workplace may need to distinguish clearly between work and personal relationships.*

Many people choose their personal friends from amongst their workplace colleagues. There will be times when it is necessary to make clear distinctions between working and personal relationships. Clashes in the workplace with someone who is also a personal friend can be particularly devastating, and can make out-of-hours contact very uncomfortable. This situation requires careful attention to response rather than reaction. For instance, you will probably have to spell out the distinction you are making to your friend, who may still be feeling alienated as a result of your workplace clash. The challenge will be to help your friend make a clear separation between the two relationships.

## Not taking charge

### 'They can't call the shots.'

As mentioned in Chapter 3, many women today are running their own small businesses. Staff, often women also, are frequently personal friends. Management style therefore tends to be very egalitarian. This style has its problems, as Carol discovered:

Carol ran a document courier company in the central business district. Her main clients were lawyers. She had successfully used a group of women friends as her employees, many of whom worked part-time as they had young children at home. Carol's management style had always been very consultative and her employees valued that highly. The company had been quite successful in the two years since she established it. However, during the last six months, activity had not significantly expanded. Unsure what to do next, and doubting that her employees had the expertise for the strategic and expansive thinking she needed, Carol called in a male management consultant to advise her on future directions.

Carol was shocked at a staff meeting one day when her employees ganged up on her in opposition to the consultant. Exploring deeper, she realised that what they disliked most was that she was accepting advice from an outsider, not jointly planning future directions with them. She didn't like to tell them that she didn't believe they had the expertise she was after. Because her employees were also her friends, Carol had always played down her right to 'call the shots'. *(Interestingly enough, she had no problem announcing her position as director to others outside the company.)*

Her staff had come to see the organisation as a place where everyone was equal. Carol was so uncomfortable about asserting her authority that she had used group consensus in most of her business decision-making. For this team of equality-minded women, working with Carol had felt like paradise. This time when she had wanted to introduce major changes, Carol's fear was that she would be swamped by other people's inertia and unable to dictate the direction in which her own company should go.

*STEPPING STONES*

On reflection, Carol realised she was using the management consultant as a bulldog who could do the growling on her behalf. She would be able to say to her staff that *he* rather than *she* required these changes. She realised that her own fear of being the boss had set up unrealistic expectations in her employees. She was not, in fact, giving them the right to run all aspects of her business. After their confrontation with her, painful as it was at the time, she recognised that she did want to *consult* with them over any changes she planned. However, she couldn't let herself be *dictated* to by them. She alone had to approve or veto plans. She had to accept that, for the sake of the company, she'd have to make some tough decisions, possibly at the expense of being liked by her employees.

*The person who bears the risk must control the decisions.*

Carol's mistake was a common one for those committed to consensus decision-making in an inherently hierarchical structure. She had given the impression that she had surrendered control to the group, though this was not and could not be the case.

There are times when we have to take charge. While consensus decision-making is particularly appealing to equalisers (and hence to many women), and it can work very well with clearly defined projects and day-to-day organisation, it will not work for all decisions. Any member of the group may have valuable input into planning, but the person who bears the risks must veto or approve future directions for the company. (See **Figure 21: Control in consensus decision-making**, below.)

At first, these cold, hard truths may disappoint an equaliser who is deeply committed to participative management. One woman in Carol's team told her, 'You've shattered my dream!'. But when the reasons control cannot be surrendered are understood, there is still great joy, creativity and self-actualisation

| CONTROL IN CONSENSUS DECISION-MAKING | |
|---|---|
| The leader cannot safely surrender authority or accountability. | The leader must make it clear that they reserve the right to veto. With the best will in the world, a group can make a decision that could be dangerous, inappropriate or too costly, or remain undecided when action must be taken. |
| The group may not have the expertise necessary to make the decision. | It is often impossible for team members to have all the facts at their fingertips and see their suggestions in the broad perspective. Personal interest will sometimes conflict with the organisation's needs. |
| The leader must be empowered. | Consensus decision-making is about empowering team members, not about disempowering the leader. |
| Group deliberations are a resource for the leader. | A group provides more brain power and greater attention than one person can give. The purpose of this method of decision-making is to optimise and harness everyone's skill and creativity. It needs clearly defined parameters, however. Group decisions in the workplace should not usually be binding on the leader. |

*Figure 21: Control in consensus decision-making*

to be gained from the inclusion and openness involved in the group decision-making style.[47]

## Not promoting your own point of view

'I'm not sure, but I think ...'

Deborah Tannen, author and Professor of Linguistics at Georgetown University, says: 'Women are more likely to downplay their certainty, men more likely to play down their doubts.'[48]

People who place a high priority on equality often have a hesitant conflict style. By taking care not to *impose* their views, they may appear not to have any views at all, even when they are quite sure of their ground.

*Hesitantly presented ideas may be dismissed.*

> At a public meeting on traffic issues that I attended, most of the speakers were men, aggressively stating their positions and views, sometimes not very logically, but certainly very powerfully. One of the few women speakers at the meeting had many more facts at her disposal. She gave a considered response to the traffic issues being addressed at the meeting. However, her speaking style was hesitant and quiet – almost apologetic. I suspect that her points did not carry much weight with the men present, but as a woman I found myself extremely influenced by what she had to say. I did wish that she had been more forceful, however. I could see how easy it was to dismiss her sound arguments amongst the surer, louder approaches of the male speakers. She also happened to be a particularly petite person.

A person with a forthright, more masculine style may misinterpret another's hesitancy as a negotiation signal. 'Ah, hah!' they think. 'There's room to move this person from this position.' They then jump into bargaining mode. The hesitant person may well back down in response to this manoeuvre. Negative thoughts are triggered: 'They never listen', 'You can never win a fight with them', 'Why do I even bother trying?', 'I can't negotiate if it means hard bargaining'. This problem of losing ground is exacerbated if the other person happens to be physically stronger. The unconscious intimidation is there as soon as anger rises, even though a physical fight would never occur.

Women are often very reticent in meetings, waiting patiently for their turn to speak. They've been too well trained by the supermarket. They queue! Men, on the other hand, are likely to have been conditioned on the football field. They jump right in, talking over someone else if necessary to score their point. In meetings, women usually have to be really hot under the collar before they'll jump in.

*STEPPING STONES*

*If you wait too long for your turn to speak, you may be ignored.*

In group discussions, meetings or one-on-one conflicts there will be times when it is very important to state your ideas forcefully. If you're overly deferential or wait too long for your turn to speak, you may be ignored. The equaliser needs the flexibility to change style temporarily when it's important to get their point across.

Shifting a debate away from the negative and towards the positive is a very potent conflict resolution skill. It often requires considerable determination, even if quietly expressed. Use it when you need to change the focus from:

▶ problems towards solutions;

▶ worst-case scenarios towards a vision of possibilities;

▶ heavy enforcement of rules and regulations towards realistic goal-setting for improved behaviour.

There are many other situations in which you might need to redirect negative energy with great clarity. Sometimes nothing less than a forthright statement will make people change direction. 'We're bogged down in detail. We need to take a look at the big picture', is the powerful redirecting statement used by one of my interviewees in a very difficult meeting.

## Too many apologies

**'Sorry, you trod on my foot.'**

Deborah Tannen does much of her research by taping everyday conversations. She reports that she often captures women engaged in a number of common conversational rituals.[49] She's found that women say 'I'm sorry' much more frequently than men. They are not necessarily apologising; rather, they are trying to restore equality in the relationship. To reprimand an employee, for instance, they will have to pull rank. They may then restore the power balance with one or more 'I'm sorrys', perhaps by apologising for a mistake they have made or could lay claim to.

> Alice had botched up some documentation again. 'I'm sorry,' said her supervisor, also a woman, 'I can't have explained clearly to you how to fill out a dispatch slip.' The supervisor knew she had already explained documentation procedures to Alice several times quite clearly.

In feminine gender culture, 'I'm sorry' is often a reciprocal ritual. In the example above, the supervisor offers her 'I'm sorry' as a softener to the reprimand. To complete the ritual, Alice really should say something like: 'Oh, I'm really sorry I left out that item. How silly of me.' If the second half of the 'I'm sorry' ritual isn't completed, there's a breakdown of equal status. In fact, the supervisor is left one-down. She's likely to walk away from the interaction upset or irritated rather than satisfied.

*'I'm sorry' is often a reciprocal ritual.*

In masculine gender culture, a man only apologises if he truly believes he is in the wrong. Apologising is usually a big deal for him. By the same token, he does not expect others to apologise without good reason.

A man's gender culture doesn't prepare him for frequent, low-intensity reciprocal apologising. When he hears a ritual 'I'm sorry' from a woman, quite likely it won't occur to him to apologise in turn. The gender differences in social rituals are generally unconscious. Neither the man nor the woman is likely to recognise that, in this situation, feminine etiquette has been breached. But when it happens, the distance widens between them.[50]

## STEPPING STONES
Respond rather than react. If you're motivated by status and apologies don't flow naturally from your tongue, you may be surprised by the effectiveness of adding a few more when you're around an equaliser. Apologising isn't grovelling in their eyes.

*Apologising isn't grovelling in an equaliser's eyes.*

If you consider yourself to be an equaliser, become aware of your own apology rituals. Don't use apologies when your reprimands would have better results without them. If you choose to use an apology, check that your point has nevertheless been clearly understood. You are more likely to see this in what the person *does*, rather than what they *say*. Hopefully you'll see the required change in their future behaviour. If you know the other person is very status-oriented and you do want to use your apology to minimise their distress, don't expect the reciprocal apology you are likely to get from another equaliser.

There are times when an apology is an admission of guilt in situations with legal implications. Be exceptionally careful what you say in these circumstances, particularly if you generally favour an apologetic, equalising style.

## STUMBLING BLOCK 2:
## TAKING OFFENCE AT INEQUALITY

### Favours not returned

**'I do so much for them. What do they ever do for me?'**

If you are frequently doing favours for someone else, you like to know you can count on that person to reciprocate sooner or later. Equalisers are more likely to be keeping score than status-watchers.[51] To preserve equality, favours can't always travel only in one direction.

> Leon was a highly competent and genuinely caring manager of the purchasing department in a bank. His offsider, Sandra, often brought her personal problems into the workplace. Leon listened supportively whenever she told him of her troubles. Sometimes her work was quite inaccurate but, knowing her difficulties, Leon made allowances. On several occasions when he could see that it would make a difference, he'd offered her some time off. One morning, Leon got a call at work. His brother had been involved in a serious motorcycle accident. Leon wanted to go to the hospital immediately, but Sandra had a rostered afternoon off. This would leave their area unstaffed, which was not acceptable. Telling Sandra what the problem was, Leon asked her if she could change her afternoon off, so he could get away. She said she couldn't, as she had appointments. Leon let her go and kept in touch with his family by phone until he could join them at the hospital that evening.
>
> The next day, Leon noticed Sandra had been to the hairdresser. It looked as though this was the appointment she'd not wanted to cancel. Perhaps Leon had not signalled clearly how distressed he was

and how much he needed the afternoon off, but he had thought that would be obvious.

After that, Leon became increasingly resentful towards Sandra and her constant neediness.

### STEPPING STONES

FOR EQUALISERS: When you need support from people who usually receive it from you, make sure you let them know. You may need to initiate a conversation about rebalancing the whole relationship, if it is too one-sided.

FOR THOSE RECEIVING SUPPORT: Be aware of misusing support. If you have received a lot of support from an equaliser, whether or not they are your superior, seize opportunities to return the support at moments when they look like they could do with it. Many competent people disguise their distress. You'll be balancing the score and that will be more important than you might realise.

## Thanking not returned

### 'Don't you ever say thank you?'

The equaliser's need for mutuality applies to thanking as well. Deborah Tannen finds that this is another important conversational ritual, particularly amongst women.[52] Often in closing a conversation, equalisers will find something to thank the other person for, expecting them to reply with a similar 'thank you'. Equality is threatened if equalisers offer their ritual thanks and the reciprocal thanks isn't forthcoming, particularly if they feel they were really the ones doing the favour.

> Sally spent many hours editing a report for a male colleague. She gave him feedback in a positive and considered way. 'Thanks for the opportunity to look at the report,' she said in closing the conversation. 'I'm glad you got something out of it,' he said. But he didn't thank her for her time and work. She was furious.

Reciprocal thanking can baffle men for a number of reasons. First, 'thank yous' don't always need to be reciprocated, so they're unsure what is expected. Second, offering thanks can, in some men's eyes, reduce their status. Being thanked, on the other hand, supports status. Helpfulness can be a hallmark of benevolent superiority. In the pleasure of being given a status 'stroke' (a term from Transactional Analysis for a gesture of positive regard or praise), men can easily misread what is required of them in exchange.

*STEPPING STONES*

*Ask for 'thank yous' if you really need them.*

Status-watchers don't thank others very often, so it's probably best not to expect it. If it's really bugging you, ask for some 'thank yous'. It may work. Many people are merely absent-minded, not ungrateful. So remind them! Perhaps Sally could have dropped a hint that she needed to be thanked: 'It took me quite a few hours to do the edit. I hope it was worthwhile for you.' This might have prompted her colleague to recognise that good manners required him to express gratitude.

The rituals we require for formal completion of interactions are culture-specific. They vary between men and women, between different social classes and between different nationalities. We each need to take responsibility for guiding other people so that they don't offend us, and we need to be sensitive to other people's customs of politeness.

## Inequality of respect

**'I deserve what they've got!'**

*Equalisers are often embarrassed about needing their superior status recognised.*

Equality can give a particular twist to status battles. Equalisers are often embarrassed about their need to have the superiority of their position respected. What they usually require is respect *equivalent to* others of the same status.

Jan, who works for a large nationwide company, told me this story:

> I was asked to be a guest speaker at our senior manager's logistics conference, a very grand affair at the Regent Hotel. It was quite an honour. I was the first woman ever to be asked to speak at this conference. About 200 men would be attending, most of whom would be bringing their wives.
>
> I arrived for the opening dinner on Sunday night. It was a four-day conference, but I was only staying for the first day, speaking that afternoon, and then leaving the next morning. I was a bit late arriving

for the dinner. Having checked me in and given me my speaker's name tag, the conference organiser told me to sit anywhere I liked. I knew there was a head table for speakers, but I didn't really feel I could just go and sit there unless I was directly invited. *Oh, great,* I thought. *All the speakers* (men!) *are at the head table except for me.* I didn't say anything, but I felt slighted.

I sat down at a participants' table, where I was indistinguishable from all the wives who were going to spend their time sitting by the pool or shopping while their husbands attended the conference. The husbands at the table no doubt classified me as another 'wife'. They were obviously uncomfortable talking to me. They probably thought that I'd have nothing to say that they'd want to hear. Perhaps also they were concerned it would have looked like flirting to their wives. These conferences can put you in a really uncomfortable social situation.

I was sitting there at the end of the table, feeling very isolated, when this man came in and sat beside me. He didn't say much and I sort of mumbled: 'Hello, I'm so and so.' 'Are you touring after the conference on Thursday, or going straight home?' he asked. Thank heavens, he was at least using some conversation opener. 'No, I'm leaving on Tuesday,' I said. 'How come?' he replied. 'Oh, because I'm speaking on Monday afternoon.' His eyes went wide. His whole manner changed. Now he was really engaged. 'Oh, you're a speaker,' he said, checking my name tag for the fine print. Then he became quite animated. We had a really good chat. He needed me to have a workplace status before he was free to talk openly. And the truth was that I needed that recognition, too. I wasn't just 'one of the wives'.

The next day, I was put on as last speaker in the afternoon. That's a terrible timeslot. The participants had to sit through an hour and a half of me and then they were free to go off and play golf or whatever. I'll bet you that because I'm a woman they felt it was okay to schedule my lecture at such a 'dead' hour. In fact, the session went very well. I got them out of their seats, gave them lots of interaction, made my points powerfully and with a bit of humour. Even the chairman said: 'That was really great.'

*[Notice that Jan responded to the status of the person in the conference hierarchy who had handed out the praise.]*

After my workshop they all went off to play golf or relax. No one asked me to join them. On my own again. It's always like that at these conferences. I should be used to it, but somehow I never am.

I went to dinner that night. Same scenario! Everyone's to sit where they want. I was about to sit down at a participants' table again, when one of the head honchos of the conference came up to me and said: 'Jan, come and sit at the head table.' I'd earned my stripes.

This story brings together a number of issues. Apparently Jan's status as a speaker was not enough to gain her automatic entry to the head table of influential men. It was not until she proved herself with an outstanding presentation that the omission was even noticed. Jan was not immune to the status slight. She herself didn't want to be seen as 'just one of the wives'. However, her real gripe was an equality issue. The other speakers had been ushered to the head table and she knew that she deserved to be there, too. As a successful woman, Jan often faces the difficulty of being isolated when playing in men's territory. She tries not to let her discomfort show, but sometimes the lack of acknowledgment is acutely painful.

*STEPPING STONES*

There are unexpected obstacles for a woman making her place in a man's world. It is important not to misread the motivation behind these obstacles. Sometimes lack of acknowledgment from men is not due to any desire to put down the woman. Men's reasons might include:

▶ sheer oversight;

▶ discomfort about change in the social dynamics of a male-only group;

▶ concern about jeopardising their relationship with their spouse or partner;

▶ the presumption that if the woman doesn't immediately include herself in social activities, she doesn't want to participate.

Many women are still following feminine etiquette more appropriate to dating twenty years ago than standing as an equal in the workplace today. For example, a woman may wait for an invitation to join a group of colleagues, particularly when she isn't sure that her right to be there is recognised. She may need considerable courage to break away from old conditioning and deliver a self-assured 'May I join you?'.

Of course, men can also hold back, waiting for an invitation. One man complained to me:

> My superior is a woman. One of her tasks is to schedule our tea breaks so that the counter is always attended. She often asks other women in my group to join her when she takes her own tea break, but she has never once asked me. I certainly wouldn't gatecrash, but I have to say I resent it that she never includes me.

Single-sexed gatherings that really have no need to be that way are a recipe for alienation if they happen repeatedly. Some workplaces now structure in women's support meetings. Men at times need that sort of solidarity, too. Such meetings have their place. But many one-sex social or working groups develop because it's easier, more comfortable or just habitual. We must create new gender-sensitive conduct for the modern workplace.

## STUMBLING BLOCK 3: CONTINUED RESENTMENT

### 'I'll never forgive them!'

In the animal kingdom, status conflicts are usually associated with the male of the species. These conflicts are generally violent and short — when dominance is established they're over. Fights also occur between females, however, and these are often far more vicious. Ritual submission signals aren't offered or may be ignored. A 'you win' gesture may not be enough for an angry female wolf that's protecting a litter, staking a territorial claim or warning another female off a preferred companion.

It's not that different for humans. Women aren't always the sweeter sex. In fact, women can be more vindictive than men, and can hang onto their anger a lot longer. If a man isn't given the respect his position deserves, he's likely to be overtly angry. He'll lash out at another man to re-establish the status to which he believes he is entitled. After the conflict, however, when one party has accepted the others' status on that issue, both men are likely

*Typically, men are quick to anger and quick to cool down, whereas women are slow to anger and slow to cool.*

to calm down quickly. Before they go home for the day, they might even have a drink together. Work conflicts don't generally carry over into men's personal relationships, yet they often do so for women.

When a woman believes the other person has been so *unfair* that she is willing to go into battle over it, that fight is likely to be particularly distressing to her. Typically, she'll have been pushed a long way past her comfort zone before she'll make this judgment. But once she has, the other person may have to work very hard to restore her goodwill. Here are a number of common conflict triggers for a woman:

▸ She feels power has been used over her unfairly or manipulatively.

▸ She believes someone has usurped or undermined her equal status.

▸ Someone won't give her the support which she feels, in fairness, she deserves.

▸ Someone has been deceitful or spread lies, destroying the trust on which her equal relationship with them has been built.

▸ Someone has abused her goodwill and tolerance, another trademark of her equality stance.

A woman probably won't get over any one of these slights in one short dispute. Unless the incident was a pure misunderstanding, she probably is quite likely to hold a grudge for a long time. Male equalisers are quite likely to have similar reactions.

*STEPPING STONES*

Possibly one of the reasons many men recover from their anger quickly is because they tend to reach a flashpoint more easily and, in the moment of loss of control, will say exactly what they think. Men and women who are more controlled deliver only a fraction of the anger they really feel. The rest is internalised as resentment. Resentment is frozen anger. It is a deadly poison in workplace relationships. It's hard to overcome other people's resentment, but we can work against it in ourselves. To head towards forgiveness you might ask yourself these questions:

---

**GETTING READY TO FORGIVE**

► Is there something you need to say to the other person in order to communicate your problem clearly?

► Is what you wish to say appropriate?

► Could you make a time to discuss the issue in private? The middle of an open-plan office is rarely the right setting.

► What else would help you get over your anger and hurt?

► Are you able to ask for what you wish?

► Do you need to broaden your tolerance (not necessarily your approval) of some negative qualities the person displays so that you can forgive the other person and wipe the slate clean?

**The real purpose of anger is to create change.**

---

# STUMBLING BLOCK 4: INTOLERANCE OF HIGH-FLIERS

### 'Who do they think they are?'

Though originally the equality value may have been founded on a desire for a conflict-free relationship, the value doesn't guarantee it by any means. Just as equality-minded people don't like to be envied, they really don't like to envy others either. Equalisers can cut others down to size quite viciously.

> Whenever Lisa, a very attractive thirty-year-old, met up with Jennifer, Lisa always seemed to come away smarting from some comment Jennifer had made. Jennifer was a master of innuendo. Her comment when they met one day for coffee was typical. Lisa was wearing a new red dress she thought suited her particularly well. Jennifer soon thrust in her dagger: 'What a wonderful colour that is on you, Lisa. Of course, I never wear red. It's far too showy.'

Ouch!

Emily had recently landed an exciting job with a radio station. She was full of the joys of working with well-known personalities and great scriptwriters. She was chatting happily about it to her friend, whose job at that time was plodding along, getting nowhere fast. 'Emily,' said her friend, 'I'm really fed up with you. You're just so full of yourself these days.'

Ouch again! Who said women are the sweeter sex?

Emily wondered what she'd done wrong. She thought she'd just been sharing her excitement. But in her friend's eyes, she was a tall poppy who needed to be cut down.

*STEPPING STONES*

How might Emily avoid this sort of problem? Perhaps she can't. If you only talk about your troubles, what sort of a friendship is that? What's Emily's friend really saying?

*It's hard for me to hear all this good stuff happening for you when my job is going nowhere at the moment.*

Emily would have reacted better to this statement. When men's and women's own circumstances block their ability to be expansive and creative, envy of others' successes comes easily. Susie Orbach and Louise Eichenbaum suggest: 'Envy ... is a cue for an exploration of other feelings.'[53]

Envy is a signpost of desire, of unfulfilled wants. If you find that you envy a friend, you may need to discuss your feelings frankly with them if the relationship is to move forward.

Emily may have been able to initiate the discussion by finding out whether envy was her friend's real issue. She could have said:

*Is it hard for you to listen to me talking about my new job? I know you're not that happy about yours at the moment.*

To respond in this way after 'You're just so full of yourself these days' requires a sophisticated level of empathy. It certainly requires a response rather than a reaction. In fact, this may be a conversation Emily could open at another time, when she has her wits about her again and can plan carefully what she wants to do to resurrect the friendship.

Women, though they may pride themselves on their ability to

be intimate, are often very poor at discussing the emotions that directly threaten their friendship. Envy, rivalry and resentment are taboo topics when the other person is their source. Left unresolved, these issues can destroy friendships and working relationships. A frank discussion may be vital if the relationship is to be saved. This can add a completely new dimension of strength and resilience to a relationship. Sometimes it will be the only way to circumvent backstabbing behaviour.

*When relationships falter over envy, rivalry or resentment, women rarely discuss the issue directly with the other person.*

## STUMBLING BLOCK 5: INSUBORDINATION

**'How can I wriggle out of doing that?'**

Society's myth is that women are more compliant than men. However, this is not what women reported in the course of my own research.[54] In response to the questionnaire statement, 'I usually do what my boss asks even if I disagree with it', only 37 per cent of women said they would, compared with 53 per cent of men. Women are an unruly lot! Yet at school, any teacher will tell you there are far fewer discipline problems with girls than with boys. 'Disobedient' has crept, apparently inaccurately, into our stereotyped images of masculinity. So what's happening as women mature in the workforce? Two of my interviewees report:

> Kate admits that she doesn't always do what her bosses ask. 'Sometimes I just tell them: "No, I'm not going to do it." Sometimes I'm a little bit more devious, like if it's filling out paperwork or reports and I think it's a waste of time, I just keep putting it off until the boss doesn't ask for it any more.'

> Chris doesn't see her bosses as better or more right than her. 'If I don't agree with what they are saying, I'll do or try to do what I think is right—but I'll be quite subtle about it. I rarely confront someone directly.'

Why this subtle subterfuge? Once they have confidence that they know the job well, women are more likely to act out of a sense of fundamental equality. The superior status of their boss seems to mean less to women than it would to men in the same position.

*Once women are confident they know their job, they are likely to query authority if they disagree.*

Relative position is not a primary focus for equalisers.

Peter, an ex-nurse, has never embraced the idea of male hierarchies. Like Kate and Chris, he values equality in the workplace. He says:

> When I was nursing, doctors would always be asking me to do something. If I disagreed with it, I'd say so. I saw that as part of the responsibility of my job. I didn't blindly just go and do it. Doctors are human, too. They can make a mistake.

Peter, now in charge of his own medical supplies company, expects his employees, both male and female, to respond to him from a commitment to their own equality. He values their professional vision. He offers and expects mutual consultation.

*Men are more likely to respect the authority of position than women.*

Peter is atypical. Most men are more likely than women to respect relative position in the organisational hierarchy. While it is always dubious to draw conclusions about human behaviour from the animal kingdom, perhaps there are some parallels. In the animal world, once established, pecking order isn't usually tested again until there's a substantial change in physical power — a young male reaching its prime, or an old animal losing its strength.[55] In the absence of such destabilising factors, each male animal accepts for the time being the position it has achieved in the dominance hierarchy. Kerbing aggressiveness under these circumstances preserves individual safety and the stability of the whole group. Status and pecking order in human male society appears to obey similar rules. However, in chimpanzee colonies, sociobiologist Robert Wright observes:

> Females settle into a hierarchy with less conflict (seniority often counts for a lot), and are thereafter less preoccupied with their status. In fact, the female hierarchy is so subdued that it takes an experienced eye to discern it.[56]

Women, our largest group of non-status-watchers, don't treat status as overly important unless they're being made to feel subservient. Those who focus on status are usually more respectful of legitimate authority. Often it's drummed into them very forcefully in childhood. Boys often receive strict discipline in team sports which focus on knowing your place and following the coach's or captain's game plan. The heavy hand of authority often comes down harder

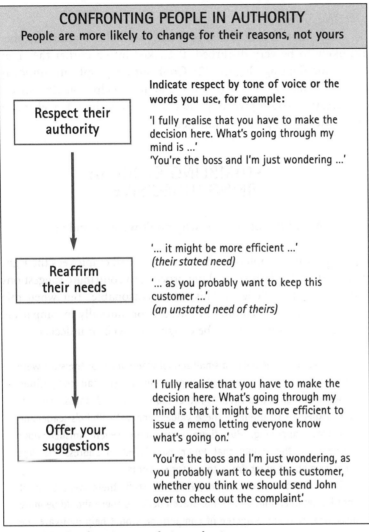

**CONFRONTING PEOPLE IN AUTHORITY**
People are more likely to change for their reasons, not yours

**Respect their authority**

Indicate respect by tone of voice or the words you use, for example:

'I fully realise that you have to make the decision here. What's going through my mind is ...'
'You're the boss and I'm just wondering ...'

**Reaffirm their needs**

'... it might be more efficient ...'
*(their stated need)*

'... as you probably want to keep this customer ...'
*(an unstated need of theirs)*

**Offer your suggestions**

'I fully realise that you have to make the decision here. What's going through my mind is that it might be more efficient to issue a memo letting everyone know what's going on.'

'You're the boss and I'm just wondering, as you probably want to keep this customer, whether you think we should send John over to check out the complaint.'

*Figure 22: Confronting people in authority*

on boys' adolescent rebelliousness than girls'. In the past, a dose of military service, sometimes compulsory, was the finishing school that prepared many young men for the world. Here they learnt that their very survival depended on obedience. Masculine culture has conditioned males to accept this rule as part and parcel of patriarchy. No wonder many men find it particularly difficult to have women around them repeatedly questioning their authority.

STEPPING STONES

Be aware that if you challenge a status-watcher's authority they are likely to be very disturbed. If backed into a corner they may come out fighting. **Figure 22: Confronting people in authority** (page 97) has some suggestions that may help you. In normal conversation you'll probably intersperse these three key elements with other appropriate comments.

# STUMBLING BLOCK 6: BEING INDECISIVE

**'Well, I'm not sure, so why don't we wait and see.'**

Equalisers often emphasise the need to give all employees the right to be part of the decision-making process, to contribute suggestions and to be acknowledged. This seems reasonable. But when this approach exposes a conflict of interests or mutually incompatible outcomes, the equaliser can be caught in a web of indecision.

Philip was the principal of a small school where most of the staff were women. The school promoted cooperation rather than competition between students, and equality rather than power and status. The staff were expected to promote these values, and with Philip's leadership this was happening. But there were some severe misbehaviour problems in the school that Philip had failed to address. He was indecisive about what limits to set for students.

Some months after Steven joined the staff, there were signs of conflict between him and Philip. Steven believed there should be more discipline, that some degree of competition would help motivate the students and he began to imply during staff meetings that Philip was too soft to be leading a school. Although some of the female staff disliked Steven's sometimes aggressive manner, there were others who admired what they referred to as a 'more manly' approach to running a school. They put their weight behind Steven to create an environment that was less compromising and more rules-bound.

Philip, who felt threatened by these moves, became noticeably harder and less empathic towards both staff and students. He began, in the words of one female member of staff, 'to play out the role of someone to be feared, rather than be the person he was at heart: someone easy to befriend.'

It's all very well for a leader to be 'first amongst equals', but sometimes tough decisions have to be made and they won't please everyone involved. Equalisers can find it difficult to adjust to a change in their previously equalising leader. Philip's rather dramatic transformation may well have been the result of considerable discomfort in adopting a more authoritarian approach for the overall good of the school. A status-oriented leader is less likely to be distressed about making decisions that others don't like. The equaliser can go through the tortures of the damned implementing unpopular decisions, even while believing it's for the best.

## STEPPING STONES

Look upon your indecision as a prompt to collect more information, opinions and options. However, there comes a certain point when all the homework is done and further indecision is ineffective for the organisation and for the problem. Excessive indecision will harm your chances of promotion within the company. Grit your teeth and get on with it. Remember, you can't please all of the people all of the time. To shore up my own resolve, I sometimes need to remind myself that what other people think of me is none of my business. You'll feel better if you explain to the relevant people the factors that have led you to the decision. If the issue is sensitive and you can't disclose that information, be honest about it: 'I'd like to tell you all the factors that were involved, but I'm just not able to do so at this time.' If an equalising manager has to issue this type of directive they will probably feel very stressed. Spare them a few supportive words.

*Medicine for tough decisions: 'What other people think of me is none of my business.'*

# SUMMARY

| EQUALITY: STUMBLING BLOCKS | STEPPING STONES: RESPOND RATHER THAN REACT |
|---|---|
| **1 ▶ Being too modest** | |
| *Hiding achievements* | Modesty isn't always the best strategy. It might be better to let the right people know about your successes. |
| *Playing down your position* | Sometimes you should clearly indicate your position even if it makes you uncomfortable. |
| *Socialising with subordinates* | Socialising out of hours needs to be combined with techniques for ensuring your position is taken seriously when you are 'on duty'. |
| *Not taking charge* | An equality-oriented team working on a false expectation of group control over all decisions may need to grasp that: ▶ group deliberations are a resource for the leader; ▶ the leader cannot safely surrender authority or accountability; ▶ the group may not have the expertise for the decision needed; ▶ the leader must be empowered. Equality-oriented teams need to understand that certain decisions must remain in the leader's hands. |
| *Not promoting your own point of view* | In meetings, equalisers may need to change style temporarily to avoid being overly deferential or waiting too long for their turn to speak. To turn the tide towards the positive will often require considerable determination, even if quietly expressed. |
| *Too many apologies* | Status-oriented people should be alert to the first half of an apology ritual so they know when it would be wise to offer their reciprocal apology. When equalisers soften a reprimand with an apology, a status-watcher may not apologise in turn. To confirm your point has been clearly understood, you may have to wait and see if their behaviour improves. |

| STUMBLING BLOCKS | STEPPING STONES |
|---|---|
| 2 ► **Taking offence at inequality** | |
| *Favours not returned* | To preserve equality, favours can't always travel only in one direction. |
| *Thanking not returned* | If you need to be thanked, you may have to remind status-watchers that you'd appreciate their thanks. Don't expect them to participate in thanking rituals automatically. |
| *Inequality of respect* | In some situations, it may be possible to address the status slight directly. |
| 3 ► **Continued resentment** | Recognise resentment as frozen anger. Ask yourself: 'What do I need in order to let go of my anger and hurt? Can I ask for it? Is it realistic? Can I wipe the slate clean so that communication is improved for the whole group?' |
| 4 ► **Intolerance of high-fliers** | Directly addressing envy, rivalry or resentment may be the best way to improve the relationship. |
| 5 ► **Insubordination** | If you challenge a superior, do it in terms of *their* needs:<br>► make your tone respectful;<br>► reaffirm their needs in the situation or remind them of others you know they have;<br>► express your alternative as a way to meet their needs. |
| 6 ► **Being indecisive** | Use indecision as a prompt to collect more information, opinions and options. Excessive indecision will harm you chances of promotion within the company. Grit your teeth and get on with tough decisions. |

# 5 STATUS: stumbling blocks & stepping stones

### PREVIEW

*STUMBLING BLOCK*

1 ▸ Domination

2 ▸ Defensiveness and low self-esteem

3 ▸ Territory protection

4 ▸ Hunger for status symbols

5 ▸ Undervaluing others

At its best, status follows in the wake of generous giving of self. Used wisely, it is shouldered alongside responsibility and a desire to assist others. It arises from skill and willingness to organise activities on behalf of others with care and vision.

In Chapter 3, we compared status with its apparent opposite, equality, and considered the different life experiences that mould these values and how status-watchers and equalisers are likely to handle power. In Chapter 4, we looked at equalisers' stumbling blocks. Now it's time to be equally ruthless on the misuse of status. In this chapter we'll mainly be addressing problems men generate, as the status value often has a higher priority for men. However, women are frequently quite status-conscious and are not immune to its pitfalls. As with Chapter 4, we'll also consider stepping stones — the insights and skills needed to overcome problems. Sometimes these solutions are relevant for status-watchers; at other times, they apply to those affected by a clumsy or self-serving use of status. Such problems occur mainly around the issue of control—either a fixation on *being in control* or acute irritation about *being controlled*. Here lurk the potential stumbling blocks of the status value.

# STUMBLING BLOCK 1: DOMINATION

## Obsession with control

'You'll do it because I say so.'

Obviously, a manager has to control. Every organisation requires systems and needs them to be followed. Where there is an obsessive need to control, however, the person interferes and directs excessively. Such a fixation can stifle other people's creativity and motivation.

OVERT OBSESSION WITH CONTROL: When people openly display excessive controlling behaviour, they often presume it is a requirement of their rank. They have misjudged the responsibilities of leadership. This misjudgment is often fuelled by underlying emotional issues such as:

► perfectionism — a need for order and system, often to avoid being overwhelmed; or

► a need to establish status based on other people's subservience.

Frequently, overt controllers are men. When the need to control is pushed to its extreme, the consequences for an organisation can be disastrous.

*Men are more likely than women to become obsessed with overt control.*

> Robert was the principal of a business college. An ex-army officer, he expected regimental obedience from his staff. Details mattered a great deal to Robert, and he would spend hours at his desk creating memos to control the trifling details of his staff's working life. There were rosters of cleaning duties, rosters for holidays eighteen months in advance, day-of-the-month duties for book-keeping tasks and so on. The aspects of control that caused the most irritation were the lesson plans from which no teacher was permitted to deviate or even discuss with him. He was fond of welcoming new staff with: 'In this college, you shape up or you ship out!' The trouble was that most people shipped out within twelve months, and his long-term staff had been well tutored by him to take no initiative at all. His reputation as a disciplinarian had spread widely in the community and good teachers no longer applied for jobs at the college.

Robert had thought he was creating high professional standards for the college. Indeed, this was his good purpose. However, as a direct result of his pedantic control, the academic reputation of the college was very mediocre.

*Many men complain about women's covert control.*

COVERT OBSESSION WITH CONTROL: Controlling behaviour doesn't only occur with people who are formally in charge of others. If the person doesn't actually have authority over another, the way they exercise their demands may be more *covert*. Many men complain about women's covert controlling behaviour. Possibly it is the presence of a focus on equality *alongside* the status value that leads women to adopt covert behaviours. Also, they are less likely to hold the rank usually necessary for overt control.

Spouses often impose implied demands on their partner. Theoretically, the relationship is equal, but one or both partners may interfere too much in the other's life. Many parents overdo their demands on teenage children. When children are young they need, and usually accept, wide-ranging guidance — from brushing their teeth to feeding the cat. But adolescents need to exercise personal choice over large areas of their lives.

*Every 'should' we place on another person is our claim to status over them.*

Male or female, most of us put some 'shoulds' on the people we work with. 'You shouldn't conduct lengthy personal conversations', or 'You should be more polite to customers', or 'You should get your statement of billable hours to the accountant by the end of each week'. These are usually legitimate 'shoulds' arising from the organisation's needs for effectiveness. Yet these demands on the other person are still a form of control. We need to recognise that every 'should' we place on another person is our claim of status over them. But what if we only think it? Even our thoughts affect the relationship, silently filling the room, creating tension and withdrawal. Most people sense when they are judged and found wanting.

*STEPPING STONES*

When is it appropriate to ask someone to change? When is it out of line? Here are three questions to ask yourself when a 'should' arises in your mind:

1. *Does the problem affect you?* If it only affects the other person, it may not be particularly functional to interfere. Everyone

needs a domain of personal choice where they can learn by trial and error what works for them and what doesn't. Personally, I keep a hellishly messy desk most of the time. The best I can say of it is that it is 'work in progress', but I know there are times when I lose things on it, or don't attend to something that's important. But it's my problem. I'd resent someone else telling me what I 'should' do about it. I already know.

When you are in charge of someone, you can be fussier if the organisation isn't getting the output from them it deserves. Nevertheless, even this may not be sufficient justification for control. Most employees today expect to have a wide area in which they have freedom of action.

2. *Can you live with the problems their way creates?* If you can, it might be smarter to see their way as part of the environment in which you have to work, rather than another area for you to try to fix. Organisations will never be perfect. When you work as part of a team, you often need to accept that others may not do a job as efficiently as you would. But you can't do everything yourself. Organisations, at least in part, are about other people's self-development. To accommodate the more cumbersome pace of working in groups, you may need to lower your expectations of others, though not necessarily your self-expectations.

*As organisations, we may need to hold lower standards than we do as individuals.*

3. *Does their way work?* If the answer is 'yes, but it's less efficient', consider whether the trade-off between a little extra efficiency and squashing initiative or inviting rebellion is worth it.

If other people, and the organisation itself, find a *significant* problem, you're on surer ground with your demand for the person to change. But consider the difference between 'power over' and 'power with'. 'Power over' the other person can lead to conflict and alienation even when you have every right to make a particular demand. Consider its sequence in **Figure 23: 'Power over' — demand behaviour** (page 106).

You may need to transform your overt or covert controlling behaviour into a relationship of 'power with'. Here each person keeps their personal power intact and respects the other person's space and integrity. From this position, both people can search

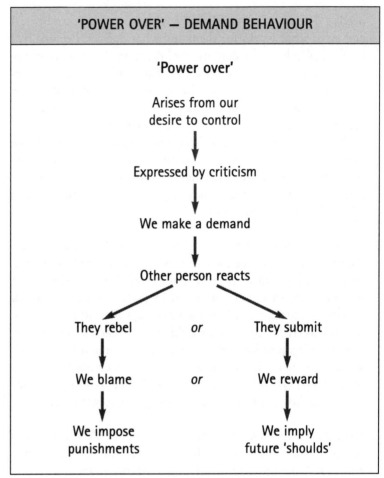

*Figure 23: 'Power over' — demand behaviour*

together for solutions to their mutual problems.

'Power with' *invites* the other person to change, rather than *demands* it. Often the most effective way to employ 'power with' techniques is to shift the focus away from the person and on to the issue and the tangible difficulties their way is creating for others. Consider also what the other person's needs are in this situation. And your own! Think about the outcome you want and the freedom you are truly giving the other person to choose their response. Of course you want a particular outcome. You believe it's better, otherwise you wouldn't bother to talk about it. You

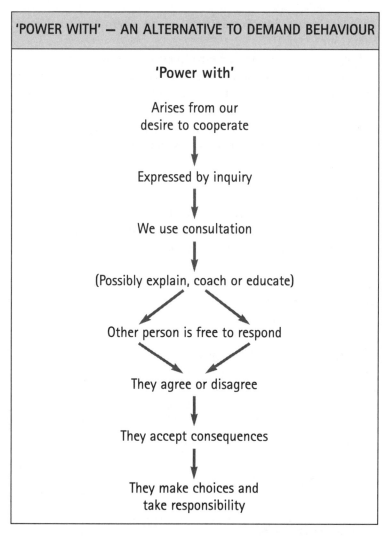

Figure 24: 'Power with' — an alternative to demand behaviour

may explain, coach or educate, but always respect the other person's right to choose not to do it your way.

Sidestepping the controlling/controlled dimension can take the sting out of cross-gender conflict. Careful attention to these factors will shift you from domination to mutual exploration. This difference is subtle, but it's one that can dramatically improve working relationships. 'Power with' has a number of elements.

*Sidestepping the controlling/controlled dimension can take the sting out of cross-gender conflict.*

Refer to **Figure 24: 'Power with' — an alternative to demand behaviour** (page 107).

When you make the move to 'power with' relating, you may experience a deep sense of personal release as you let go of the emotional issue you have tied up in control. You can hold a lot of energy in judging the other person as 'wrong' and in demanding overtly or covertly that they do it your way. To trigger this shift in consciousness, you may need to explore your own motivations with regard to control.

*EXERCISE*

Figure 25 below contains some questions inspired by the work of Will Schutz.[57] Think of someone in your life on whom you place spoken or unspoken 'shoulds'. Consider the questions below with your relationship to that person in mind. Place a tick in the column next to the issues that definitely or probably apply to you. You may need to delve into your unconscious motivations, so take your time — it will help you stir the processes of awareness.

| EMOTIONAL ISSUES OF CONTROL<br>My control over: (insert name) . . . . . . . . . . . . . | |
| --- | --- |
| I choose to control because the other person *wants* me to direct their behaviour. | |
| I choose to control because the other person *needs* me to direct their behaviour. | |
| If I am not the one in control, I think the other person will control or undermine me. | |
| If I don't tell the other person what to do, there will be chaos. | |
| The other person would tell me if they don't like me taking charge. | |
| I sometimes use control to mask my feelings of inadequacy. | |
| I believe that I can see how things should be and that the other person doesn't measure up. | |
| Other issues are involved. These seem to be about:<br>. . . . . . . . . . . . . . . . . . . . . . . . . . . . . . . . . . . . . . . . . . . . . .<br>. . . . . . . . . . . . . . . . . . . . . . . . . . . . . . . . . . . . . . . . . . . . . .<br>. . . . . . . . . . . . . . . . . . . . . . . . . . . . . . . . . . . . . . . . . . . . . . | |

*Figure 25: Emotional issues of control*

Beware! If lots of people don't measure up to your standards, it says more about you than it does about them. For example, a director of a large club went through nine public relations officers in two years. Nine! Were they all that bad?

The honest exploration of these questions may bring up some motivations that you can recognise as unfair to the other person and dysfunctional in yourself. Such reassessments can lead you away from 'power over' and towards true 'power with'. Of course, sometimes only a clear order will be appropriate: Sexual harassment must stop. Stealing cannot be condoned. Non-productive time at work needs firm correction. Discrimination or victimisation must not be overlooked.

## Arrogance

**'You're not capable of understanding my job.'**

When status swamps other values, the person may become over-inflated with their own sense of self-importance. They may give the impression they think they are better than everyone else. Whenever you're around them, you notice that you feel somehow inadequate. You may not realise that it is part of their image-building process, because you're so uncomfortable being at its receiving end.

Arrogance in both the sexes has been around a long time. Men have relied on their position and expertise, women on their beauty and social class. In the past, gender differences were clear. In the modern workplace, however, women with inflated egos are likely to use the crutches for self-esteem that were once exclusively men's. Here are some of the ways arrogance in either sex can present itself in the workplace:

► ambition beyond skills;

► stretching the truth about one's level of expertise;

► withholding information to get an edge on others;

► using greater knowledge as a reason for feeling superior;

► using intellectual agility to discount other people's perspectives.

The manoeuvres of arrogance may be difficult to pin down. It's one-upmanship developed into high art. Take, for example, this antique dealer who gave a lecture on purchasing antiques:

> The dealer chose to limit his subject to buying antiques at auction. Few people in the audience would have wanted to do this, but it was an area in which he could display a clear superiority. He told the audience about how he was educating one amateur enthusiast on the subject. Until the amateur had read various key textbooks and studied all the sales catalogues, the dealer wouldn't discuss anything with him. The amateur did his homework well. He was ready to make his first purchase at auction. He had his eye on a particular piece and visited the dealer again to discuss his intentions. The dealer proudly announced to his audience how he'd taken the wind out of the amateur's sails. He'd told the amateur that only he, the dealer, could ever really assess the piece despite all the study the amateur had done so far. Why? Because only he had ever had a similar piece pass through his hands. This extra knowledge, he informed the amateur, was something you'd never get out of a book.

It was one-upmanship, but the dealer seemed quite unaware of the arrogant picture of himself his story was creating. Moreover, by implication the audience were being given exactly the same message — they could never know what they were doing and could never be taught. Only a man of his experience could safely purchase an antique.

*Why do we tolerate arrogance better in men than in women?*

Well, he might be right. Antique dealing is a complex field, but this man had no concept of a coaching relationship. He built his image on others' ignorance. He'd done it at the expense of his enthusiastic student and done it again to his audience. He'd managed to present a forty-five minute lecture without revealing any information on what was a good buy and what to look out for.

We don't like arrogance in men, but many of us find it even more irksome in women. It conflicts with the stereotype of the good woman as modest and self-effacing. One man I interviewed reported it as a major stumbling block for one of the women in his department of the public service. He says of her:

> My impression is that she hides ruthless ambition under a tiny build and softly spoken voice. I don't know if she'll ever settle down to be a good manager. She certainly isn't doing her job effectively in our department. She spends a major portion of every working day preparing

applications for higher positions. Of course, you have to address your skills in résumés, but I overhear this woman making the most outrageous claims about her skills. The gap between the reality of her managerial skills and her statements in these job applications is huge.

*STEPPING STONES*

If you always feel inferior in the company of a particular person, it is likely they are using superiority as a stance to maintain control. You'd love to take them down a peg or two, but you are unlikely to succeed. They're usually very skilled at the game. If you can ignore the arrogance, they may let you in as friend and colleague — at least to some degree. One of the purposes of their style is to hold people at bay.

Sometimes the arrogant person is masking shyness, distancing themselves from others as a means of self-protection. If you can take your personal spotlight off the arrogance and focus on the positive qualities they possess, you may succeed in getting them to drop the worst of their status-building at your expense. Non-sarcastic humour may be just the tool for breaking down their icy exterior and reaching through to them.

*Humour is a great tool for breaking down an icy exterior.*

When we are unable to acknowledge an occasional desire in ourselves to act superior to others, we are likely to be very intolerant of this behaviour in others. If other people's arrogance particularly inflames you, look within yourself and come to terms with your own pride, however well checked. When we know what triggers our own self-importance, we can usually sidestep overt arrogance and one-upmanship in others and find something else to relate to them about.

## Shaming

**'You ignorant, stupid, good-for-nothing fool.'**

I use the word *shaming* here to mean behaviour, usually a verbal attack, which causes the other person to lose face. To defend their sense of superior position, some status-watchers who are highly sensitised to control and unskilled in interpersonal relationships will use shaming tactics to diminish the other person. The shamer, bolstered by righteous indignation, may become venomous if respect and obedience are not offered as required. Shaming may include:

▶ put-downs disguised by humour. (When challenged, the shamer's response is often 'Can't you take a joke?');

▶ guilt trips for minor misdemeanours. Women, particularly, can be suckers for this one. They take to guilt like a duck to water;

▶ public exposure of another's faults;

▶ insults;

▶ name-calling.

The use of shaming tactics is seriously dysfunctional behaviour and rapidly destroys productive working relationships. The damage that shaming causes can't always be fixed by an apology. Few people recognise that if someone calls them *gutless*, a *slut* or an *idiot* that it's not that person's real opinion of them. If the target person has experienced heavy shaming in their childhood they may not have the resilience to withstand its onslaught. Instead, they sink into helpless desperation. Ultimately they may have no other solution but to look elsewhere for work. It takes considerable ego-strength to withstand shaming.

*What is the psychology behind a person who shames others?* Daniel Goleman believes that the shamer becomes flooded by:

> ... an unpleasant wash of fear and anger that seems inescapable and, subjectively, takes 'forever' to get over. At this point ... a person's emotions are so intense, their perspective so narrow, and their thinking so confused that there is no hope of taking the other's viewpoint or settling things in a reasonable way.[58]

*Shaming others can be a defence against being out of control.*

When someone uses shaming tactics frequently, others will see them as a bully. Sometimes the situation is confined to one other person where there is a serious personality clash or where the shamer particularly has to prove themselves.

Shamers use attack as their method of defence. Often its deeper cause is fear. For example, they may:

▶ fear that they will be controlled by others. Control is a competition and they must win;

▶ fear that they will lose control over the situation. They are compensating for feeling overwhelmed by its complexity;

▸ fear that they will lose status. In situations of tension, when status-watchers feel constantly under attack, they become hyper-vigilant in the protection of status. They read hostility into neutral or relatively mild comments;

▸ fear that if they don't attack by shaming others, they will themselves be shamed. Being ashamed is an emotion they cannot tolerate, and they will avoid it at all costs. They are constantly on guard for loss of face.

There's a lot to be said for coming to terms with a *little* shame early on in life. Being able to acknowledge you're wrong, at least occasionally, is a sign of emotional maturity. Sometimes the original impulse towards shaming behaviour arises from having been grossly shamed in childhood and a determination never to let that feeling arise again. The problem will be compounded if the person has a strong predisposition to aggression and a drive to assert superior status.

*Being able to accept you are wrong is a sign of emotional maturity.*

While shamers are often men and their targets are often women, shamers and their targets can, of course, be of either sex. When a man shames women repeatedly, deep down he probably feels threatened by them. Often the real threat is not even in the present situation but lies in unresolved issues from childhood — perhaps his relationship with a mother who was hostile or who felt forced to accept abuse from her husband. Identifying with his father, he adopts his father's dysfunctional abuse of women. When a woman shames men repeatedly, she is probably also dealing with unresolved childhood issues — often with her father. *There is no mandate in the workplace to address directly core issues such as this. In 99.9 per cent of cases, do not mention it!*

## STEPPING STONES

FOR TARGETS: Sometimes by intuiting the real cause of the shamer's behaviour, you can lessen its impact on you. Sometimes, you can be instrumental in resolving the other person's deeper problems by showing, through your behaviour, that not all people match the negative picture they have created. We are all trying to resolve, in current relationships, incompatibilities and traumas from our past. Mostly we don't need therapy, though we may need to be led skilfully away from inappropriate behaviour.

While other status-watchers are likely to move straight into reciprocal attack, equalisers may feel overwhelmed when the other person is shaming them. Both reactions do not serve the resolution of conflict. Instead, if you can respond appropriately, you can help the other person regain self-control and engage in a more mature response.

If you are at the receiving end of shaming, **Figure 26: Handling a verbal attack** (page 115) suggests a set of procedures that may help.[59]

FOR SHAMERS: If you recognise that shaming others is something you tend to do, there are a number of factors to consider. Remember, shaming can be a repetitive cycle. It creates the problem it addresses. Alienation from others makes being discounted or despised more and more likely. Become alert to your own contempt. Sam Keen, author of *Fire in the Belly*, suggests:

> In the beginning *do* nothing. Observe. Watch your conduct, your feelings, your interactions with the objective eye of a scientist. Study the ways you blame others or allow others to blame you ... The second step is taking responsibility for your habitual roles, feelings, actions and values.[60]

Shaming often happens when you're furious, when the lid has blown off all restraints. Controlling your anger, particularly in moments of extreme frustration, will be a very important skill for you to learn.[61] Discipline yourself to talk about how it is for you, rather than how stupid, crazy and so on you think the other person is.[62] As you notice your anger mounting, discharge some of your pent-up energy in an acceptable way, perhaps by going for a jog in your lunch break or shifting your attention to a less stressful task, such as filing.[63]

| HANDLING A VERBAL ATTACK | |
|---|---|
| Receive | Listen and say nothing for the moment. Give the other person room to discharge emotions. Respect the other person's communication of feelings, if not their methods. |
| Notice | Observe your own reaction. |
| Centre | Tune into yourself. Breathe deeply. |
| Listen again | Ask yourself what you are picking up from the communication. Separate feelings from factual content. Extract valid concerns, even if inaccurate. Try to let abuse pass you by. |
| Reflect back | Check you have really understood their complaint – both their feelings and factual content. Use an active listening response, such as: 'Let me check with you if ...', or 'Are you saying ...' |
|  | For example, you've just been called a lazy incompetent and respond with: 'Are you saying that you are angry *(feeling)* that I didn't phone the suppliers yesterday *(content)*?' |
| Clarify and explore | What are the other person's needs and concerns? Explore what is behind the words being used. Ask questions to shift the focus from anger to exploring the issues. |
|  | For example: 'Are you worried that we won't be able to return the goods?' |
| Repeat the cycle | Work through again from *Receive* to *Clarify and explore* perhaps several times. Ensure the person knows you have understood both feelings and facts. Anger escalates when the other person doesn't feel heard. Anger generally abates as they register that their message is getting across. |
| Move | Acknowledge their needs and concerns before you explain yours. Wait until the worst of their anger has subsided before you justify your actions. Consider your next step. Would it be best to make an 'I' statement, or take time out if you or they are out of control, or address fears, or develop options together? |

*Figure 26: Handling a verbal attack*

## STUMBLING BLOCK 2:
## DEFENSIVENESS AND LOW SELF-ESTEEM

**'I don't want your help. I can stuff it up by myself'**

*Defensiveness can arise from acute irritation and anxiety about being controlled.*

Defensiveness can arise from acute irritation and anxiety about *being controlled*. An inadvertent remark, for example, may lead a wary status-watcher to believe that the other person is pushing for an inappropriate status. Their defensive response is often an unconscious battle to climb, maintain or defend a position. Their reactions can come as quite a surprise to an equaliser who believes they are conducting an innocuous conversation. An equaliser is unlikely to be tuned into the status/control issues below the surface. Sensitised to equality rather than status issues, they are more likely to become defensive if they feel they have been underestimated. The defensiveness of status-watchers may not result in the extremity of tactics discussed in the section on shaming, but the person may seem quite *prickly*. Their response appears to throw blame on you for something they believe you are implying, even if you intended nothing of the sort.

> John, branch manager of a car sales company, was visiting head office. Marie, who was in charge of clerical functions there, asked him most politely to take back a box of invoice books she had just received from the printer. True, the box wasn't light. True, deliveries were 'below' him as far as his job description was concerned, but to Marie it seemed the commonsense way to get the box from head office to the branch. It would save arranging for a courier and John was going back to his office, anyway. John glared at Marie as if he'd never been asked to deliver a box in his life before and never wanted to be asked to do it again. Marie stood her ground and John took the box. They both went down about ten notches in each other's estimation.

### STEPPING STONES

*We tend to react to prickles with prickles of our own.*

WHEN THE OTHER PERSON IS DEFENSIVE: We tend to react to prickles with prickles of our own, when what is really needed is reassurance. Ask yourself what is the other person's underlying fear. Their prickles may alert you to a status issue you hadn't recognised.

► Praise the person for something you really do believe they do well.

► Improve your relationship with conversations about non-work-related issues, if they'll allow you to get close enough to do so.

► Take opportunities to indicate that you do respect the position they hold in the organisation.

Recognise also that many men grumble along the way to saying yes to a request. Women are more likely to have been conditioned to be cooperative, and will at least *appear* to respond positively when asked for a favour — unless they have a serious issue with the request. It's important not to let prickles and grumbles put you off. Ask for what you want and accept that others may not say *yes* or *no* as charmingly as you'd like. To work successfully with a defensive person, you need to develop a certain level of tolerance towards their behaviour. Too much sensitivity to pleasing them all of the time will get in the way.

*Before you react defensively, check out the intent.*

### WHEN YOU ARE DEFENSIVE:

*Short term:* If you have a tendency to misinterpret situations and react defensively, first check with others whether they perceive a slight was intended. If you're checking directly with the person, make sure your tone of voice is as neutral as possible to start with. In other words, you're trying to postpone your hurt and anger until you know you have a case. You might ask: 'Are you saying that my report wasn't adequate?', or 'I'm not sure I'm understanding you. Would you run that by me again?' John, the car sales manager in the earlier example, might have collected information on Marie's intent if he'd asked: 'Do you really need me to deliver the box?' Checking the intent of a comment may avoid an immediate problem, but it doesn't address the deeper roots of defensiveness.

*Long term:* Generally, defensiveness is a self-esteem issue. It can arise from a lifetime of comparing yourself with others and being very unsure of where you stand in the status stakes. There is a solution, though it may take a major shift of awareness.

Self-esteem can be based *internally* on who you are as a person, or *externally* on what you achieve. Many men build self-esteem exclusively on status, defining it by the things they've acquired, such as position or possessions. Women often base their self-esteem on other people's feedback — 'I am not okay unless someone tells me I am.' When it rests on who you are, it is indestructible. No one can take that away from you. When it rests on outward shows of status or support, its nature is precarious. Any threat to those externals defining self-esteem will look like personal attack.

*Nurse the candle flame of faith in yourself.*

How do you work on building your internalised sense of self-esteem? It can be a lifetime's exercise. Use each incident where you have fallen into defensiveness as a reminder to measure your self-worth with yardsticks of self-love, your real competencies and respect for your struggle and persistence. Nurse the candle flame of faith in yourself. Not faith that you'll never make a mistake or have nothing to learn, but faith that you are fundamentally of good will and doing the best you can in the circumstances. **Figure 27: Building indestructible self-esteem** (page 119) offers some pointers. You might want to photocopy it to stick on the fridge or the back of the toilet door!

## Wrangles over promotion defeats

### 'I deserved that promotion, not that idiot!'

Status-watchers see the world through a lens of hierarchy. If they feel they've been cheated out of a promotion, they can become extremely angry and vindictive. Equalisers won't take this lying down, either. The difference, though, is that status-watchers perceive a challenge to their rightful place in the hierarchy. Some of the nastiest and most protracted conflicts can arise in these circumstances.

*A woman being promoted over a man challenges the traditional pecking order.*

Some people hold an unrealistically high opinion of themselves as a form of self-protection. This inaccurate self-image is shored up by a belief that they are underrated and badly done by. They defend themselves vigorously against any negative feedback, such as being passed over for promotion. If a man has this inflated self-image and it is a woman who is promoted ahead of him, the conflict seems to take on a particularly vicious edge. This situation challenges the traditional pecking order, and adds extra fuel to the wrangles, appeals and continued resentment that sometimes follow.

| BUILDING INDESTRUCTIBLE SELF-ESTEEM | |
|---|---|
| Generalise from positive experiences | Consciously build your sense of personal worth using your positive experiences. Internalise the good things that happen to you and generalise from them. Tell yourself they've happened because you're a fine person. Treat the bad things as lessons to be learnt, not as reflections on you as a person. Stop beating yourself up for past failures. |
| Form a loving relationship with yourself | Look at your own image in a mirror. Make eye contact and say as if you mean it: 'You're a decent human being, doing the best you can. I really care about you.' (If this person were a stranger, would you be as hard on them as you are being on yourself?) |
| Apply pressure to self-destructive tendencies | Keep fighting your own self-destructive behaviours. Admire yourself for the effort as well as the outcome. In order for you to respect yourself, you don't have to be perfect, you just have to try — today! |
| Take in praise | If other people praise you, don't knock it. Say thank you. No 'yes, buts ...'! Listen. Take it in. Allow yourself to be touched. Let yourself trust that they are seeing truth. |
| Build your real competencies | Work to develop your skills; for example, master a computer program, improve your sales technique, take up photography. Find something you'd like to do better and practise. Sign up for a course in something. As your competency or knowledge grows, value that in yourself. This is solid, unshakeable ground for increasing self-esteem. |
| Set yourself a big goal and take small steps | Do you have goals or secret dreams? Take one step today, no matter how small, towards making them a reality. Regularly ask yourself what's the next step, and do it. The point is not your final achievement of the goal. You may or may not ever get there. Your indestructible self-esteem comes from engaging yourself in the process of travelling on the path. |

*Figure 27: Building indestructible self-esteem*

## STEPPING STONES

If you have to tell someone they missed out on a promotion, you can expect an uncomfortable interview. Though it can be an anguishing process for someone to reassess their own competence, it is usually kinder in the long term to tell the person why they didn't get the promotion. Describe their weaknesses in terms of skills they can work on, so that you offer them a real chance to get something positive from the experience. For example, 'This position needs a person who has good communication skills. That's not your strong suit, yet. Have you thought about doing a conflict resolution or leadership effectiveness course?', rather than, 'You didn't get the job because no one wants to take orders from you'.

*Weigh carefully the cost/benefit ratio of an appeal.*

If you've missed out on a promotion you feel you deserve, consider an appeal very carefully before you act. Weigh up the inevitable costs against the uncertain benefits. Appeals in government departments and institutions that have formal procedures for such complaints can take years to conclude. If you stay in the same department, don't underestimate how the permanent breakdown of relationships with your co-workers will affect you. Your career and your enthusiasm for your workplace may be sucked into a black hole. Those people who do finally win rarely feel that the vindication compensated them for the emotional drain and financial payout of mounting their appeal.

Accepting that you didn't get a promotion you felt you deserved is never easy, particularly if you perceive the other person was promoted because of a gender bias. The issue about whether a person is a man or a woman is often highly relevant in these decisions today. We've got a long way to go before there is true gender equality. As we try to redress the problem, women will sometimes have preferred status. It's been the other way round for a very long time and often still is!

We will sometimes fall victim to societal forces — both the old and the new — that are beyond our control. If it happens to you, it's important for your sanity not to take it too personally or to tie up your energy in protracted retaliation. Taking it out on the person who was promoted damages you more than it hurts them. You've got a life to get on with. Resentments freeze us in the past.

# STUMBLING BLOCK 3:
# TERRITORY PROTECTION

### 'Get off my patch!'

Status is often defined by personal territory. Territory is the area over which you have control, the 'patch' over which you have power or ownership. It may be *physical territory* — your office — or *non-physical territory* — your job responsibilities, or the number of people under your supervision. Some status-watchers can invest enormous amounts of time and energy in disputes over territory.

Anna, a very successful woman executive in the corporate world, commented:

> The men that I work with, in every environment, mark the outer boundaries of their territory. Women don't have this personal territory thing to anything like the same degree. We're so busy protecting everybody else and their personal territory. My husband noticed it in me the other day: 'You never eat your food hot,' he said. 'I've got children,' I replied. If I had expectations of hot food, I'd spend my life disappointed.

I interviewed Laura, who had become deeply embroiled in a territorial dispute in her company:

> Laura was a sales representative for a pharmaceutical products and supplies company. In response to a survey of clients' needs, the company decided to bring together all their laboratory supply accounts into a new specialist sales territory serviced by one representative. They asked Laura if she would be interested in applying for this job. It fitted nicely with her eight years of experience and her Bachelor of Science degree, so she applied. She was delighted when she was accepted for the new position.
>
> Within the first month of taking over the new territory, one of the other sales reps, Gary, stopped talking to Laura. He'd pass her in the corridor and look the other way, though she'd worked with him closely for three years. In the creation of the new territory, he'd had two major accounts taken away from him. Apparently it hadn't occurred to him that his own territory would alter with the restructure. He'd also been asked to apply for the new position and had chosen not to.

Gary was very friendly with Steve, the company's chief accountant. Although Gary's issue lay in the sales manager's domain, not the chief accountant's, Steve chose to involve himself in Gary's problem. Instructed by Steve, Gary wrote a formal letter of complaint, saying how successfully he had worked on the accounts, that he believed that 'other reps [meaning Laura] were being handed accounts on a platter', and that he believed the accounts should be returned to him.

Gary didn't discuss his issues with Laura. She had no idea why Gary wasn't talking to her. No one told her he'd lodged a formal complaint. When she finally heard about the problem through a secretary, management meetings about the issue were well under way without any input from her. Told by her sales manager, Trevor, that she could only communicate on the issue in writing, she addressed her letter to him. She pointed out that the territory she had been given had been created in response to market research, and that the territorial realignment had been open knowledge before she'd even taken up the position.

Her letter had some effect. Steve and Trevor decided to hold their next meeting with Gary and Laura present. It took place a couple of days later in Steve's office. Gary and Steve sat together. Trevor sat away from everyone. Laura also sat by herself. Steve opened the discussion. 'I believe that Gary would get the best results from the disputed accounts', he said. Laura was shocked and hurt. How would Steve know who was going to get the best results, she thought. He wasn't the sales manager, not even a sales rep. He didn't even work at the same branch. Laura knew she was just as good a salesperson as Gary, and she had a great deal more experience in laboratory supplies. She felt Gary and Steve were ganging up on her while her own boss, Trevor, who she ought to be able to count on for some support, sat on the sidelines, trying not to make a decision or side with anyone. Laura felt that she'd been left out on a limb.

As her frustration and her sense of isolation mounted, Laura burst into angry tears. 'I'm not going to have my territory changed just because somebody else wants it. Gary and I and all the other reps don't *own* our accounts. The company does.'

'We are trying to do what's best for the company', said Steve.

'The company saw fit to give those accounts to my territory and not his. Gary should just accept it', Laura replied. 'He's not carrying the target for those accounts, I am. It doesn't even affect what's happening to his commission bonuses.' She was clutching onto her own sense of 'mine, not his!' and the status that came with the expansive scope of her new field.

In the end, Laura won, or thought she had at the time. She went back to the work with renewed gusto. However, two months later Steve raised her targets, which cut back her commission by 40 per cent. Her sales manager, Trevor, again appeared powerless to stand up for her rights. Laura was furious. She lost all respect for the people involved and left the company within twelve months.

Disputes over territory issues can be very vindictive and need to be handled with the utmost care, so that neither the individual nor the company loses out. In the example above, the dispute was handled poorly, and the end result of this argument was losses all round. Although Laura was ambitious, she had no concept of how much Gary's territory meant to him, the methods he would use to try to regain it, or the punishments for not restoring it that he could indirectly arrange.

### STEPPING STONES

The sad part about Laura's story is the opportunity that was lost to nip the whole saga in the bud. Gary chose not to talk directly to Laura about his concerns. Laura didn't address a difficulty she could see existed in her relationship with Gary. Trevor didn't consult with Laura as soon as he'd received Gary's complaint. He even turned down her request to discuss the issue, instructing her to write down her side of the story. Steve's interventions didn't serve the company in the long run. Trevor had no skills to handle Steve's invasion of his territory of control as sales manager. Laura's own territory issues made her dig her heels in at the meeting. Laura confided to me that had she been approached differently she might have been willing to come to some arrangement about the disputed territory.

Anyone, man or woman, with any sensitivities, would have hated the position Laura found herself in. This company's culture appears to be extremely paternalistic. The conflict replicated dysfunctional family patterns. Steve, as final authority for the company, played the role of authoritarian father. Trevor played the role of ineffectual mother. The squabbling kids, Gary and Laura, tried to play off one parent against the other. Conspiracy and secrecy added fuel to the fire. No wonder Trevor was silent in the meeting. With dysfunctional forces like these at play, who'd dare open their mouth? Status, territory and poor communication are a deadly mix.

What are the lessons here?

▶ Talk more openly about territory issues as they arise.

▶ Recognise the legitimacy of someone's concerns over territory infringements.

▶ Use every possible means to develop win/win outcomes that don't leave one person dissatisfied.

When one person loses in an argument of this type, they are likely to plot sabotage behind closed doors.

Andrew Acland believes that territorial disputes often arise because territory represents security, and in times of change people want to hang on to the known. Therefore he suggests:

> The best way to wean people away from old territory is to ensure they have new territory in which to invest their security and stake their claim.[64]

In times of change, we are balancing what we gain against what we lose. To avoid territorial hostilities, managers may need to ask honest and probing questions, such as: 'If you move into that office, will you feel like you have lost something?' Recognising that territory is a status issue, it's important to help the person perceive that their new territory has at least equal status to their previous 'patch'.

When a company is downsizing, territorial disputes can be particularly painful. Open and clear explanations of policy decisions need to be issued by management. Employees need to be given support and honest information about their future with the organisation and their intended role.

## STUMBLING BLOCK 4:
## HUNGER FOR STATUS SYMBOLS

### Salary biases

**'Why should they get paid more than me?'**

Echoing our animal forbears, vestiges of the need to establish and maintain dominance abound in our workplaces. Status is marked by various signs, a key one being salary. A status-watcher is usually very focused on salary, because it is a sign of status, not only within the organisation, but in society as well. Sometimes it can be overdone, particularly if the person refuses to take into consideration the complex arrangement of relative salaries based on length of service, age, responsibility, sensitivity to private information, and so on. While from time to time your salary will need your attention, outrageous and repeated demands may not be well received.

*A key sign of status is salary.*

But unfortunately there is another aspect to this status issue. While they're unlikely to voice their prejudice openly, some male managers make decisions about other people's salaries based on the belief that men are better than women and that men are entitled to a higher pay because they have a greater worth to the organisation. Equal pay awards set in place by unions now counteract this inequity, at least in theory. In practice, it still can creep in to the workplace in debatable situations. As the prejudice is often unconscious, it's hard to correct.

The following story was told to me by Catherine, an extremely intelligent and efficient middle manager in her fifties:

> I was supervising a young graduate straight out of university. He was very raw, and often quite slow to pick things up, but I was showing him the ropes. By chance, I found out that he was being paid more than I was. I went to my boss, demanding to know why. 'Well, er ...' he bumbled. 'He's a man.'
>
> 'You've got to be joking,' I said. I was really shocked.
>
> 'Well, er ... he's a graduate,' said my boss.
>
> 'But he can't do the work!' I replied. 'We ought to be paid according to our value to the company. The criterion for that isn't credentials and it certainly shouldn't be gender.'

'Catherine,' he said, 'this young man is good value to the company. If we can tempt him with a really good salary package to stay on here, we can train him for future management.'

Catherine was incensed. 'Why not train me? I've been here for six years already. You know I'm really competent.'

'Catherine, you do a really good job where you are. Why rock the boat? The truth is, you're a woman. I don't know how long you'll stay. You might want to retire soon or just get sick of working. I know you're in a relationship.'

'If I haven't given any sign of leaving for six years, why would you even think I would now? At least you could ask me about my plans before you put on a youngster at a higher rate of pay than me, someone I have to supervise, yet who has better promotion prospects than you're prepared to offer me. And all for no other reason than that he's a man!'

### STEPPING STONES

*Address negative stereotyping.*

Many men today realise that women are in the workplace for the long haul. They are also recognising that while their styles may be different, there is no basic difference in competence between men and women. However, women and these fair-minded men still often have to address negative stereotyping of women in others. They may need to:

▶ bring the issues out in the open, expose faulty thinking to the light of day, and make sure such issues are discussed;

▶ point out the flaws in the argument;

▶ point out, if necessary, that actions arising from such faulty thinking are politically dangerous.

Women may need to state that they'd like to be considered and trained for promotion, and indicate clearly what their family commitments and plans are.

If you are negotiating your own salary, consider whether salary biases are working against you. Find out what others at your level are being paid in other organisations, so that you don't undersell yourself and have the courage to ask for what you're worth.

There's nothing wrong with negotiating hard for what you want. Salary reviews are negotiations. Prepare a strategy. Many men handle them by asking for more than they are willing to settle for, and presume other people are doing the same. You might start by asking for more than you really want, but, if this is very uncomfortable for you, make it clear that you are asking for what you *do* want. If the bargaining continues, you may want to indicate that the sum you're asking for assures your high level of commitment to the organisation and that you may not feel the same if the figure is not met. Obviously, you would need to know that you are a valued employee for this approach to have the required effect.

Equalisers' motivations in asking for a salary review are likely to be a little different from status-watchers'. Equalisers may be asking for more money in order to run their households, for example, rather than to prove their worth to others. They're likely to fight for what they believe is equitable, rather than for what they need to outclass others.

This difference in motivation may partly explain why men are likely to come out of salary negotiations with more money than their female counterparts.

Those in charge of salary reviews must be particularly watchful of unbalanced salary arrangements in the organisation. They can be the cause of deep unrest amongst staff. Those in charge need to weed out their prejudices and level out differences based on different negotiating styles and motivations. They'll need a flexible and considered approach, playing it tougher on excessively high demands and fairer with moderate demands.

## Too much fuss about status symbols

**'I have the right to a bigger company car than them.'**

Status-watchers will negotiate hard, not only for salary, but for other status symbols such as the flashy car, the high-backed chair, the larger office, the secretary screening calls. The squabbles over these types of issues can become petty and ugly.

Carol's supervising role in her organisation entitled her to one of the five window seats in the open-plan office. Always rather sensitive to glare, she erected a small screen between her desk and the window, which prevented her seeing the view. The whole issue of preferred

*Status-watchers will negotiate hard for the high-backed chair*

seating was unimportant to her. But the other women lower in the hierarchy who sat in the central area of the office were incensed that she had 'wasted' her window position. Some wanted to swap places with her, but there was no fair way to choose who should take over the coveted position. Carol stayed put, having decided that any swap would arouse accusations of favouritism.

Equalisers tend not to be as motivated by the acquisition of workplace symbols of success, though few of us are truly immune to their allure.

### STEPPING STONES

Status symbols can be very useful rewards. They are proof that you are important to the organisation. Yes, disputes can become unpleasant, but it's easy to become unfairly judgmental about these status-watching issues, particularly for equalisers. If a private office generally accompanies the position yet it's not being offered to you, that isn't fair. When others in an equivalent position have a parking space supplied by the organisations yet you don't have one, a complaint is not unreasonable.

For those of you who may be receiving complaints from status-watchers or observing unfair treatment, remember to treat the person with respect. The same cautiousness needed in salary reviews is needed in negotiations over status symbols. Consider whether the demand for the privilege is:

► fair in relation to other people;

► wise as an acknowledgment of the person's efforts;

► affordable to the organisation.

If it passes these criteria, go along with it. Life has to have some perks.

# STUMBLING BLOCK 5:
# UNDERVALUING OTHERS

## Discounting other people's skills and abilities

'She couldn't do that. She's only a secretary.'

Status-watchers, with one eye usually on their own status, can easily and quite unconsciously discount others' skills and abilities. This attitude is extremely frustrating for those affected by it, and often results in the repression of people's potential.

Young people and migrants are frequently the targets of this type of discrimination. Women also complain that men under-value and under-utilise their skills. In my work with government departments, where the change of status from 'temporary' to 'permanent' is an important step, I hear women complaining that such offers are more frequently made to men than to women. This gender-biased underestimation can also take the form of:

▶ workplace training and education being offered to men ahead of women;

▶ young males being mentored while young women are left to fend for themselves;

▶ women being expected to make the tea, clean up, or work as a support to men;

▶ women not being invited to attend meetings, presumably because the contributions that they could make are not recognised.

*STEPPING STONES*
Discounting other people's skills and abilities is insidious and unkind. In today's workplaces we need to be more and more scrupulous about providing equality of opportunity. We can guard against being prejudiced and lobby for change in organisations where prejudice occurs. However, these issues may be very difficult to fight alone. Large organisations often have equal employment opportunity divisions to address these problems. In organisations without a formal department, the disadvantaged group — for instance, women or migrants — may need to network closely with each other to explore every avenue for change.

Positive change may require long and careful work. Helpless resentment will not achieve the goal.

It's a major step forwards when management show they understand that women's complaints about being undervalued are real by putting into effect programs that redress the balance, such as quota systems for women in management positions. But such initiatives are not trouble free. Often, male status-watchers don't really understand the problem and therefore these programs can appear to them to be unfairly biased towards women. They need to accept that equity systems have their place and probably will for many years to come.

Options such as rotating 'acting' positions of responsibility give women a chance to learn the ropes of greater responsibility and show what they can do. Attitude shifts gradually follow such demonstrations. However, people may need to be presented with many exceptions to their biased stereotypes before they really break them down.[65]

*Management policy to reduce gender bias may have to be enforced to produce attitude shifts.*

Sometimes, one gender-sensitive supervisor can start a trickle-down effect for the whole organisation, but usually senior management's policy is the stepping stone needed here.

## Rejection of unproven authority

**'I'm not taking orders from them. What would they know?'**

Men generally appear to accept workplace hierarchies more readily, but not always when the boss is a woman.

Kerry responded to my question about this issue by saying: 'If the orders are coming from a woman, men find that very difficult to take.' Cherie, an architect, says:

> As a woman I am not always taken seriously. Quite often my opinion is not regarded as being worth as much as a man's. I have to present in a masculine way and show I'm exceptionally skilled if my opinion is to be valued. Even then, with some clients it's as if they listen *in spite of* the fact that I'm a woman.

Men can be very threatened when a woman is placed in charge of them in the workplace. Older women can also be most uncooperative if they have to receive instructions from a younger woman. (Seniority often features in women's status issues.)

Status-watchers who preserve the integrity of lines of authority can become very irritated when instructed to do something by someone who doesn't directly supervise them, even though that person has higher status in the organisation. Equalisers may think status-watchers are nitpicking, whereas status-watchers have learnt it keeps them out of trouble. For example, a factory supervisor (let's assume he is a man) may baulk at receiving instructions from the human resources director. He demands the correct chain of command, because he's learnt that he could find himself in hot water with his department manager if the manager hasn't received the instruction, too. Tactics used by both men and women to undermine disputed authority can include:

▶ trying to 'out talk' the manager — even if they don't really know what they are talking about;

▶ sneering in private;

▶ refusing to accept orders;

▶ sabotaging plans;

▶ discounting the manager's point of view;

▶ sexual innuendos.

It's nasty stuff!

*STEPPING STONES*

One newly appointed woman building supervisor handled the problem by working on the relationship first:

Anna toured her new site with an attitude of respectful inquiry. 'Show me exactly what you do' was a common opener she used with the various tradesmen. Then she discussed the job with them in a way that indicated she knew exactly what she was talking about. For several days she issued no direct instructions. She knew she'd arrived when, having been engaged in paperwork all morning, she finally emerged from her office and one of the tradesmen jovially called out to her: 'Where were you? You haven't been down today to see what I'm doing.' Indirectly, he was indicating to her that he accepted her authority.

Establishing permission to direct is not automatic. Position in the hierarchy may not be sufficient. Leaders may need to earn the right to direct others. Passing various tests of knowledge and joking comfortably in response to sexual innuendo are often vital components of the acceptance process for women.

*Leaders may need to earn the right to direct.*

While they'll give lip service to obedience, some men will never believe women have the right to issue orders. They never really hand over that permission to direct. Why not? Hierarchies in the animal world and to a large extent in the workplace are masculine structures. When women are involved, there's an immediate clash in the 'natural' order of things. Many challenges to women leaders arise from fundamental discomforts felt by men towards women in a higher status than themselves. As we move away from the rule of biology, where physical strength determines status, and into the arena of mind, where men and women stand on equal ground, many men will need to work on transcending ingrained biases.

▼▼▼

Men's behaviour is not always motivated by status values, nor is women's behaviour solely directed by equality values. Many women will become preoccupied with status, especially if they face resistance in promotional opportunities. When women do place status over equality, they can be perceived as acting out masculine stereotypes. When men use equalising behaviours such as modesty, hesitancy and apologising, they may be judged more feminine and therefore weak.

Our workplace culture is in the process of transformation and such judgments are probably temporary. What we perceive as 'masculine' or 'feminine' is constantly evolving. When:

▶ equality includes empowerment;

▶ status includes genuine respect for others; and

▶ self-respect isn't based on being better than others, but on an internal yardstick of self-worth;

we will have minimised clashes between equality and status, and travelled some way towards closing the gender gap.

# SUMMARY

| STATUS:<br>STUMBLING BLOCKS | STEPPING STONES:<br>'POWER WITH' NOT 'POWER OVER' |
|---|---|
| **1 ► Domination**<br><br>*Obsession with control* | Control, overt or covert, is likely to invite rebellion or stifle creativity. Ask yourself:<br><br>► Does the problem affect you?<br><br>► Can you live with the problem their way creates?<br><br>► Does their way work?<br><br>Shift from 'power over' to 'power with'. |
| *Arrogance* | Avoid trying to take arrogant people down a peg or two. Concentrate on the positive qualities of the person. Use non-sarcastic humour. Don't judge women more harshly than men for arrogant behaviour. Come to terms with your own pride so that you can be more tolerant of self-importance in others. |
| *Shaming* | Shamers can learn to observe their reaction, control the moment of explosion, use 'I' statements and safely release elsewhere the tension of pent-up feelings.<br><br>A target person can try to bypass insults and reflect back to the shamer both the factual content and the feelings they sense behind the abuse. They could acknowledge the other person's needs and concerns, before explaining their own; address fears and focus together on the issue and its solutions. |
| **2 ► Defensiveness and low self-esteem** | Try not to respond in kind. Don't treat grumbles on the way to saying yes as defensiveness. Reassure, build a relationship and indicate respect.<br><br>Your own defensive reactions need to be examined for validity. To work on building indestructible self-esteem:<br><br>► generalise from positive experiences;<br><br>► form a loving relationship with yourself; |

| STUMBLING BLOCKS | STEPPING STONES |
|---|---|
| | ▶ apply pressure to self-destructive tendencies;<br><br>▶ take in praise;<br><br>▶ build real competencies; and<br><br>▶ set yourself big goals and take small steps. |
| *Wrangles over promotion defeats* | Address disappointment by pointing out behaviours the person can improve on. Weigh carefully the cost/benefit ratio of any appeal. Continued resentments freeze us in the past. |
| **3 ▶ Territory protection** | Discuss territory issues openly. Recognise the legitimacy of territorial concerns. In times of change, if possible, don't leave one person dissatisfied. Try to balance territory lost against territory gained. |
| **4 ▶ Hunger for status symbols** | |
| *Salary biases* | Stand up for what's fair and right. In salary negotiations, collect information about what others at your level are earning elsewhere. Recognise that salary reviews are negotiations. Plan a strategy. Recognise your salary must fit a complex web of relative salaries within the organisation. |
| *Too much fuss about status symbols* | Status symbols have their place. Is the demand fair, wise and affordable? |
| **5 ▶ Undervaluing others** | |
| *Discounting other people's skills and abilities* | Lobby for policy changes. Get managers on side. Install programs which will correct bias in the long-term. |
| *Rejection of unproven authority* | Work towards the moment when permission to direct is handed over. Meet tests with equanimity. Some men need to work on transcending ingrained biases against women who have authority over them. |

# PART III
# AGREEMENT AND COMPETITION

## EIGHT COMMON CONFLICTS

### Agreers' complaints:
► 'They're so hard to get on with!'

► 'They'll never make time to discuss it properly!'

► 'They keep harping on about ...!'

► 'They're such a sour puss!'

### Competers' complaints:
► 'You have no respect for what I've achieved!'

► 'If you can't stand the heat, get out!'

► 'I'm tired of being a reserve! I want the chance to prove myself.'

► 'I've missed promotions three times. I must be a failure!'

## Synopsis — where are we now?

In Part I, Chapter 1, we discussed how we are moving towards a melding of masculine and feminine approaches in the workplace. We looked at how far changing culture is able to support this process, and where biological predisposition permanently embeds some differences between the sexes. In Chapter 2, we considered underlying differences between the sexes in the priority given to a number of key values and their effect on conflicts.

In Part II, Chapters 3, 4 and 5, we discussed the values of equality and status, and their links to gender differences. A higher priority on one or the other value will alter attitudes to power and the way power is exercised.

Here in Part III, we will explore underlying differences in our style of interacting with each other — agreement or competition. As with equality and status, these differences are frequently gender-related.

| PERSPECTIVES | FEMININE STEREOTYPE | MASCULINE STEREOTYPE |
|---|---|---|
| Use of power: | Equality | Status |
| Interacting style: | Agreement | Competition |
| Focus of attention: | Feeling | Actions and objects |
| Comfort zone: | Interdependence | Autonomy |

The arrows above indicate the discussion areas for the next three chapters.

A NOTE ON TERMINOLOGY:   While the agreement value aligns with the feminine stereotype and competition with the masculine, agreement also ranks on a man's list of priorities, just as competition ranks on a woman's. Some men loathe competition and always move towards agreement — even at the expense of standing up for themselves and clearly stating what they need. Some women are particularly competitive and draw extra flak because they cross their gender's stereotype.

Therefore, in order to keep our discussion broad enough to be realistic, I often talk about 'agreers' and 'competers' who may be either male or female. I am applying these labels to them *only while they are engaged in the activity of agreeing or competing*. It isn't a permanent description, as we don't always seek to agree or to compete.[66]

# QUIZ

Circle the number in the column that best reflects your response to the following statements:

## Quiz 1

|  | RARELY | SOMETIMES | OFTEN |
|---|---|---|---|
| Conflict in a group, or a lot of pressure to compete, diminishes my ability to function well. | 0 | 1 | 2 |
| I let people have their way to avoid disagreements, even when it doesn't really suit me. | 0 | 1 | 2 |
| If someone is rude, I'd rather ignore the problem than bring it out in the open. | 0 | 1 | 2 |
| It upsets me when people put each other down, even if it's in jest. | 0 | 1 | 2 |
| I agonise over using confrontation to get what I want. | 0 | 1 | 2 |

Total:

+          =

## Quiz 2

|  | RARELY | SOMETIMES | OFTEN |
|---|---|---|---|
| I thrive on the challenge of competition. | 0 | 1 | 2 |
| I am drawn towards heated debates. | 0 | 1 | 2 |
| I treat people the same way they treat me. If someone is aggressive, I will react in a similar way. | 0 | 1 | 2 |
| It annoys me when people are overly sensitive to light-hearted sarcastic remarks. | 0 | 1 | 2 |
| I think it is acceptable to use aggressive tactics to get ahead. | 0 | 1 | 2 |

Total:

+          =

Add up your circled numbers for each quiz separately then compare the two scores.

If your score was higher in Quiz 1, you probably focus strongly on *agreement*. If you scored higher in Quiz 2, you probably put more of a priority on *competition*. If your scores were equal, you may swing between the two polarities, depending on the situation.

The next three chapters will tell you more about these qualities.

# 6 AGREEMENT–COMPETITION: interacting style

## PREVIEW

- ► Characteristics: agreement
- ► Characteristics: competition
- ► Interacting style
- ► He-men and she-women
- ► Moulding stereotypes
- ► What is the good intention?
- ► Spotting the underlying values
- ► Flight, fight or flow

This chapter focuses on differences in interacting style that arise from the different emphasis we place on agreement and competition in our hierarchy of values. Agreers focus on the rapid restoration of harmony, competers focus on what it will take to cross the finish line first. These differences can create productive diversity in the workplace. However, each approach is also prone to misuse, which we'll consider in Chapters 7 and 8.

In this chapter, we examine some of the factors that mould agreement and competition values. We review each value's expression in the workplace, its positives and good intentions. The aim is to become more comfortable with the value that is not our usual style. In the extremity of conflict, competers usually fight, agreers flee. We consider a third option — flow, which is fundamental to an empowered win/win resolution.

# CHARACTERISTICS: AGREEMENT

Agreers exhibit a number of characteristics. Generally, they:

▶ *Keep the peace.* Calm, friendly relations are usually very fundamental to the agreer's sense of personal wellbeing. Arguments are something to be avoided wherever possible. Often their desire to keep the peace leaves them very disconcerted when others around them are in conflict, even when the arguers accept their tiff as healthy and productive. Acutely sensitive to atmosphere, they need outer calm to maintain inner peace. Many agreers also believe strongly in democratic principles. The equality value explored in Part II is one they are usually very comfortable with. They are often drawn to conflict resolution techniques as tools to avoid feeling devastated and defeated by conflict. With these skills and their underlying agreement value, they can become excellent mediators.

▶ *Emphasise similarities and common ground.* Agreers will often focus on the similarities and common ground they share with others. They'll talk about a similar experience, take a friend's side in an argument. This tendency often helps them to build bridges between themselves and other people. But sometimes they'll masquerade agreement by suppressing real and important differences, or change views depending on who they are with at the time.

▶ *Are urgent about concluding disagreements.* Many agreers are acutely sensitive to hidden as well as open disharmony. Re-establishing the peace has a very high priority for them as any disagreement makes them very uncomfortable. To handle this discomfort, they may too readily accept a speedy compromise in which they lose out.

   Those with conflict resolution skills are less likely to reach agreements that severely disadvantage them, but nevertheless they are usually anxious to address conflict early. They will express this urgency through the active pursuit of win/win solutions.

▶ *Modify behaviour and suppress needs readily to fit in with others.* Agreers may minimise real conflict and avoid issues if they lack the communication skills to address the problem. They adapt their behaviour and often compromise their own needs in order to please others. Their reaction to conflict is more often 'flight' than 'fight'.

▶ *Need harmonious teamwork for job satisfaction.* They tend to enjoy team projects, but work performance and satisfaction may fall away badly if they are part of a conflict-ridden group.

# CHARACTERISTICS: COMPETITION

Competer's style contrasts with that of agreers in a number of significant ways. Competers are likely to:

▶ *Enjoy the challenge of competitive strategies.* Competers enjoy the possibility of winning over others or over circumstances. For instance, they enjoy the challenge of securing a difficult-to-negotiate contract. They generally tolerate the politics of self-promotion quite well. Many define their self-worth on their ability to 'give as good as they get'. Their reaction to conflict is more often 'fight' than 'flight'. They welcome the team spirit that can develop as a group unites in common purpose.

▶ *Value competition because it drives people forward and tests worth.* Workplace leaders who value competition may engineer situations that create competition between employees to encourage the best performance possible. For instance, they may set sales or production targets, or provide over-quota bonuses and top producers' rewards.

▶ *Accept some aggression as part of the 'rough and tumble'.* Competers often display an aggressive style in their inter-actions. They will show anger when thwarted in their goals or when others stand in their way. They withstand anger in others, rarely falling to pieces as an agreer might. They may meet the other person's anger with their own, even more aggressive display. They believe aggression is a necessary aspect of drive and initiative. Competers may not recognise that their aggression is not well tolerated by less combative clients and colleagues.

▶ *See interaction with others as inevitably competitive.* They may regard most workplace and social situations as subtle, and sometimes not so subtle, battles—their aim being to prove they are at least as good, if not better, than someone else. Not all competers will display open aggression. When crossed, some may manipulate or plan a counter-attack behind the scenes.

▶ *Use and receive one-upmanship as a comfortable, light-hearted way of relating.* Competition can take the form of light-hearted one-upmanship. Knocking and put-downs are often a standard part of competers' casual conversation. The worth of other people is judged by their ability to participate in the banter. Competers will often use an attacking style when they are actually building an alliance with the very person they appear to be putting down.

## INTERACTING STYLE

Baden Eunson, author of *Dealing with Conflict*, says:

> ... males tend to see life as a contest, where one's worth has to be continually reasserted and defended against assault. This can mean a competitive rather than a cooperative approach to problem-solving. Non-physical contest, such as argument or negotiation, take on this combative ... aspect as well, with men seeing them as arenas for using logic as a weapon, and experiencing the thrill of a contest. Females, some researchers contend, experience reality in quite a different way, approaching disputes as a chance to cooperate.[67]

I'm not at all sure women see disputes in such a positive light. But many I know have an intense dislike of conflict. For them, work's chief rewards come through friendship and affiliations. While work for men is often about winning, work for women is more likely to be about lifestyle. They can be acutely distressed if relationships sour.

*Men's work is often about winning. Women's work is more likely to be about lifestyle.*

Nessa was a sales rep for a large domestic appliance wholesaler. Her sales manager had briefed her when she was first employed. 'Go out there and get to know your clients better than anyone else,' he'd said. Nessa was delighted with her role. It was a carte blanche to build harmonious relationships between her company and its major retailers. Her manager's brief gave Nessa full scope to use her unusually charming personality and considerable creativity and intelligence.

Nessa designed in-store campaigns. She spoke at in-house conferences. She demonstrated new products, and won over buyers and sales personnel. She worked twelve-hour days and there was always more she could do than she had time for.

Nessa regretted that she had little time to do much for the distributors, the middle men in the chain from wholesale to retail, but contented herself with the thought that this had not been part of her brief. 'Create the appetite with the retailers. The distributors will look after the supply details,' her boss had said. She also regretted that she didn't visit the smaller retailers. But overall she knew she was doing a fantastic job. Sales figures boomed under her policy of extraordinary service to the retailers with the greatest capacity.

In a company reshuffle, Nessa found herself with a new sales manager. He gave her no instructions following his appointment, so for the first week or so she went on as she had before. But she began to feel anxious about his lack of communication. She felt she was being ignored.

One day, desperate for some contact and feedback, she complained to him about it: 'You've been here three weeks now and you haven't even talked to us sales reps.' Perhaps it wasn't the most tactful statement, but his response was way beyond what she expected. He was furious. 'How dare you question my management', was what he said to her face. 'I'll white-ant her. She's a threat. She's out of here. Watch me!' was his private comment to a colleague, who was shocked at his vehement reaction to the company's golden girl.

In two months, all staff were to be assessed by their managers in the yearly performance review. Meanwhile, Nessa's sales manager continued to say nothing about the direction of her strategies. He was in destructive competition mode. Nessa had become the enemy. He watched her running towards a cliff edge, waiting silently until she tumbled over. He solicited comments on her performance only from her underserviced distributors and smaller retailers. Of course they were negative. Even Nessa knew they would have to be. Well-armed against her, the sales manager used this feedback to write a scathing review of her performance.

On review day, he called Nessa into his office and read his report to her. Nessa was stunned. 'Don't you have anything positive to say?' she stuttered. 'No. Nothing', he replied. 'Are you trying to get rid of me?' she asked bluntly. 'Up to you', he smirked. 'I'm pulling you off all the big company accounts immediately.' He'd scored against her, he'd won, he was delighted.

A number of marketing directors and buyers from the major retailers rang the manager, horrified that the best sales rep they'd ever dealt with had been withdrawn. He was implacable. No amount of positive feedback would make him change his mind.

Like many caught up in underlying values conflict, Nessa explained the problem as a personality clash (her shorthand for 'I can't fix it'). Her high need for harmonious relationships, particularly with her own boss, made this new situation intolerable for her.

Within a couple of weeks, Nessa had a new job lined up and left the organisation. Two people were appointed to fill her one position — both of them men.

'I couldn't believe I could be the brunt of that sort of internal competition. I do everything I can to be nice to people', she said to the human resources officer during her exit interview.

Was Nessa's sales manager motivated by competition or by status? Nessa apparently had crossed the line when she complained he wasn't talking to the sales reps. He had lost face. The way status and competition can be played out can look similar, and a problem with status can trigger competition.

Here's a rule of thumb that can sometimes help. Consider the goal. What is the person trying to achieve? At its most extreme, when status is the issue the person wants a slave. When competition is extreme, the person wants the other's blood. In the workplace, of course, the values aren't quite as dramatic. But the metaphor helps us make the distinction. Nessa's sales manager didn't just want her submission to his authority, he wanted her out of the company.

David, a public relations campaign director, read this story and commented:

I've been in almost exactly the same position as Nessa. This guy was gunning for me. He was my immediate superior, but quite frankly he wasn't that good at the job. He was very good at political knee-capping, however. He took client after client away from me; vetoed my creative ideas in meetings, then blamed me when campaigns didn't work. I'm not the sort to fight back with those types of tactics. I knew I was good at my job. I got out of there before he ruined my reputation in the industry. I personally think he was terrified that I'd be better at his job than he was, and that if he didn't keep knocking me down, the powers that be would see that.

Competition has no need to be the destructive force it was for Nessa's and David's bosses. Used more wisely, it can focus drive and ambition for high success. Most men accept it as a necessary part of their working world. Some men particularly enjoy it, even thrive on it. Wins bolster self-esteem. Competing establishes status, provides their goals, keeps them alert. It's a socially acceptable expression of healthy aggressiveness.

Women rarely feel the same way about competition. Agreement usually takes a higher priority. Most women thrive on warm association rather than hard-nosed competition. Pitted against someone else, the typical woman is likely to be shocked that she has found herself in that position and becomes extremely anxious. Her ability to perform effectively takes a nosedive. All of her energy is sucked into the disagreement and concentrated on how best to extricate herself. Workplaces dominated by masculine competitiveness are seen by her as alien, dangerous territory — *enter at your own risk*.

## HE-MEN AND SHE-WOMEN

Bearing in mind that any discussion involving stereotypes is a minefield in which we must tread very carefully, a number of agreement and competition qualities creep into our images of men and women. **Figure 28: Agreement and competition stereotypes** (page 145) highlights some common distinctions made between feminine and masculine style. However emancipated we feel we are from gender stereotyping, we are still likely to believe that the

| AGREEMENT:<br>feminine stereotype | COMPETITION:<br>masculine stereotype |
|---|---|
| accessible | active |
| accommodating | aggressive |
| affiliative | assertive |
| amiable | athletic |
| appreciative | blunt |
| approachable | bold |
| charming | candid |
| compassionate | dynamic |
| compliant | excelling |
| considerate | forceful |
| cooperative | refining |
| flattering | sparring |
| sweet-tempered | stubborn |
| submissive | them-and-us |
| tender | tough |

*Figure 28: Agreement and competition stereotypes*

left column lists more feminine qualities and the right, more masculine ones. That's stereotypes for you, they catch you unawares!

We've come to see agreement as a more feminine attribute and competition as a more masculine one. This difference generates considerable gender-related conflict. Misunderstanding and alienation arise from mismatched goals — the agreement-style woman searching for areas she and the other person can agree on, while the competitive man is enjoying the debate he's set up. He wants to score points, but he wants an opponent who'll play along, trying to score their own points. She's so busy minimising the disagreement, she doesn't meet his need for a worthy opponent. She expects that if she's accommodating, he'll make reciprocal concessions. But that's not the way a competition game works. The woman can end up feeling boxed in, seething or exploding with more real malice than he ever directed at her. The man can end up being made to feel a bully if he handles her explosion with a return volley. If she arrives at hatred, that's likely to threaten him even more. She now becomes an enemy, not just a sparring partner, in his eyes. The primal reactions of flight and fight are seriously in play.

*Misunderstanding and alienation arise from mismatched goals.*

This type of scenario is common, yet avoidable. Understanding differences in style is a crucial tool for avoiding these strings of reactions that can end in crisis.

# MOULDING STEREOTYPES

## Social conditioning

Agreement and competition implies marked differences in interacting style. We see the channelling of competition for men and agreement for women arising in childhood. Though a good number of boys and girls will bypass the conditioning of their respective subculture, enough are affected to reflect in our stereotypes of the 'typical male' and the 'typical female'.

Boys generally display far more aggressive, 'push and shove' behaviour when they play. Little girls are likely to play more cooperatively, acting out family roles. Fantasy games such as 'tea parties' and 'babies' rely on the cooperative division of duties. As they grow, boys delight in and are encouraged to participate in body contact sports, which demand the pitting of physical strength against someone else. Girls' organised sports, such as basketball and hockey, rely far more on skill and fitness than opposing physical strengths.

In their teenage years, boys continue building self-esteem through competition. Parents, school and society direct them towards action and achievement. Though the same pressures are now increasing on girls, too, traditional values for girls still hold their ground. Being sweet, helpful and obliging are more often rewarded by parents, particularly fathers, than scholastic achievement.

*People will often compete via mental agility, logic and by outwitting their opponents.*

This emphasis on cooperation is likely to carry through to womanhood. Most women are horrified if they walk into a business meeting of colleagues and find they've been cast in the role of opponent by male peers out to score a touchdown. Many men test the measure of their status, power and self-esteem by competition. In earlier times, the chief way of competing was through muscle, then via weapons. Today, most people competing in the workplace do so via mental agility, logic and by outwitting their opponents.

## Movement in the stereotypes

Competition appears to be a genetically inherited trait in many species of animal. Perhaps it has also had a survival value for humans. Competition serves and protects the group, especially in procurement, defence and attack.

However, the urge between nations to compete is rapidly losing its survival value as population numbers explode and technological advancements escalate. Our mounting concern for our environment, wildlife, the planet's resources and the weapons of mass destruction now available make unbridled competition an unsustainable strategy.

Yet today, many women are releasing in themselves the assertive drive that underpins competition, shaking off stereotypes and often tumbling into many of competition's attendant pitfalls. Unreined, it can feed exploitation, greed, acquisitiveness and pride. Previously this drive in women had been suppressed in the public arena under an overwhelming cultural pressure to conform to their specific gender role.

The shift to a more service-oriented, people-oriented culture is a major change occurring in the modern workplace. It's a shift that women can celebrate as it demands their particular areas of expertise. Women's entry into the workforce marks a unique opportunity to temper the forces of competition with those of agreement and community building, qualities that have traditionally been attached to feminine behaviour.

Although humans may be genetically programmed for competition, it's likely that we're also programmed for agreement. Modern biologists are reviving the notion of the 'superorganism' — a group of individuals whose collective behaviour resembles the integration and organisation of a single organism. The cooperation displayed in ant and bee colonies, or in the sophisticated pack hunting of wild dogs, shows us the building blocks of agreement that are also inherited from our genetic forbears.[68]

We build our stereotypes based on our assumptions and experiences. They are the generalisations we employ to make sense of things. But they won't always serve us when it comes to the particular situation.

# WHAT IS THE GOOD INTENTION?

Well-rounded individuals are responsive to both their agreement and their competition tendencies, though they may favour one side of themselves more than the other in particular circumstances. If we reject outright a real part of ourselves, when we meet it in others we create a 'sound barrier', through which it can be impossible for us to take in what the other person is really trying to say.

*Agreers often affirm the value they place on harmony by their disdain of a competitive style in others.*

Agreers often affirm the value they place on harmony by their disdain of a competitive style in others. Suppressing their own aggression and wish to win, they don't tolerate in others the qualities they reject in themselves. Agreers who reject the competitive stance of others may face a number of negative consequences:

▶ They are likely to fail to consider the valid point behind the competition.

▶ They may feel quite strongly about their position on a particular issue, but find themselves unable to express their ideas in a heated arena.

▶ With their own voice unheard, agreers are left feeling frustrated, suppressed and dangerously isolated. They can feel as though they've walked into a roaring lions' den armed only with a few futile words.

Competers have a different, but similar, problem. They have found that life is better when they deny or suppress their peace-loving, compliant side and use aggressive competition to ensure their needs are met. In rejecting their softer side, they may:

▶ show little sensitivity to other points of view;

▶ make poorer decisions in the workplace; and

▶ walk over people who can't easily get their message across.

### Three stepping stones for finding the good intention

The following three steps for finding the good intention apply not only to agreement and competition, but also to any set of values that is not our own.[69]

STEP 1     Recognise how you may have suppressed your urges for a style opposite to your preferred style. Acquaintance with your suppressed urges dissolves the 'sound barrier' when others are doing things you don't approve of.[70]

STEP 2     Acknowledge the good intentions of the style that is not your own. This opens a chink of empathy, one of the most helpful ingredients of good conflict resolution.

STEP 3     Start listening. You may need to invite reticent agreers to talk to you. It's important not to later use what they say as ammunition against them, or you're unlikely to hear the truth from them a second time.

        An agreer may need courage to probe behind the anger or attack of competers to see the valid points they are making.

Agreers' good intentions often start from the premise: *Other people will be considerate towards me, as long as I'm nice.* Competers generally base their behaviour on the premise: *Other people probably won't look after me, especially if I appear to be a pushover. I must watch out for myself.*

It's important to remember that self-interest is not a crime. Agreers sometimes need to give themselves, as well as others, permission to pursue it more actively.

Rising to the challenge and keeping the peace are two very useful forces in the workplace. Both individuals and organisations must repeatedly find the right balance between them. Good decision-making becomes even more powerful when the perspectives from both sides are considered. This synthesis is only possible when the good intentions of agreers and competers are respected and understood.

*EXERCISE*

Stop for a moment and think of someone you know, or know of, who is strongly motivated by the agreement value. For a behaviour or decision they've made that you found difficult to cope with, consider at least one good intention that may have motivated them. Choose from the list on the following page and add others that come to mind.

| Agreers'<br>good intentions | Probable<br>motivation<br>for ............ :<br>(name) |
|---|---|
| Avoiding arguments where possible | |
| Creating friendly work climates and bonded relationships | |
| Responding to the needs of the team | |
| Minimising conflict | |
| Facilitating joint planning | |
| Building trust | |
| Other good intentions:<br><br>............................................................<br>............................................................<br>............................................................<br>............................................................<br>............................................................<br>............................................................ | |

*Place crosses against relevant motivations*

*Figure 29: Agreers' good intentions*

Now consider someone you know, or know of, who you'd classify as a competer. Think of a time when something they did annoyed you. Did they have a good intention that arose out of their competition value? Were there other good intentions that motivated them as well?

Remember, there's nothing wrong with proving you are intelligent or have the best solution to a problem. We all need to do this from time to time. It is possible to support this intention while emphatically *not* supporting a method of achieving it that makes another person appear stupid.

| Competers' good intentions | Probable motivation for ............. : (name) |
|---|---|
| Thwarting a perceived attack | |
| Pursuing a clear goal in the face of opposition | |
| Responding to a challenge with plenty of energy | |
| Proving they're intelligent, street-smart, a winner | |
| Coming up with the best answer | |
| Inviting a relationship with playful teasing or baiting | |
| Other good intentions: .............................................. .............................................. .............................................. .............................................. .............................................. .............................................. | |

*Place crosses against relevant motivations*

Figure 30: Competers' good intentions

## SPOTTING THE UNDERLYING VALUES

Do you notice people's underlying values, or do you pay attention only to the surface? People's mannerisms provide us with many clues to understand them. We may react unconsciously — we just don't like them, or we're just not relaxed with them — if their style is not our own. The challenge is to notice they're *different*, but not make them wrong for it.

People frequently signal agreement or competition with their body language and verbal style. Consider the differences in these two values that the following mannerisms suggest:

**Body language:**
▶ leaning back or leaning forward

▶ rough or gentle physical contact

▶ side-by-side or face-to-face

▶ avoiding or maintaining eye contact

▶ fixed expression or smiling frequently

▶ non-responsive or responsive to facial expressions

**Verbal style:**
▶ combative or friendly

▶ statements or questions

▶ extreme or partial generalisations

▶ demands or requests

▶ enjoying or bored by sports talk

▶ assertive or avoiding

▶ not apologising or apologising after confrontation

▶ interrupting or not interrupting

▶ report- or rapport-talk

These differences in mannerisms often align with gender. As we discuss them in detail, we're once again in danger of stereotyping the sexes. So, bear in mind that you probably know many highly combative women and many nurturing men, and in observing them note whether they tend to use mannerisms more typical of their opposite sex.

## Body language
Body language is learnt, usually unconsciously, by copying significant others. Frequently, these people will be of the same sex. This is how gender subcultures perpetuate. However, we need to remind ourselves that race and nationality are other strong

defining factors for culture, so while the following distinctions are frequently observed in western culture, some nationalities may behave differently.

### LEANING BACK OR LEANING FORWARD

When sitting in a chair, men usually lean back while listening, women usually lean forward. For men, leaning back signals: *I'm at ease, in non-combative, non-competitive mode. I am not geared up for action.* Women's leaning forward indicates: *I'm right with you, I've entered your personal world, I've united with you.* As we generally read body language unconsciously, we may be completely unaware of the misinterpretations we have made about the other person in cross-gender relating.

### ROUGH OR GENTLE PHYSICAL CONTACT

Some men have a tendency for rough physical contact with each other — the bone-crushing handshake, the powerful slap on the back. The heartiness sometimes seems to be a way to display manly strength or test the other person's ability to cope with physical pain! Women's touching tends to be more gentle, with an underlying purpose of nurturing, indicating agreement or a shared point of view.

Men often misinterpret women's physical touching as sexually provocative. One man complained bitterly to me about a female colleague: 'When we're talking, if I touched her half as often as she touches me, I'd be up on a sexual harassment charge.' In most workplace situations, women may be wiser to control their tendency to touch and stroke men, even when they know them well.

### SIDE-BY-SIDE OR FACE-TO-FACE

For men, a face-to-face stance is confrontational and can be read as an invitation to compete. When men are talking comfortably with each other and power issues are not on the agenda, they're likely to avoid face-to-face contact. They often prefer a side-by-side stance, or at least place themselves at oblique angles to each other. Women, on the other hand, do not view face-to-face contact as confrontational. Deborah Tannen, a linguist, recorded video clips showing that when two women are talking, they're more likely to sit face-to-face. Women read this body language as 'open'.[71]

*Women read face-to-face contact as open, men as confrontational.*

If a woman expects a man to adopt the same approach with her, she may misinterpret his averted body position as 'closed'. In fact, he may be turning away precisely because he wants to relate to her in a non-confrontational way.

Deborah Tannen found these contrasting patterns are visible in children, too. When filming small boys planning a joint task, they tended not to face each other for their conversation, whereas the girls sat opposite each other in positions that facilitated visual contact.[72]

### AVOIDING OR MAINTAINING EYE CONTACT

Though there are many individual variations, men look into another person's eyes more rarely and for shorter periods than women. The direct glance is confrontational for many species in the animal world and it seems that it also holds this implication in men's competitive subculture. A woman who is unaware of gender and cultural differences may well believe a man is discounting her opinions if he doesn't make eye contact reasonably frequently. Men may misinterpret women's greater tendency to make eye contact as confrontational.

It's also worth noting that between men and women, eye contact can be regarded as sexually provocative. In many Asian cultures, for example, eye contact in the workplace is regarded as extremely inappropriate for between-gender conversations, and for conversations between superiors and subordinates. Asian women are likely to express the modesty prescribed by their culture through a lowered gaze.

### FIXED EXPRESSION OR SMILING FREQUENTLY

*Many men find an overenthusiastic response rings false to them.*

Women are more likely to greet another person with a smile — a non-verbal indicator of non-aggressiveness. Men are less likely to greet someone by smiling at them. This should not be misinterpreted as unfriendliness, however. Men tend to smile less frequently in conversations and to hold back on showing enthusiasm. Many find that an overenthusiastic response rings false to them, especially when talking about work situations. A lot of women cultivate friendly enthusiasm with smiles, head nods and intense listening to indicate their genuine interest clearly, unaware that this behaviour probably alienates more undemonstrative men.

### NON-RESPONSIVE OR RESPONSIVE TO FACIAL EXPRESSIONS

Possibly because of the avoidance of continuous eye contact, men are often less responsive to the other person's facial expressions.[73] Even when they have noticed that the other person is smiling at them, they are less likely than women to return the smile. One man explained to me why he was less responsive to others' facial expressions: 'I'm trying to maintain independent, coherent thought.'

## Verbal style

Conversational rituals are comfortable and effective in many contexts. Yet different styles of communication between men and women can account for considerable alienation and misunderstanding. Competition and agreement drive different verbal expressions. Maxims such as 'Don't rock the boat' and 'All's fair in love and war' are typical of these differences.[74]

### COMBATIVE OR FRIENDLY

Women's interaction style tends to be more nurturing, supportive, compassionate and easygoing. Women will often prefer to use their boss's first name, if the environment accepts this familiarity. First names generally indicate a non-combative, friendly relationship.

Men's interaction style tends to be more combative, aggressive, disciplinary and active. They'll often use surnames without the 'Mr' in front. This is a common form of addressing people they are acquainted, but not overly familiar, with. Workplace manoeuvres can become a form of competitive sport. Men might refer to their team leader as 'coach' and those outside the team as 'the enemy'.

*Workplace manoeuvres can become a form of competitive sport.*

> Teresa and John worked for a large real estate development company. They had just returned from a trip to Hong Kong where they completed a successful merger with another company. Teresa's report: 'I'm delighted that we've succeeded in joining with this company. We've welcomed them into the fold.' John's report: 'Got 'em. Made a killing. Another one in the bag.' They were both talking about the same transaction.

John puts zest into his experience by pretending he's in a war zone. Teresa puts zest into hers by focusing on her success in achieving cooperation with another organisation. The difference in *verbal* style is harmless. But *treating* the other person like an enemy can turn them into one. The long-term viability of

*Negotiations that leave one party severely disadvantaged are conflicts waiting to happen.*

relationships depends on mutual respect. Negotiations that leave one party severely disadvantaged are conflicts waiting to happen. On the other hand, negotiations that are not favourable to yourself because you have been 'too nice' and let someone take advantage of you, will not serve you or your organisation either. Teresa and John's directors probably did well to send both of them to Hong Kong to do the negotiating. They may well have been a good foil for each other.

### STATEMENTS OR QUESTIONS

Women ask more questions. Men make more statements. When a woman makes a statement, she will often do so with a rising inflection or a tag ending to indicate she is seeking agreement: 'It's hot today, isn't it?'

I interviewed corporate trainer, Mike Davis. He noted this difference in a workshop he attended:

> For once I had the luxury of being a participant rather than the lecturer, so I could really observe interactions more closely. There were thirty-five people present. All but five were women, and one woman came up to me after the first day and said, 'Look, there are hardly any men here, but did you notice how they dominated the discussion?' I hadn't, so the next day I decided to watch everyone's contributions closely. The men definitely made a little more than their share of the comments, but that was not as significant as something else I observed. They tended to make a statement as frequently as they asked a question. The men tended to put forward a suggestion with a statement format like 'We should ... take a break.' The women would put forward their suggestion with a question format like 'How about we take a break?' Also, if a man wasn't happy with an answer to a question he'd raised, he was more likely to follow it up and persist with it. The women were more likely to show gratitude for the answer offered, appear to accept it and try and work it out in some other way.

### EXTREME OR PARTIAL GENERALISATIONS

*Women generally create less dogmatic sentences.*

Baden Eunson, in *Dealing with Conflict*, tables the tendency in men to shape more forthright unequivocal sentences, sprinkling them with 'always', 'never', 'all' or 'none'.[75] 'We *never* do it that way', 'You're *always* complaining', '*Every* time you answer the phone, you forget to say the company name'. Women tend to use less black-and-white sentence construction. They'll incorporate conditional quantifiers such as 'a bit', 'often', 'sort of' or 'generally'.[76] They are more likely to make fewer definitive statements, softening them with 'maybe', 'perhaps', 'I think' or 'I believe'. They create sentences more likely to be agreed with, because they are less dogmatic.

Men often appear less threatened if they trigger opposition. Keeping the peace is not their major priority. When things become heated, they may use language that is potentially more crushing than language women would generally use. These differences seem closely related to agreement versus competition style.

### DEMANDS OR REQUESTS

Men are more likely to presume compliance to requests. They might use phrases such as 'Over here!' or 'File this'. Women are more likely to say 'Please come here' or 'If you wouldn't mind, could you file this?'. The careful padding of a request is required by women for politeness. Men's bald requesting can sound rude and demanding to a woman's ears. Women's style of requesting carefully avoids a challenge, whereas, at least to women, men's style can appear to invite it, though in fact they are probably merely hoping not to have their authority questioned.

### ENJOYING OR BORED BY SPORTS TALK

Sports talk is men's competition talk. Discussing the weekend's games and the chances for their favourite team in the upcoming finals is an important aspect of men's social rituals with each other. Sports are men's civilised version of defending territory. Although many efforts have been made to eradicate violence from sports, many men wouldn't deny that they enjoy watching a 'good punch-up'.

Most men enjoy talk about sport because it is the one common interest they share. It allows for bonding on safe topics. A show of enthusiasm, knowledge and opinions can amount to a confirmation of allegiance to manly pursuits. As a conversational tool it conveniently bypasses rank and social class. Many women switch off once the conversation topic turns to sport. Women tend to bond by self-disclosure on intimate topics.[77]

*Sports talk allows men to bond on safe topics.*

A male interviewee reported:

One manager with a very autocratic managerial style destroyed the respect of his male employees because he didn't appreciate the significance of sport in their lives. On a night when every red-blooded male in the country was dying to watch the football final on television, he ordered his team to work back and strip down a machine — a job that could have been done any time that week. He was not responding to their very real needs, and his men regarded his demand not just as inconsiderate, but as criminal! That was the final straw for these men, who'd already put up with a lot from this manager. The next week, over a relatively minor problem about overtime payments, they were out on strike, demanding his dismissal.

Women beware! Ignore men's sports culture at your peril. Many women have found that if they want to talk men's talk they need to keep at least moderately up-to-date on the sports scene. Expatriate Australian author, Jill Kerr Conway, on a return visit to Australia in 1996, caused quite a stir when she advised her Sydney audiences that women in business should 'watch those wretched football games' and 'learn the language of football'. Following the code (rugby league, AFL, soccer, etc.) and the preferred teams of male colleagues makes a woman seem more like 'one of the boys'. Personally, I really enjoy tennis and can usually manage several minutes of pleasant social chatter with men after a big tournament, but I acknowledge that an interest in football or soccer would really serve me well.

### ASSERTIVE OR AVOIDING

Many men have no problem stating exactly what they want and exactly what they disagree with, even when they know it will cause conflict. Many women will go to great lengths to avoid confrontation. Rather than directly confront, a woman may try manipulative, indirect methods to get another person to do something. If that person starts to feel used, they may become very irritated and instigate the fight the woman is trying to avoid.

Ingrid worked with her husband, Ben. They were establishing a new supermarket and had borrowed heavily from the bank to finance it. The opportunity arose to open a second branch, but they would need to borrow even more money. Ben wanted to go for it. When he tried to discuss it with Ingrid, all she had said was: 'It's up to you.' In fact, Ingrid was very worried about expanding at this stage, but she couldn't state her point of view openly. Instead she used a 'sniper' approach. Each time a bill came in she'd make a big fuss about how expensive it was. She complained about the interest on the present loan, and about the increase to the wages payments since they'd employed an extra part-timer. She carried on about the cost of a new computer they'd ordered. Ben had had enough: 'For heaven's sake, if you don't think we should open up the branch, will you just come out and say so! You've been whining about money ever since the idea came up.'

Many women are very inexperienced when it comes to a direct, confrontational approach. It doesn't fit the stereotype of femininity to which they conform. Harriet Goldhor Lerner, author of *The Dance of Anger*, says:

> Our very definitions of 'masculinity' and 'femininity' are based on the notion that women must function as non-threatening helpmates and ego builders to men lest men feel castrated and weakened.[78]

This, Lerner believes, is why many women avoid fighting, asserting their viewpoints, requesting explanations from others and clearly stating what they want. They regard all these as 'potentially destructive acts that might hurt or diminish others'.[79]

However, I also collected a number of complaints from women on men's avoidance of confrontation. Karen reports:

> I've had a real problem with my boss regarding the allocation of holidays. He's given permission for one guy who has no children to take two weeks off during school holidays. I've got three kids and I really need to take my holidays at that time. But he won't even let me talk about it. I tried tackling the issue with him face-to-face. He walked away before I'd even explained my problem properly. Later that week I rang through to him at a time when I was pretty certain he wouldn't be that busy. 'Got to go, Karen,' he said, and hung up on me. I thought I was being really calm and clear about it all. It doesn't seem to me to be an insurmountable problem. At the moment I have no idea how I'll cope with babysitting during the school holidays. Yesterday he discussed some work stuff with me like we didn't have a problem. Why can't we just deal with it?

*Women often complain that men won't discuss issues.*

As long as this boss refuses to reopen the holiday issue, he has his preferred solution. The status quo suits him, and helps him retain the upper hand. Quite possibly he is trying to avoid disappointing the man he'd already granted leave to. By not allowing Karen to tell him about her greater need, she is unable to force his hand.

*Men may avoid confrontation because it helps them to:*
▶ *hold the upper hand;*
▶ *keep the social wheels on track.*

Men can also avoid confrontation in order to keep the social wheels on track. Many men lack skills to confront assertively without aggression. Their upbringing has given them only two responses, fight or flee. Girls rehearse life situations over 'tea parties' and 'babies' games, and as a result are generally comfortable with their feelings and able to discuss their feelings with others. Boys, on the other hand, rarely discuss or acknowledge feelings in play. Many men are uncomfortable and unpractised in feelings talk.[80] Many women find men's conflict avoidance behaviour very odd. Emilia, who works in a stock-broking office, says:

> I don't pretend to be someone that I'm not and I don't try to suck up to a person I don't like. But that's how George and some of the other men in the office do it. They are really nice to your face, then they will turn around and stab you in the back. It seems to me to be a male thing because a woman would be franker about her dislike. I don't invite people I don't like out for lunch. I don't see any point in wasting their time and mine, but the guys do that. I don't know why they do it. It's a crazy thing.

It seems men can be far more tolerant than women of people they find difficult. Emilia's comment reminded me of another I'd collected in a totally different area of work, a woman designer involved in a long-term building project.

> If a woman doesn't like another woman, both people know exactly where they stand. But you can sit around a mess room table with a bunch of guys and they'll be bitching about someone and if he walks in, it's 'Mate, how are you?', and I think, *But you were just saying that you hated that guy.* They never actually come out and say it.

Making a stand and opening up a confrontation can be a very big deal for men. They're in danger of inviting 'kill or be killed' to the lunch table. They find it smarter not to! Harry, after reading a draft of this book, warned me: 'You'd better believe it, men can also make it quite clear they're giving you the cold shoulder.'

I was chatting with Caroline about aggressiveness in the men in her workplace and she had this to say:

> They never yell at a woman. They are aggressive in other ways. I've been treated with disdain — you know, that sort of very off-hand 'flick that bit of dust off your shoulder' kind of attitude. 'Get away you, you've annoyed me.' They cut your conversation off in mid-stream. My boss does that. If I'm having a disagreement with him and he cannot come back at me with a good argument, he just walks out of the room or changes topics.

Men may appear more comfortable with open conflict than they actually are. Despite surface appearances, conflict makes many men *highly* uncomfortable, often because they lack skills to work through the conflict to an acceptable solution. Nurtured in a culture where if you fight you're supposed to win, not fighting may appear to be the safer option.

Other factors may be relevant, too. A number of men have reported to me that they hate having to control their adrenalin rush to fit in with the confines of acceptable behaviour. Often to avoid open warfare they resist engagement in a conflict situation by refusing to discuss a contentious issue. Thus on the surface of things, they may appear to cope better than women with unresolved conflict. In fact, the type of moderate discussion required to resolve conflict in the workplace is something men may find more difficult than women do, hormonally armed as they are for attack and physical combat. For them it's rather like driving a car with both the accelerator and the brake pressed hard to the floor.

## NOT APOLOGISING OR APOLOGISING AFTER CONFRONTATION

After a confrontation, a woman is very likely to apologise. A man is far less likely to do so as a matter of course. He will need to have a particularly good reason. No wonder women often complain: 'Why do I always have to be the peacemaker?' Peacemaking by apology is not a standard part of men's gender subculture. Competers don't apologise for competing. They don't feel themselves to be in error. They are just doing what they do. Agreers who have confronted someone, however, feel they have something to apologise for. The confrontation has blotted their copybook.[81]

Sometimes it really does seem that competers are using an entirely different rule book from agreers — not just with conversational style but also with ethical concerns and acceptable behaviour. Understanding these differences (and a little bit of humour) helps us to tolerate one another.

### INTERRUPTING OR NOT INTERRUPTING

*Women often interrupt to add to the conversational topic, men to change it.*

Style differences can affect even innocuous conversation. Generally, men readily change topics to one they are more comfortable or preoccupied with at the time. Another man will probably interrupt in turn to reinstate his conversation if he wants it to continue. However, if a woman finds herself repeatedly talked over, unable to complete her sentences or maintain her chosen focus of discussion, she may seethe with indignation, yet say nothing.

In workplace meetings, this tendency to hold her peace can make a woman look powerless. In comparison, men who rarely interrupt in meetings can nevertheless be highly respected. Other men will really listen to their point of view. Perceived status plays a big part in whether an interruption will get a fair hearing. Smeltzer and Watson report on research which found that in negotiations, women's interruptions were singularly less successful than men's. They defined unsuccessful interruptions as 'oral messages to which nobody responded and the initial speaker continued unabated'.[82]

*Men often prefer to have the uniqueness rather than the similarity of their experience acknowledged.*

Women's interruptions are often motivated by the desire to agree and add to the same topic. Despite this, some men will feel usurped. Men often prefer to have the uniqueness rather than the similarity of their experience acknowledged. They may feel as if the woman is trying to outdo them and to minimise the reality of their experience. Other women, however, are likely to feel supported by such interruptions because the report of a similar experience indicates that they not alone. It confirms their reality.

Men may change topics or not follow up on hints to be questioned for a number of considerate reasons. They may perceive the other person is upset and want to help them save face by 'keeping it all together'. They may perceive that the next logical step in the conversation is to tear down the other person's argument. Consequently, they change topics to avoid an unpleasant confrontation.

Of course, we are always making allowances for individual style. We tolerate talkative extroverts, though we can reach our limits with these people, too, particularly when they totally dominate a conversation. Some people's speaking style is halting and they are quite happy to have a more fluent person complete their sentence. This isn't quite an interruption, it is more of an add-on, and it indicates that the other person is following their line of thought. However, I've noticed that competers often interrupt to correct something they feel isn't true or accurate. It's liable to make an agreer clam up in resentment. Agreers sometimes pause in a conversation for support or encouragement to explore an unresolved issue more deeply. They can feel violated if the topic is changed in this space.

### REPORT- OR RAPPORT-TALK

The same woman who rarely gets a word in at a meeting may chatter nineteen to the dozen in private conversation. In fact, excessive talk is often a complaint that men make about women, though it is generally not borne out by careful studies registering who speaks the most in mixed gender conversations.

Deborah Tannen makes the point that men are more likely to use talk to impart information, while women are more likely to be establishing connections or negotiating relationships. She labels the contrast, *report-talk* versus *rapport-talk*.[83] It explains why women are often seen as the more talkative sex, because outside of a formal meeting they are using talk to build rapport and will do this far more expansively than a man. Women will talk at length in situations in which men would be very brief — in private conversations with friends or on the telephone. Women enjoy sharing the small details of their lives with friends and workmates. It's part of their rapport-building process. Men don't build rapport that way, and so judge women as time-wasting when they observe it happening. A woman is quite likely to judge a man as cold and impersonal if they see each other on a daily basis and he doesn't exchange personal disclosures with her.[84]

## Unspoken rules

These differences in conversation styles between men and women can be summarised as follows:

*Men often complain about women's supposed excessive talk.*

The unspoken rules of female-to-female conversation include:

▶ don't change topics;

▶ if one person is discussing an issue, it's her air-time until she has said all she wants to say;

▶ encourage the other person to share her deepest feelings and concerns;

▶ empathise with her feelings about the issue.

The unspoken rules of conversation amongst male peers are often:

▶ go for what you want;

▶ compete for the air-time;

▶ save others from a disclosure of painful or too intimate emotions;

▶ run with commonly held opinions;

▶ don't explode.

The traditional rule of men-to-women conversation was:

▶ the woman defers to the man and allows him to direct the conversation.

We are in an often very uncomfortable process of establishing new cross-gender conversational patterns. How would we like it to be?

Men would like women to:

▶ really listen;

▶ offer advice, but only when men have chosen to talk about a problem (generally, men won't willingly talk about a problem if they don't want advice);

▶ hold back on sharing similar experiences when the man is talking about important experiences of his own;

▶ not delve too deeply into painful areas, their own or the other person's, particularly if there are more than two people present;

► jump into a meeting discussion if they have something to contribute;

► say they disagree if they do, not imply by silence that everything is okay.

**Women would like men to:**

► really listen;

► interrupt to add to the discussion, but not to change topics;

► continue to negotiate in conflicts they find difficult rather than close down the conversation;

► understand that if a woman is talking about a problem it is not necessarily because she either blames the man for it or wants him to tell her how to fix it;

► hold back advice unless specifically asked for it, or at least really acknowledge how the woman feels about the problem first;

► recognise that in mixed gender situations at work, and especially at meetings, quieter women may need to be offered frequent opportunities to speak.

## FLIGHT, FIGHT OR FLOW

### Fight or flight: Pre-programmed responses

Agreement and competition styles are rooted in some fundamental differences in body responses to conflict. Perceived threat triggers a flurry of activity in the sympathetic nervous system. Blood diverts from the digestive system and skin to the skeletal muscles. The adrenal glands secrete the hormone epinephrine. The liver releases glucose into the blood stream. Bronchial tubes dilate to take in more oxygen. The body is ready for instant action — fight or flight.

There appears to be a connection between testosterone and the fight response. In other words, the more testosterone in the blood stream, the more likely the body's readiness for action will take

*There is a connection between testosterone and the fight response.*

the form of *fight*.[85] Lesbians who inject testosterone report that the hormone seems to make them more aggressive. One woman who weekly injects the artificial testosterone chemical Cipionate reports on the changes in her personality it has produced:

> I am less likely to let people mess with me. And I know why [men] get so angry when you cut them off in traffic. Before I was like, 'Oh what's the matter with them?' Now I'm more, 'You must die for what you've done!'[86]

While male hormones appear to have something to do with the decision to fight or flee, many other factors come into play. This includes comparison of physical size, power relationships, and the split-second assessment about which response will best serve the situation.

Fundamental world views will also influence the response to conflict. Competers see conflict as a contest. As such, they are more likely to direct the body's activated state towards fight. They must prove who is stronger, or who is right. They jump into the action in order to win. Quite often they'll see opposition as a personal affront and attack out of a need to protect their own self-respect, dignity or status.

*Competers see conflict as contest. Agreers see conflict as cataclysms.*

Agreers, on the other hand, are more likely to see conflicts as potential cataclysms to be avoided if at all possible. Their response to perceived threat is more likely to be fear than anger. They respond with flight—either physical withdrawal or withdrawal of the claim that appears to precipitate the conflict. To reduce conflict they may suppress their own needs. Sometimes they fear that in a direct confrontation they would lose, so they avoid the conflict as best they can. Their challenge is to learn to state their needs clearly, and to engage in difficult situations rather than avoid them.

## Flow

*Flow invites the opportunity for positive change.*

Fight and flight are two options. There is a third alternative: flow. Ultimately we want to be able to flow with conflict, viewing it neither as contest nor as cataclysm, but as an opportunity for positive change.[87] The following eight points offer a creative response to conflict. Flow means you will:

1. *Engage with the other person rather than flee.* You consciously involve yourself with the other person's energy, flowing with it

| FLIGHT OR FIGHT | | |
| --- | --- | --- |
| | Agreers: Flight | Competers: Fight |
| Conflict is: | Cataclysm | Contest |
| Belief: | My needs don't matter as much as safety | Your needs are not important |
| Expectation and approach: | I lose, you win | I win, you lose |
| Primary emotion: | Fear | Anger |
| Method: | Passive | Aggressive |
| Potential problems: | Lack of support; unmet needs; anger at unjust treatment; disunity; low self-esteem | Lack of support; long-term enemies; alienation from others; frustration: bitterness and isolation |
| Pay-off: | Avoids unpleasant situations | Vents anger and achieves goals in the short term |

*Figure 31: Flight or fight*

and directing it towards the positive. A reframing question is an excellent way to do this verbally without backing down or using a combative approach. For example, 'Can we try looking at this from a promotional perspective, as well as a profit one?'

2. *Know you are at the power centre of events, not a helpless victim of them.* You are stable and steering the direction of change towards the positive. While you may not have chosen the circumstances in the first place, you are always free to choose how you respond to them.

3. *Manage your own emotional distress carefully.* It may be more appropriate to deal with hurt and anger at another time or place. It's usually not acceptable to explode at a customer or a superior in the workplace. This doesn't mean that you *suppress* your feelings, bottling them up, never to be dealt with. Rather you *contain* them and postpone their expression. If you are in danger of exploding in anger or crying, you could try saying: 'Could I get back to you on this in a few minutes?' Leave the room or hang up the phone and then do something that

discharges the feeling in a 'safer' environment. For example, pound on your desk behind your closed and soundproofed door! Or vent your feelings with a trusted friend who'll listen and then help you move on from there. The right friend for this sort of support won't make your enemies their enemies. 'Enemies' and flow don't go together.[88]

4. *Work with, rather than against the problem.* Try not to let the problem intimidate you. Don't resist the problem. Acknowledge it. View it from all angles and then begin to brainstorm solutions.

5. *Trust in the process of communication.* Enjoy your flexibility and responsiveness as you engage with the difficulty.

6. *Share power or work towards that ideal.* If you don't involve others in the search for realistic solutions, they may not be convinced their best interests are being served.

7. *Seek agreements that are as fair to all concerned as the situation will allow.*

8. *Unfold the opportunity.* Make this conflict lead to something better than you had before it happened. A favourite phrase from Tom Crum's workshops is 'Ah, conflict. What an opportunity.'[89]

For most people, flow is a learnt response, and agreers and competers arrive at insight from different directions and for different reasons. (See **Figure 32: Arriving at flow**, page 169.)

▼▼▼

Many women today have enormously high expectations of what they want to achieve. Once opportunities were limited by class and gender. Now, both men and women become caught in setting themselves higher and higher goals. We get swept into a competitive rat race, in which we constantly compare ourselves with others.

We use our workplace position, our salary, our job's social respectability and the annual turnover of the company to inform ourselves of our own worth. To build self-esteem, we pressure ourselves to compete against others who are competing against us —

| ARRIVING AT FLOW | | |
|---|---|---|
| | AGREERS' INSIGHTS | COMPETERS' INSIGHTS |
| Attitude to conflict: | Knowing that conflict is a necessary and inevitable aspect of interaction, I will develop the skills to deal with problems directly and to achieve an outcome that will benefit both both me and the other person. | Perhaps there's a better deal for both/all of us. We can all participate in the search for it. I'll consider your legitimate wishes as well as my own. |
| Belief: | I can assert my right to get what's fair. | I'll push for what is fair and truly reasonable, rather than whatever I can get away with. |
| Expectation and approach: | I win, you win. | If you lose, ultimately I do, too. If I make you back down now, I may turn you into my adversary rather than my colleague. Solutions that benefit you also reap more benefits for me in the long term. |
| Primary emotions: | Courage and persistence. | Respect for others and restraint. |
| Method: | Assertive movement towards engaging in the conflict. | Aggression controlled and directed towards fair resolution. |
| Potential problems: | I may not be able to persuade people who use win/lose tactics to adopt my approach or to really hear me. But I'll know I stood up for myself. | At times I compromise even though I am not forced to. I might not always strike the most advantageous deal financially, but I prefer to conduct my affairs this way, as I don't believe that in the long term I really lose out — even financially. |
| Pay–off: | I get more of what I want more often; whatever happens I am rewarded with feelings of self-esteem; my self-confidence grows as I repeatedly engage in conflicts. I once would have withdrawn from. | Dealt with properly, conflict brings me improved relationships and more productive outcomes; my fair dealings with others bring me integrity and self-respect; I am in control of myself. |

*Figure 32: Arriving at flow*

people who often appear to have everything under control. Generally, we don't get to know about other people's inner struggles. We only know about our own.

We might ask ourselves: *What is success?* Will the next promotion, the next pay rise, the next contract really make the difference? The apparent explosion of opportunity as we move into the twenty-first century has made us greedy — like kids in a lolly shop, wanting everything.

You may want to consider the following: Does *success* need redefining for me? Will I wait until I come to the end of my life before I ask: 'Was I true to myself?' Did I create balance between work, income, family, health, friendships, humanitarian and ecological concerns?

We live in times that demand the broadest perspectives in order to choose right action. Both men and women are discovering that the win/win approach focuses them on the big picture.

# SUMMARY

*CHARACTERISTICS*

| AGREERS | COMPETERS |
|---------|-----------|
| Keep the peace | Enjoy the challenge of competitive strategies |
| Emphasise similarities and common ground | Value competition because it drives people forwards and tests worth |
| Are urgent about concluding disagreements | Accept some aggression as part of the 'rough and tumble' |
| Modify behaviour and suppress needs readily to fit in with others | See interaction with others as inevitably competitive |
| Need harmonious teamwork for job satisfaction | Use and receive one-upmanship as a comfortable, light-hearted way of relating |

*GOOD INTENTIONS*

| AGREERS | COMPETERS |
|---|---|
| Avoiding arguments where possible | Thwarting a perceived attack |
| Creating friendly work climates and bonded relationships | Pursuing a clear goal in the face of opposition |
| Responding to the needs of the team | Responding to a challenge with plenty of energy |
| Minimising conflict | Proving they're intelligent, street-smart, a winner |
| Facilitating joint planning | Coming up with the best answer |
| Building trust | Inviting a relationship with playful teasing or baiting |

*BODY LANGUAGE*

| MANY WOMEN | MANY MEN |
|---|---|
| Lean forward to indicate openness | Lean back to indicate openness |
| Frequently touch others in a gentle way to indicate support | Rarely touch others and when they do, are hearty, even rough |
| Imply non-confrontation by a face-to-face stance | Imply non-confrontation by a side-by-side stance |
| Maintain frequent eye contact | Avoid frequent eye contact |
| Smile often | Smile rarely |
| Respond closely to facial expressions | Respond infrequently to facial expressions (particularly smiles) |

*VERBAL STYLE*

| MANY WOMEN | MANY MEN |
|---|---|
| Speak respectfully about others unless they actively dislike them | May talk about people they have no real problem with as though they were an enemy |
| Use more questions | Make more statements |
| Use less black-and-white sentence construction | Make more forthright, unequivocal statements |
| Pad requests with 'please', 'would you mind ...' etc. | Make requests with the same sentence structure as demands |
| Place little focus on sports talk | Use sports talk to build intimacy |
| Avoid confrontation because they fear a battle | Avoid confrontation if it helps them win or preserves social decorum |
| Apologise following confrontation | Tend not to apologise following confrontation |
| Interrupt to support or add to a topic | Interrupt to change topics |
| Build relationships with rapport-talk, using intimate and extensive conversation | Speak in report-talk mode – less intimately and sometimes more briefly |
| Expect and use the following conversational rules: | Expect and use the following conversational rules: |
| ▶ don't change topics; | ▶ go for what you want; |
| ▶ if one person is discussing an issue, it's their air-time until they've said all they want to say; | ▶ compete for the air-time; |
| ▶ encourage the other person to share their deepest feelings and concerns; | ▶ save the other person from a disclosure of painful or too intimate emotions; |
| ▶ empathise with the other person's feelings about the issue. | ▶ run with commonly held opinions; |
| | ▶ don't explode. |

# 7 AGREEMENT: stumbling blocks & stepping stones

### PREVIEW

*STUMBLING BLOCK*

1 ▶ Arguments lost

2 ▶ People pleasing

3 ▶ Failure to achieve positive results from conflict

4 ▶ Stuck on sticky steps if not tough enough

5 ▶ Leadership expertise undervalued

On the whole, agreement-oriented people are great to be around. When agreers take the path of least resistance, other people's lives go pretty smoothly. The agreer, however, may be drowning in a private sea of frustrated emotions and disappointment.

Having considered in Chapter 6 the differences in style between agreers and competers, we now turn to some of the problems agreers can create for themselves and other people. We'll look at how they can improve their interacting style with skills such as assertive 'I' statements, a win/win approach and collaborative negotiation. When agreers are able to draw on these conflict resolution skills, they can minimise their difficulties while remaining true to their underlying values.

## STUMBLING BLOCK 1: ARGUMENTS LOST

**'I thought it was obvious I disagreed. That didn't stop him!'**

Agreers pick up the subtle signs of disagreement in others and adjust their expectations and their options to take these into account. This method for maintaining successful relationships can work like a charm when the other person is also an agreer, but it can be disastrous if the agreer isn't receiving the same consideration they're giving. This problem is very common in male–female interactions.

*Men generally expect that you will fight your own fight.*

Under a polite veneer, the woman believes she is sending subdued messages of opposition. She may become resentful if the man doesn't respond. A male competer readily looks after his own interests and so he assumes she's looking after hers. He doesn't recognise that her cautious agreement is convention only. She expects that he'll understand from her tone that she really wants something else. She may have made her point once, but it could well have been a week ago. He cannot even remember now exactly what she said. She wants *him* to balance fairly her needs against his. He expects *her* to fight her own fight. If she's not fighting now, he presumes she really doesn't care about whatever it was she said the other day.

*When an agreer argues with another agreer:*

▶ each person relies on the other to understand their position;

▶ each person generally cares about the other not losing out;

▶ they both search for acceptable solutions;

▶ they will probably discuss the problem and the options together.

They are likely to head into a win/win approach quite naturally. Getting this approach going with a competer is not nearly so straightforward.

*When a competer argues with another competer:*

▶ each person expects the other to fight for what they believe in;

▶ they are not surprised if the argument becomes heated;

▶ they do not back down in the face of opposition;

▶ each person persists in trying to get their own needs met.

Thus when agreers argue with competers, not only is there a clash about the *substance of the problem* ('Will we or won't we run the advertising campaign?', 'How will we handle an underachieving employee?'), but there is also a style clash to be addressed. It is usually the agreer who backs down.

Agreers may see only two alternatives: losing repeatedly to competers or sacrificing their own principles by 'playing dirty'. There is a third way, however — *appropriate assertiveness*.

*When competers and agreers argue there are two problems: the issue and the style clash.*

## STEPPING STONES: APPROPRIATE ASSERTIVENESS

Agreers can remain true to their core values and not lose out when arguing with a competer. This might imply that they:

1. Adjust their expectations. Agreers cannot rely on the competer to tune in to what they need and consider their needs. Also, they cannot presume that they will be *offered* the space to put forward their point of view. They may have to grab it.

2. Master a win/win approach and use the approach very assertively.

3. Don't go along with things they really disagree with in order to please.

4. Oppose dominating or narrow-minded approaches.

5. Are not always 'nice'.

6. Show their anger clearly, but in a controlled way.

7. Plan strategically to 'call in the troops' if their own efforts are not sufficient.

Who are 'the troops'? It might be a superior who'll arbitrate the decision; a friend who'll take their side and have a quiet word in the other person's ear; an accountant who can present figures to prove the case; a mediator who'll create a structured conversation in which it will be very hard for the other person not to participate; a lawyer who'll tell the agreer where they stand according to the law. If, for instance, serious gender injustices fail to be addressed after persistent efforts, people have recourse to government bodies such as an anti-discrimination board.

When they first resolve to become assertive, many agreers are a bit clumsy and heavy-handed about it. Pent-up frustrations from past losses are liable to spill into the present situation. Unsure about how much pressure it takes to win, they push far too hard.

Their judgment on how far it's fair and responsible to take an issue can be defective. Their new-found assertiveness dramatically changes the dynamics of their relationships, and others around them may resist major adjustments. Gradually things do settle down, as the person carves out a network of mutually respectful relationships.

8. Use 'I' statements, which are an invaluable tool for an assertive win/win style.

**'I' STATEMENTS:** A well-formulated 'I' statement is often an excellent opener to an assertive approach to a difficult issue.[90] It aims to communicate clearly and cleanly.

> **Clear:** Your statement of the problem is precise and explains what is the matter.
>
> **Clean:** Your statement does not attack or blame the other person, and does not aim to hurt.

The 'I' statement should minimise the defensiveness of the other person, though of course this can't be guaranteed. Many people compose their opening 'I' statement for a difficult confrontation before the event, so they can think it through carefully. 'I' statements are generally composed in three parts:

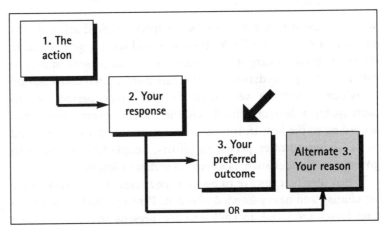

*Figure 33: 'I' statement elements*

Sometimes you won't deliver all three parts at once. However, it's best to prepare the whole statement, to set your thinking straight. Of course, as the conversation progresses, you'll have to compose on your feet. Delivering one 'I' statement effectively helps you with the next. If tempers start to rise, resist the temptation to blame. Come out with the best spur of the moment 'I' statement you can muster, even if it's not as perfect as the one you could have delivered if you'd thought about it all night. Chances are it will still be less inflaming than a 'You should have …', 'You never …' type of sentence. Your aim is to keep the emotional heat turned down so that you can hang on in there and assert what you need. Here's some more detail on the construction of 'I' statements.

1 ► *The action.* Find an *objective description* of the action that is causing you the problem. Sometimes it helps to start off your description with the word 'when'. Carefully choose non-emotive language. It's often very helpful to avoid using the word 'you' in this description. When people hear 'you' they can feel accused and will want to defend themselves. People hate being told what's wrong with them, but it's not quite so hard to hear what's not working for you. For example, you're less likely to spark a defensive reaction with, 'When I'm not able to finish what I'm saying …', rather than, 'When you interrupt …'. By removing 'you' from the sentence construction, you're forced to describe your own problem without implying that it's the other person's fault.

2 ► *Your response.* Here the key is *no blame.* When we feel angry, we often want to blame the other person for our pain, inconvenience or annoyance. It's usually a lot safer to avoid blame by 'owning' our own emotions. For instance, rather than saying, 'You make me so angry', say, 'I feel angry'. This will help prevent the other person becoming defensive.

Alternatively, you might indicate your response with a statement about what you feel like doing. Men, in particular, are often better at this than at stating how they feel. This method can also deliver a clear, clean message to the other person about your response. For example, 'I feel like walking out on the meeting'.

The response part of the 'I' statement formula delivers valuable information. Often when something has happened to upset us, the other person is unaware of how we feel. They may not realise that their actions are irritating us. In many cases, the other person will respond by changing their behaviour to accommodate us.

If the conflict is entrenched, or it's over an issue that is significant to both parties, things may not be that simple. Sometimes it's wiser to edit how much you tell the other person about what you're feeling. It may not be helpful to tell your boss you're feeling overwhelmed if you're on probation in a new job, for example. You may want to deal with that part of your problem privately. But you may be able to talk with them about your frustration in not being given clear instructions about certain tasks.

**3 ▶** *Your preferred outcome.* Do your best to place *no demand* on the other person to do it your way. Don't back the other person into a corner or sound like you're unwilling to negotiate. Sometimes, when we're upset, we expect the other person to fix the situation. We may be tempted to say, '… and I want you to keep quiet until I've finished'. If you begin this third part of the 'I' statement with the words, 'And what I'd like is that I …', you are forced to construct a sentence about *what you want to be able to do, rather than what you want the other person to do.* You might say, 'And what I'd like is that I can complete what I want to say'.

Conflict Resolution Network has taught this method for many years now and students have found it produces a constructive search for mutually acceptable solutions. Of course, you may have to present an ultimatum further down the track if you're not getting anywhere, but it's rarely a good opening move.

**Alternate 3 ▶** *Your reason.* Another useful alternative for the third part of your 'I' statement is to *explain* why you have the problem. Start with the word, 'because'; for example, 'When I don't have clear instructions, I feel frustrated because I may be wasting time'. If your reason affects the other person, too, stating it may be quite sufficient to make them change. A 'because' statement usually includes a need or concern that, because of the other person's action, is not being addressed.

*EXERCISE*

Think of a situation that annoys you and, using the guide in **Figure 34: 'I' statements** (page 179), construct an 'I' statement. You may or may not ultimately use it. If in doubt, run it by a friend explaining the guidelines given here. Have them check your statement over. Is it clear? Is it clean? Consider together if it would be wise to actually deliver it. Often others can see whether your statement is clear and clean more easily than you can.

Remember that an 'I' statement, no matter how well it is constructed, is not a cure-all. It is simply a discussion opener. You may well need to construct more of them as the conversation progresses. You may have to assert yourself to have the situation addressed and, if necessary, point out the consequences of it not being addressed. In doing so, be clear you are not making a threat. You are delivering information on cause and effect. This consequence information indicates the solution you will take if the other person is unwilling to contribute to problem-solving.

*Convey consequence information if the other person is unwilling to contribute to problem-solving.*

| 'I' STATEMENT ELEMENT | SAMPLE LEAD WORDS | SAMPLE STATEMENT: | COMPLETE YOUR OWN EXAMPLE BELOW |
|---|---|---|---|
| 1. The action *(objective description)* | When ... <br><br> ✗ you | When ... changes to our plans have been finalised before I have a chance to contribute. | |
| 2. Your response *(no blame)* | I feel ... *or* I feel like | I feel ... powerless *or* I feel like ... leaving the team | |
| 3. Your preferred outcome *(no demand)* | And what I'd like is that I ... | And what I'd like is that I ... have more involvement in the decision-making process. | |
| Alternate 3. Your reason | Because ... | Because ... I'm very concerned that you don't find my input useful. | |

*Figure 34: 'I' statements*

Some men will perceive a woman as being aggressive no matter how carefully she words her 'I' statements. I suspect this is because some men are so used to women's non-resistance that any attempt she makes to stand up for herself is seen as being 'out of role'. Yet passive 'in role' behaviour offers no real answers for comfortable relating either. Passivity invites intimidation and bullying.

## STUMBLING BLOCK 2: PEOPLE PLEASING

**'She'll promise the moon — while you're in her office.'**

Agreers are people pleasers. They can find themselves agreeing with whoever they are talking to at the time. Some will promise the earth and deliver nothing. The mismatch between what they say and what they do loses them respect. If an agreer is supposed to be representing a group of people, they must maintain that group's perspective in any official capacity. The agreer must not appear to blow with the wind. Unless they have clearly established their impartiality, they are likely to be perceived as a turncoat. They will increase divisiveness and possibly find themselves alienated from people on both sides of the issue.

*Agreers in managerial positions sometimes allow discipline amongst staff to become lax.*

Agreers in managerial positions sometimes allow discipline amongst staff to become lax, rather than tackle the problem head on. Some agreers are unable to stop an avalanche of work. Many women remain silent in the face of gender discrimination or harassment. Agreers can't let themselves be so fearful of confronting or so hurt by a preliminary skirmish that they cannot mobilise any skills to get in there and deal with the issues.

*STEPPING STONES*
Conflicts are generally best addressed early. If issues that could have been addressed are ignored, they can lead to further misunderstandings, mounting tension and, ultimately, a crisis. **Figure 35: Levels of conflict** (page 181) can help you grade a particular conflict in your own life. If you'd rate the conflict at misunderstanding, tension or crisis, it's high time to take some assertive action. If an issue arises at the discomfort or incident level, consider whether you should be addressing the problem. If

you can do it without being too prickly, you offer the other person your self-disclosure and the opportunity to restore an unencumbered relationship — a rare and special gift!

Are you putting up with a situation that has a significant gender component? **Figure 36: Examples of assertive openers** (page 182) offers some assertive openers you might use to begin to address the problem.

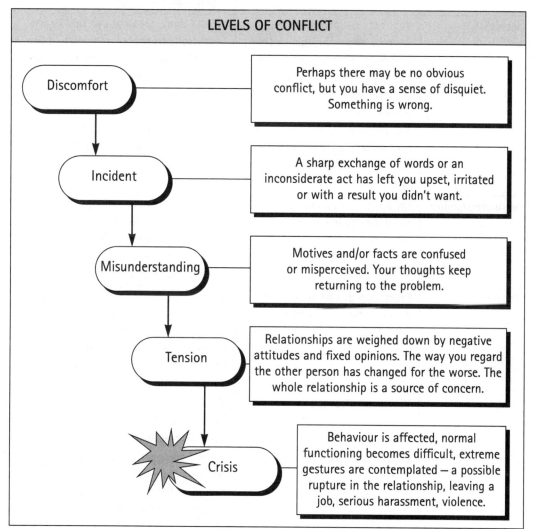

## LEVELS OF CONFLICT

**Discomfort** — Perhaps there may be no obvious conflict, but you have a sense of disquiet. Something is wrong.

**Incident** — A sharp exchange of words or an inconsiderate act has left you upset, irritated or with a result you didn't want.

**Misunderstanding** — Motives and/or facts are confused or misperceived. Your thoughts keep returning to the problem.

**Tension** — Relationships are weighed down by negative attitudes and fixed opinions. The way you regard the other person has changed for the worse. The whole relationship is a source of concern.

**Crisis** — Behaviour is affected, normal functioning becomes difficult, extreme gestures are contemplated — a possible rupture in the relationship, leaving a job, serious harassment, violence.

*Figure 35: Levels of conflict*

| LEVEL OF CONFLICT | ISSUES | EXAMPLES OF ASSERTIVE OPENERS |
|---|---|---|
| Discomfort | Repeated compliments on physical appearance in workplace settings. | When our conversations start with a compliment on the way I look, I worry that I don't have your respect as a work colleague. What I'd like is that I can stay focused on the job in hand rather than my image. |
| Incidents | Your requests are not acted upon by peers. They blame time frames or technical constraints, but you suspect they give your requests lower priority because of your gender. | When I don't get what I've said I need, I feel really frustrated and what I'd like is that I clearly know in advance what is and is not possible. |
| | You are being called names you find demeaning, e.g. 'girlie', 'darling', 'love', 'Teddy', 'Sonny boy'. | When I'm called 'darling', I feel discounted and what I'd like is that you use my name. |
| Misunderstanding | Unwanted sexual overtures, e.g. touching, standing too close. | When I'm physically too close to you, I get annoyed about it, and what I'd like is that it's easy for me to maintain a discreet distance, because then I can focus properly on what you're saying. |
| Tension | Promotion denied because of gender rather than ability. | When I missed that promotion, I was really perturbed, because I knew I was better qualified for the job than the man/woman who got it. What I'd like is that I understand the basis of your decision-making. |
| | Your good ideas are ignored. | When my ideas aren't discussed at all, I feel irritated, and what I'd like is that I see them seriously considered. |
| | Others take credit for your ideas. | When I don't get credit for my ideas, I feel really angry. I really want to be known as the originator of ideas which were mine to start with. |

*Figure 36: Examples of assertive openers*

| LEVEL OF CONFLICT | ISSUES | EXAMPLES OF ASSERTIVE OPENERS |
|---|---|---|
| Crisis | Demands for sexual intimacy with or without the promise of job advancement. | When I believe I have to offer sexual favours to move up in the organisation, I'm overwhelmed with a serious and possibly legal problem. I need to be absolutely sure that my workplace and private life are completely separated. |
| | The other person is determined to undermine you because you have challenged their status. | When my plans are shelved without my input, I feel I'm not being treated with the respect I deserve. What I need is that all problems to do with my area of supervision are openly discussed with me from the start. |

*Figure 36: Examples of assertive openers (continued)*

# STUMBLING BLOCK 3: FAILURE TO ACHIEVE POSITIVE RESULTS FROM CONFLICT

If we avoid addressing conflicts, we lose the opportunity to search for new and better solutions to problems. Moreover, relationships may stall at a certain emotional distance. In our personal lives, it may mean we hold at bay the potential for deepening love and commitment. In the workplace, it often hampers our ability to work successfully and joyfully together as a team.

## The win/win approach

Sometimes problems seem like a giant jigsaw puzzle. Win/lose solutions are an incorrect assembly of the pieces. It takes care and thought to get all the parts into the right position so that a win/win picture can emerge. This requires a win/win approach and the expectation of finding an acceptable win/win outcome.

*A win/lose situation is often like a jigsaw puzzle with the pieces incorrectly assembled.*

In my experience, agreers convert to this approach more easily than competers. This may be because agreers face a higher cost from its alternative — the win/lose style. They're usually on the losing side. They pay the penalty of unmet needs and loss of self-esteem. Over time, agreers are likely to nurse a long list of grievances. Increasing distress pushes them to search for another way to do things.

Initially, women may be more open than men to adopting this win/win approach.[91] Sarah, one of the women I interviewed for this book, discussed this gender bias. She says:

> I found that men handle situations very differently from women. Usually, if I need advice I ask a suitably experienced woman, because I am likely to find that a man will offer me advice more confrontational than suits my style.

I believe that this gender bias is slowly changing as workplace ethics shift to accommodate the increasing influence of women.

*We're tempted to switch from win/win when the other person is playing win/lose.*

It certainly can be very difficult to maintain win/win strategies when the other person is playing a win/lose game. It's tempting to switch tactics under such circumstances and play by their rules rather than your own preferred ones. Some of the factors that may tempt you to switch tactics include:

▶ being walked over or taken advantage of;

▶ looking like a fool in the eyes of others important to you;

▶ supporters who advise you to match the other person's win/lose style: 'You should give 'em hell!';

▶ your own rising anger at the other person's dirty tactics and your desire for revenge.

You will often need to shore up your resolve for the win/win approach, for to be taken seriously by a win/lose fighter you may need to be extremely assertive, very clear and even, at times, openly angry. The win/win style is not passive and it need not be sanitised of all emotions. If necessary, scream in 'I' statements. 'I really hate it when I can't finish what I'm saying!' 'I' statements are less damaging to the other person than blaming, but can still get your perspective across extremely clearly. Fight to restore fairness, not to make them grovel.

The win/win approach can incorporate firm and binding outcomes. Safeguards with preset penalties can be incorporated into the original agreement: 'If you don't make up your time off, your pay will be docked.' Objective measures of compliance can help keep both parties honest, as non-compliance is visible to scrutiny by others: 'Report in when you get back to the office.'

*ELEMENTS OF THE WIN/WIN APPROACH*
The win/win approach demands two commitments:

1. To work towards better solutions that give everyone more of what they really need in the long term.

2. To engage in as much consultation and joint decision-making as the situation will allow.

A win/win approach is not the same as a win/win outcome. The commitments above do not guarantee a perfect result. But even if the result is less than a perfect win/win outcome, the use of the method makes a vast difference to long-term relationships. How do you go about it?

*A win/win approach is not the same as a win/win outcome.*

▶ Consider the relevant needs of relevant people.

▶ Invite options, open yourself to innovative and expansive solutions.

▶ Involve in the process those people affected by the outcome.

▶ Compose a solution that meets as many needs of each person as possible.

When you know how you really want to play the game, you will become wonderfully inventive about new options. You may not even see problem situations as conflicts any more. They'll look much more like opportunities for positive change.

## Development of a wider range of options
The search for solutions that meet both people's needs can inspire better solutions than either person could have thought of alone.[92] When you trust this process, you mobilise the creativity that conflict can produce. True, you may not succeed in always giving everyone *all* of what they want, but you can usually succeed in giving people *more* of what they want.

You have to hang in there, insist on following a win/win rather than a win/lose approach, and consider a broad range of needs.

Often you'll build an innovative overall solution from the building blocks of smaller agreements. This requires collaborative negotiation skills. They work brilliantly, but they do take practice. (See **Figure 37: Collaborative negotiation skills**, below.)

| COLLABORATIVE NEGOTIATION SKILLS | |
|---|---|
| Negotiate hard on the problem and soft on the person | This means being considerate of the other person's feelings and valid concerns. This suits an agreer's naturally empathic response. |
| Defuse angry emotions early on | Paraphrase the point they are trying to convey under their anger, so they know you've understood.[93] |
| Focus on needs, not positions | Generally, rather than standing firm for your solution, stand firm for the needs that it meets. Be open to a superior solution if it addresses more needs of more people. |
| Include the other person's objections | Rather than rejecting their point, add it to the problem that must be solved. Avoid using the word 'but' while you're negotiating. Instead, use 'and': '*I* want that report completed **and** *you* need to get away at 5.30 tonight. What are our options?', or 'I have a major problem with the headline for our ad **and** it's too late to alter it. Let's start from there.' |
| Determine who's behind the scenes | Is someone behind the scenes putting pressure on your opponent or on you? Are they getting what they need? Can their stake in the outcome become part of your frank discussions? |
| Is it fair? | Can you find an objective yardstick, preferably one you will both agree on? For example, equivalent use of time, money or other resources, equal inconvenience, balanced exchange of favours. |
| Emphasise common ground | Skilled win/win negotiators build a climate of evolving agreement. Point out areas of agreement as they emerge. In the beginning it may be no more than, 'Okay, we've agreed to meet at 3 pm to talk', or 'We both agree the situation can't go on as it is.' Later, note more substantial sub-agreements on the way to the full solution: 'Well, we've agreed that a new fax machine is part of the answer.' |

*Figure 37: Collaborative negotiation skills*

| COLLABORATIVE NEGOTIATION SKILLS (continued) | |
|---|---|
| Help the other person save face | Build in wins for the other person. Make them public if the problem is being viewed by others. Competers, in particular, often need face-saving solutions – and that's okay. |
| Make it easy for the other person to say yes | Build in wins for the other person that are easy for you to offer and valuable for them to receive. Prepare figures or tables that make it easy for them to understand why you want what you do. Offer to do any time-consuming chores related to the solution you want to implement. |
| Negotiate the deal to your advantage, too | You need to consider your needs as well, including face-saving if it's relevant. Aim to have the agreement include things that are easy for the other person to give and valuable for you to receive. |
| Choose solutions that recognise the ongoing relationship | Burning your bridges is rarely a good idea. This usually means keeping some control over your anger, no matter how justified you feel. |
| Make clear agreements | Contracts that suit both parties are self-perpetuating. By documenting your emerging agreement together, each person can clarify their thinking and be sure their needs are met. Include check-back dates to see how the plan is working. You might outline the agreement in a memo to the other person, so they have a record, too. If it's a serious or ongoing workplace problem or negotiation, it's worth keeping clear dated notes on discussions. |

*Figure 37: Collaborative negotiation skills (continued)*

## STUMBLING BLOCK 4: STUCK ON STICKY STEPS IF NOT TOUGH ENOUGH

*'I'll never make it to the boardroom*
*unless I play as dirty as they do.'*

### The glass ceiling for agreers

Deidre was stuck in middle management. She felt the only way she could go further in the organisation was to change her style radically:

> I've watched who gets promoted here. It is definitely not your feminine-style person. Some women, of course, conform to the masculine culture. They've already learnt the game. Men who don't conform [male agreers] get shunted aside at some stage. Their deviation from the corporate male norm is too obvious. Women who don't conform may get away with it a bit longer precisely because they are women and have been tolerated because of their different gender. But for senior executives there's a very masculine, cutthroat way you have to behave. To go any further in this organisation, I will have to turn myself into a carbon copy of them and I'm not prepared to do that. I guess that means I'm never going to make it to the boardroom!

The glass ceiling is not solely a problem for women. It strikes agreers irrespective of gender. Many fall by the wayside during their executive apprenticeship. For agreers to succeed, they have to suppress their gentler, agreement-oriented side. They may enjoy this development of inner strength — at least for a number of years. But, sooner or later, many experience a profound sense of loss as a result of their alienation from a core value. Softer values in their personality struggle upward for air.

### Token males

Some women make the decision to work within the male model with all its constraints. They train themselves to become token males and thus often fall into a catch-22. They're stuck on sticky steps if they're not tough enough and still stuck even if they are. One male executive in a financial institution noted:

> The problem with women who have worked their way up to more senior positions in our organisation is they are so hard. You just don't like them.

Many women find that a chameleon-like transformation to blend with a male culture didn't get them where they wanted to go anyway. When women become assertive beyond a certain point they are seen as 'out of role' and aggressive.[94] This in itself may prevent them reaching senior management level. Marie reports:

> One woman in our research company has a BSc and she's just done her MBA. She got honours. She also has her masters in science and she's doing more science subjects this year. She has made it to lower management, but she's pretty outspoken. If she disagrees with someone, she'll let them know and they don't like that. She is very articulate and a hell of a lot more qualified than most of the others. She can beat anyone in an argument if she knows her subject. She knows enough of the boy's rules to play their game, but she's missed out for the second time on promotion in her department. I really believe that they see her as a threat.

A woman who has developed a tough exterior is often a disconcerting enigma to men. Greg told me about an aggressive woman in his office:

> She can dish it out but she can't take it. We were all working our guts out to meet a deadline. She was carrying on about how we were going to miss it and what a disaster that would be. I said to her: 'If you keep thinking like that, we will miss it.' She burst into tears. I guess I'd sounded firm, but she was going into panic mode. I was trying to keep her in reality.

Other women are probably less surprised than Greg to find the feminine vulnerability under the armour donned to lead in a masculine-style workplace.

# STUMBLING BLOCK 5:
## LEADERSHIP EXPERTISE UNDERVALUED

*'They just don't value what I've got to offer.'*

*Male-oriented senior management cultures often don't value what women have to offer.*

A 1995 survey of 194 top organisations in Australia found that 'women represented 4 per cent of all board members, 1 per cent of executive directors and 5 per cent of non-executive directors'[95] Amanda Sinclair at Melbourne University carried out a study which revealed that the number of women in senior management in large companies is actually dropping.[96] It's too simple to say that there is not available talent; there is now a large pool of women middle managers to draw on. The issue seems to be more insidious than this. Male-oriented senior manager cultures often don't value what women have to offer. An age factor is relevant. Men condoning discriminative practices are often older. Younger men are more likely to accept women as equals at the top.

A socioeconomic factor is involved, too. Many women in lower paid and lower skilled employment have greater difficulty moving up through their workplace hierarchy than highly educated, professional women.

The Karpin Report, a significant review of management practices in Australia, found that, overall, women were not influential decision-makers in the economy and that they were not given appropriate roles in management.[97] The report warns that two skills in particular — skills that agreement-style women often bring to business — are missing, and that it's mattering more and more. These are:

1. *Empathy — a natural strength that usually underpins an agreement style.*

All managers need to develop skills in cross-cultural awareness and interaction. Leaders of the future must increase trade with and employ very diverse ethnic groups. Good relations with other nations and cultures must be backed up at home. Nearly 25 per cent of the population of Australia is of non-English speaking background.

L. Lippman, in *The Aim is Understanding: Educational Techniques for a Multi-Cultural Society*, writes:

When people come from different cultural climates, apart from having a different way of perceiving their environment, they will have different expectations from the same social situation. This can make personal interaction difficult or even painful unless the individual is trained to understand the subjective culture of other groups or is at least prepared to acknowledge that people from other cultures may have different terms of reference and different value ... systems from his [or her] own.[98]

## 2. Consultation — the skills of the empowered agreer.

Today's workforce is generally well educated and has expectations of meaningful and fulfilling work. Senior management needs to recruit people who have consultative skills and are able to supervise such employees effectively. Expertise in building agreement is often undervalued, so the contribution of this by highly skilled women often goes unrecognised.

### STEPPING STONES

The solution to these problems requires a major rethink on what makes a good leader for today's workforce. This is covered in more detail in Chapter 8, 'Competition: Stumbling blocks and stepping stones'.

▼▼▼▼

In the past forty years, feminism has altered women's expectations of success. The majority of women in the workforce today have been spoon-fed the idea that 'in this day and age, women can make it'. Working from this premise, many women feel that they have failed. But perhaps what has happened is not that women have failed, but that they have *failed to be like men*. Their problem is not one of performance, but of opportunity.

There needs to be many more ways of being an effective executive. Women should be able to move into executive roles without having to conform to traditional masculine managerial stereotypes. Similarly, men need to be given the okay to use an agreement-based style when appropriate. Workplaces only stand to benefit from a new, more inclusive leadership style.

# SUMMARY

| AGREEMENT: STUMBLING BLOCKS | STEPPING STONES: APPROPRIATE ASSERTIVENESS |
|---|---|
| 1 ► Arguments lost | Employ an assertive style. Develop expertise in making clear, clean 'I' statements. |
| 2 ► People pleasing | Become proactive in crisis prevention, addressing issues early on in the conflict cycle, long before they become entrenched or explosive. |
| 3 ► Failure to achieve positive results from conflict | Use a win/win approach and collaborative negotiation skills to design more creative solutions. |
| 4 ► Stuck on sticky steps if not tough enough | Avoid potential weaknesses in leadership qualities, such as an excessive need to please, diffidence, or inability to hold ground in the face of opposition. |
| 5 ► Leadership expertise undervalued | Encourage the recognition of empathy and consultative skills that can flow from an agreement style. |

| THE WIN/WIN APPROACH |
|---|
| ► Consider the relevant needs of relevant people |
| ► Invite options, open yourself to innovative and expansive solutions |
| ► Involve in the process those people affected by the outcome |
| ► Compose a solution that meets as many needs of each person as possible |

# 8 COMPETITION: stumbling blocks & stepping stones

## PREVIEW

*STUMBLING BLOCK*

1 ▶ Leadership style relies too heavily on warrior skills

2 ▶ Fear of being seen as an outsider to the pack

3 ▶ Alienation from others

4 ▶ Poor listening skills

5 ▶ Lack of support for those who could be potential threats

Before we look at its problems, let's remember that the spirit of competition is responsible for some of the finest qualities people can display. When we unite to face a common enemy, be it an invader in times of war or a competitor in the marketplace, we place ourselves in testing circumstances that will ultimately prove our worth. We learn courage in facing the threat to our lives or financial security. We learn endurance, as few things worth fighting for come easily. We learn to shoulder responsibility as others rely on our skills, and we learn trust as we rely on other team-mates to do their part.

Despite all this potential for good that can come from competition, competers can get it horribly wrong. They can destroy organisational unity with an excess of individualism. They can make too few people their allies and too many the enemy. They can ignore ethics, fair play and friendship if they allow the desire to win to override all else.

While not all those who value and enjoy competition will fall into the following traps, many do. These stumbling blocks can form the bases of intractable conflicts. Competers' stepping stones include understanding the long-term benefits of a win/win approach and incorporating good listening and arguing skills in the interests of a fair fight.

## STUMBLING BLOCK 1: LEADERSHIP STYLE RELIES TOO HEAVILY ON WARRIOR SKILLS

**'She'll never cut it when the going gets rough.'**

As indicated in the previous chapter, most senior managers in the workforce today are men. Statistics for 1995 indicate that less than 15 per cent of general managers in Australia were women.[99] Half of these women were working in their own businesses rather than being employed by others. The lack of opportunity for promotion forces many potential women leaders out of large organisations. There's a strong element of competition here. Women's rise in the workplace often threatens male-only territory and can challenge masculine identity.

The choices men are making about who will join them at the top have far-reaching consequences. Though supposedly promotion is based on merit, when merit is *defined* by a man who is strongly embedded in his leadership culture, only other *men* may be seen to be merit-worthy. In male-dominated cultures, leadership style can be very unbalanced, embracing too few of the leadership skills needed for our sophisticated work climate.

By not promoting women into senior management, organisations lose some of their best employees and fail to attract the cream of the workforce—both men and women—who no longer accept outdated management practices. Organisational structures are in transition. Hierarchies are becoming flatter. More people have higher expectations of meaningful, responsible work and more real authority. They are far less accepting of the traditionally masculine 'command and control' management style. In fact, women often display the new skills expected by staff more readily than men.

*A highly competitive culture is self-perpetuating, keeping out anything unlike itself.*

A highly competitive culture is self-perpetuating, keeping out anything unlike itself. Competitive leaders recruit senior managers who display the traditional qualities of the hero warrior — the victor of battles. These qualities include:

1. dominance;

2. courage;

3. confidence;

4. tactical analysis.

The trouble is that you have to go into battle to prove you possess these warrior qualities. If you're very skilled at developing real agreements well before crisis point, you may not notch up nearly enough visible victories to capture your boss's attention.

Women's agreement-oriented subculture generally encourages a very different set of leadership skills. These are:

1. consultation;

2. an ethic of care;

3. communication and conflict resolution expertise;

4. whole system awareness.

The gentle revolution is still essential. Many men still need to learn that the contributions from masculine and feminine perspectives can serve to balance each other, equalling better leadership. Today's management environment needs both sets of skills. Together they suggest a new set of management criteria. Let's consider what this would be and why.

*The leadership contributions from masculine and feminine perspectives balance each other.*

## Real authority

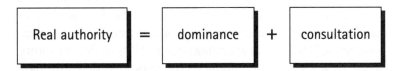

DOMINANCE
Dominance is a quality essential to good leadership. Senior managers in a competitive environment need the skills to ensure their company dominates its rivals or that it at least increases its share of the market.

Women are generally less aggressive than men and fail to impress when dominance is judged only by a competitive approach. If dominance is equated with a command and control management style, again many women will fail to seem promotable because they are unlikely to lead in this way. Some women may find, therefore, an easier road to the top in community-oriented organisations focusing on social services rather than the commercial marketplace.

Workplaces are certainly not under-supplied with women who display many of the other qualities necessary for leadership dominance, such as:

► high energy;

► charisma;

► ability to visualise direction for themselves and for their organisation;

► intelligence;

► knowledge in their specific area;

► creativity in using and making opportunities.

Wherever the criteria for judging dominance rely mainly on pugnacity (readiness to fight at a moment's notice), however, many women are failing to qualify as leaders.

### CONSULTATION

Command, control and aggression, while essential in some crises, are less acceptable for today's workforce. Staff expect to be treated as respected members of a work community with significant rights. While not abandoning responsibility to their investors, company leaders are beginning to recognise that they also have responsibilities to their workers. This awareness is becoming an important part of long-term sustainability. Today's well-educated, upwardly mobile employees have high expectations of return from their labour input. They want more than a pay packet. They are not just running on a dominant leader's vision. They seek a vision of their own. They are no longer content to be mindless cogs in the organisational machine. Individual goals must be harnessed to organisational ones. Otherwise, says futurist Charles Handy: 'If there is no common goal people put their own goals first.'[100] The leader is required to facilitate an ongoing process of planning future directions in consultation with employees. Wise leaders will probably also create opportunities for employees to develop new skills, support employees' ongoing education, provide attainable progression paths, provide meaningful work by delegating duties and responsibilities, and build work structures that give employees a creative input.

To achieve these new goals, consultation should become standard in the sustainable organisation's toolkit. While many men pay lip service to consultation, they don't seriously practise it themselves. When they truly consider consultation expertise as a necessary prerequisite for promotion, they will find many more women to be worthy leaders. Many women's refined consultation skills have been well honed in their agreement-building subculture.

*Consultation should become standard in the sustainable organisation's toolkit.*

Does a consultative approach work when women are leading men? I interviewed Louise Crossley. She found the consultative approach highly effective in her role as station leader at Mawson in Antarctica. There was only one other woman on the base.

I think previous male station leaders had used more of a military leadership model — very command and control. My style was more inclusive. I never talked about 'my station'. It was always 'our station'. I always tried to generate a sense that each of us was part of the team and that each of us had a useful function. A lot of people acknowledged that they appreciated it.

On one occasion when we were unloading the supply ship, we'd been working absolutely flat out for four days, eighteen hours a day. Daylight the whole time. It'd gone really well, no stuff-ups, no accidents. People had that wonderful sense of satisfaction that you get from working as a team, knowing that their efforts were important, that the whole thing was greater than the sum of everybody's parts.

Then, I realised that I actually made one mistake. We'd planned to keep an empty container onshore for rubbish. The one I'd earmarked for this got filled with rubbish from the unpacking. I should have noticed, but I'd mistaken the container.

'Damn,' I said to somebody, 'I really stuffed up on that, we should be keeping that container, but it's already full. Okay, It will have to go back to the ship!' Somebody else overheard me: 'Don't worry, Louise,' he said. 'We'll fix it for you.' And so these guys who'd been sweating their guts out for four days turned around and transferred the contents of this huge container to a different one that we didn't want to stay.

It was extraordinary generosity of spirit beyond the call of duty. That sort of thing only happens when the people feel it's their plan, too, not just yours, and they regard you as being someone that they want to please. I might be quite wrong, but I get the feeling that that wouldn't have happened with a man in charge using a command management style. They may have emptied the wanted container if they'd been ordered to, but they would've done it resentfully at that point, not out of their own desire to complete a totally successful operation.

I think their attitude also had something to do with the fact that I was willing to acknowledge that since *I'd* stuffed up, I'd live with the problem. *[True consultation implies you don't have all the answers and that you can look to your team to solve problems on your behalf.]*

*Your personal credibility is your only authority.*

In a lot of situations my willingness to consult rather than command, which was my style anyway, generated credibility. In Antarctica, your personal credibility is your only authority.

To achieve *real authority* in the modern workplace, organisations must now recruit people with both dominance and consultation skills.

## Right action

Right action = courage + ethic of care

### COURAGE

The workplace is today's battleground of traditional masculine culture and is still looking for warrior leaders who demonstrate courage. There is undoubtedly some wisdom in recruiting for this quality. Senior managers — male and female — must have the courage to ask the difficult questions and take firm steps when required. The leader is a change agent and staff who are satisfied with the status quo may resist or even obstruct the process of change. Successful leaders must be street-wise. Even if personally they are not competitive, they must defend themselves against competition effectively, and be alert to it even when it's subtle or manipulative. Every successful leader needs to be capable of protecting their own and their organisation's interests. All these are tasks that require considerable courage.

Women leaders probably need more courage and strength than their male peers. They have to counter the resistance of male work cultures that have not yet adapted to the presence of women. Eva Cox, author of *Leading Women*, says that women as change agents are often caught in a double bind — being ignored if they don't speak out and being scorned if they do.[101]

Courage does not have to imply a willingness to deal unmercifully with the opposition. Women can and do succeed without going in for the kill. Maria Bordoni, Australia's first governor of a maximum-security male prison, says she believes that one of her strengths is her ability to make tough decisions quickly. 'I'm tough and decisive, but I'm tough and fair at the same time. People will take that,' she says.[102]

If a woman is still working on her 'nice girl' image — passive, compliant and supportive — she won't look like she can cut it at the top, despite the fact that that very image may have been instrumental in her reaching lower levels of management. Middle management usually requires considerable face-to-face contact. An emphasis on agreement helps middle managers excel in straightforward non-confrontational contact. It's not surprising therefore that in Australia in 1992, 71 per cent of all women with any managerial status were at the lowest level.[103]

Although women's ready compliance can make them useful supervisors, it may ultimately cause much physical and mental distress if structures, systems or arrangements are unsuitable.[104] To move above middle management, agreers may need to radically rethink an overly compliant style. It is not necessary to sell out the agreement value to achieve this. A liberal injection of assertive win/win strategies in their management methods can do the trick. A balance is needed between being too nice and too tough, and this balance probably has to change with the position held in the organisation.[105]

*By the time women are ready for senior management, they should have let go of the need to please and to be liked all the time.*

By the time women are ready for senior management, they should have let go of the need to please and to be liked all the time. Their agreement style should instead rest on respect for others and a determination to make fair and effective decisions. With this base firm, courage and strength flow to the task at hand.

## ETHIC OF CARE

In the modern workplace, courage should not mean ruthlessness. Organisations must demonstrate through their leaders, that they care: care about their workers as individuals; care about their customers and the quality and safety of its products and services; care about their impact on the community.

Women are especially likely to balance courage with this ethic of care. Men tend to base their morality code on rules, rights and justice, whereas women are more likely to formulate their moral principles on duties of humanitarian concern, nurturance and responsibility. Both styles have their place in sound management practice. While rules must be adhered to for smooth functioning, workers cannot be treated as fodder for the organisation to chew up and regurgitate. The law increasingly supports an ethic of care. Unfair dismissal laws, obligatory redundancy procedures and anti-discrimination legislation must be carefully and considerately administered in the modern workplace.

What does an ethic of care look like? A senior woman executive told me:

> Bad stuff was happening to another person within the organisation. I could see some colleagues colluding in putting him down, or at least not prepared to rock the boat in his defence. I'm not prepared to leave it at that. People can be damaged by other people's silence.

*Ethical decision-making is increasingly necessary for the twenty-first century.*

This woman was clear about her limits and what she stood for, and she spoke up forcefully on her colleague's behalf at an executive meeting. Of course, men can — and do — display caring, nurturing qualities, but these contributions are often undervalued by other men and are forced underground in a highly competitive culture. Organisations can no longer afford to sideline those men and women who speak up for humanitarian, ecological and other non-profit based principles. Ethical decision-making is increasingly necessary for success in the twenty-first century. Women will have an important part to play in this process.

What we must really look for from competent leadership is right action. It requires both courage and an ethic of care.

## Enabled and empowered teams

### CONFIDENCE

We expect our leaders to be confident. But how are we judging this? By what they say about themselves? Men and women tend to communicate differently about their successes. Men are likely to attribute a success to their own ability. Women tend to speak of a success as being due to luck, to someone else helping them, to a whole team.[106] Politeness and self-perception demand they wait for someone else to tell them that their success is actually a result of their own ability. Their conversational rituals mismatch those of the usual male workplace culture. If judged by a male yardstick, women can appear to lack self-confidence, even to look incompetent, and their ideas are likely to be dismissed if tentatively presented.

Perceived competence is critical. Women who want promotion may need to pay more attention to becoming *visibly* competent. In fact, to receive a promotion in a male-dominated environment a woman will usually have to be more competent than a man at the same level. Recruiters must become astute enough not to make any final judgments about confidence based solely on what the person says about themselves. Real confidence is based on competence that is measured by performance and results.

*Real confidence is based on competence which is measured by performance and results.*

### COMMUNICATION AND CONFLICT RESOLUTION SKILLS

No one wants an insecure leader telling them how to run the show. However, too much self-confidence can close the mind. Self-confidence gives leaders the ability to persuade, but they must also have the ability to *be persuaded*. They need to be good listeners, open to new ideas and feedback on what is and is not working.

Good decision-making by the leader and the team rests on constant two-way information sharing. To inspire empathy and trust, the leader must be able to communicate their own ideas and rationale clearly. They must have an ability to self-disclose, even about some apparent failures. They and their team must be ready to respond quickly to changing circumstances. Good communication is vital if the team is to have the flexibility to shift priorities and portfolios.

Leaders are only as good as their team's output. If that output is seriously blocked by internal conflict, the leader's first task is conflict resolution. Modern managers are rarely required to be the hero–warrior — out in front leading the charge for an infantry with set tasks to perform without question. They are very much part of the team they lead. Flatter organisational hierarchies mean devolved decision-making and hence more possibilities for overt conflict. In such team environments leaders must possess excellent conflict resolution and mediation skills in order to iron out their own and others' difficulties rapidly and repeatedly.

Sometimes self-confidence gives a false impression of professionalism. People with strong communication and conflict resolution skills may be overlooked. Confidence must combine with strong communication skills if leaders and their subordinates are to stand together as *enabled and empowered teams*.

## Strategic thinking

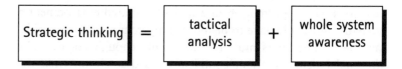

| Strategic thinking | = | tactical analysis | + | whole system awareness |

*TACTICAL ANALYSIS*
Effective leaders are tactical thinkers. Often this is misinterpreted in a male-dominated culture as mastering brinkmanship. Tactical thinking requires considered planning of the steps required to achieve a goal. An ability to plot a logical and time-ordered sequence of actions is absolutely vital when organising many people and resources. With increasing responsibility, all leaders,

male and female, will need to focus on and perhaps develop these skills. But good leadership is not just a matter of mastering complex cause-and-effect sequences, or developing effective tactics for one-upping other people.

## WHOLE SYSTEM AWARENESS

Good leadership also requires focus on the whole system. This is not a logical, analytic process. It is an intuitive function. Some brain research appears to indicate that genetic predisposition may favour women in this regard.[107]

While the 'left' brain seems to present information in logical and analytic sequences, the 'right' brain presents information about a system as a single unit, a flash of intuition or creativity. The global sense of 'all about the team' or 'all about the project' is often received as a kinaesthetic response (a feeling) or a visual image (a mental picture). 'It doesn't feel right', 'I just know we should be doing x', 'I can't tell you why, but that way lies danger', are statements that can't always be analysed. They are flashes of understanding before all the detailed information has been received.[108]

Many men who value analytic skills dismiss intuitive information received in this all-at-once, global way. Yet intuition is an important leadership ability, and difficult to acquire. It enables someone to step outside a narrow context and see the larger whole. It comes from an inner perception of forces and reactions.

*Many men who value analytic skills dismiss intuitive information.*

People often lack the means to talk about conclusions reached this way, which means that others must take them on trust. This can reduce the usefulness of their contributions as a team player. Yet they may be able to describe their process if they learn to explain situations in terms of patterns of interacting rather than linear cause–effect sequences. This is the basis of systems analysis, now often used to describe group process. A description may go something like this: 'If this happens, that could happen because of this *tension* here, or that *block* there, exerting this kind of *force*.' The language of systems thinking is particularly useful for intuitive people. Once mastered, they'll have a higher credibility with more analytic thinkers. Describing intuitive leaps in terms of perceived patterns means others can follow your thinking. You are pointing at what you are 'looking' at, so that other people can 'look', too.[109]

Without whole systems awareness, leaders can lose themselves in a myriad of details, become bogged in tasks that are the most urgent rather than the most important, or create an excellent plan of action for going in the *wrong* direction.

*Strategic thinking* of great leaders has always relied on both tactical analysis and whole system awareness for receiving and monitoring information.

We can represent the balance between traditionally masculine leadership skills and the still undervalued feminine ones as a *leadership wheel*. While our best leaders will be strong in all aspects, organisations will benefit greatly by putting together teams of leaders with differing strengths, if the full range of those strengths is valued.

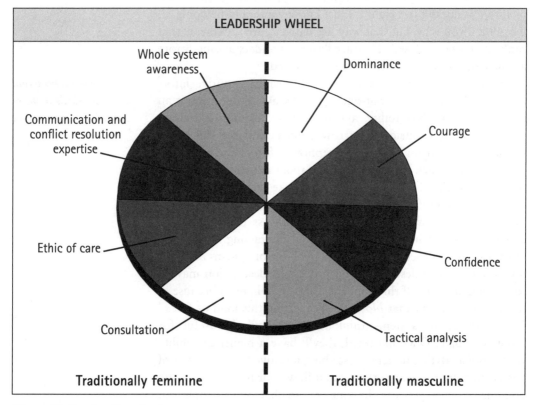

*Figure 38: Leadership wheel*

*STEPPING STONES*

There are some important questions to ask yourself about your workplace:

- ▶ Are the qualities the management team displays out of balance?

- ▶ Would the promotion of more women bring some missing skills, abilities or ethics to the collective leadership function?

- ▶ Does there need to be a shift away from a competitive masculine-style culture in order for agreement-oriented contributions to be acknowledged?

One way to encourage a culture shift is by changing methods of performance review — getting peers and subordinates, as well as superiors, to rate employees' performance on a balanced set of leadership skills. This type of performance review can give important feedback for self-development and indicate those people suitable for promotion. It is often employees lower in the hierarchy who notice and value leadership skills such as consultation, an ethic of care, communication and conflict resolution skills, and whole system thinking.

## STUMBLING BLOCK 2: FEAR OF BEING SEEN AS AN OUTSIDER TO THE PACK

'I can't push an unpopular idea. I have to survive.'

Many men cut themselves off from important facets of their character in order to run with the boys. They often feel they need to present themselves as excessively tough, even sexist, to be acceptable to their peers and superiors. A competitive environment can be a very dangerous place. Sarah, a competent and astute executive in a large financial planning company, has an interesting perspective:

*Many men cut themselves off from important facets of their character in order to run with the boys.*

> I find that most of the time men are very risk averse. They hate failing, whereas women seem to have less to lose and will fall down, get up and try again — because they're not as competitive. Peer pressure is a terrible thing for men. They have to be one of the boys. If any of them do try to push a particular cause, the others will give them a hard time

about it. Under such circumstances, their concern can squeeze them into mediocrity.

John, a managing partner where Sarah is employed, relates how it was for him:

Sarah, our HR manager, had come up with a pretty comprehensive training schedule for the year, involving all the staff. It really was an excellent plan, but Tony, our senior partner, couldn't see the sense in training everyone in both communication skills and our new computer programs. It came up in an executive meeting and we were both getting pretty hot under the collar about it. The way Tony argued it would have made me look like I was overindulgent if I backed her plan all the way. I just couldn't afford to be seen like that, by Tony in particular, but by the other partner, too. As it was, it must have looked like I had a thing going with her to fight that hard for her ideas. I hate letting Sarah down. I know she was relying on me to back her up in the meeting. But that's boardroom politics! If you want to survive you have to play your cards right.

In interviewing Megan, I heard a similar tale:

I wanted my title changed. The title itself was pretty trivial, but I needed to know I had my boss's support. Other people in our organisation working at the same level, or even below it, had the title 'director'. I'd canvassed the market to see what my equivalent role in other organisations was called. 'Marketing Director' was completely appropriate, whereas my title was 'Marketing Manager'. The change had to be requested by my boss and then approved at the national office. Every few weeks I'd ask him what was happening. He'd promise to chase it up with head office but still nothing happened. The saga went on for fourteen months.

Finally, when I handed in my notice, my boss asked: 'Megan, why?' I told him: 'To tell you the truth, one of the reasons, though it's not the only one by any means, is because we never resolved my title. I needed to see how far you and the national directors were prepared to support me. I give you a lot. I give you total support. I never say 'no'. I don't let anything fall. I juggle every ball. I give a lot of energy, a lot of commitment and a lot of loyalty, but where is the pay-off? Changing my title was a simple thing to do and nobody came through. So why should I come through for you?

He said: 'Well, I think that they won't give you the title until you have a formal marketing qualification.'

I've got a Bachelor of Economics with a major in accountancy, but it's true I don't have formal marketing qualifications. At this stage of my life, spending a year doing a post-graduate degree is not what I want to do. I said: 'I find that a pathetic reason. One, you haven't ever communicated it to me. Two, a piece of paper is useless. It isn't going to help me do the job. I'm already doing it. I've done it successfully for two years.'

'Megan, I'd have supported you if I could. I did ask about it two or three times. But after a few knockbacks, I thought I was getting the message to pull my head in. Title changes are obviously unpopular in the national office.' 'But you didn't even find out what was going on,' I said. 'No, I didn't,' he admitted. 'Quite frankly, I didn't dare. If I start rocking the boat, I could be the next manager who's asked to take a redundancy package. I've climbed too far up the ladder to let myself be thrown off now.'

In our corporate cutthroat culture, it's extremely difficult for men to stand up and support an unpopular idea — especially if it comes from a woman. Also, the unwritten policy at the top is often to keep women out of top positions — even in Megan's case where her new title would have been window dressing and didn't involve more pay or any change in her responsibilities. The men above Megan's boss would be making the decisions about *his* future. If they want to make it to the top, men have to fit the mould of the men above them.

*If they want to make it to the top, men have to fit the mould of the men above them.*

### STEPPING STONES

A number of women reported to me how shocked and disappointed they'd been by the inability of their male peers and superiors to promote them or their ideas. We do need clear awareness of the competitive pressures men experience in furthering their own careers.

Women often end such insoluble problems by leaving to start up their own small businesses. One woman who was national credit manager for a large organisation tried unsuccessfully for five years to become general manager. Eventually, she resigned to run her own credit services agency. Some of her former male adversaries now choose to use her services, admiring the very qualities they criticised her for in corporate life.

What is needed here is a huge culture shift. Toning down internal competition seems to be the only effective way of making it safer for both men and women to stand up for what they believe in. This is no short-term fix. It requires a slow and considered revolution in the workplace culture. It starts with beginning to value and promote agreement-building expertise. Skilled agreement-builders welcome a diversity of opinions and build solutions that incorporate this diversity wherever possible. Many women have these skills to offer. So do many men. However, men may have had to keep their diverging points of view secret for fear of standing outside the 'party line' of the dominant male culture.

Is it realistic to expect such change? Clare Burton in *The Promise and the Price* states her belief that through our practices at work, we are altering gender relationships:

*Men and women don't come with their gender identities sewn up.*

> ... that men and women don't come to the workplace with their gender identities sewn up ... that what we do and how we do it at work re-creates, reproduces, reorganises, reconstitutes our masculine and feminine identities.[110]

Yes, it can be done. It starts by knowing where we're going.

## STUMBLING BLOCK 3: ALIENATION FROM OTHERS

**'Our workplace is a war zone.'**

A competitive style of itself need not cause a problem. Sparring often takes place in an environment of friendly camaraderie. Things go wrong when the underlying undercurrent of empathy is diverted by aggressive behaviour that seriously damages others.

Managers whose negotiation tactics have isolated them from others make less effective decisions, not only because they encourage safe mediocrity, but because they ignore the needs of others. They make other people 'the enemy' — a dangerous tactic in a competitive climate where trust, support and respect are needed to survive the long haul. Competitive workplace environments are extremely stressful for both men and women, because you always need to be on your guard. The shorter lifespan of men who are more constantly exposed to this type of stress, and for longer (women tend to retire earlier), may well attest to its toll.

Negotiation is a core activity of organisations, particularly negotiation about the use of scarce resources (e.g. departmental salary or marketing budgets, office space). Empathy is lost when people play the game by power politicking, blocking opportunities for others, manoeuvring themselves into the most advantageous position to gain as many resources as possible, or by accumulating power at the expense of others.

Alienating tactics also include restricting the flow of information so that others are disempowered. Boasting excessively about achievements is another strategy used to stay on top of the heap, but it doesn't win you real friends.

The competition gets stiffer the higher you climb. Katrina reports her experiences with senior management:

> Men, in my observation, seem to be aggressive at all levels of the organisation. And it's not just tactics to gain power or get the next promotion over someone else. Even amongst the men that are actually up there, at that top level, there is a high degree of competition still. You go to meetings and watch them spar with one another. Even at the board level.

Those women that do break through the glass ceiling don't find that life is sweet near the top. They talk of 'being stuck on sticky steps', as described in Chapter 7.

### STEPPING STONES

A competitive culture doesn't necessitate alienating tactics, but it does encourage them. A win/lose mentality can easily prevail between people who should be on the same team. There are other ways: valuing different styles, honouring different skills, genuinely making efforts to understand and support other people's needs, and tackling issues with a win/win approach. Competers are often very challenged by the win/win approach.[111] Accustomed to looking out for themselves, they may need to be shown how they will have greater long-term benefits from cooperation than from competition. They'll need to be reassured that the win/win approach is about *them* winning, while encouraging the other person to win, too.

Some competers dismiss the win/win approach on first acquaintance. To them it appears to negate the benefits of competing. They incorrectly presume they lose the right to stand up for themselves.

The win/win approach shouldn't block goal-setting, drive and perseverance, or street-wisdom, even in a highly competitive workplace. In fact, the approach supports dynamic and worldly-wise achievement. Good win/win negotiators are constantly using the litmus test of *tell me why that's fair*. They're less likely to be tripped up by enemies, and less likely to run out of steam because, deep down, they hate the methods they're using to get there. Win/win is a good way to travel wherever you're headed, especially if it's right to the top.

|  | WIN/LOSE | WIN/WIN |
|---|---|---|
| Who wins: | One wins, one loses out. | Both get more of what they want by developing new options. |
| Conflict style: | Demanding: Low respect for opponent's needs. | Negotiating: Respectful of opponents' legitimate needs. |
| Use of anger: | Aggressive: Hard on the people and hard on the problem. | Assertive: Soft on the people and hard on the problem. |
| Use of power: | Power over: Participants test their power to make the other(s) concede. | Power with: Solutions selected for mutual fairness and advantage. |
| Place of trust: | Trust is often very low. Power enforces compliance. | Mutual trust is often high. Where trust is low, compliance is monitored and penalties are preset. |

*Figure 39: Win/lose, win/win comparison*

The win/win approach relies on good communication—first, in openly exploring the needs and concerns of the parties involved, then in asking for other people's opinions on how to meet those needs and concerns. Of course, when your opinion is invited, this can set up the expectation that your solutions will be used. While ideally each person's opinion is sought, each person's opinion cannot necessarily be acted upon. Someone who's been asked for their opinion may well be very angry that their point of view is not the prevailing one at decision-making time. They are far more likely to accept a less than perfect win/win *outcome* when they have had full and considerate explanations of the whole problem and its constraints (e.g. budget or time limits).

The win/win approach can be deeply satisfying for those involved. After a particularly successful outcome, a born competer can be completely won over to the method by the cooperative spirit of the process. One male manager reported:

> The win/win approach is actually a huge relief. Now I see I don't have a duty to come up with all the answers. I don't have to offer advice. I just have to go back to everyone's needs and work with that.

Once this style becomes a conscious choice, both agreers and competers will use it far more consistently and effectively. More men are choosing a win/win approach, even though it challenges self-images of manly toughness. Best practice in management is supporting this transition.

Changing an overly competitive climate may seem an overwhelming task. Yet it starts with small and manageable steps. Ask yourself: 'Do I contribute to an undesirably competitive culture in my organisation or do I minimise it?'

## STUMBLING BLOCK 4:
## POOR LISTENING SKILLS

**'You haven't heard a word I've said.'**

Consider how you deal with a clash. Often when people are in competitive mode, they don't really listen. When someone is angry and you are the object of that anger, the instinctive response is to defend yourself. One person voices a complaint, perhaps with considerable emotion. The other is silent, but not because they're listening. They are waiting for their turn to retaliate. When it comes, they throw into the arena a piece of information from their own agenda, designed to top, overwhelm or lay more blame than the blame being laid on them. Acrimonious interchanges mount. The number of topics over which they disagree multiplies the longer the conversation continues. The conflict becomes more serious and more difficult to resolve. It's rather like a macabre tennis game where both people are sending and returning many different balls on the one court — a nightmare! (See **Figure 40: Competitive disconnected conversations**, below.)

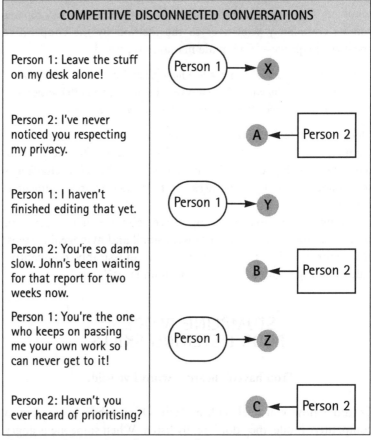

*Figure 40: Competitive disconnected conversations*

*STEPPING STONES*

Looking at Figure 40, if person 2 was really listening, they'd take the first ball put into play, ball X, and bounce it around for a while — ask a relevant question to get some more information about it, toss it backwards and forwards, and investigate the angles. The interchange would look more like that shown in **Figure 41: Connected listening** (below).

The secret of good listening is not only waiting for your turn to speak but *taking in* what the other person has said, staying with their topic and their feelings. An appropriate response may be a question that gathers more information about what they are trying to communicate. It may be the equivalent of 'message received and understood'. You may respond with your understanding of what they said and perhaps include how you believe they feel about it. It's often useful to put this in question format: 'Are you saying that you don't want me to read the

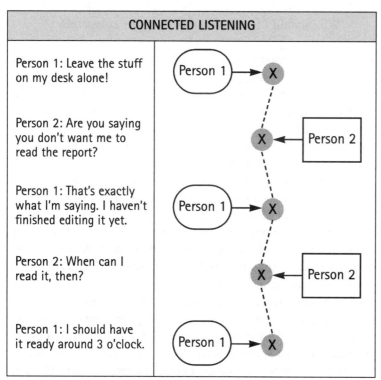

*Figure 41: Connected listening*

report? If someone is very angry with you and apologising isn't appropriate, try instead an information-seeking question, such as the one in the example: 'When can I read it, then?, or 'Tell me why you have a problem'. Make sure you really listen to the answer! Listen to their criticisms, but look beneath what they say to their thwarted needs, no matter how badly expressed.[112]

*Many men need a much better grasp of the basics of empathy-building in difficult circumstances.*

Many men need a much better grasp of the basics of empathy-building in difficult circumstances. I am certainly not saying that all women are strong in empathy-building, but generally I have found that more men do need more training in empathy-building techniques than women, in particular the skill of active listening.

## STUMBLING BLOCK 5: LACK OF SUPPORT FOR THOSE WHO COULD BE POTENTIAL THREATS

'Why should I be her mentor? She's the competition.'

*In times of downsizing and economic down-turn, men's wariness of 'the competition' shoots upwards.*

It is not only market forces that drive a capitalist economy. Fear does too! Fear of losing your job, fear of not keeping up with the mortgage, fear of being unable to support your family in the style to which they have become accustomed. Scarcity of work and the need to share limited resources impact on masculine competitiveness. In times of downsizing and economic downturn, men's wariness of 'the competition' shoots upwards.

An intelligent, assertive woman in the workplace is often perceived by men as a direct challenge to their status and power. If she is promoted, she's likely to have to put up with such comments as, 'She must be sleeping with the boss', or 'She only got the job because she's a woman and they had to fill the quota'. She is more likely than men to have her authority resisted.

The glass ceiling keeps women out of the competition, and to crack it women generally need support. Most women who want to achieve a management position in a corporate environment are going to need a mentor. In *Smashing the Glass Ceiling*, Pat Heim and Susan Golant quote a recent American survey which found that of the seventy-six women executives interviewed, 100 per cent arrived at where they were with the support of a mentor. In

an equivalent group of men, only 34 per cent had used a mentor.[113]

The mentoring process — whether formal or informal — is fraught with difficulties in a competitive environment. First there is the resistance to supporting any woman who might compete for scarce jobs at the top. If the mentor and mentee are male and female, both will probably be accused at some stage of having an affair. Mentoring requires time spent together. If you frequently go to lunch or meetings with someone of the opposite sex, comments and innuendos generally abound. It is particularly difficult for women to acquire a male mentor under these circumstances.

Few organisations encourage mentoring as standard practice. Most women must find their mentor outside their own organisation, and therefore this important process is often haphazard and informal. Most women miss out on this sort of support altogether.

*STEPPING STONES*

Most women and most young people of both sexes need coaching and support to progress within an organisation. Alastair Rylatt, author of *Learning Unlimited* says: 'Mentoring and coaching are two processes that have a direct impact on the quality of workplace learning.'[114] If organisational policy rewards learning relationships, both parties can more easily lay aside fears of competition and sexual baiting. What is implied in mentoring may need to be clearly spelled out. Mentoring tasks include:

▶ training or encouraging training and updating of technical skills;

▶ encouraging constant upgrading of managerial skills;

▶ allocating tasks and duties that stretch the person and will support their upward mobility;

▶ encouraging participation in policy meetings within the company and professional exchange with others outside the company in the same field.

If these supportive roles are not respected and encouraged from the top right down through the organisation, the penalty is low staff loyalty, missed opportunities to train on-the-job and loss of future leaders.

# SUMMARY

| COMPETITION: STUMBLING BLOCKS | STEPPING STONES: ENCOURAGE A CULTURE SHIFT | | |
|---|---|---|---|
| 1 ► Leadership style relies too heavily on warrior skills | BALANCED LEADERSHIP QUALITY | CONTRIBUTION FROM TRADITIONALLY MASCULINE PERSPECTIVES | CONTRIBUTION FROM TRADITIONALLY FEMININE PERSPECTIVES |
| | Real authority = | dominance + | consultation |
| | Right action = | courage + | ethic of care |
| | Enabled and empowered teams = | confidence + | communication and conflict resolution expertise |
| | Strategic thinking = | tactical analysis + | whole system awareness |
| | Broader criteria for leadership will include qualities in which many women excel, and address glass ceiling issues. | | |
| 2 ► Fear of being seen as an outsider to the pack | Tone down internal competition. Value and promote agreement-building expertise. | | |
| 3 ► Alienation from others | Value different styles, honour different skills, tackle issues with a win/win approach. | | |
| 4 ► Poor listening skills | Understand the basics of connected listening. | | |
| 5 ► Lack of support for those who could be potential threats | Internal competition can have devastating consequences for long-term effectiveness and sustainability. To counter this, make mentoring and coaching part of the culture of the organisation. | | |

# PART IV

# FEELING FOCUS AND ACTIONS-AND-OBJECTS FOCUS

## EIGHT COMMON CONFLICTS

*Feeling focusers' complaints:*

▶ 'You've got no heart.'

▶ 'You've got no idea how I feel about this.'

▶ 'My feelings may not be logical, but they're real to me.'

▶ 'I just wanted your ear, not your advice.'

*Actions-and-objects focusers' complaints:*

▶ 'How can you say that my idea's not well thought through?'

▶ 'I can't get anything done if six people have to agree to it first.'

▶ 'You're just being stupid. Use your brain!'

▶ 'Problems at home are no excuse for not getting on with the job.'

## Synopsis — where are we now?

In Part I, we discussed the transition in our workplace priorities towards what have traditionally been regarded as feminine values. This is the gentle revolution. In Parts II and III, we considered the problems that arise when people give differing priorities to equality versus status, and agreement versus competition. We also looked at the gender links between these values and the stepping stones to resolving the conflicts they generate.

Part IV explores the issue of where we focus our attention — on *feeling* or on *actions and objects*. The matrix below points to where this part fits in the scheme of the book.

| PERSPECTIVES | FEMININE STEREOTYPE | MASCULINE STEREOTYPE |
|---|---|---|
| Use of power: | Equality | Status |
| Interacting style: | Agreement | Competition |
| → Focus of attention: | Feeling | Actions and objects ← |
| Comfort zone: | Interdependence | Autonomy |

The arrows above indicate the discussion areas for the next three chapters.

In Chapter 9, we consider the positive contributions of these values, as well as the differences between them. Chapters 10 and 11 deal with feeling focus and actions-and-objects focus in turn, and we take a look at the problems that face each approach.

A NOTE ON TERMINOLOGY: While we'll consider the tendency of these values to be associated with a particular gender, the heading 'stereotype' in the figure above reminds us that *we are dealing with images of the sexes that live inside our own heads and which do not always match up with reality*. To broaden the discussion, I frequently use gender neutral descriptions, *feeling focusers* and *actions-and-objects focusers* (sometimes abbreviated to *actions focusers*), to include the many people who do not fit their sex's stereotype on these issues.[115]

# QUIZ

Circle the number in the column that best reflects your response to the following statements:

## Quiz 1

|  | RARELY | SOMETIMES | OFTEN |
|---|---|---|---|
| People seem to trust me and come to me with their problems. | 0 | 1 | 2 |
| I prefer people-oriented tasks to mechanical or computerised ones. | 0 | 1 | 2 |
| I try to socialise with my colleagues and talk about things other than work. | 0 | 1 | 2 |
| I trust instincts more than logic. | 0 | 1 | 2 |
| People tell me that I am too sensitive or emotional. | 0 | 1 | 2 |

Total:

+        =

## Quiz 2

|  | RARELY | SOMETIMES | OFTEN |
|---|---|---|---|
| I am uncomfortable when someone wants to unburden their emotions with me. | 0 | 1 | 2 |
| I like to stay busy with lots of activity. | 0 | 1 | 2 |
| I prefer to keep personal worries and concerns to myself. | 0 | 1 | 2 |
| I'm good at not letting my feelings get in the way of my judgment. | 0 | 1 | 2 |
| People say they can't keep up with me. | 0 | 1 | 2 |

Total:

+        =

Add up your circled numbers for each quiz separately then compare the two scores.

If your score was higher in Quiz 1, you probably focus strongly on *feeling*. If you scored higher in Quiz 2, you probably put more of a priority on *actions and objects*. If your scores were equal, you may swing between the two polarities, depending on the situation.

The next three chapters will tell you more about these qualities.

# 9 FEELING – ACTIONS-AND-OBJECTS: focus of attention

While almost no one completely excludes either feeling or actions and objects from their focus of attention, many people are drawn more to one approach than the other — a difference that is often linked to gender. In this chapter, we begin with the characteristics of these two focus areas and the good intentions behind them. Both approaches have important contributions to decision-making, even if the issues as viewed from each area may look very different. In the second half of the chapter, we consider *mapping* — a conflict resolution skill that bridges the gap between a feeling focus and an actions-and-objects focus, validating both approaches.

## FEELING FOCUS AND ACTIONS-AND-OBJECTS FOCUS AT CROSS-PURPOSES

Bob was senior administrator of a large hospital. He attended a meeting with Eliza, chief of nursing, and a newly appointed architect, to discuss the renovations needed to a wing of the hospital. Plans were spread over the meeting table. Wanting to be helpful in explaining the brief, Eliza said to the architect: 'Why don't I take you down to the wing and show you the problems we have getting trolleys round the corner. I'll introduce you to a couple of the orderlies and they can tell you all about it.'

'He doesn't need to go down there, Eliza,' Bob snapped. 'He can understand the situation perfectly well. He has the existing plans in front of him.'

Eliza persisted. 'No, I need him to see the wing. Mistakes have been made in the past and we've had to redraw plans because the architect hasn't really understood the situation.'

'Don't be ridiculous, Eliza. It's a *design* problem. He doesn't have to chat up the locals to get the picture.'

Eliza's contributions were repeatedly brushed aside by Bob. Their styles were diametrically opposed. Eliza knew that if she were the architect, she'd want to know the whole picture first before drawing up the plans. To her, this was vital. For instance, she guessed that, when using trolleys, female nurses and orderlies probably needed a larger turning circle than male staff who were probably stronger. She felt that redesigning the wing according to the needs of staff was a wonderful opportunity to show employees that the hospital cared about their working conditions. She was concerned about staff morale while construction work was going on and reasoned that if the staff felt they had input into the design, they'd accept the problems involved in its execution. She was concentrating on the process, the people and their emotions.

Bob was very competent at reading plans. He didn't see how employees were important to the design. He felt it would be a waste of the architect's time and the hospital's money to chat with staff. Bob had worked hard to make sure that all the data and measurements the architect needed were already in the brief. He was focused on hard facts. Care for his staff was shown in the commitment to enforcing short building deadlines so that there would be minimum disruption to hospital routines.

Eliza's feeling focus and Bob's actions-and-objects focus were at odds.

Many feeling focusers participate in their most engaged, connected conversations when they are focused on emotions —

*Deep feelings are
not a general topic
of conversation
between men.*

their own and other people's. They generally become close by
sharing how they feel. Fears, concerns, love and rapport — or lack
of it — are typical topics.

Many action-and-objects focusers regard discussion of deep
feelings as a weakness and will only hold meaningful conversations on them with their partners or close family, if at all. They'll
generally choose to discuss their feelings with women. Deep
feelings are not a general topic of conversation between men.

Many men are at their most connected and spontaneous when
their attention is on actions: plans, goals for achievement, sports;
or on objects: how something operates, the comparative merits of
one car or computer over another. They build relationships based
on discussions of shared interests or by striving together towards
mutual goals.[116]

Ken Wilber describes the distinction I am making here as two
different domains of attention — the interior and the exterior.[117]
Most people switch attention repeatedly from one domain to the
other, but many of us have a strong preference for or a prime focus
on one particular domain.

These preferences often (but not always) align with gender, or
at least with our stereotyped images of masculine and feminine.
From the many possibilities, I have chosen the labels *feeling* and
*actions-and-objects* to describe these two domains of focus.[118] You
might prefer a different pair of labels, depending on the particular
issue you are trying to come to grips with. Other common terms
used to describe these two approaches are listed in **Figure 42: The
feeling–actions split** (page 225).

| THE FEELING–ACTIONS SPLIT | |
|---|---|
| Feeling focus | Actions-and-objects focus |
| Feelings | Facts |
| Emotion-oriented | Action-oriented |
| Subject-oriented (subjective) | Object-oriented (objective) |
| People-oriented | Task-oriented |
| Process-oriented | Goal-oriented |
| Problem prevention | Problem correction |
| Feeling | Thinking |
| Intuition | Logic |
| Intuitive reasoning | Analytic reasoning |
| Awareness of wholes | Awareness of parts |
| Emotional intelligence | Sensorimotor logical/spatial intelligence |
| Internal (or interior) | External (or exterior) |
| Comfort with ambiguity and uncertainty | Comfort with certainty and measurability |

*Figure 42: The feeling–actions split*

For instance, the conflict between Eliza and Bob at the hospital could also be described as one of *process* versus *goal*. In the workplace, stereotypically feminine concerns focus on the wellbeing of the individual and the support they need to perform their job. Stereotypically masculine concerns focus first on output, on performance, on action. They are likely to address the wellbeing of the individual only if output is suffering as a result.

Each focus needs the balance of its opposite. Without this balance, each approach will generate the stumbling blocks and conflicts that we discuss in more detail in the following two chapters.

As we move now to the characteristics of each value, it's wise to remember that people don't always, or don't in particular circumstances, fit their sex's stereotype.

# CHARACTERISTICS: FEELING FOCUS

People with a feeling focus often display certain characteristics. Usually they:

▶ *Believe that feelings, and sometimes intuition or creativity, are what really matter.* These are the preferred topics of a feeling focuser's conversation when building rapport with another person. However, they generally require a climate of trust in which such self-revealing talk is possible. Concern about the feelings of others demonstrates important workplace values — politeness, respect, caring and compassion.

▶ *Closely observe their emotions, creativity and intuition throughout the day.* As emotions arise, they draw the feeling focused person's attention, even when they might prefer to be able to ignore them.

▶ *Are relatively willing to disclose vulnerable feelings.* Feeling focusers may be more comfortable talking about their vulnerable feelings, such as fear, anxiety, guilt and sadness, than their defensive ones, such as anger, irritation or envy.

▶ *Believe workplace climates and processes should support employees.* They believe that people are an organisation's most important asset. Employees have the right to be happy at work. If workplace processes require attention in order to achieve this, that should be management's top priority. They consider costs incurred to support employees to be money well spent.

▶ *Believe discussion of feeling cements a team.* They feel that solid teams and good working relationships arise from shared emotions. Though not always as open as discussions with family, they may be broader than purely work-related concerns. Workplaces may be self-defeating if conversation is so controlled that such exchanges cannot occur.

▶ *Use emotions as a guide to action.* Emotions, both their own and other people's, can be important reference points as a guide to action. Feeling focusers may justify intuitive preferences with a logical, reasoned line of thought built after their initial response.

▶ *Tolerate ambiguity and uncertainty relatively well.* Ambiguity and uncertainty are common inner experiences, as feelings can take time to emerge and are often clouded by conflicting emotions. When in doubt, feeling focusers may wait long periods for the waters to clear before deciding what action to take. Alternatively, they may be too open to influence, expressing one opinion with one person and being swayed to an opposing viewpoint with another.

▶ *See life as fundamentally an inner journey.* Many feeling focused people see the world from their inner perspective. Events unrelated to them personally may hold little importance for them. They care that those close to them emotionally are doing well. Some will also wish ill to those they dislike.

▶ *Try to extract emotional meanings from their experiences.* As the feeling focused person matures emotionally, they are likely to reflect on situations they are involved in and the lessons offered to them and look at how this can help them grow. Once they find meaning, the emotions generated by the experience are usually laid to rest and the person feels they can move forward.

## CHARACTERISTICS: ACTIONS-AND-OBJECTS FOCUS

The usual attention point for actions-and-objects focusers is external reality, rather than their internal world, as is the case for feeling focusers. This outer focus may lead actions-and-objects focusers to display many or all of the following characteristics. They:

▶ *Are happiest when they are doing something.* Actions people enjoy activity. They like to be busy, even though they may complain about it. They may use activity to block self-reflection. On inactive holidays or when ill they can become quite depressed because the emotions they have blocked begin to surface.

▶ *Focus on the external world, or the world of ideas.* Their interest and conversation is drawn to topics such as plans for activity, mechanical equipment such as computers and cars, physical strength and sports. More intellectual actions focusers are likely to have an abstract, philosophical or moral bent, unrelated to personal feelings.

▶ *Resist the expression of vulnerable emotions.* Actions focusers are usually comfortable with their own self-protective feelings of anger, disapproval or irritation. They will talk about and act from these emotions, often in highly charged ways. However, they shy away from emotions such as fear, anxiety, and sadness, believing that to display these emotions will leave them vulnerable and open to criticism. They may not know what to say or do when someone else is experiencing these emotions and may carefully avoid the issue with surface conversation. They will often defend themselves from experiencing such emotions by keeping themselves busy. They are likely to convert vulnerable emotions, such as grief or guilt, into defensive emotions, such as irritability or anger or the desire for revenge. If unable to accomplish this, they can become immobilised or irrational in the midst of vulnerable emotions.

▶ *Focus almost exclusively on tasks and output when in the workplace.* Actions focusers can become very goal-focused. People and their emotions are relevant only insofar as they are relevant to a particular goal. They may discount the feelings of those around them, taking the view that personal emotions should never stand in the way of maximum productivity at work.

▶ *Build rapport through the exchange of concrete information and conversations about activities and objects.* These conversations, which often include technical tips, may be highly animated because the actions person is totally engaged and involved. If both people are actions focused, verbal duels on mutually interesting topics are likely to generate real connection.

▶ *Use logical thought to plan action.* These people are often very analytical. Logical, reasoned thought is their mental vehicle for dealing with strategies, people, machinery, money and so on. Though logical reasoning is an inner process, it is best used for cause-effect sequences in the realm of actions and objects. Logical analysis is not nearly as sensitive or helpful to the world of feeling.

▶ *Are often willing to take risks.* The actions person is sometimes the one who will go out on a limb, taking risks for a project their analytic skills have told them ought to work. They will often be pushed into risk-taking by a desire to counteract ambiguity or uncertainty.

▶ *Believe life is about mastery of objective facts and circumstances through action.* Life's experiences are there to teach mastery of the external world. What is the best car to buy for a certain price? What is the most effective way to negotiate the best deal? Once they have figured this out, the experience is complete.

▶ *Aim for competence and want others to trust and respect their abilities.* Competence is frequently the basis of their self-esteem, which is directly linked to their successful completion of tasks or skills development. They enjoy displaying their mastery and having others praise their skills.

## WHAT IS THE GOOD INTENTION?

Feeling focused people and actions-and-objects focused people often find themselves at odds. Joe commented:

> At work, the men always seem to be complaining that the women are too emotional, while the women are complaining that the men have no idea what really matters to others. Many of the men say that women are too warm and fuzzy, and not hard-headed enough to make the tough decisions needed in business. I've heard women say that some of the men's solutions have given no thought to the long-term costs of damaged relationships. The men see their own decisions as quick and a woman's as impulsive. The women see themselves as far more supportive. They don't seem to understand the support that's implicit in men's actions or their considered silence on sensitive issues.

It's often very difficult for feeling focusers and actions focusers to appreciate each other's point of view. But often the conflict between them cannot be solved until the other person believes their perspective has been heard, understood and respected. We each need to cultivate an understanding of the good intentions of people whose primary focus is different from our own. In situations where there is a clash between focuses, it is generally true that

*Conflict often cannot be solved until the other person believes their perspective has been heard, understood and respected.*

each perspective has a contribution to make. A good solution will nearly always incorporate something from both perspectives.

*EXERCISE*

Consider someone you know, or know of, who you would classify as a feeling focused person. Think of a time when something they did annoyed you. Did they have a good intention that arose from their feeling focus? Were there other 'good intentions' that motivated them as well?

| Feeling focusers' good intentions | Probable motivation for ............ : (name) |
|---|---|
| Considering other people's feelings | |
| Supporting someone through a difficult time | |
| Responding to anxiety, concern or injustice | |
| Communicating what really matters to them | |
| Building rapport | |
| Working through emotions in order to move forwards | |
| Other good intentions: ................................................ ................................................ ................................................ ................................................ | |

*Place crosses against relevant motivations*

*Figure 43: Feeling focusers' good intentions*

Now consider someone you know, or know of, who is strongly motivated by an actions-and-objects focus. For a particular behaviour that you've judged harshly, consider what their good intention could have been.

| Actions-and-objects focusers' good intentions | Probable motivation for ............ : (name) |
|---|---|
| Getting the job done | |
| Moving forward quickly | |
| Solving problems, taking responsibility | |
| Dealing objectively with difficult situations | |
| Making conversation on non-emotional, non-threatening topics | |
| Avoiding being overwhelmed by emotions | |
| Other good intentions: ................................................ ................................................ ................................................ ................................................ ................................................ | |

*Place crosses against relevant motivations*

*Figure 44: Actions-and-objects focusers' good intentions*

You may not get very far with either the feeling focused or the actions focused person until you first acknowledge the worth of their perspective. They're then more likely to open up to hear how it is from your side. Bear in mind that although their primary attention point is feeling, feeling focusers may be very competent in their work and that actions focusers, although not as closely attuned to their own or other people's emotions, generally don't choose to act in ways that hurt others once they understand that it would.

Appreciating others' differences can help us appreciate and grow ourselves. Negative judgments about others are often negative judgments about repressed areas of our own nature.[119] Many psychologists believe that, in order to display the qualities

*Appreciating others' differences can help us appreciate and grow ourselves.*

we presently espouse, we may be suppressing our potential for their opposite. Wholeness and integration comes when we know how to manifest both a feeling and an actions-and-objects focus.

## SPOTTING THE UNDERLYING VALUES

### Verbal style

People's language often provides important clues about their underlying values, the messages they received as a child, the beliefs they presently hold and how they communicate with themselves.

We can often spot these underlying values in everyday conversation once we are attuned to them. We can hear the values in common expressions such as: 'I don't want to hurt her feelings', or 'Just give me the facts'. See **Figure 67: Language driven by feelings and actions-and-objects focus values** (page 403) for other common signals that may indicate these values are affecting the situation.

### Body language

*Women tend to use the other person's facial expressions as a key to understanding emotional meaning.*

Women tend to use the other person's facial expressions as a key to understanding emotional meaning. When a woman communicates a positive verbal message to another woman, they'll watch each other smile. When delivering a negative message, they will closely monitor frowns or lowered eyebrows. Often, however, whether the message is positive or negative, the only change in men's facial expressions is raised eyebrows. Because of this, a woman may badly misinterpret a man unless she's listening closely and knows him well. Even then, she may find his lack of transparency with regard to feelings uncomfortable and alienating.[120]

The feeling focusers also unconsciously note very subtle signals such as tone of voice or a quiver in the voice; muscle movements, sometimes only a minute twitch; contraction or dilation of the eye pupils; or blood moving into and out of the skin areas. Men may be handicapped in this process where their subculture encourages the disguise of feelings, particularly vulnerable ones such as disappointment, hurt or rejection.[121]

## Diffused or spotlight attention

Feeling focused people tend to expand their attention when they are serving the needs of others. It is by diffusing their awareness to include other people that they express caring, nurturing and support. When their energy is broadly focused in order to include others, they can have difficulty maintaining a priority on their own needs and personal rights.

Often feeling focusers live in a state of permanently open focus, which affects their ability to maintain their personal boundaries.[122] They can become overwhelmed by the needs of others. If they have to turn down someone's request, they may do so defensively because they're very uncomfortable. 'No' isn't a simple *no*, it feels like a rejection of the other person and their needs. Says John Gray:

> Under stress a woman tends to expand her awareness and become even more conscious of others ... [a man] becomes more focused.[123]

Actions-and-objects focused people are more likely to beam out their energy like a spotlight. Their attention is held by the task or goal at hand. Actions focusers can appear to be self-centred when the needs of others are not in their sharp focus of attention. They may be accused of self-centredness, when the truth of the matter is that they would do anything for you *if only they'd thought of it*. Their mind is elsewhere — on a task or goal or all-consuming problem.

A person can be considered to be well integrated when they are able to apply their energy in either open or focused awareness, depending on the circumstances.

*The open awareness of feeling-focused people can mean they may have difficulty holding their own ground.*

# MAPPING

The conflict resolution skill of mapping is of enormous help when a feeling style clashes with an actions-and-objects style. Mapping is a method of clarifying the differing needs and concerns that are driving the conflict. It builds up a picture of the whole problem in context, and makes place for people's deeper values, as well as their immediate concerns. It is a very useful process when two or more parties to the conflict are together.

Someone who understands the method can usually initiate the mapping process quite easily. Although mapping is often done using pen and paper, the steps do not always have to be written down. Instead, the points can be brought up in discussion by asking questions and making statements about everyone's needs and concerns. Sometimes one person will do a map of a conflict alone as a preliminary to tackling the issue together, making informal guesses about what is motivating the other people involved.

Mapping meets the feeling focuser's need for understanding and acknowledgment as well as the actions focuser's need to objectify the situation and consider the problem via an analytical, logical and practical process. The person initiating the process can start with a feeling (e.g. distress, anger at injustice), then ask, 'Why do you feel that way?', and with a little probing they will arrive at the feeling focuser's needs and concerns. Or they can start with the actions focuser's 'solution' — their preferred action in the circumstances — and ask, 'Why does that seem like the best answer to you?', and once again they will arrive at needs and concerns. Even though they are seeing the problem from two very different perspectives, mapping helps them arrive at equivalent conflict source points. Mapping may help both parties with practical work-based issues and with deeper values clashes. It's also a very useful tool for group planning.

### Identifying needs and concerns
*WHAT DOES THE ACTIONS PERSON NEED?*
*WHAT DOES THE FEELING PERSON NEED?*

*Actions-and-objects people thrive on practical, down-to-earth details.*

Actions-and-objects people thrive on practical, down-to-earth details. They need clear goals to strive for, otherwise they lose motivation. Reaching sales or production targets, particularly when there is a bonus for success, will often supply the needed incentive. Extrinsic job rewards such as pay increases, a company car, a larger office are other goals that often help keep motivation high. They may also need freedom to achieve, efficiency both from those they rely on and themselves, and for their actions to be trusted, appreciated and accepted by others. Where this fails to happen, they perceive it as a personal attack on their self-worth. In a conflict situation, they will be guided by the concrete facts of the case.

Feeling focusers need their emotions to be understood and acknowledged by others. They feel personally attacked if their emotions are ignored or discounted. Their prime motivation at work is more likely to come from the good feelings generated by the job itself — intrinsic job rewards. Their key workplace needs are work they feel is worthwhile or helpful, acknowledgment for effort, connection with others while working, and harmony and compatibility with colleagues. In a conflict situation, their distress is likely to focus on uncomfortable relationships and how the conflict inconveniences, angers or disturbs the people involved.

Katrina and Kevin's conflict has elements that are commonly reported when feeling focus and actions focus are in opposition:

*Feeling focusers are likely to be motivated by the good feelings generated by the job itself and other people's acknowledgment.*

Katrina, a young university graduate in environmental studies, is employed by a local electricity supply council. The council was preparing recommendations on preferred routes for new power lines. Kevin, Katrina's boss, asked her to collect and edit reports from various sections of the council and to create a briefing document for an independent environmental impact study. It was an important project and Katrina really enjoyed applying her theoretical expertise to a real-life situation.

She prepared a draft and handed copies out to Kevin and other team members for their comments, suggesting a two-week deadline for feedback. One morning, before this period was up, she found a bound copy of the report in her in-tray. She was shocked, and then even more horrified when she realised it had already been distributed to senior management.

When Kevin had received his draft, he'd made his corrections, added a technical report of his own and then sent it on for final layout without telling Katrina or giving her the chance to incorporate suggestions from other team members. There wasn't even an acknowledgments page, which she'd intended to add once the input was finalised. Only Kevin's name appeared as originator of the report. Katrina now wants all copies of the report recalled and a revised version with a complete acknowledgments section issued.

When Kevin sent the report off for reproduction and binding, he hadn't understood that others in his team were also correcting the draft. He now feels he would lose face by withdrawing the report. As he puts it:

'They've read it already. What's the point? I wanted management to get this report a.s.a.p. We've been working on it long enough. What's more, I want them to take the recommendations seriously. I'm the one who'll have to speak about it at the next council meeting, so it's best if my name is on it. We've always done it that way. It's been okay with everyone. Why change now?'

Kevin is exasperated by Katrina's position on the issue.

'What's she so worried about? The report's fine. It doesn't need everyone's name on it. They don't take final responsibility anyway, I do. It's my department.'

Right now Kevin and Katrina are at an impasse. Kevin, as Katrina's supervisor, can simply refuse to do anything about the problem and he will have what he needs in the short term. But he respects Katrina and her contributions, and wants her continued loyalty. He's willing to take a look at the issues before he lays down the law. He does have a key ingredient to conflict resolution — a willingness to resolve.

The purpose of mapping at this point in their argument is to go behind each person's position and find out what supports it. The major focus in mapping is:

> **Step back from conflict about solutions**
> **and**
> **get down to needs and concerns.**

It's a shift from *confrontation* to *exploration*. When you're mapping, ask questions that draw out the needs and concerns behind each person's stand. If it's impractical to ask them directly, put yourself in their shoes and consider how they'd be likely to answer. To develop a full map, you'd look at the needs and concerns of all relevant parties. Let's start with Katrina's and Kevin's needs and concerns.

Kevin, or a third person acting as mediator, might ask Katrina: 'Why is recalling the report important to you?'

Skill is needed to ask 'why?' questions in a non-confrontational way.[124] The tone of your voice should imply genuine inquiry and consideration.

Katrina states her *need* is recognition. Needs are the gap between what she has now (inadequate acknowledgment) and how she wants it to be (sufficient acknowledgment).[125] 'Why?' questions can also illuminate *concerns* or fears. Katrina is concerned about hurting other people's feelings. Other contributors don't have their name in the report and she had implied to them they would.

Kevin's *needs* are for the report to carry weight and be available to people now so that further action can follow quickly. His *concern* is that he will lose face if he withdraws it for what might seem to his superiors to be a petty issue.

You may also uncover concerns with a question such as: 'What's concerning you/worrying you/making you anxious about all this?' Don't bother to list separately an answer you've already covered under *needs*. You wouldn't need to write up 'lack of recognition' under *concerns*, for instance, if you've already written 'recognition' under *needs*. Your search for concerns will often expose issues not already noted, such as the drafting teams' possible concern about how reliable Katrina is.[126]

## Values exploration

You may also uncover relevant values with 'why?' questions. It is not necessary to distinguish them from needs and concerns, but it is worthwhile watching out for them, as people don't shift their values quickly and get angry if solutions do not accommodate them.

*You may uncover relevant values with 'why?' questions, as well as needs and concerns.*

So, why does Katrina need recognition and feel concerned that others might be offended? She has a number of underlying values that are important to her. They revolve around her strong desire to nurture the drafting team.

1. *Fairness.* Katrina believes that she and the rest of the team deserve acknowledgment for their efforts.

2. *Team spirit.* All team members have pulled their weight and she wants them to have the reward of acknowledgment. She is also concerned about her working relationship with these people if she lets them down. The team thought they were still in the midst of a process to which they were all very committed. It has been cut short by the early release of the report.

What values are uppermost for Kevin? Perhaps something like the following is going on for him.

1. *Status.* Recalling the report to add an acknowledgments page will seem strange. Kevin is concerned that it might signal to others that he has had to respond to problems in his department. Perhaps it will make him look like a bad manager or, worse still, that Katrina has him under her thumb.

2. *Efficiency.* Writing and distributing a memo, and getting people to locate the report and return it, is time-consuming and inefficient.

3. *Credibility.* With only his name on the report, Kevin is more certain its recommendations will receive a fair hearing. Katrina is developing a reputation for being a greenie, which might prejudice some people against the report.

When you are leading a mapping process, to address a value properly you'll need to relate it back to the particulars of the situation. You need to know if more or less of something concrete will satisfy the value in question. We'll look in detail at how you do this in Chapter 15.

### Drawing and using your map[127]

*When mapping, start with a general description of the problem area*

1 ▶ *Define the problem are to be resolved.* Kevin and Katrina would describe their individual problems differently. For their map, they'll need a broad definition of the area of concern that they would both agree on. When mapping, describe the problem in neutral language. 'The release of the report' will do. Avoid 'Will we … or won't we …' sentence structures; for example, 'Will we or won't we recall the report?'. These structures are divisive. Don't allow the conversation to get bogged down in defining the problem. Remember, too, you could do more than one map if there appears to be a number of quite separate issues.

2 ▶ *Name the parties.* The next step in building up Kevin and Katrina's map is to put the key players on the chart. In this case there are four. Kevin, Katrina, the drafting team and senior management. It's fine to group a number of people together if their needs are substantially the same on this issue.

**3 ►** *List needs, concerns and, if appropriate, values.* Explore what's relevant for each person or group and summarise it on the map.[128] Sometimes lists will be much longer than the examples developed here. There is no particular need to list values separately unless the apparent infringement of a strongly held value is the crux of the issue.

Kevin and Katrina's map might end up something like the one shown in **Figure 45: Katrina and Kevin's map** below.

**4 ►** *Design new options.* Mapping alone doesn't solve the problem, but it takes the focus away from opposing positions and places it on all the factors that need to be considered. With the map in front of you, you could begin by discussing needs shared in common, key issues and new insights. Mapping often initiates a very creative process in working out new ways to meet more of everyone's needs.

Mapping minimises the confrontation that can arise when discussing the problem and exploring new options. If you draw a

*Mapping often initiates a very creative process in working out new ways to meet more of everyone's needs.*

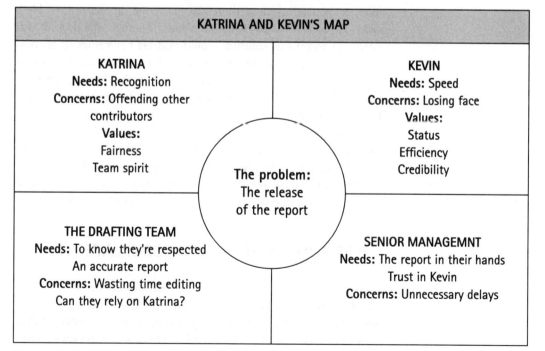

*Figure 45: Katrina and Kevin's map*

map on paper together with a person you're in conflict with, the ideal physical position is to sit or stand side-by-side, both facing the same direction, towards the emerging map. After just a few minutes of work, you're likely to find that you start pointing at the paper as the location of the problem instead of at each other.

Using mapping as part of the conflict resolution process creates an opportunity to look beneath original positions. By moving down to the level of needs, concerns and values, and then coming back up again to their concrete implications, we are able to understand why someone holds the position in the conflict that they do. It may be a chance to explore any flaws in logic. It can set guidelines and limits for alternative solutions. The exploration, if done together, is likely to restore some goodwill — a necessary foundation for designing new solutions that satisfy all or more of everyone's needs, concerns and values.

A solution acceptable to both Katrina and Kevin might be found: perhaps a morning tea celebration with the writing team. Kevin would deliver a 'well done, folks' speech, explaining his 'final responsibility' and therefore his name on the report. He'll need to consult with Katrina about whether she'd find this adequate and if this solution would address her values of fairness and team spirit, in these circumstances. Planning the event together would be an important part of the healing process. Perhaps in the wider organisation, there are some other ways that Kevin could offer to make Katrina's contributions more visible.

The mapping process makes the scope of the problem clearer and provides the opportunity to tailor solutions to its various aspects. As well as pointing towards solutions, mapping provides an opportunity to understand other people's concerns more deeply and often suggests alternative work practices to avoid conflict in the future.

## ADOPTING A FLEXIBLE WORKPLACE STYLE

The polarities of feeling and actions-and-objects need balancing. There are times when a focus on how people are feeling (process), particularly when it's starting to go wrong, is more important than a focus on tasks, goals or end results. There are many times when it's wiser to shelve anxiety or petty squabbles and pull together to get the job done. The two perspectives bring complementary skills. There are times when it's the feeling focuser who pinpoints an empathy breakdown, while the actions person may well identify organisation and planning issues more easily.

The tension between these opposing focuses can also be exciting and stimulating. Most people in workplace environments where there has only been one sex report the advantages of adding employees of the opposite sex to their staff. The shift to empathy building when women are added to men's teams or to a greater task focus when men are added to women's teams are frequently reported benefits.

*Most people report the advantages of adding employees of the opposite sex to the staff.*

If one person is expressing more of one approach, the other person is likely to express more of the opposite approach to create a balance. If one person is very emotional, the other is likely to react by becoming more practical, demonstrating more of an actions-and-objects focus, even if this wouldn't be their preferred response when with other people. This movement from one value to the other is a fluid dance. Inability to shift is rigidity.

As we are propelled into new situations, our interests and values change. If feeling focusers reach upper management, their focus in the actions-and-objects field may well increase because this is what the job demands. Actions-and-objects focusers who find themselves in a human resources management role will need to shift their perspective towards a greater feeling focus if they are to carry out their duties effectively.

Any measure that shows women in general are better at some skills and men are better at others is merely a measure of where their focus of energies and interests are at that point in time. Neither the individual nor the organisation is set in stone. No organisation today can afford not to be adaptable to change. It is likely that an organisation will be far more adaptable if it has in place processes that enable management to:

*Neither the individual nor the organisation is set in stone.*

▶ recognise the differences in focus of individual staff members;

▶ facilitate an environment that acknowledges the good intentions of conflicting members of the team; and

▶ consciously apply techniques designed to resolve conflict creatively and productively.

# SUMMARY

*CHARACTERISTICS*

| FEELING FOCUSERS | ACTIONS-AND-OBJECTS FOCUSERS |
|---|---|
| Believe that feelings, and sometimes intuition or creativity, are what really matter | Are happiest when they are doing something |
| Closely observe their emotions, creativity and intuition throughout the day | Focus on the external world, or the world of ideas |
| Are relatively willing to disclose vulnerable feelings | Resist the expression of vulnerable emotions |
| Believe workplace climates and processes should support employees | Focus almost exclusively on tasks and output when in the workplace |
| Believe discussion of feeling cements a team | Build rapport through the exchange of concrete information and conversations about activities and objects |
| Use emotions as a guide to action | Use logical thought to plan action |
| Tolerate ambiguity and uncertainty relatively well | Are often willing to take risks |
| See life as fundamentally an inner journey | Believe life is about mastery of objective facts and circumstances through action |
| Try to extract emotional meanings from their experiences | Aim for competence and want others to trust and respect their abilities |

*GOOD INTENTIONS*

| FEELING FOCUSERS | ACTIONS-AND-OBJECTS FOCUSERS |
|---|---|
| Considering other people's feelings | Getting the job done |
| Supporting someone through a difficult time | Moving forward quickly |
| Responding to anxiety, concern or injustice | Solving problems, taking responsibility |
| Communicating what really matters to them | Dealing objectively with difficult situations |
| Building rapport | Making conversation on non-emotional, non-threatening topics |
| Working through emotions in order to move forward | Avoiding being overwhelmed by emotions |

*BODY LANGUAGE*

| FEELING FOCUSERS | ACTIONS-AND-OBJECTS FOCUSERS |
|---|---|
| Read facial expressions, tone of voice and body movements closely to interpret others' feelings. | Are less aware of facial expressions, tone of voice and body movements. |

*ATTENTION*

| FEELING FOCUSERS | ACTIONS-AND-OBJECTS FOCUSERS |
|---|---|
| Diffused, broad, expands under stress | Spotlight, sharply focused, contracts under stress |

| MAPPING | |
| --- | --- |
| Feeling focusers' common needs | Actions-and-objects focusers' common needs |
| Their emotions understood and acknowledged | Information on facts and plans |
| Intrinsic job rewards | Extrinsic job rewards |
| Work they feel is worthwhile or helpful | Clear goals |
| Acknowledgment for effort | Freedom to achieve |
| Connection with others while working | Trust |
| Harmony | Efficiency |
| Compatibility with colleagues | Appreciation and acceptance |

'Why' questions will often draw out needs and values. 'What's making you anxious?' may specifically draw out concerns.

### Drawing and using your map
▶ Define the problem area.
▶ Name the parties.
▶ List the needs, concerns and, if appropriate, values for each party.
▶ Then design new options together.

# 10 FEELING FOCUS: stumbling blocks & stepping stones

---

**PREVIEW**

*STUMBLING BLOCK*

1 ▶ Extreme emotional reactions

2 ▶ Difficulty confronting others

3 ▶ Focus too open

4 ▶ Low resilience to other people's bad moods

5 ▶ Stuck in resentment

---

Psychologist Daniel Goleman, author of *Emotional Intelligence*, defines emotional intelligence as:

> ... abilities such as being able to motivate oneself and persist in the face of frustrations; to control impulse and delay gratification; to regulate one's moods and keep distress from swamping the ability to think; to empathise and to hope.[129]

We all need an intelligent balance between head and heart. Men and women are likely to follow different paths towards that balance. Masculine culture with its emphasis on actions and objects is likely to steer men away from their feeling life. To develop their emotional intelligence, many men first need to get in touch with their feelings and then to apply skills in handling them. Feminine culture can saturate women in feeling, but may not necessarily show them how to handle strong emotions effectively. They may need to develop greater objectivity about their feeling life in order to balance it with the rest of their activities. Both men and women need aware contact with feeling and enough distance to direct its development and control its use.

This chapter deals with common problems that can arise when feeling takes priority over workplace activity. These stumbling blocks can be relevant to either sex. Generally, they're the problems of those who are already highly alert to their feeling life, usually women. However, people whose workplace focus is usually on actions and objects may also encounter these stumbling blocks if, for instance, they find themselves overwhelmed by conflict.

# STUMBLING BLOCK 1:
# EXTREME EMOTIONAL REACTIONS

## Expressing strong feelings

'Oh, oh, here we go. It's that time of the month.'

Often women are accused of having pre-menstrual tension (PMT) whenever they get upset about anything. This can seem very unfair. One woman I interviewed defended strongly her right to her feelings.

> I can't just hide strong feelings and concentrate on my work when I'm bubbling away inside. I go crazy if I try. Thank goodness, we don't have to hide our feelings and emotions these days. We can talk about them. We can deal with them. There's nothing wrong with being upset. Everyone has emotions. You get upset, you air it and it's gone.

Daniel Goleman would largely agree. He says:

> Our deepest feelings, our passions and longings, are essential guides, and ... our species owes much of its existence to their power in human affairs.[130]

### STEPPING STONES
Women who affirm the right to express their strong feelings in the workplace will undoubtedly irritate 'old school' men, who respect emotional restraint. What you do about that is up to you, the situation and how badly you want promotion or the job. In many masculine-dominated workplaces, free expression of emotions does not come without cost.

Jeanette really does have a PMT issue, but she handles it well:

> I have learnt to recognise the start of my PMT by the sudden feeling of impatience and a change in my tone of voice. Ever since I figured that out, I've been very careful not to dump on other people at those times.

While no workplace can ever be a mood-free zone, we are expected to minimise the impact of our moods and reactions on other people. We must acknowledge and take responsibility for them. They are not someone else's fault.

## Crying

**'I just want to get through this without bursting into tears.'**

There are hormonal reasons why women cry more easily than men. When things are going wrong, many women become tearful. They may even cry at times when they're very angry.

Men can overreact when a woman cries. Things usually have to be desperate for their own crying impulse to be triggered. Therefore, they may feel very guilty that they've provoked tears in someone else, or they may feel manipulated. In either case, the crying issue may overshadow the original problem. Jill told me:

> I try not to be emotional at work, but I've been caught out. I had some very strong feelings on an issue that I was trying to convey to a branch manager, and I actually started to cry. Nevertheless, I thought I made my point fairly clearly. Later, he said, 'I'm sorry I made you cry this afternoon', but he hadn't heard my argument at all.

Some men are very disdainful of women who cry at work. A number of women reported the issue as significant. Here are two such reports.

> I cried in front of my supervisor during a very distressing confrontation with a colleague. Later my supervisor labelled me as 'over-emotional' in my performance review. To get a label like that for a one-off event seems grossly unfair.

> If I get sufficiently angry about not being listened to, I get tearful. Yet I know this is the worst technique. If I wasn't being listened to before I started crying, then certainly I'm completely dismissed afterwards.

*STEPPING STONES*

It may be wise for a woman to do her best to control tears in workplace conflicts with men. Sometimes making an assertive statement can keep tears at bay. Talking her way through the problem, even though it's difficult, generally brings the best long-term outcome. If she feels her control slipping, she might do best to postpone the discussion with some reasonable excuse and try for a dignified exit. Then quickly disappear to the nearest ladies room!

*For overwhelmed feeling focusers:* Help them name exactly how they feel.

HELPING A FEELING FOCUSER WHO'S OVERWHELMED: To return to equilibrium, feeling focusers may need to explore their emotion. However, if the circumstances are public, a business meeting for example, they'll probably be far too embarrassed and prefer to have attention taken away from them, rather than drawn towards them.

If privacy permits, you might invite them to explore how they feel with an opener such as: 'You look as though you're really upset.' Help them name exactly how they feel. In the process of talking it all out, they'll often find their own solutions.

*For overwhelmed actions-and-objects focusers:* Shift their focus back to a plan of action.

HELPING AN ACTIONS–AND–OBJECTS FOCUSER WHO'S OVERWHELMED: Being caught up in strong feelings can immobilise actions focusers. Actions focused men are less likely to sob and more likely to show extreme distress by physical agitation or a reddening of the eyes, with much looking up to the ceiling—a technique which seems to block the crying impulse. However, the strongest actions focused woman has been known to break down in tears in extreme circumstances, much to the surprise of colleagues who thought they knew her well. Strong feelings plunge actions focusers into alien territory. While it's important to acknowledge what they are feeling, the workplace may not be the right place for further processing. Often the actions person is best supported by gradually shifting their focus away from feelings and back to a plan of action. Ask questions such as, 'What alternatives do you see?', or 'How might that work out?', to lead them back into their area of greater strength and comfort.

## Deeply offended by criticism

### 'How could you criticise me like that?'

Criticism hurts. Both men and women suffer when criticised, but those more in touch with their feelings may be seriously rocked. Actions-and-objects focusers are more likely to fend off criticism by lashing out at the criticiser. Feeling focusers, on the other hand, will mull over the painful words and become stuck in mental rehearsals of defences that they may never deliver. Rosina's reaction to Alan's criticism is a good example:

> Rosina ran a computer systems consultancy, drawing from her pool of consultants when she was able to offer them work. A new client, Ace Hardware, needed a warehousing and point-of-sale system. Rosina had taken Alan along to the initial meeting, intending to put him in charge of the project.
>
> At the meeting Ace widened their brief, necessitating extensive adaptations to standard programs and staff training. As Alan was already too busy for the year to manage all these aspects, Rosina put another consultant in charge, allotting Alan a smaller but significant role. Alan confronted Rosina about it:
>
> 'I'm really irritated you didn't put me in charge of Ace, Rosina. I went with you to that meeting. Without me there you wouldn't have got half as much work from them. It's not like you pay me to do that, you know.'
>
> Rosina was distraught. She always tried so hard to be fair to her consultants. No one, herself included, was ever paid for initial client meetings. Alan knew that. It wasn't her fault he didn't have the time for a major role in this contract. How could he criticise her!
>
> Rosina was too overwhelmed with Alan's criticism to reply. She let the matter slide, nursed her hurt and resentment, tried even harder to be perfect and quietly vowed she'd never take Alan to another initial meeting.

*STEPPING STONES*

A robust conflict, with open exploration of the issues involved, might have served Rosina and Alan better. Alternatively, had Rosina openly postponed discussion, both she and Alan may have found it easier to reopen the subject in the right situation.

**IF ROSINA WERE TO INITIATE FURTHER DISCUSSION:** Though revisiting a conflict can be nerve-racking, Rosina could still acknowledge Alan's irritation well after the event. She needs more information to see the issue through to a better conclusion. However, she'd have to keep the challenge out of her tone of voice and perhaps start with less sensitive topics first. She could find out:

▶ if Alan was in fact implying that Rosina had been unfair, or whether he was simply indicating that he was disappointed;

▶ if he wanted some financial compensation for having attended the initial interview and improving the contract.

A mapping process could help: formally with pen and paper, or informally through detailed discussion of each other's needs and concerns.[131] It is possible for them to reach some good solutions together. See **Figure 46: Coping with criticism** (page 251) for other techniques they could use. Rosina must make sure her own needs are met. In particular, she must ensure that the project is fully and effectively supervised. A conclusion to their discussion that doesn't achieve this will not suit her at all.

**IF ALAN WERE TO INITIATE FURTHER DISCUSSION:** Alan may not realise the damage his outburst caused. However, if he's astute, he'll find some excuse to telephone Rosina and drop an apology into the conversation. He need only apologise for those aspects of the problem he didn't handle as well as he could have. Most feeling focusers deeply appreciate the other person clearing the air and don't expect them to grovel. Alan will have to guard against going back into attack mode once the topic reopens.

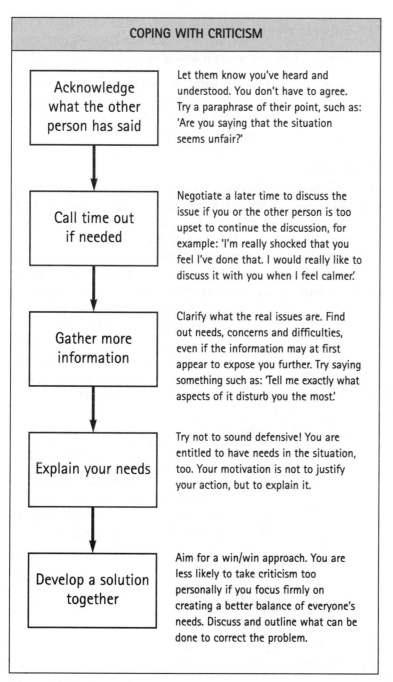

**COPING WITH CRITICISM**

**Acknowledge what the other person has said**

Let them know you've heard and understood. You don't have to agree. Try a paraphrase of their point, such as: 'Are you saying that the situation seems unfair?'

**Call time out if needed**

Negotiate a later time to discuss the issue if you or the other person is too upset to continue the discussion, for example: 'I'm really shocked that you feel I've done that. I would really like to discuss it with you when I feel calmer.'

**Gather more information**

Clarify what the real issues are. Find out needs, concerns and difficulties, even if the information may at first appear to expose you further. Try saying something such as: 'Tell me exactly what aspects of it disturb you the most.'

**Explain your needs**

Try not to sound defensive! You are entitled to have needs in the situation, too. Your motivation is not to justify your action, but to explain it.

**Develop a solution together**

Aim for a win/win approach. You are less likely to take criticism too personally if you focus firmly on creating a better balance of everyone's needs. Discuss and outline what can be done to correct the problem.

*Figure 46: Coping with criticism*

### Self-inflicted emotional injuries

**'I'm hopeless. Trust me to get it wrong again.'**

If a moderate piece of criticism devastates you, you may be responding to your internal 'critical parent' — that inner voice that's always telling you what you did wrong, how bad or hopeless you are, how weak or how slovenly.

*STEPPING STONES*

*It's not what comes into your mind that's important, it's what you do with it once it arrives.*

Most self-punishing thoughts are unhelpful. You will strengthen your emotional intelligence if you take charge of your carping thoughts. Remember, it's not what comes into your mind that's important, it's what you do with it once it arrives.

One technique I use successfully is an imaginary 'cancel' stamp. Whenever a negative thought arises that is totally unhelpful for getting on with my life, in my mind's eye I stamp 'cancel' in bright red across the thought.

Sometimes, to avoid hearing the over-critical voice within, people blame the person who criticised them. Their snappy reaction may invite even harsher words to drive the point home. The only way we grow and improve is to remain open to feedback and, when appropriate, correct what we can correct. If we short-circuit this process, we may doom ourselves to being second-rate employees and managers.

# STUMBLING BLOCK 2: DIFFICULTY CONFRONTING OTHERS

## Kindliness exploited

'I just can't tell them what they're doing wrong. But it's driving me mad.'

Feeling focusers are prone to paint a surface veneer of agreement over discord, keeping their true feelings on the matter hidden and thus undealt with. Olly has this problem. He is a kind, sensitive man — definitely a feeling focuser. He reports:

> I work in an advertising agency and daily deadlines must be met. Jack, my colleague and friend, finds it impossible to complete tasks in the order of priority set by management. He often asks me to help him meet his deadlines, yet he's not really overworked. I always say 'yes', but then my own work suffers. I know he could fix this problem with better time management.

*STEPPING STONES*

Sometimes the kindest thing you can do for another person is to give them considered and appropriate criticism. It's the information and support they will need to succeed. If you're too gentle with some people, they'll exploit you. They know they only have to hint at hurt or anger and you'll back down. Retain your concern but don't let yourself be manipulated.

*Retain your concern for others, but don't let yourself be manipulated.*

If the other person switches to an attack on you, you will have to be quite firm to bring the conversation back on target. For example: 'Right now, we need to look at how you are going to get these reports in on time, not on my managerial style/what I did last month/last week/what I didn't do yesterday.' You will have to be quite skilful at times in recovering your ground. Bear in mind that just because the other person chooses to throw at you real or imagined faults you have, you need not play the same game in retaliation.

If you get a defensive response to a legitimate criticism, sometimes it's best just to make your point and not worry that they seem to be ignoring it. Don't necessarily demand an admission or an apology. Often you'll see you've made a difference by their future actions.

## Initiating difficult conversations

### 'Do I leave it alone? Or do I go into battle?'

Deciding whether or not to confront someone about a difficult issue is a dilemma many feeling focused people will face. Their strong preference is to avoid confrontation. Once they're in the grip of strong emotions, their decision about whether or not to confront someone and how best to do it may not be very rational.

> Sonja, a very effective salesperson in her early fifties, worked for a city real estate agency. On their books was a building nearing completion that would be sold as strata office units. Sonja had briefed herself thoroughly on the project and knew she could sell off the plan effectively. When an insurance company responded to the agency's advertisement, she asked to be assigned to this new client. However, the agency head, a man, insisted that a younger, very attractive salesperson be sent out to see the client. Sonja was furious, as she knew the younger woman didn't know nearly as much as she did about the project.

Should she or shouldn't she confront the agency head? Should Morris confront the partners in the large law firm where he works?

> Morris, a lawyer, had been with the firm for eight years. His next career step was to become a partner. Sally, also a lawyer, had been in the same firm for five years. Morris had often given her a helping hand, reminding her of relevant precedents, sometimes tightening up some sloppy clauses she'd let through in contracts. A vacancy arose for a partner. Sally was offered the partnership. Morris believed that she had been nominated in order to demonstrate affirmative action and the advancement of women in the organisation. He felt victimised, demoralised and unfairly treated.

Whether or not to confront can become a serious dilemma that requires focused thinking. **Figure 47: Should I confront?** (page 255) and, if relevant, **Figure 48: Should I confront gender discrimination?** (page 256) may clarify the issues.[132]

*STEPPING STONES*

| SHOULD I CONFRONT? |
|---|

| What is a good outcome here? | What is the most positive thing I can expect in this situation? |
|---|---|
| What is the best approach? | Confront?<br>Bypass?<br>Ignore? |
| To confront or not to confront? | Weigh up how important it is to address the issue:<br>1 ► Is behaviour repeated?<br>2 ► Is there an audience?<br>3 ► How much does it bother me? |
| Guidelines for direct approaches | ► Confrontation should come from the desire to re-educate rather than demolish<br>► Try to establish a climate of trust, so that you are seen as trustworthy and worth listening to<br>► Try non-sarcastic humour<br>► Try not to blame the other person for having misinformation<br>► Present sound logical reasons for your preferred alternative<br>► Try working together towards a common goal |

*Figure 47: Should I confront?*

| SHOULD I CONFRONT GENDER DISCRIMINATION? | |
|---|---|
| **What's the cause of the discrimination?** | *Is it:*<br>▶ ignorance?<br>▶ prejudice?<br>▶ a tactic? |
| **If it's ignorance …** | *Consider:*<br>▶ How often do you see this person?<br>▶ Do their opinions affect what you want to achieve? |
| **If it's prejudice …** | *Consider:*<br>▶ What would it take to get them to adopt a win/win approach with you?<br>▶ Are there some allies who'd support you?<br>▶ Can you manoeuvre behind the scenes to re-educate and correct?<br>▶ Should you arrange a substitute person for yourself or request that the other person be replaced? (May be necessary in a major negotiation)<br>▶ How might you create a climate where even smaller discrimination problems, such as gender-biased language, are discouraged?<br>▶ Is it time that you or someone in authority made a statement that prejudice and bigotry will not be tolerated?<br>▶ Should you expose this prejudice to public view?<br>▶ Is it so unacceptable that you must insist on enforcing government legislation or workplace rules? |
| **Guidelines for direct approaches** | *Consider:*<br>▶ ignoring it<br>▶ making a joke<br>▶ pointing out that you've spotted the tactic<br>▶ substituting negotiators |

*Figure 48: Should I confront gender discrimination?*

# STUMBLING BLOCK 3: FOCUS TOO OPEN

## Under stress, an inability to prioritise tasks

### 'Get your priorities right!'

Feeling focusers may be very task-oriented at work, but under stress they can lose their ability to prioritise. They may be desperately trying to respond to everyone's needs.

Their attention *expands* to include all pressing issues at once, leaving them immobilised. By contrast, under stress, actions focusers are more likely to *contract* their attention, narrowing it to concentrate exclusively on the most important issue. This causes its own problems, which we discuss in the next chapter. The feeling focuser's failure under stress to set and stick to priorities is one of the actions focuser's common complaints. One woman described to me how stress affects her:

*Under stress:*
*► feeling focusers'*
*attention expands*
*► actions-and-objects*
*focusers' attention*
*contracts.*

> When I'm stressed and my desk is full of unattended papers, I just can't sort or prioritise them. I have to start with the first paper and work my way down the pile. It may not be an efficient method, but that's what I have to do.

### *STEPPING STONES*

Feeling focusers can be enormously helped by making a list of all pressing issues, so they can see the shape of the whole. Then they need to spend some time prioritising, and delegating where possible. Discussing the various pressures upon them can help, time consuming though it is. When others are sympathetic to their stress, feeling focusers can usually move forward.

## Excessive inclusiveness

### 'If only you'd get to the point!'

Feeling focusers are sometimes excessively inclusive when presenting reports to colleagues. While each detail seems very important to them because it affects relationships and decision-making, actions focusers often prefer to make quicker assessments based on just the main facts. An over-inclusive feeling focuser can really annoy them and make them tune out.

*STEPPING STONES*

Feeling focusers should tailor their report to the person receiving it. Are too many details going to bore or irritate an actions-oriented listener? Sometimes, you will look more efficient if you present the bare facts first. Wait to be asked for the extra information. In more formal presentations, numbering your points often helps actions people follow your line of reasoning.

## Feeling/intuitive reasoning versus logic

### 'Where's your evidence?'

In our stereotyped images of men and women, feminine reasoning is seen as emotional and intuitive, masculine reasoning as logical, deductive and sequential. These differences aren't always gender linked, but the conflict between the two styles can be the source of endless frustration and perplexity. Adherents of each style fail to communicate with each other because they are working on completely different planes.

*STEPPING STONES*

To bridge the gap, intuitive reasoners may be able to explain to logical reasoners more about the patterns and relationships they see. For instance, if discussing whether a proposed organisational change will work, they might talk about the restraining and driving forces affecting the situation. Intuitive reasoners are often very good at picking up on these; in fact this is what their so-called intuition is really based on. When communicating with feeling focusers, logical reasoners need to be aware that logic won't always be relevant when discussing an emotional response.[133]

## Too available for emotional support

### 'There are other things for you to do in this office besides listen to everyone's troubles.'

Feeling focusers regard discussions on the ins and outs of emotion-arousing situations as very important. Their ready accessibility can be abused by an overly dependent staff member. To the actions focuser this tendency often appears to be gross time-wasting. While feeling focusers generally accept that at work,

work comes first, this can be very difficult if a colleague is going through a very distressing period in their personal life. Some feeling focused supervisors will see it as their role to give that person all the support they need.

*STEPPING STONES*
Part of teamwork is carrying each other through the rough spots. Feeling focusers, who are often naturally very nurturing, especially when the other person is extremely vulnerable, need to monitor the time they spend lending emotional support to a colleague.[134]

## Destructive gossip

**'Did you hear what she did the other day?'**

When people won't grapple with an issue directly they'll sometimes substitute confrontation with destructive gossip. Gossip becomes destructive when we talk 'against' others, not just talk 'about' them.[135] When we talk 'against', we are emotively negative rather than objective in our discussion of a problem. Talking 'against' can be a tempting way of expressing anger indirectly.

Another way people misuse gossip is by reporting something negative that a third person has said about the person they are speaking to: 'I just thought you should know what so and so is saying about you.' Often it would be far better if the person didn't know at all and the rumour stopped before it reached their ears.

*STEPPING STONES*
Destructive gossip can poison the atmosphere at work. This doesn't mean that talking 'against' is never appropriate. But perhaps a third distinction is helpful here — talking 'through'. People may indeed need to talk through their difficulties with a third person. Guide such a conversation towards a deeper understanding or a conflict-resolving action. It then becomes a positive step and sometimes a necessary one for de-stressing.

When you're angry with someone, try wherever possible to deal with your anger directly with them. Brushing up on your conflict resolution skills and steering the conversation with a win/win approach will bolster your courage.

*Try to deal with your anger directly with the other person who has aroused it.*

## Confusion between empathy and identification

**'I'm so sorry for you. I feel just awful!'**

> Fiona was shop steward for her assembly line. As union representative, she felt it was her duty to vigorously defend her fellow members in every dispute, large and small, that arose on the shop floor. Unfortunately, it gave her the reputation of being a troublemaker and interfered with her chances of promotion.

The distinction between Fiona's own and other people's needs had become blurred. Feeling focusers feel *with* others, but sometimes too much. Their own emotions mirror the other person's. They have trouble maintaining a caring objectivity. Here feeling focusers fall into a common trap — confusion between empathy and identification.

### STEPPING STONES

Empathy is a conscious process of understanding the other person's feelings while remaining separate, however deeply involved you are.

Identification is merged attachment. If you start feeling as bad or as angry as the other person, you have moved into identification. Too much passion on someone else's behalf can easily backfire. Had Fiona, the shop steward in the example above, identified less with others in difficulty, she may have been able to take a win/win approach and solve problems in a way that enhanced rather than diminished her own career.

# STUMBLING BLOCK 4: LOW RESILIENCE TO OTHER PEOPLE'S BAD MOODS

**'I can't cope with their grumbles.'**

*Open awareness and permeable personal boundaries can leave you vulnerable to other people's moods.*

Is it hard for you to disconnect from other people's bad moods? The feeling focuser's tendency towards open awareness and permeable personal boundaries can leave them vulnerable to every passing storm in another person's emotional world. Often people's mood swings are not really sparked by their own problems, but because they too readily absorb the emotions of those around them.

If feeling focusers ask someone to do something for them and that person grumbles, many will flip straight into resentment. Yet grumbles in the workplace are common occurrences. Actions focusers are liable to grumble on their way to saying yes to a request. Feeling focusers, trapped by their desire to please, will often say yes more readily, but they, too, can become disgruntled later if they should have been saying no all along. We all need to allow some space for other people's grumbles.

Unproductive reactions to other people's grumbles include:

► becoming a *persecutor* by being bitchy or aggressive;

► becoming a *rescuer* by spending excessive time consoling or agreeing with the other person about injustices;

► becoming a *victim* to their mood by reacting to or absorbing their mood.

## STEPPING STONES

When you make requests of actions focusers, you're asking them to change gears, to pull their focus out of one area and place it in another. Ignore these revving-up grumbles as best you can and show your appreciation for the task they ultimately perform. When dealing with feeling focusers, take account of how hard it may be for them to say no to you. Give them some support if they start to grumble. They may have taken on more than they can handle.

Take charge of preventing other people's bad moods from affecting your own. Here are some suggestions as to how:

► *Develop your sense of humour*, even if you have to keep it to yourself. Try to lighten your own mood.

► *Acknowledge the emotions, but deal with the facts.* Summarise what you hear the other person saying and feed it back to them. 'I understand that you are really angry we missed the deadline. It looks like we'll have to pay a fine.'

► *You don't have to stand there and take abuse.* If humour or dealing with the facts isn't working and the other person is becoming more rather than less inflamed, remove yourself from the situation. Use a postponing rather than a dismissing statement to excuse yourself: 'Let's talk about this when we're both calmer.'

*Exercises of the imagination create a pathway into the unconscious.*

The following exercise may improve your ability to withstand other people's emotional upsets. Find a glass jar with a lid. Choose an object to represent the person or the situation that is throwing you into emotional turmoil. A pencil stub or paper clip will do. Make a small ceremony about putting the object in the jar and screwing the lid down firmly. Image that you are keeping the situation or the person contained and energetically separate from you.

Exercises such as this create a pathway into the unconscious. If you visualise something clearly, the subconscious mind acts as though it's true. Some golfers practise an inner game to improve their style, picturing themselves hitting a hole in one. Exercises of the imagination can help us alter the way we relate to other people and events.[136] Create your own personal image of self-protection from any emotional meteorites coming your way.

## STUMBLING BLOCK 5: STUCK IN RESENTMENT

**'It's three months since that incident, but I feel as bad as the day it happened.'**

Actions focusers are often more mercurial than feeling focusers, and are likely to explode at a moment's notice. Usually they'll calm down rapidly — if they've won their point. What they say when they are angry is not necessarily something they even believe when they are calm. The important thing at the time was winning the argument. If a feeling focuser takes offence and doesn't let go of their resentment, they are likely to continue a dispute long past its natural conclusion.

Until people learn to see their emotions through to their conclusion, or at least a move forward, they can rehash the same old negative thoughts for weeks, months or even years. Actions focusers often find it easier to prevent their replayed emotion intruding too much in the workplace, whereas feeling focusers can wallow in negative emotions if they lack skills to move past them.

What keeps people stuck in a negative emotion?

► *Contact:* Sometimes people fail to move forward because their pain gives them the opportunity to talk to someone else about something meaningful. They mistake intimacy for talking about their pain.

► *Emotions still partially unconscious:* Sometimes people get stuck in resentment because they never accurately name what they're feeling. Once an emotion is clearly named, the emotion itself transforms and takes you a step forward in letting go of your distress.

► *Pay-offs:* Sometimes the pay-offs from *having* the problem keep the person stuck. There may be some financial benefit, or an emotional one such as righteousness.

► *Defines who they are:* Sometimes people know themselves by the enemies they have and the injustices that have been done to them. Letting go of their resentments leaves a void.

Of course, we won't always be able to settle disagreements in perfect harmony. *Conflict can be traumatic.* Conflicts are likely to leave feeling focusers harassed and exhausted, and most unlikely to look for friendship where they have just done battle. Thereafter they may become hyper-alert to any attack from that direction.

> Leah was a trainer in a large government department. Her colleague, Vicky, had asked to attend some of the courses she was running for the general public. 'I'd love to see you work and I'm sure I'd get a lot from the course.' Leah was flattered.
>
> It had all seemed very innocent and friendly, until Leah heard some weeks later that Vicky had just put in a request to their boss to teach the very subjects she had watched Leah teach, knowing full well that the organisation did not need two teachers in this area. Leah was outraged. She loathed Vicky's method of underhanded competition. She felt betrayed.

There will always be some people who will break our trust. Leah may not ever wish to resolve her issue with Vicky, but she doesn't deserve to be consumed by her own resentment. Leah needed someone trustworthy with whom she could let off steam.

## STEPPING STONES: DEBRIEFING SKILLS

*Debriefing someone after a skirmish requires good listening skills.*

Sometimes you'll need to debrief after a skirmish. Ideally, you'll find yourself a supportive listener. You'll need someone who validates your feelings without making you wrong or being too much on your side. You need to be able to trust that person to keep your confidences and not to use them against you later.

The feeling focused person can be very dependent on other people's good listening skills to help them wade through their turmoil. Emotional trauma in the workplace is more likely to continue to distress a feeling focuser than someone who is more actions focused. If others can help them label exactly how they are feeling, the energy trapped in the emotion will be released — sometimes with an audible sigh or cleansing tears. An insight or a realisation often follows swiftly.

Managers with a feeling focus often have a head start in developing good debriefing skills for staff conflicts. Dealing with the distress of conflict can become a management and self-management tool. Good debriefing includes both a feeling and an actions-and-objects assessment.

You could lead someone through a debriefing process like the one described in **Figure 49, Debriefing after conflict** (page 265).[137] Of course, you can also use its principles to debrief yourself once you know what you're doing.

## Willingness to resolve

*The key step to moving on from conflict is a willingness to resolve.*

How can you move on from conflict? The key step is a willingness to resolve. It demands a willingness to let go of bad feelings left over from the conflict and to overcome the desire for revenge — even if it is as subtle as withdrawing contact. Of course, with some people you may have to set limits. But you need to be sure your motive is necessary self-protection, not retaliation. Putting willingness to resolve into practice may require you to face a number of your own issues:

### ARE YOU BLAMING OTHERS FOR THE WAY YOU FEEL?
**'How dare he make me feel like this.'**
When you resent or blame others for how you are feeling, you perpetuate the problem, because you have placed control outside yourself. *They* have to do something for you to feel better. When

| DEBRIEFING AFTER CONFLICT | |
|---|---|
| **What do you now see were your needs in this situation?** | ▶ What were your motivations?<br>▶ Are there some other ways you could ensure your needs are met more frequently or in the long term? |
| **What do you understand their needs to be?** | ▶ What were the other person's or people's motivations?<br>▶ Are there some legitimate needs that the other person has that you can support? |
| **Can structures, methods or procedures be improved?** | ▶ Did the system work well?<br>▶ Could something be improved or changed to help avoid a similar problem in the future?<br>▶ Consider flow of information, lines of responsibility, better equipment, longer lead times, etc. |
| **What can you learn from this experience?** | ▶ What do you need to have respected by others?<br>▶ What do others need you to respect?<br>▶ Has everyone said everything they need to say?<br>▶ Did you say or do anything that didn't work well?<br>▶ What did you say or do that did work well? |

*Figure 49: Debriefing after conflict*

you don't take responsibility for your own emotions, you're stuck until the other person makes the first move.

*STEPPING STONES*
When you can see yourself as accountable for your own actions and reactions, you can:

▶ reconsider what the other person's motivations may have been and choose a new response;

▶ feel your pain *at the time* and then move on;

▶ dislike the other person's *behaviour* thoroughly, but not embellish the problem with permanent judgments about how awful the *person* is or use revenge to pacify your anger.

### ARE YOU NURSING RESENTMENT TO PROTECT DAMAGED SELF-ESTEEM?
**'I'll never forgive him.'**

When someone's actions or words wound you deeply, you may reclothe your damaged ego with a garment of resentment.[138] You make a negative judgment about the other person and feel better about yourself. While resentment may be a short-term fix, it does little in the long run to build indestructible self-esteem or to rebuild the damaged relationship. The other person usually picks up on your resentment, even when you don't express it openly. They may not know quite why, but they dislike you, and are therefore more likely to do and say more heartless things. One person's resentment can make a very uncomfortable workplace atmosphere for all who come in contact with the troubled relationship.

### STEPPING STONES
If you really intend to support your team by not contributing to workplace tensions, it's not sufficient to just bite your tongue, you need to clean up the mess that's inside you.

### HAS YOUR PERSONAL HISTORY SENSITISED YOU TO CERTAIN ISSUES?
**'He's as uncaring as my brother. He was so cruel to me when we were kids.'**

Willingness to resolve is often blocked by your own personal history. John Welwood, in *Journey of the Heart*, says:

> Old wounds continue to control our behaviour only because we have withdrawn our awareness from them. Since we have essentially gone to sleep in these places, we must first wake up to how our wounds affect us if we want to free ourselves from their grip. We can do this by using the external conflicts they create to develop greater awareness of the internal conflicts we feel around our needs.[139]

*STEPPING STONES*

In the process of resolving workplace issues, a private and intensely personal resolution of old wounds can also occur. Many of us put more hours and more energy into our work than we do into anything else in our lives. We deserve to use the issues we encounter there for our personal growth and release. A present issue that reminds you of past traumas is an opportunity to handle the situation afresh with the skills and strengths you've gathered with the passing years. You will have released yourself from the bondage of the past if you can handle today's problems well.

▼▼▼▼

The feeling focused person achieves self-mastery when they understand their emotions, and accept both the positive and negative aspects of themselves. This doesn't mean *acting* from their negative side, but it does mean *being aware* of it. When reactions such as anger, envy and the desire for revenge are out of awareness, they are out of control.

Soliciting a win/win approach when the other person is in the grip of destructive feelings may require courage and great emotional strength on your part in order to break out of ingrained habits of attack/defend and win/lose thinking. It may also require giving up assumptions about how things are, and how things should be. Transforming negative emotions into win/win approaches to resolution demands that your emotional intelligence is finely tuned, robust and resilient.

# SUMMARY

| FEELING FOCUS: STUMBLING BLOCKS | STEPPING STONES: AN INTELLIGENT BALANCE BETWEEN HEAD AND HEART |
|---|---|
| **1 ▶ Extreme emotional reactions** | |
| *Expressing strong feelings* | Free expression of emotions does not come without a cost. Minimise the impact of your moods and reactions on other people |
| *Crying* | HELPING THE FEELING FOCUSER: If privacy permits, explore the strong emotion. |
| | HELPING THE ACTIONS FOCUSER: Steer them back to a plan of action. |
| *Deeply offended by criticism* | Acknowledge what the other person has said, call time out if needed, gather more information, explain your needs, develop a solution together. |
| *Self-inflicted emotional injuries* | Take charge of carping, self-punishing thoughts, but remain open to feedback, correcting what you are able to correct. |
| **2 ▶ Difficulty confronting others** | |
| *Kindliness exploited* | Considered and appropriate criticism may be the deeper kindness. |
| *Initiating difficult conversations* | Keep the conversation on target. Weigh up: Is the behaviour repeated? Is there an audience? How much does it bother you? |
| **3 ▶ Focus too open** | |
| *Under stress, an inability to prioritise tasks* | Prioritise, plan and delegate where possible. |
| *Excessive inclusiveness* | Present basic facts. Wait to be asked for the extra information. |
| *Feeling/intuitive reasoning versus logic* | Explain the patterns and relationships you see affecting a situation in terms of restraining and driving forces. Remember that logic may not override strong emotions. |
| *Too available for emotional support* | Monitor the time you are spending giving someone emotional support, taking care it doesn't get out of hand. |

| STUMBLING BLOCKS | STEPPING STONES |
|---|---|
| *Destructive gossip*<br><br>*Confusion between empathy and identification* | Head conversations towards understanding and conflict resolution.<br><br>Understand the other person's feelings while remaining separate. |
| **4 ► Low resilience to other people's bad moods** | UNPRODUCTIVE REACTIONS: Avoid becoming a persecutor, rescuer or victim.<br><br>Develop your sense of humour.<br><br>Acknowledge the emotions, but deal with the facts.<br><br>You don't have to stand there and take abuse.<br><br>Create your own personal image of self-protection. |
| **5 ► Stuck in resentment**<br><br>*Willingness to resolve* | WHAT KEEPS YOU STUCK: Contact, emotions still partially unconscious, pay-offs, enemies and injustices defining who you are?<br><br>Are you blaming others for the way you feel?<br><br>Are you nursing resentment to protect your damaged self-esteem?<br><br>Has your personal history sensitised you to certain issues? |

> Transforming negative emotions into win/win approaches to resolution demands that your emotional intelligence is finely tuned, robust and resilient.

# 11 ACTIONS-AND-OBJECTS FOCUS:
## stumbling blocks & stepping stones

> ### PREVIEW
>
> *STUMBLING BLOCK*
>
> 1 ▶ Task at the expense of people
>
> 2 ▶ Poor skills in the domain of feeling
>
> 3 ▶ Contracted awareness under stress
>
> 4 ▶ Snap decisions
>
> 5 ▶ Low tolerance for ambiguity
>
> 6 ▶ Self-esteem achieved from what they do rather than who they are

Researchers often note the feeling–actions split in men's and women's preferences. In reviewing the evidence, Moir and Jessel in *Brainsex* opt for a nature rather than nurture explanation:

> Boys want to explore areas, spaces, and things because their brain bias predisposes them to these aspects of the environment. Girls like to talk and listen because that is what their brains are better designed to do.[140]

In a mixed-sex group, boys' mean scores tend to be higher on tests of spatial ability; girls average out with higher mean scores on sensitivity to emotional stimuli. But there are wide variations in scores and an enormous overlap between the sexes. So we must consider men *and* women when discussing those who place a high priority on actions and objects. Actions focusers face the danger of being consumed by goals and tasks, and, in the process, becoming too angry, too distant, too clever or too busy. These are the stumbling blocks we address in this chapter. Remember, not all actions people will have these problems and certainly not all of the time. They are often, but not exclusively, men's problems, just as the feeling stumbling blocks in the previous chapter are often, but not exclusively, women's problems.

## STUMBLING BLOCK 1:
## TASK AT THE EXPENSE OF PEOPLE

'I can't see how spending money on conflict resolution training will improve productivity.'

Alice Eagly's research found that:

> Men fared consistently better in first-level (low end management) positions which often require technical knowledge. Women held the advantage in middle-level slots, in which communicative skills are especially important. Few studies addressed upper management, where women remain under-represented.[141]

Most organisations prefer to promote to senior executive level their task-oriented people. Many of the most successful women executives are atypical of their sex, preferring task-oriented roles. When the choice seems to be between broader concerns and task-oriented goals, those who do stand up in the boardroom for issues such as staff development and ecological concerns are often outvoted. When considering major decisions, actions focusers often view the issues as solely task related. As a consequence, the organisation is often short-changed.

### STEPPING STONES
The ability to outvote others places a responsibility on the majority to listen carefully to minority voices. Actions focusers need to recognise not only the strengths, but also the weaknesses of their own perspectives if they are to be effective decision-makers. Smart actions focusers will therefore see that one of their decision-making tasks is to respond with serious consideration when wider community and ecological concerns are raised. Don't shoot the messenger just because you don't like the message!

*Don't shoot the messenger just because you don't like the message.*

## Goal at the expense of process

'At least you could ask me how my holiday was before we get started.'

Actions focusers are goal-oriented. They want to know: *What needs to be done?* Feeling focusers are more oriented to the process — in particular, the human interactions involved in achieving a goal. They want to know: *Is everything alright?* Both focuses provide useful watchdog services, though they may not want to hear each other's news.

Mandy's manager had a very low focus on process. Their conversation went like this:

*Mandy:* I want some more time with you to discuss what I'm doing. I don't feel I'm getting enough support for the projects you've set me.
*Mandy's manager:* I give you lots of time. What do you mean?

Frustrated, Mandy decided that, over the next month, she would carefully document how much time her manager actually gave her to discuss the projects he had assigned her. She recorded a total of thirty minutes. At the end of the month, she politely confronted him with her findings. He was surprised the figure was so low. Now he could see she may well need more support than that. In the months that followed, he gave her more discussion time, but she still found she had to ask him for it. Mandy could accept that, so long as he responded positively to such requests.

Mandy found there was an additional benefit in getting this extra time with her manager. He praised her more often, commenting favourably on her good ideas. She felt appreciated now she was getting regular feedback and became more productive.

*The ability to focus on goals is an important key to organisational success, but it can also mean you miss the pleasure of the journey.*

### STEPPING STONES

The ability to focus on goals is an important key to organisational success. But there are moments when a focus on process, particularly if it's going wrong or could go wrong, is more important. Single-mindedness can be a great source of strength, but it may limit the leader's ability to take in diverse opinions.

Focusing only on goals can also mean you miss the pleasure of the journey. Putting some focus onto the human element might add creative buzz and camaraderie—the best antidote to burnout.

# STUMBLING BLOCK 2:
# POOR SKILLS IN THE DOMAIN OF FEELING

Consultant Jutta Townes, in an article entitled 'Training the Emotions', says: 'There is little doubt that emotional competency correlates with productivity.'[142] The obverse is also true. Productivity is affected when people lack skills for processing their emotions effectively.

## Low frustration threshold

**'For goodness sake, don't start telling me off before you hear the whole story.'**

Sometimes people with a strong task orientation have a low tolerance for frustration. Stress lowers our anger threshold, and highly motivated, task-driven people are often stressed. If what they are doing is blocked or threatened, some actions focusers will explode in anger. They may well be unaware of its destructive impact on others, particularly on feeling focusers who can be devastated.[143]

*Stress lowers our anger threshold.*

Men are often better than women at recovering from someone's angry outburst. When they're working together, men are often quick to anger, but they are also quick to cool. In men's subculture, displays of anger can become a rite to establish mutual respect.

While 'quick to anger, quick to cool' and ritual fighting characteristics are common and well within the range of normal behaviour, if you often seem to be on a short fuse, something is seriously the matter.

*STEPPING STONES*
To overcome a low frustration threshold, sometimes a change of attitude is required. Are you setting unrealistic deadlines for yourselves and others? Do you need to accept that others may not have the same capacity or standards as you?

Some understanding of the way our bodies reflect and hold our emotions can also be helpful.[144] We can store unresolved anger in our body as chronic muscle tension. Given even a mildly irritating situation, the body will offload some of its excess, often on an innocent bystander. It's not okay to kick the cat, take your aggression out on the road or yell at your spouse or children. Regulate your body tension by going for a run, enthusiastic housework, punching a pillow or a workout at the gym instead. Consciously releasing the tension of a hard day in safe, appropriate ways can become a valuable self-management tool to reduce inappropriate explosions. **Figure 50: Controlling explosions** (below), offers some guidelines for handling anger with consciousness and competence.

Avoiding inappropriate explosions doesn't mean that you'll say nothing. But before you confront someone, ask yourself the following questions:

▶ Why am I angry?

▶ What do I want to change?

▶ What do I need in order to let go of my anger?[145]

| CONTROLLING EXPLOSIONS | |
|---|---|
| Stop and take stock | Notice the body sensations you experience as your anger starts to rise, e.g. muscle tension, body heat, heart pounding. Get to know your own triggers and when to be particularly vigilant. |
| Choose not to explode | There is a moment before you explode when you actually have a choice about whether to let it blow completely or to control your response. The old technique of taking three deep breaths really works. |
| What do you want to be different? | Consider what is it that you want to be different, and how you will best achieve it. |
| Use an 'I' statement | If you do explode, make it a personal rule to yell 'I' statements, not insults. They're less likely to cause lasting harm and they sound a lot better to eavesdroppers. You might use the 'I' statement structure:<br><br>'When you ... I feel (or feel like doing) ... And what I'd like is that I ...'[146] |
| Release body tension elsewhere | If expressing your anger is inappropriate, release pent-up energy later with physical activity. |

*Figure 50: Controlling explosions*

At moments of impasse, your commitment to resolution may have to be strong enough for two — yourself and the other person.

## Unexamined anger

**'I'm not the one who's screwed up — you are.'**

Actions focusers tend to place most of their attention 'out there' in the world and often fail to consider what inner motivations may be feeding their angry reaction to an external problem.

Anger that is partly motivated by internal causes can affect anyone, but particularly those whose personal world of feeling remains unexamined. Internal issues do have their uses. They can direct our focus and become the fuel for a sustained campaign for positive change. Many feminists who have won significant rights for women have used internal anger to sustain their long battle. The external problem was manifest inequality. But undoubtedly some also had internal issues — a personal history of physical or emotional abuse that maintained their rage at injustice, for instance. Unionists working for respectable pay and conditions or activists fighting for the rights of suppressed minorities may also be fuelled by both externally and internally driven anger. The mix is volatile, but harnessed to something worthwhile, it can push a team, organisation or a whole society to greater achievement and equity.

*While internal issues can fuel a sustained campaign for positive change, they can make the person very abrasive to work with.*

Often, however, someone with sustained, unexamined anger will be too abrasive for other people to enjoy working with them — they are too volatile and quick to blame other people or events.

### STEPPING STONES

To handle your anger with emotional intelligence and to use it wisely, you need to have some understanding of its underlying as well as surface causes. Here are the three most common categories of anger motivated by internal issues:

► *A response to suppressed needs.* For example, you don't recognise your need for support, so you become very irritated when you don't get it.

► *A response to unresolved personal history.* For example, a client's belligerent style triggers childhood memories of powerless rage at a drunken parent.

▶ *A response to unacceptable qualities in yourself that inflame you when you see it in others.* For example, demanding perfection of yourself in your own work, you are highly irritated when someone's standards of work are lower than your own.[147]

When you acknowledge what's really going on for you, the internal issue loosens its grip. You can then separate the internal from the external, and keep your response to the external event in proportion.

## Payback for being rejected sexually

### 'Turn down my advances and I'll see you suffer!'

While anger often serves a very worthwhile purpose, there's no doubt it can be misplaced. Many people find themselves out of their depth in deeply emotional conflicts with sexual overtones. Where sexual involvement has been invited by one person and rejected by the other, a particularly vicious vendetta can follow, if they refuse to feel their pain or disappointment and externalise it as anger and blame. Commonly, it is men who make overtures to women and then give the woman a hard time if she rejects them. But it is not always that way. One of my male correspondents reported:

> A lady behaved in a way that embarrassed me because I did not respond to her wanting a relationship with me. She went on to develop an extreme hatred towards me.

A woman manager told me her story of how sexual anger had undermined her ability to manage one part of her organisation:

> While in fact I was in charge of Jim, in the lab he was king. I couldn't say 'Do it!' because, as the expert, he had a right to refuse. It was very much a matter of us negotiating. To begin with, we'd worked well together. We were very good friends with a good male/female dynamic going. We never dated, it was just a dynamic. Subsequently, I became very friendly with another member of the team and I guess Jim sensed my withdrawal. He began blocking my plans at every turn. I couldn't negotiate with him anymore. If I asked for something from the lab that

was out of the ordinary, he'd work out a good reason for saying no. Our conflict slowed down the progress of a whole lot of areas in the organisation that were dependent on his lab's output.

Some men can only relate to women through a sexual dynamic, even in the workplace. Some women will enjoy the game, while being clear that they don't intend to allow the relationship to go further. Many, however, will feel extremely threatened by it. Reasons for this may include:

▶ they may not be sure enough of their own assertive abilities to keep the other person in check;

▶ flirtatious conversations may make them feel they are being disloyal to their partners;

▶ they may not be comfortable enough with their own sexuality to engage it in any workplace transaction.

If the woman refuses to flirt, this type of man has no cooperative way of relating to her. If she's lucky, he might ignore her completely, but often his whole relationship with her is coloured with intense dislike and competition.

*If the woman refuses to flirt, some men have no cooperative way of relating to her.*

*STEPPING STONES*
Inability to divorce a working relationship from a sexual one is immature. Using the frustration of a failed conquest as a reason for directing a sustained attack on another person in the workplace is abusive. It is unacceptable workplace behaviour that ultimately tends to rebound on the perpetrator; for example, with a well placed payback, dismissal, or a charge of harassment.

Sexual conquests are no way to build an ego. Address your own job competencies, making a real effort to improve your skills. In doing so, many inappropriate grudges will fall away.

## Failure to recognise and deal with fear

'Scared? Don't be ridiculous. I'm a man!'

Actions focusers, both men and women, are likely to be strongly influenced by prevailing masculine norms. They are moulded by that subculture to conceal vulnerable feelings. In a downturned economy, probably the deepest fear is losing your job. In one organisation, the employees' fear of losing their jobs and their inability to discuss it was so extreme that they would avoid the routes that took them past the desk of six people recently issued with redundancy notices. Other workplace fears of the actions focuser may include:

► being overwhelmed;

► losing control;

► financial loss;

► threatened self-esteem;

► having to accept guilt;

► facing their own incompetence;

► other people's incompetence reflecting on them;

► dealing with conflicting loyalties; for example, to work and to family.

### STEPPING STONES

*Actions focusers often disguise fear by becoming obsessive about organisation and control.*

Actions focusers frequently disguise fear by becoming obsessive about organisation and control. They will often project anger when fear is the real issue, as anger is exempt from the masculine embargo on feelings.

As these substitutions are rarely a conscious process, the actions person may find it particularly difficult to examine their own fears successfully. Many feeling focusers complain: 'If only they'd talk about what's the matter!' Sometimes, with absolute privacy and trust, actions focusers can discuss their deeper issues and be greatly helped by the process. But frequently the workplace can't offer the safe space that's needed. Help may have to be offered indirectly. For example, counselling for retrenched employees may indirectly lower the fear of remaining staff.

Fear and anger are the two sides of one coin. If you only look at one side, you don't know yourself fully. If your usual response is anger, ask yourself: 'What am I also scared about?' If, on the other hand, your usual response is fear, ask yourself: 'What should I be angry about in this situation?' When you acknowledge both your fear and your anger, you can consciously address your real needs for support, security and self-esteem that is not based on an inflated self-image or the need to be perfect.

## Insensitivity to other people's feelings

'All that feelings stuff is garbage.'

A logical reasoning style is by far the most effective in the realm of actions and objects. Its sequential method handles cause-and-effect chains. It tends to switch people off from feeling, so they can get on with the job. When logic and reasoning are over-applied, however, the downside is emotional remoteness or a cold rationality. Actions focusers can keep themselves so involved in the external world and its demands for a reasoned approach that they never really tune into other people's feelings. They have little concept of what's really happening internally for another person, and may indeed be equally switched off to their own inner feelings.

> Ed was discussing a personal problem with a work colleague, Margaret. Her sister was very ill with cancer. It had always been hard for Ed to show compassion for anyone other than his immediate family. Talking with Margaret about her sister's illness, Ed blurted out: 'Well, you know she's going to die, don't you?'
>
> Margaret was incensed. 'That's the last thing I want to hear. How can you be so insensitive?' Ed's immediate reaction was to defend himself and justify his comment. Suddenly he saw very clearly that he was about to justify the indefensible. Instead, he said: 'I'm sorry. I just didn't think how a comment like that was going to hurt you.'
>
> Reflecting on the incident, Ed recognised that he often became righteous when caught out for being insensitive. He began to look at the ways he disconnected from his compassion and why he needed to do this. 'You know,' he said to me, when discussing the incident, 'the truth of the matter is that I feel *too much*, not too little. But letting myself really acknowledge that flies in the face of everything I learnt about how to be strong and manly. I was telling her the sort of thing I have to tell myself in order to stay tough and together.

Masculine subculture with its demand for silence about feelings perpetuates the perception that men are insensitive. In fact, many men are far more alert to what's going on for the other person

*Many men are not equipped to talk about deeper emotions.*

than they're given credit for. They *understand* well enough, but they're just not equipped to *talk* about deeper emotions. A worker on an emergency response and rescue team reported:

> I know that young guys coming through would like to discuss some of the emotional difficulties of the job. We know what they're going through when they can't save someone. It really throws you. But we don't say much because the whole culture of the team is that you don't ever talk about anything personal or emotional.

### STEPPING STONES

*The key strategy in the realm of feeling is to acknowledge and validate how the person feels.*

The key strategy in the realm of feeling is to acknowledge and validate how the person feels. This is the essence of being a good listener. It's one of the most useful skills that managers, in particular, would do well to develop. A willingness to listen can break down the rigidity of traditional hierarchical structures. When you are willing to *truly* listen, you'll see people as *people* rather than *positions*. Good listening skills get managers the right information and help develop the loyalty and trust needed for effective teamwork.

Many men are in a process of examining the way their culture disconnects them from deeper feeling. It has alienated men from their partners and fathers from their children. With no outlets for talking with their male friends who would understand their experience best, men are more likely than women to severely abuse drink and drugs. But the gentle revolution is under way for men, too. Their straightjacket of emotional restraint is slowly peeling off.

## Solution focused when the other person just wants to be heard

'What you should do is ...' 'Yes, but ...'

I caught the following complaint on my tape recorder:

> I often find when I am talking with a particular male colleague at work that we are talking at cross-purposes. If, for instance, I've got some anxieties, he sounds to me like he's putting me down. In fact, what he's doing is trying to allay my fears. But there's no need. I'm quite

comfortable both with my fears and with expressing them. The problem is that *he's* not comfortable with me feeling that way. He seems to think that I've only spoken to him about them because I want him to fix them up.

Most people prefer to find their own solutions to problems. Actions focusers often won't talk about a problem until they've run out of ideas. So they believe that if another person is *talking* about a problem, then they must want advice now. However, feeling focusers often use talk to *clarify* their process well before they've exhausted their options.

*STEPPING STONES*
Advice such as, 'There's no need to be upset' or 'Don't be silly' can alienate feeling focusers. They feel that their problems are being dismissed as inconsequential. Though it's very tempting for any actions person to offer advice, your solutions may be rejected with 'yes, but ...' — a very annoying sentence construction to the practical actions focused person!

If someone is using you as a sounding board, don't try to hurry their conversation along too quickly. Remember, listening alone may be the best support you can offer.[148] There is a place for your input, but it's usually further down the track and is best phrased as extra information rather than instructions. For example: 'You know what I saw someone do in similar circumstances ...', or 'I've tried ... and it's worked', or 'One possibility you might want to explore is ...'. You leave the power to take up your suggestion or not with the person. People learn far more when they work with solutions they have chosen.

*Phrase input as extra information rather than instructions.*

# STUMBLING BLOCK 3:
# CONTRACTED AWARENESS UNDER STRESS

**'What do I have to do to get your attention?'**

Under stress, actions focusers are likely to *contract* their attention, excluding everything but their most important task. At such times they'll be particularly annoyed by interruptions and even if they

*Under stress, actions focusers are likely to contract their attention.*

appear to be listening, it's likely you don't really have their attention.

Despite the fact that they hate interruptions themselves, many men will barge into someone's work space demanding this or that because they need it *right now*, without even considering what problems they may be creating for the other person. Many women seem to be particularly unconscious about the problem an interruption can create for someone who is deeply focused on a task. Mostly, women accept interruptions well. Perhaps it goes with the territory of bringing up children!

### STEPPING STONES

FOR ACTIONS FOCUSERS: When your attention is contracted, find a polite way to let people know, and schedule a time to talk when you have completed your task or when you're prepared to lay it aside. For example: 'Would it be okay if I come to see you at four o'clock? I can't give you my full attention at the moment as I'm really caught up in what I'm doing right now.'

FOR WHEN YOU NEED TO INTERRUPT AN ACTIONS FOCUSER: Respect their thinking space. This doesn't mean you should never interrupt, but you might avoid irritating them if you:

- ▶ interrupt respectfully — 'I'm sorry to interrupt …';

- ▶ request permission — 'May I ask you something?';

- ▶ check your timing — 'Does it suit you now to talk about …'.

One woman I interviewed handles her actions focused boss with finesse.

> When my boss is in task mode and under stress, the tone of her voice changes. We frequently liaise over the phone and I listen carefully for clues to her mood so I know where I stand. I always start conversations with a short sentence stating my need and the time required. For example: 'I have two quick questions. Is now okay for you?' Issues of lesser importance are handled via her two in-trays, one of which is reserved for urgent correspondence that she attends to daily.

## STUMBLING BLOCK 4: SNAP DECISIONS

**'How dare you not consult me before going ahead.'**

Colins and Chippendale, in their book *New Wisdom II*, report:

> The majority of men will prefer to make snap decisions and act on them and deal with the consequences later.[149]

Regardless of gender, the person more attuned to actions and objects will prefer quick decisions. In certain situations this may well be the best approach. Sometimes, however, they'll act too quickly — a sharp retort, a cancelled contract, a bridge burnt with an important customer.

*STEPPING STONES*
Actions focusers are less likely to discuss things before they make their move. Sometimes they're concerned they'll look insecure and ineffectual. Yet often it would be wiser for them to at least check with others first. This will not only make for a more informed decision, but it may also bring them greater commitment from colleagues for what they're doing.

# STUMBLING BLOCK 5:
# LOW TOLERANCE FOR AMBIGUITY

**'What do you mean, there's no straightforward answer?'**

Actions focusers can find themselves at the mercy of their logical, analytical side, having to be pragmatic, compelled to know the answers and be right, and to appear to be always in control. It's often particularly hard for them to say, 'I don't know'. Our society often equates knowledge with wisdom, yet sometimes a clear statement of *not knowing* shows the greater wisdom.

Einstein talked of 'living in questions'. Our learning edge is uncertainty. Demanding watertight answers for all questions before attempting a new activity may retard innovation and learning. Many assumptions are best held lightly and consciously when we are in the midst of radical change.

*Logical reasoning processes can hold a false promise of certainty.*

Actions focusers can be left stranded if they rely exclusively on a logical reasoning process with its false promise of certainty. The responsibilities to the members of the workplace mini-community grow increasingly more complex. The nature of work, the percentage of workers to non-workers in the wider community, the number of hours each week deemed ethical to work is in uncomfortable flux.

## STEPPING STONES
Managers will increasingly have to develop a global approach — an awareness of the whole sociological system in which work occurs. Managing complexity often requires the person to be comfortable with this non-linear thinking style. Global thinking can lead us to see a larger purpose for business, one beyond the return of capital. It is equally about quality of life. These new considerations continue to include wages and profits, but could also address fulfilling work, cooperative effort, the provision of a helpful product or service, the development of workers and a community focus.

Human values, respect for macro-economic considerations and environmental concerns are all seamlessly interwoven when we see the world from a broad perspective and respond to the interdependency of each part.

Actions focused managers will sometimes need to incorporate very consciously a more global, less analytical approach, allowing themselves to be more open to intuition and less bound by the necessity of logical deduction. Feeling focused managers tend to be more comfortable with ambiguity and uncertainty, and may find it somewhat easier to be responsive to complex times and the responsibilities of corporate citizenship.

Managing well the highly complex interrelationships of the modern workforce, however ambiguous and 'untidy' they may be, can be as crucial to success as statistics.

*Complex relationships, however untidy, can be as crucial to success as statistics.*

## STUMBLING BLOCK 6:
## SELF-ESTEEM ACHIEVED FROM WHAT
## THEY DO RATHER THAN WHO THEY ARE

'Who am I? $100 000 a year and I work bloody hard for it, too.'

Many actions people build self-esteem exclusively on accomplishment. Pushed to the extreme, 'doing' can become their whole reason for 'being'.[150]

### Workaholism

Workaholism is a form of addiction, leaving people little time for inner reflection and the digestion of experience. Richard Moss, in a workshop teaching authenticity and spiritual maturity, brought me up short in one day. 'Busyness is the narcotic of the mediocre,' he said. As a confirmed twelve hours-a-dayer, his statement felt like a blow to my solar plexus! 'What do you mean?' I asked, hoping my workaholic ways weren't under attack. They were! Action focusers particularly may need to make time for reflection on their life, their feelings and the rich contents of their inner world. Without it, life can become increasingly meaningless.

*Busyness is the narcotic of the mediocre.*

One man who was retrenched from a very senior position confided to a friend after it had happened:

> I don't have to play roles any more. I don't have to pretend that I'm all gung ho and dying to do the next thing, which wasn't really how I felt about the work at all.

Our notions of successful masculinity have led men and the women who copy them into workaholic patterns, blinding them to the injustice of excessively long working hours to prove themselves as individuals and as family providers.

*STEPPING STONES*

To be all that we can be as human beings, we need to protect and nurture all life, including our own. It is only in knowing and accepting our inner selves fully that we can finally give up measuring and proving our self-worth with brittle yardsticks such as accomplishment, status, power, money, intelligence or physical stamina.

When someone's sense of inner worth is secure, they are able to throw themselves into work wholeheartedly to expand the expression of their potential or simply because they love to serve. Actions focusers in this instance may be *workaphiles*, but they will not be *workaholics*. They are not addicted. They see their family, friends, nature, creative arts or spiritual communion as paramount in their list of priorities. Knowing the importance of these things to their inner life, their work achieves its natural balance.

▼▼▼▼

Men are beginning to reclaim their emotional life that has been stolen by their need to conform to outdated masculine stereotypes. They are beginning to tell the truth, even to each other, about their fears, confusions, hopes and grief. They are beginning to see the problems that arise from being too angry, too distant, too clever or too busy.

When we start looking at our emotions in depth, often there are no answers — a huge challenge to the outcome-oriented person. Emotions can be dark and confusing, and seem to be, dare I say it, feminine. Action focusers may need to be vigilant in order to reclaim the whole of who they are: feeling *and* actions focused, internally and externally directed, analytic and global thinking, masculine *and* feminine!

# SUMMARY

| ACTIONS FOCUS:<br>STUMBLING BLOCKS | STEPPING STONES:<br>RETHINK THE WAY CULTURE DISCONNECTS<br>YOU FROM DEEPER FEELING |
|---|---|
| 1 ► Task at the expense of people | Listen to what feeling focusers have to say about people's concerns. |
| *Goal at the expense of process* | Take in diverse opinions. Enjoy the journey. |
| 2 ► Poor skills in the domain of feeling | |
| *Low frustration threshold* | CONTROLLING EXPLOSIONS: Stop and take stock, choose not to explode and ask yourself: ' What do I want to be different? How will I best achieve it?' Become a master of making 'I' statements.<br><br>Consciously release the tension of the day in safe, appropriate ways |
| *Unexamined anger* | CONSIDER INTERNAL CAUSES OF ANGER: Suppressed needs, unresolved personal history, unacceptable qualities in yourself. |
| *Payback for being rejected sexually* | Divorce working relationships from sexual ones. |
| *Failure to recognise and deal with fear* | If angry or too controlling, ask yourself: 'What am I also scared about?' |
| *Insensitivity to other people's feelings* | Acknowledge and validate how the other person feels. |
| *Solution focused when the other person just wants to be heard* | Listening may be the best support you can offer. Phrase input as information rather than instruction. |
| 3 ► Contracted awareness under stress | DON'T PRETEND TO LISTEN: Schedule a time when you'll give the other person's issue your full attention.<br><br>RESPECT ACTIONS FOCUSERS' THINKING SPACE: Interrupt respectfully, request permission, check your timing. |

| STUMBLING BLOCKS | STEPPING STONES |
|---|---|
| 4 ▶ Snap decisions | Consultation does not indicate insecurity. It builds wider commitment. |
| 5 ▶ Low tolerance for ambiguity | Complex issues in modern organisations may not lend themselves to a logical reasoning process or to certainty in decision-making. |
| 6 ▶ Self-esteem achieved from what they do rather than who they are | Allow some time for internal reflection and digestion of experience. Recognise the priority of other self-sustaining aspects of your life. |

> **Reclaim the whole of who you are.**

# PART V
# INTERDEPENDENCE AND AUTONOMY

## EIGHT COMMON CONFLICTS

### Interdependent people's complaints:

▶ 'Why didn't you ask us before you rearranged the office?'

▶ 'You haven't considered how that's going to affect everyone.'

▶ 'A one-hour monthly staff meeting at which we are lectured does nothing to bond us as a team.'

▶ 'Our supervisor won't even talk about flexi-time. He doesn't consider our personal needs at all!'

### Autonomous people's complaints:

▶ 'Committee work is so frustrating!'

▶ 'He's supposed to be the manager of this department. So why doesn't he get on with it?'

▶ 'I want to be my own boss. I'm sick of taking orders.'

▶ 'Why should I have to account to you for how I spend my time. I'm paid for results, not time spent on the job!'

## Synopsis — where are we now?

In Part I, we discussed the gentle revolution as a significant re-evaluation in the workplace, raising the priority of values once regarded as typically feminine. We considered movements in our gender stereotypes and the fact that both men and women may place a high priority on some values that have been traditionally regarded as typical of their opposite sex. In Parts II, III and IV, we considered in detail the pairs of values: equality–status, agreement–competition, feeling–actions-and-objects, and the conflicts and possible solutions when these values oppose each other. In Part V, we'll examine the last of these pairs: interdependence–autonomy.

| PERSPECTIVES | FEMININE STEREOTYPE: | MASCULINE STEREOTYPE: |
|---|---|---|
| Use of power: | Equality | Status |
| Interacting style: | Agreement | Competition |
| Focus of attention: | Feeling | Actions and objects |
| Comfort zone: | Interdependence | Autonomy |

The arrows above indicate the discussion areas for the next three chapters.

In Chapter 12, we focus on understanding and accepting the differences in people's zones of comfort — how close to or independent of others people prefer to be when working with and relating to other people. We examine the effects of this on teamwork styles. In Chapter 13, we consider common stumbling blocks of a highly interdependent style and the stepping stones for solutions to conflicts coloured by these issues. In Chapter 14, we take the same approach for the autonomous style of relating.

A NOTE ON TERMINOLOGY: To broaden discussion and give gender-neutral descriptions of behaviours, I sometimes use the terms 'autonomous players' and 'interdependent players' when referring to people of either sex who place a high priority on that value.

# QUIZ

Circle the number in the column that best reflects your response to the following statements:

## Quiz 1

| | RARELY | SOMETIMES | OFTEN | |
|---|---|---|---|---|
| I'm happy to stop what I'm doing when someone needs my help. | 0 | 1 | 2 | |
| I believe two heads are better than one in coming up with a solution. | 0 | 1 | 2 | |
| I resent being given written instructions without any discussion first. | 0 | 1 | 2 | |
| I am sensitive to group dynamics and often notice underlying tension before others seem to. | 0 | 1 | 2 | |
| I form close bonds with the people I work with. | 0 | 1 | 2 | Total: |
| | | + | = | |

## Quiz 2

| | RARELY | SOMETIMES | OFTEN | |
|---|---|---|---|---|
| I tend to refuse other people's help. | 0 | 1 | 2 | |
| I would choose a job as an independent consultant over working in a large team. | 0 | 1 | 2 | |
| People tell me I am too opinionated and don't take other's ideas into account. | 0 | 1 | 2 | |
| If I feel I'm doing my job well, other people's approval is unimportant. | 0 | 1 | 2 | |
| I avoid volunteering for group activities. | 0 | 1 | 2 | Total: |
| | | + | = | |

Add up your circled numbers for each quiz separately then compare the two scores.

If your score was higher in Quiz 1, you probably focus strongly on *interdependence*. If you scored higher in Quiz 2, you probably put more of a priority on *autonomy*. If your scores were equal, you may swing between the two polarities, depending on the situation.

The next three chapters will tell you more about these qualities.

# 12 INTERDEPENDENCE– AUTONOMY: comfort zone

Although the values of interdependence and autonomy are frequently gender related, obviously this is not always the case. As you read, consider how closely you and those you know fit or diverge from the stereotypes. Knowing there are many exceptions, we often do see that:

▶ women generally place a higher priority on *interdependence* (social relationships, closeness and intimacy);

▶ men generally place a higher priority on *autonomy* (individualism, adventurousness and independence).

## ROOTS OF INTERDEPENDENCE

Susie Orbach and Luise Eichenbaum, in their book *Between Women*, point out that:

> Connectedness, attachment, affiliation, selflessness, have been and still are, to a great extent, the foundations of women's experience. A woman knows herself and gathers a sense of well-being through her connection and attachment to others.[151]

A girl child's first relationship is with her mother, and it is one of merged attachment, which the process of growing to adulthood may do little to tarnish.[152] This relationship can set the pattern for all future relationships. She finds herself and knows herself through her responsiveness and attachment to others. She becomes closely attuned to other people's needs, and meeting those needs may well become the same as meeting her own. Indeed, she may have difficulty distinguishing between the two.

## ROOTS OF AUTONOMY

Susie Orbach and Luise Eichenbaum say:

> Women live in a network of relationships and know themselves through these relationships. Men, on the other hand, know themselves in the *difference* — i.e. in the way they distinguish themselves from others.[153]

*Women know themselves through their network of relationships.*

A boy child must separate emotionally from his mother in order to establish his manhood. As he moves into puberty, a mother is likely to touch, hold and cuddle her son less than she might a daughter. This supports his movement towards independence. He is likely to continue the process of learning to stand on his own by emphasising adventurousness, independence and a focus on self as distinct from family.

Nancy Chodorow, in *Feminism and Psychoanalytic Theory*, says:

> A son's male core gender identity develops away from his mother. The male's self, as a result, becomes based on a more fixed 'me'–'not me' distinction ... By contrast, the female's self is less separate.[154]

Boys' growing focus on autonomy may be tempered by their experience of team sports, which teaches them to harness individual effort to a common goal.

*Boys' growing focus on autonomy may be tempered by their experience of team sports.*

In their teenage years, both boys and girls usually push towards independence. Boys generally push harder than girls. Boys with natural aggressiveness often give it free rein during these turbulent years and, for some, aggressive individualism characterises the whole of their lives. They are always pushing for independence and control, making them good bosses but difficult employees.

Daniel Levinson, in *The Seasons of a Man's Life*, writes that as a young man enters adulthood he generally does so with 'a Dream', a vision of who he wants to be. Men's Dreams include a yearning for separation and autonomy. They tend to contain a purely occupational component that guides them, like a template, as they enter the work force.[155]

Young women, too, form Dreams of how they want their lives to be. However, usually these are more of a vague image of themselves in a particular kind of environment or community, revolving around a yearning for attachment.[156] Researchers Priscilla Roberts and Peter Newton suggest:

> Women approach the tasks of adulthood fettered by relational requirements, whereas men approach the same set of tasks intoxicated with occupation.[157]

So far, we have discussed the gender link between the interdependence and autonomy values. As with the three previous pairs of values, there are many exceptions.

Some men will rank interdependence more highly than autonomy, particularly at certain times of their lives, or because the nature of their job demands it. When they do, they are likely to feel rather different from the norm for men, and may be viewed by others as weak. Although interdependent people can develop a very good sense of self and not be weak at all, there is a danger of being (or being seen to be) overly influenced by others.

Some women will rank autonomy more highly than interdependence. If this causes conflict, a man who expects a woman to be subservient to him, or even just dependent on him, may feel threatened and become very angry. Autonomy is becoming a much higher priority for many women today, but often still in the context of emotional, if not financial, reliance on others, usually family.

# CHARACTERISTICS: INTERDEPENDENCE

The interdependence value will influence a range of attitudes and behaviours in the workplace.

Interdependent players may:

▶ *Believe we don't get anywhere alone, nor do we have to.* Those with interdependence as a high priority are likely to perceive that their connections with others are vital for their own sense of wellbeing and personal development. They easily connect with other people.

▶ *See people as a resource for support, information and advice.* They are relatively comfortable asking others for what they need, as long as they sense a bond exists between themselves and the person they are asking.

▶ *Accept responsibility to care for others.* Care of others is a very high priority for interdependent players. When others, even those with whom they normally have little association, are in need of support, they are very likely to respond with help. When circumstances make that difficult, they, too, can become distressed.

▶ *Place their personal goals second to group goals.* Interdependent people often find the same satisfaction in meeting other people's needs as they would in meeting their own. They are relatively willing to adapt their behaviour for the good of the group in which they feel included.

▶ *Prefer a consultative approach.* When in charge, interdependent players use a consultative rather than an authoritative approach under most circumstances, often trusting the wisdom of the group rather than their personal viewpoint. They may rebel under authoritarian control, if they have no opportunity to contribute to decision-making.

▶ *Prefer collective group activity.* Interdependent players often express a stronger preference for working in teams than those who place a higher value on autonomy. Teamwork may be important in its own right, bringing enormous satisfaction when it's working well.

▶ *Closely observe the patterns of interconnections between people.* They are likely to be particularly alert to emotional bonds between people: who has rapport with whom, who is in conflict with whom.

▶ *Use their social context to define themselves.* Interdependent players gain their sense of self-worth and enjoyment of life through others. They are more likely to describe themselves in terms of relationships; for example, 'I'm a member of our sales team', or 'I'm a mother … a wife … a partner'.

# CHARACTERISTICS: AUTONOMY

While autonomous players may relate very well to other people, unlike interdependent players they are likely to have a clearly defined sense of self as separate from others. They will express this in a number of ways.

Autonomous players may:

▶ *Aim to be an independent, powerful contributor to the organisation.* While they may be very willing to align with team endeavours in their workplace, they still see themselves as separate and independent.

▶ *Like the freedom to make independent contributions.* Autonomous players dislike feeling accountable to others. They want to be free to make their own contribution to output and efficiency. If other people offer too many suggestions or try to change the way the autonomous player does things, they may resent the intrusion and feel disempowered.

▶ *Make tough decisions and see them through.* These people are often very effective change agents, because they are less concerned than their more interdependent colleagues about whether other people like them.

▶ *Prefer to have total responsibility for a task.* Their autonomy is supported by work situations where they can have full responsibility for a task. Large projects that are broken down into sub-goals to be achieved by one individual often suit them better than team goals.

▶ *Form strong personal opinions.* The personal opinions and values of autonomous players are relatively independent of what others around them think. They are likely to defend their opinions vehemently if challenged.

▶ *Rise to leadership positions easily.* Those who have used their autonomy value to develop a strong sense of self and trust in their own opinions and viewpoints often emerge as natural leaders and are frequently seen as promotable in an organisation.

▶ *Protect individual rights.* They may have a higher sensitivity to any infringement of the rights of individuals than the interdependent person. They may also be very alert to power issues.

▶ *Value self-sufficiency and ego-strength, and expect others to act responsibly.* They admire those who manage on their own without the support of others — financial, practical or emotional. They strive for this themselves and may expect others in their workplace to do the same.

## WHAT IS THE GOOD INTENTION?

We judge others through the lens of our own gender culture. As we become alert to differences in gender style, we become aware of our own filters on reality and the unexplored limits we impose both on ourselves and on others. Excessively interdependent people can indulge in self-righteousness about their consultative, interactive style, while excessively autonomous people can be equally self-righteous about the responsibility they exercise.

*We judge others through the lens of our own gender culture.*

While interdependent and autonomous players probably have very different agendas influencing how they relate to each other, good conflict resolution demands they respect each other's viewpoint. The following exercise could sharpen your awareness of what may be driving another person to the conclusions they are reaching.

*EXERCISE*

Stop for a moment and think of someone you know, or know of, who you would classify as *interdependent*. Think of a time when something they did annoyed you. Did they have a good intention that arose out of their interdependence value? Were there other 'good intentions' that motivated them as well?

| Interdependent players' good intentions | Probable motivation for ............ : (name) | |
|---|---|---|
| Planning with a team or wider system focus in mind | | *Place* |
| Inviting interaction and support from others | | *crosses* |
| Offering interaction and support to others | | *against* |
| Trying to be patient with or tolerant of others | | *relevant* |
| Self-revealing and open to others | | *motivations* |
| Encouraging emotional closeness | | |
| Other good intentions: ....................................................... ....................................................... ....................................................... ....................................................... ....................................................... ....................................................... | | |

*Figure 51: Interdependent players' good intentions*

Now consider someone you know, or know of, who is strongly motivated by their need for *autonomy*. For a particular piece of behaviour, statement or decision you've judged harshly, consider at least one good intention that may have been a motivating factor.

| Autonomous players' good intentions | Probable motivation for ............ : (name) |
|---|---|
| Being self-reliant | |
| Avoiding being a burden on others | |
| Enjoying being different and individual | |
| Taking responsibility or leadership | |
| Responding to their own sense of timing | |
| Preventing themselves being diminished by another's opinion of them | |
| Other good intentions: .................................................. .................................................. .................................................. .................................................. .................................................. .................................................. | |

*Place crosses against relevant motivations*

*Figure 52: Autonomous players' good intentions*

## SPOTTING THE UNDERLYING VALUES

The purpose of recognising each other's differences is to help us forge meaningful and productive relationships based on mutual respect, less clouded by negative judgments. When interdependence or autonomy values are at issue, they influence people's communication patterns. By observing these variations, we are able to pick up important clues about a person's underlying values. Consider whether they:

▶ *Seek someone else's advice or make decisions alone.* The interdependent player will want to wait for someone else's advice or perspective before making an important decision. The autonomous player sometimes will say or imply: 'I want to do it myself.' It's possible to spot differing values in common phrases people use. (See **Appendix 3, Figure 68: Language driven by interdependence and autonomy values**, page 403)

▶ *Seek people out or withdraw when distressed.* This difference in men's and women's communication patterns goes to the core of the interdependence–autonomy split. In his book *Men are from Mars, Women are from Venus*, John Gray frequently says that when men and women are faced with a problem, a woman goes to the *well* to chat with others and collect a range of perspectives on the issue, while a man goes off alone to his *cave* to think it out.

▶ *Use either rapport-talk or report-talk.* Talk for women, says Deborah Tannen, is a means of building rapport, establishing connection and developing relationships. By contrast, men mainly use talk to pass on concrete information, and to establish independence, status and power.[158]

▶ *Have different needs.* Interdependence-driven needs include caring, respect, understanding and the opportunity to interact. Autonomy-driven needs include trust, appreciation, acceptance and the opportunity for individual achievement. These differing needs will often be evident in the phrases people use.

▶ *Work from different morality bases.* A person whose sense of identity is based on connection and relationship is more likely to form morals based on responsibility, nurturance and care. Someone who defines themselves in terms of separation and autonomy, on the other hand, is more likely to build morals based on justice, laws and rules.

▶ *Guide decisions of ethics and rules with situational concerns or with abstract principles.* The interdependent value structure demands a system of ethics and rules that has flexibility. Interdependent players need to consider the whole context, including how applying the rule may disturb the pattern of interrelationships. Interdependent players, often women, are more likely to argue from the particular to the general. They will back up arguments with personal examples. Their ethics are situational. They are more likely to discover the exceptions that indicate the rules should be modified. They expect open lines of communication for this type of discussion.

Autonomous players, often men, are likely to consider and seek to apply the general principle or standard rule — not that rules are inviolate. Their final decision is likely to be swayed by a need to protect the individual freedoms that the principles support and their recognition of the dangers of making up one's own rules in a team situation. They are more likely to back up arguments with an abstract line of reasoning based on an ethical system of right/wrong, this works/this doesn't work, or 'this is how we've always done it'. This avoids ambiguity and uncertainty in the application of principles and work practices.[159]

*Autonomous players are more likely to back up arguments with an abstract line of reasoning.*

## TEAMWORK STYLES

When teams are functioning well, it may be difficult to spot the differences between masculine and feminine styles. But when a team is not functioning smoothly, autonomy and interdependence issues tend to come to the fore.

One woman reported her observation to me:

*When teams are functioning well, it may be difficult to spot the differences between masculine and feminine styles.*

There aren't many men who'll automatically act as members of a team. The moment you start putting them under any sort of pressure, the first thing they do is go 'individual'. They have to *learn* how to become part of a team. If female teams split, they will fracture into smaller groups, but they're still in groups. When teams of men fracture, it tends to be every man for himself.

Men's teamwork, often learnt through competitive sports, is about striving together to be the best and not letting their side down. The team leader holds the vision and directs his group towards its achievement. Women's team structures tend to be less leader focused.

Though men's and women's teams will rarely be as starkly contrasted as the following table suggests, consider the trends in **Figure 53: Teamwork differences** (page 302).

There are various team styles. A more hierarchical, even military style may be the best when:

| TEAMWORK DIFFERENCES | |
| --- | --- |
| Women's teams are more like this: | Men's teams are more like this: |
| Primary purpose is agreement, solidarity and mutual support within the group. | Considerable competition with others outside the team. |
| Informal assignment of many roles and duties. | Most roles and duties formally organised. |
| Flagging members (often because of a sick child or temporary ill health) are accommodated as a matter of course. | Flagging members told to pull up their socks because they're letting down the team. |
| Special time to talk about team relationships is desired for bonding and deeper intimacy. | Bonding takes place while they're getting the job done. 'Why talk about it?' |
| Leaders are expected to solicit opinions and advice from team members. | The leader is expected to inform team members. |
| The leader rarely issues orders. Work gets done through cooperation on what's needed. | The leader issues the orders. |
| Orientation is the group itself. | Orientation is the individual, as part of a group. |

*Figure 53: Teamwork differences*

▶ there is a need for controlled, immediate responses to emergencies;

▶ many in the group are uncertain or unskilled;

▶ key information must be kept confidential and only a small group possesses sufficient facts to make the policy decisions.

In the Karpin Report, *Enterprising Nation*, Cutler, Ingleson and Barlow note that organisational structures are becoming less pyramidal.[160] They point out that different skills are needed to run the horizontal organisation. Its executives must lead rather than direct. People-related skills are vital; in particular, the ability to work in teams, to coach, to support and to motivate other people. There is a far greater need for networking between different parts of the organisation. Flatter, leaner organisations lend themselves to an interdependent approach, where whoever is available and able does whatever needs to be done. Roles tend to be variable.

*Flatter, leaner organisations lend themselves to an interdependent approach.*

Louise Crossley, station leader at Mawson, Antarctica in 1991, felt she ran a very different style of team from her male predecessors.

> The men were used to having the station run like a military camp. I ran it like a commune. Essentially my approach was 'we're all free, consenting adults here. We can work out a way of sharing the jobs *and* caring for each other *and* handling all the issues.' I talked a lot about the good of the whole community.
>
> I didn't have any concrete goals. Everybody else, however, had a work program, set tasks and supervisors for their particular specialty. In a sense, my achievement was the sum of the achievements of all the other people on the station. For your military-type leader, that's not the way it goes. That sort of person needs personal achievements, so they take on the achievements of everybody else. They'd say: 'It's *my* science program.'
>
> I tried to get it right for everyone. I put a lot of effort into trusting people and demonstrating that I cared about them. When I did have to lay down the law, it was usually on safety issues. It was very important for me to make the point that the issue was safety and not control. Being a woman running a group of men meant they wouldn't have let me control them anyway.
>
> We had a great year, but I think it also had to do with the group of people. My style of leadership, which I think is a fairly feminine style, worked really well.

## EFFECTIVE TEAMWORK

An interesting balance between interdependence and autonomy was suggested by a group of firefighters who seemed to me to have raised the elements of effective teamwork to the level of high art. They have to be highly disciplined, obeying instructions instantly and performing precisely the role they were assigned that day. In a fire, their lives depend on each other, both as individuals and as team. I asked them what they saw as the keys to effective teamwork. Their experience suggests useful principles for all team-builders in the workplace.

## Mutual support

*Victor:* 'Team' for us is 'you can't be competitive', because 'my life depends on you and yours depends on me'. It's very much a brotherhood. Sometimes there's not much you can do when a fire's really beyond control. If there are five of us standing around nearby and one of us asks, 'Have you seen so and so?', and we realise he's missing, we'd all go, 'He must still be in there!'. There'd be a rush to go back into the fire and help our mate, no matter how dangerous it was.

*Backing each other up means moral support as well as task-oriented help.*

Backing each other up is the key. This means moral support as well as task-oriented help. For Dawn, the only female member of the firefighting team, support is crucial in her needs from the team.

*Alan:* You have to feel comfortable enough to say to your boss or to your fellow workers: 'Look we've just had two deaths and I don't know how to deal with it'. You don't want to hear: 'Ah, you're a wimp, what's wrong with you? I'm all right. So what's your problem?' You want to talk it through with someone.

It's often the boss that makes it okay to talk about those things, but women team members are also likely to support the discussion of deeper, more troubling emotional issues.

## Communication

*Alan:* The first thing in teamwork is *communication*. Gary joined us a few weeks ago. He's just come out of the training college and he needs to have a lot of things explained to him. He knows that he can ask anybody on shift if there's something he's not sure about.

*Gary:* That sort of thing is not a problem for me, but I think it might be for a quieter sort of person. You've got to have a reasonable amount of self-confidence, because when you ask a question, you are showing that you don't know how they're really doing things. A lot of the time, what you've been taught is not the same as it is on the job.

These firefighters carried their less experienced members, accepting their mentoring role and creating an environment in which it was fine to ask questions and reveal lack of knowledge.

## Trust

*Milton:* Each of us has to really pay attention to what we're doing and what we're supposed to do. I have to trust that the others are going to do the right job. If I'm going in to a fire, I've got to know there's someone behind me who's able to help me out.

Mutual trust is part of good teamwork in any workplace. Respect for the other person's ability to do the job they are assigned encourages autonomy within the confines of that job description.

## Respect for everyone's abilities

*Steve:* You've got to respect everyone's abilities. The other day, I was reading some of Gary's literature on metal fires that he got from training college. I hadn't seen it before. It was good stuff. That's going to be an area where I know I can trust Gary. One member of our team, Ernie, has been an electrician. When I go in to do a job with him and a switchboard needs isolating, I'm obviously going to refer to him. I know he knows what he is doing.

Using and respecting each person's special abilities is an integral part of good teamwork. It builds the individual's sense of self-worth by encouraging their particular contributions to their team.

## Respectful familiarity with the team leader

*Jim:* You don't want to go to a job where your boss annoys you, and in the back of your mind you're thinking: 'Oh, he doesn't know what he is talking about!'

*Mark [the station officer]:* As a boss, I hope I do get questioned, because other people can see things that I don't see.

Heads nodded as Mark said this. The firefighters really appreciated his openness to their comments. Mark obviously ran a very successful firefighting team and didn't do it along traditional authoritarian lines.

*Mark:* Teamwork is also relying on others to think independently. A lot of times you've got to think for yourself. I've got to know I can rely on any one of these people to do that.

Mark's expectation of independent thinking from his team was well balanced by the group's respect for his leadership expertise, and their clear understanding and acceptance of their assigned roles when on duty.

### Team as community

Did these firefighters arrive at this team relationship because one of their group was a woman?

Dawn: I can't say that it had no effect, but I think that the chief reason our team's the way it is is because of our boss. I think our welfare is very much paramount in his thoughts. He believes in community and does what it takes to build and maintain one.

*Excessive independence prevents the miracle that strong teams can create. Excessive dependence prevents it, too.*

When safety depends on the team, the issues become very clear. Most of us don't face life-threatening situations on a daily basis, but nevertheless there is something to learn from what comes to the fore in extreme circumstances. Excessive independence prevents the miracle that strong teams can create. Excessive dependence prevents it, too. With the right balance between interdependence and autonomy, we can create united teams of self-motivated, cooperative, loyal and effective members.

## STAGES: SOCIETY, WOMEN, MEN

### Society evolving

Two significant forces at work in modern society affect autonomy and interdependence. First, Craig Schindler and Gary Lapid, conflict resolution consultants and co-authors of *The Great Turning*, suggest:

Those of us living in the twenty-first century will have to adjust to the reality of interdependence — global, national, personal — whether we like it or not, and whether it happens through conscious policies or painful resistance. The paramount issues of human survival require us to move beyond narrow factionalism to a politics of interdependence.[161]

Second, Charlotte Waterlow, in the *Hinge of History*, points out:

> Women are, for the first time in history, associating with men as colleagues and friends – in every profession, in every activity, even in the armed forces and the astronaut's spacecraft. At some deep level of this non-possessive, non-dominant, non-sexual, non-service relationship with women is a profound challenge to the male psyche ... And it is having a corresponding effect on women, ridding them of age-old attitudes of dependence and low self-esteem.[162]

*'Women are, for the first time in history, associating with men as colleagues and friends.'*

Many women today pride themselves on their autonomy. They no longer rely on men for identity, status or a sense of importance. They're more career-minded and more self-sufficient. They are reaching for autonomy in ways never previously attempted. They can be much more outspoken than in previous generations. One female interviewee reported:

> If there is something I feel strongly about, something I'm going for that I believe is right for me, I'm not that fussed if the other person doesn't agree with me or doesn't like me as a result. I think many women today are learning to have the courage to stand up for their principles and their goals.

This still bewilders and angers the traditionally-oriented male. We are in transition. The independent, outspoken woman concerned about the advancement of her own career, steps outside of her expected gender role. Research conducted by Candy Tymson and myself suggests that women in managerial positions may be even more concerned about autonomy than their male peers (see Appendix 5, pages 407–408).

## Stages in women's lives

More and more women today are creating independent, autonomous lifestyles. They are establishing careers and expect to be treated by their relationship partners as professionals with a significant and valued role apart from that of wife, lover or mother. Nevertheless, women often still rely heavily on others for validation, support and even permission to pursue their autonomy.

Women may reassess and redefine their roles many times during their life. They repeatedly have to come to terms with the conflict between their professional and their feminine identity. Their

*Women may reassess and redefine their roles many times as they move through life.*

solutions to dilemmas may well be different at different times in their lives, as they shift their priorities between interdependence and autonomy. As they move through life, they won't always want or need to achieve the delicate balance between work and family. As they mature and family responsibilities, though just as compelling, become less time-consuming, they may broaden their horizons — take up new studies or start a new career.[163]

The female partner of an unemployed or under-employed man can find that her job, once merely a support to the family income, now becomes its major source. Many women come to these challenges deeply fearful that they cannot meet life's sudden demand on them for autonomy, particularly if their relationship with their partner has broken down and they are forced to provide not only for themselves but also for dependent children. Generally, their strength grows in response to need.

## Stages in men's lives

Men who overburden themselves in adopting the traditionally masculine role — always the man of action, always in control, both in the workplace and at home — leave themselves little space for the development of their feminine side. The traditionally masculine stance in life is incredibly time-consuming and exhausting, and often excludes internal reflection and true interdependence with team-mates and partners. Others who are close to these highly autonomous dynamos may be given very little space to develop their own strengths.

*Men's goal in early adulthood usually revolve around mastering the conventional masculine role.*

Men's goals in early adulthood usually revolve around mastering the conventional masculine role. Once achieved, an important transition can take place. Sometimes quite painfully, the conventional role is dropped or reduced. Suppressed aspects of their personality can begin to emerge. It can be a time of turning inwards and a time of feeling secure enough to be less of what the world demands and more of who they really are.

Frequently in mid-life, when many goals have already been achieved, men will grow disenchanted with the workplace. It may show up as daydreaming about early retirement or alternative lifestyles such as 'back to nature', or as the pursuit of creative arts. Often workplace demands and the need for financial security force men to suppress these yearnings. They may be left with a sense of alienation from a lifestyle they once found satisfying. Because this is also an alienation from their emerging feminine side, often they will project irritation and negative judgments onto the women in their lives. Men sometimes respond to their inner angst by having affairs, by breaking up their marriage or with conflict and domination over female colleagues at work. These 'solutions', however, do not resolve the inner emptiness, only postpone it.

To move forward, men have to come to terms with their suppressed feminine qualities. In times of economic recession, this transition may be forced by retrenchment or a failed business. Sometimes it is caused by ill health. Dragged out of their traditional masculine role and their sphere of action, men may be dumped into a more internal, reflective and often excruciating process. Peter O'Connor, in *Understanding the Mid-Life Crisis*, writes that this distress may be escalated by an inability to accept ambiguity and uncertainty.

If men use their mid-life crisis for their own development, they will usually raise the priorities of their feminine values. They are then equipped to mentor workmates and partners, nurturing, challenging and empowering them to discover and develop their own talents.[164] Men may then explore their own latent gifts in the creative arts or begin to focus on community service.

*If men use thier mid-life crisis for their own development, they will usually raise the priority of their feminine values.*

In order to move through the various stages of adult development successfully, both men and women need to become soul detectives, looking for those places where unexpressed aspects of the personality want to burst through; recognising and honouring the rebalancing of independence, control and autonomy against needs for intimacy, connectedness and community.

▼▼▼▼

In pursuing ongoing personal development, we may choose the path of strengthening the culturally defined values of our given gender; alternatively, we may wish to integrate values that traditionally have been assigned to the opposite sex. If the former, more traditional path is chosen, gender balance is often sought through partnership. On the other hand, if the latter path is chosen, the aim is not to lose anything that is biologically given, but rather to diversify, to round out our talents. We don't deny the strengths we already have, but rather empower our less-developed aspects. Integration in this instance will mean the expression of the values that have been suppressed.

This path is usually one of first acknowledging the gendered role, then gradually drawing through its suppressed opposite. Speaking very generally, we could say that men achieve personal integration (as opposed to integration achieved through balanced relationship) by absorbing more interdependence values, women by taking on more autonomy.

On this path to integration, we don't feel 'all male' or 'all female'. But there's no 'bump' as we move between the masculine and feminine sides of ourselves. Integrated energy is neutral and it can be used in different ways, sometimes for interdependence, sometimes for autonomy.

# SUMMARY

*CHARACTERISTICS*

| INTERDEPENDENT PLAYERS | AUTONOMOUS PLAYERS |
| --- | --- |
| Believe we don't get anywhere alone, nor do we have to | Aim to be an independent, powerful contributor to the organisation |
| See people as a resource for support, information and advice | Like the freedom to make independent contributions |
| Accept responsibility to care for others | Make tough decisions and see them through |
| Place their own personal goals second to group goals | Prefer to have total responsibility for a task |
| Prefer a consultative approach | Form strong personal opinions |
| Prefer collective group activity | Rise to leadership positions easily |
| Closely observe the patterns of interconnections between people | Protect individual rights |
| Use their social context to define themselves | Value self-sufficiency and ego-strength, and expect others to act responsibly |

*GOOD INTENTIONS*

| INTERDEPENDENT PLAYERS | AUTONOMOUS PLAYERS |
| --- | --- |
| Planning with a team or wider system focus in mind | Being self-reliant |
| Inviting interaction and support from others | Avoiding being a burden on others |
| Offering interaction and support to others | Enjoying being different and individual |
| Trying to be patient with or tolerant of others | Taking responsibility or leadership |
| Self-revealing and open to others | Responding to their own sense of timing |
| Encouraging emotional closeness | Preventing themselves being diminished by another's opinion of them |

*SPOTTING THE UNDERLYING VALUES*

| INTERDEPENDENT PLAYERS | AUTONOMOUS PLAYERS |
|---|---|
| Take advice | Make decisions alone |
| *Stressed or distressed:* Seek people out | *Stressed or distressed:* Withdraw from people |
| Use rapport-talk | Use report-talk |
| *Needs:* caring, respect, understanding, the opportunity to interact | *Needs:* trust, appreciation, acceptance, the opportunity for individual achievement |
| *Morality based on:* responsibility, nurturance, care | *Morality based on:* justice, laws, rules |
| *Ethics and rules are situational:* argues from the particular to the general | *Ethics and rules are abstract principles:* argues from the general to the particular |

| QUALITIES OF EFFECTIVE TEAMS |
|---|
| ▶ Mutual support<br>▶ Communication<br>▶ Trust<br>▶ Respect for everyone's abilities<br>▶ Respectful familiarity with the team leader<br>▶ Team as community |

| Effective teamwork blends interdependence and autonomy |
|---|

# 13 INTERDEPENDENCE:
## stumbling blocks & stepping stones

### PREVIEW

*STUMBLING BLOCK*

1 ▶ Too dependent on others

2 ▶ Merged attachment to others inhibits personal power

3 ▶ Alienated if others won't make real contact

4 ▶ Creating 'them' and 'us' situations

5 ▶ Disadvantaged when negotiating

6 ▶ Alienation from true self in bureaucratic workplaces

Interdependence causes problems for many women and for a considerable number of men. Establishing an identity separate from others can be a lifelong struggle, with many stumbles on the way. Conflicts can highlight lessons we must learn and motivate us to define for ourselves a workable balance between interdependence and autonomy.

## STUMBLING BLOCK 1:
## TOO DEPENDENT ON OTHERS

Interdependence implies *mutual dependence*. When support doesn't go both ways, we're either too reliant on others or we are being excessively helpful. Both are inappropriate forms of dependency.

## Excessive reliance on others

**'You're so much better at it. Will you do it for me?'**

A number of quite intelligent women habitually play 'helpless and incompetent', particularly around men. When relationships are dependent rather than interdependent:

▶ we may expect that others should know what we need without us asking;

▶ we may rely on others for things we ought to be able to do for ourselves;

▶ we may manipulate others to help us when they don't really want to.

*STEPPING STONES*
Interdependent players may need to regularly monitor their dependent behaviour, asking openly for what they want from others, being clear about how much help they're really asking for, without demanding, expecting the answer to be yes or manipulating. They can take steps to enhance their own self-reliance. For example, taking a course in computer skills or writing notes on what's required to accomplish a complex sequence of actions. Whenever they manage alone a task they would once have relied on others to help them complete, they can celebrate their growing competency.

## Excessive helpfulness

**'I do everything for you. Why aren't you grateful?'**

*An interdependent player's dependency on others may be masked by excessive helpfulness.*

An interdependent players dependence on others may be masked by excessive helpfulness. They may become too supportive of other people's problems to the detriment of their own work. Gratitude and contact are the rewards they're after. If they don't get enough, they can become very resentful. This is where their real dependency shows its true colours.

Extreme over-helpfulness has been termed *codependent* behaviour.[165] This label is used when people have great difficulty meeting their own adult needs and wants because they are fixated on taking care of others. It is a coping mechanism that can start in childhood in response to an abusive or dysfunctional parent. Codependency is often seen in people who are the children of alcoholics. Codependency support groups (an offshoot of twelve-step Alcoholics Anonymous programs) help people address these issues.

*STEPPING STONES*
Interdependent players need to raise their awareness of motivations such as the need for gratitude and contact, and explore other ways to meet these needs. They may also have to become more aware of how their own work may be suffering as a result of being too helpful to others. Many codependent people are numb to their own needs and wants. They are too 'other' focused. Considering 'What do I need that I could ask for?' and then asking for it — often — establishes better habits of mutual dependence and modifies an excess of helpfulness.

## Over–involvement in other people's work processes

**'I have to get approval for everything I do.'**

Fundamental differences in interdependence and autonomous styles of teamwork can be a source of considerable tension in the workplace. Interdependent players may prefer to work with another when one person could do the job perfectly well alone. They may supervise their subordinates too closely, even though their issue is not really control.

The interdependent manager may well be irritated by an autonomy-minded employee who doesn't come to them and discuss things, not just because the manager fears an inappropriate decision or wishes to plan jointly, but because they are fulfilling significant social needs while chatting about issues related to work.

Those who place a high value on autonomy are particularly likely to be annoyed if they have to refer many small decisions to their interdependent supervisor. They want the freedom of independent action. While interdependence is, or should be, a core value for a well-run organisation, it is not the only consideration. Many autonomy-minded people find the lengthy conversations required for serious consensus decision-making tedious and unproductive.

*STEPPING STONES*

Appropriate compromises must be made. Highly interdependent players may need to consider whether it would be beneficial to modify their style to suit the needs of other employees and the organisation.

My natural style tends towards discussion on even minor decisions. In my early days as a manager, I recall being asked by a less interdependent colleague to communicate more of my questions and requests on paper, which could travel backwards and forwards via in-trays. Each sheet might shuffle between trays a number of times before the activity was completed. It proved to be one of the most useful changes I made to my management style. We interrupted each other's work far less frequently and projects moved forward without being at the mercy of us having to make time for face-to-face contact.

Over-involvement often disguises a problem with delegating tasks and responsibilities. Developing clear guidelines with the other person so that both of you can work independently may reduce the problem significantly.

## Excessive concern about what other people think

**'What if they think I'm stupid/cruel/promiscuous!'**

*Over-dependent people have a wavering sense of self-esteem that is at the mercy of the good opinion of others.*

Over-dependent people have a wavering sense of self-esteem that is at the mercy of the good opinion of others. Often they're perfectionists so that they'll always be blameless. Some of these issues appear in a story told to me by a female executive:

Our managing director instructed me to take over the branch accounts of one of our directors, Lionel, because he was hopeless with money. Lionel complained about the arrangement to the other directors, saying that now he didn't know what was happening with the accounts. No one took much notice. They knew he needed my help. Several times, Lionel and I had minor clashes. Then I found out he'd started dropping hints to the auditors that I didn't know what I was doing. Well, that wasn't true. I'm a perfectionist with the books I keep. You have to be.

It all came to a head at the annual Christmas party when Lionel apparently told his wife, none too quietly, that I was so hopeless there was only one reason why the MD must be keeping me on. Wink, wink, nudge, nudge! The rumour travelled like wildfire. The following Monday, the MD called me into the office and said: 'I thought I'd better tell you, because you are going to hear it from someone anyway. My wife asked me how long I'd been having an affair with you. I'm really sorry.' When I left his office I burst into tears.

No one could understand why I was so angry and so distressed. I told the other directors I wanted a public apology from Lionel. They agreed the incident shouldn't have happened, but as none of them believed the rumour anyway, they felt I was overreacting. Not one of them ever approached Lionel to say: you owe this woman an apology. Never.

One director, who was very nice, did say to me: 'I have to tell you I'm disappointed. I thought you were stronger than that.' So it became a test of character. Are these things supposed to bounce off you as though they don't matter?

This woman's dependence on other people's good opinion of her didn't stand up well against Lionel's smear campaign. Her inability to confront him directly and her desire for other people to do it for her are fairly typical faults of over-dependent people.

*STEPPING STONES*
There may be times when we all need to remind ourselves of the 20–40–60 rule:

At 20, you worry about what other people think.
At 40, you don't give a damn what other people think.
At 60, you realise they never did!

Perhaps others aren't as shocked or judgmental as we suppose.

*Perhaps others aren't as shocked or judgmental as we suppose.*

# STUMBLING BLOCK 2: MERGED ATTACHMENT TO OTHERS INHIBITS PERSONAL POWER

Those who have mastered interdependence will generally choose to work alongside others. They'll value networking and close association, even warm friendships, with work colleagues. In contrast to those whose comfort zone is in autonomous independence, they'll meet more of their needs *in* relationships.[166] They will have broken the childhood bonds of merged attachment,

*When childhood's merged attachment is outgrown, interdependence allows a fair measure of autonomy.*

combining interdependence with a fair measure of autonomy. When merged attachment is still a problem, interdependent players know themselves only through others, and adjust, deny and lose themselves in the attachment. They may repress their own self-development needs in order to please other people. Often this is specifically a woman's issue. Her fear of abandonment constricts her in exploring autonomy and self-expression. Her neediness for others may even cause her to discourage close friends from adventure into greater independence and career moves.[167]

## Negative self-talk

**'They're just waiting for me to trip up so they can throw me out.'**

Personal power requires that we are in charge, not necessarily of who does what in the workplace, but in charge of ourselves and our responses.

We grow in personal power as we learn not to pull ourselves down with negative self-talk. Many very senior, very successful people hide beneath their *positional* power, struggling against self-talk messages such as: 'I'm a fraud and I'm going to get found out soon' or 'They don't like me unless I go that extra mile for them'. Interdependent players still in a state of merged attachment to others are often driven by self-talk fuelled by low self-worth and a fear of abandonment.

### STEPPING STONES

*Bad feeling about a situation often come from negative self-talk rather than the experience itself.*

Bad feelings about a situation often come from negative self-talk rather than the experience itself. Identify your negative self-talk. Challenge it. Replace it with positives. For example, 'Things always go wrong for me' could become 'I made the most sensible decision I could based on the information I had'.

Then, despite the fact that your affirmation will still be tenuous at best, act out of it: 'I'll ask for some help to get the project done on time', or 'I won't apologise for disagreeing'.

Sometimes, we cast ourselves in powerless roles quite unnecessarily. We may be repeating powerlessness habits learnt from our family when we were growing up. Here Susan explains how she helped Hilton, a senior executive in her company, to break free from his dependency trap:

Hilton had fallen out of favour with the head of our organisation, Terry. Terry is gorgeous and people love him to love them. His favour is very important. Noel, who's Hilton's subordinate, had usurped Terry's ear. I invited Hilton to look at the problem from a family perspective. 'What would Terry's role be?' I asked him. 'Father,' he replied. 'And Noel?' I asked. 'Step-son,' Hilton answered. 'What about you?' I said. 'Son,' he answered. And then I said: 'If he's the father and you're the son, what power position do you have?' 'I'm powerless!' he said.

It was quite a profound realisation for him. I said: 'If you are in a powerless position, what can you do about it?' He thought for a moment. 'I can change my relationship with Terry — stop playing the child. I can ask him out for a meal. I can make regular appointments with him to keep him up-to-date on my projects. And if I can get the communication between us flowing a little bit better, I might be able to get him to discuss with me what has been bugging him.' In the space of a few minutes, Hilton was moving from powerlessness to taking charge of his situation.

In his book *Unlimited Power*, Anthony Robbins uses this interpersonal orientation in his definition of power:

Ultimate power is the ability to produce the results you desire most and create value for others in the process. Power is the ability to change your life, to shape your perceptions, to make things work for you and not against you. Real power is shared, not imposed. It's the ability to define human needs and to fulfil them — both your needs and the needs of the people you care about. It's the ability to direct your own personal kingdom — your own thought process, your own behaviour — so you produce the precise results you desire.[168]

Authoritarian leaders may not recognise the real power of the competent interdependent player. Power is frequently seen as the ability to get somebody to do something *against* their will. Mastering interdependence means getting somebody to do something because you have provided them with information and they can see that it is a good idea. This is the difference between manipulation and influence.[169] It's more subtle and quite different from power *over* another. It's power *with* them.

## Lack of clear boundaries

**'I can't say no.'**

*Boundaries are the way we use our energy to protect ourselves from others intruding into our personal space.*

Boundaries are the way we use our energy to protect ourselves from others intruding into our personal space. Good boundaries are part of having a clear self-identity. Interdependent players may have a poor sense of self-identity, another problem of merged attachment. If we have diffuse boundaries, we get upset when others are upset, deeply disturbed when others are angry and we are unable to distinguish clearly between our own needs and someone else's needs. We may feel guilty if we are unable to do what another person wants us to, even when there is nothing we can do about it. We may be unable to say no to requests from others, even though we cannot or do not want to respond.

*STEPPING STONES*
To establish a separate self, we must be able to separate our own needs from other people's needs. While at times we may postpone our own needs, we will be comfortable asserting what we want. This is personal power–interdependence style.

*Personal power for the interdependent person means helping others is a choice, not an obligation.*

In the process of pulling away from others, the interdependent player may appear to undergo a personality change. Suddenly, the person that others could always rely on to be accommodating and helpful seems to have deserted ship. Personal power for the interdependent person takes a huge leap forward if this transition stage is successfully accomplished and the sense of moral obligation about serving others' needs has fallen away. Then helping others becomes a choice, not an obligation.

## Sexual harassment

When someone makes an inappropriate push for intimacy, the interdependent player with defective boundaries is likely to become angry and defensive. These emotions help them to erect a temporary wall between themselves and the other person, as a substitute for the missing clarity of self as separate from others.[170]

While highly interdependent people may lack strong boundaries, highly autonomous people may have boundaries that are too impervious to messages coming from other people. Both can compound sexual intrusiveness problems.

Sally was secretary to the director of an advertising agency. This is how she spoke of her issues with her boss:

> He always seemed to have this sexual tension thing going. He would touch me, stroke my shoulder or my face, but I didn't feel that it was okay to say, 'Don't do that!' because he wasn't doing anything overtly sexual. I'd try stepping back from him, but he never really got the hint. I know I have a real problem with boundaries and I hated myself for not being able to say something. Once, when his hand started moving down towards my breast, I was finally able to say 'Don't!'. I had to allow him to be really intrusive – overtly sexual – before I could open my mouth.

Some women reject unwanted sexual overtures extremely well, often using humour. If the man doesn't get the hint to lay off, they are comfortable about giving him a sharp reprimand. However, not all women can handle unwanted advances. They feel threatened by repeated sexual approaches, even if they are only verbal (see also page 277). Autonomous men whose own sense of personal boundaries is much more secure may not recognise how distressed these women become. If a man presumes that all women find it straightforward to set their limits, he leaves himself wide open to accusations of sexual harassment when he flirts with someone who can't deliver a clear message to back off. Of course, there are a few men who'll ignore even the clearest message on the subject! They're not alert to the signals that don't suit them.

*Some men don't recognise how distressed women can become by unwanted sexual approaches.*

### STEPPING STONES

Many women find it very difficult to set their limits clearly. This can be particularly difficult for shy women and those whose upbringing has encouraged passive acceptance of intrusive behaviour. Often women let the harassing behaviour go on for a long time, which makes it more difficult to address the issue as they appear to have accepted such behaviour in the past. If you are upset about such an incident or incidents, this means the other person has overstepped your boundaries. You have the right to define them clearly. As many men's cultural conditioning and role modelling sets an accepted pattern for this sort of behaviour, they may simply not realise that you find their behaviour intrusive and may respond well when informed how you feel. Sometimes, you can ask a third person to have a quiet word to them.

Some men who engage in sexually harassing behaviour don't limit their target to just one person. If you suspect that the problem is widespread, talking to other women may help you develop the most appropriate strategy. Carrie Herbert, author of *Sexual Harassment in Schools*, tells the story of a group of women who banded together to anonymously name a harasser in their workplace. After working hours, they wrote on the mirror of the men's toilets in lipstick: 'John Western sexually harasses secretaries.' From then on, he modified his behaviour.[171]

While group action and formal procedures for reporting harassment are two options, you should probably try direct action first.

▶ Under most circumstances, aim to be polite but firm. If that's not working, you cannot worry excessively about hurting the other person's feelings. You probably are going to make them upset or angry and you'll have to allow for that.

▶ Name clearly the behaviour that's the problem and how it makes you feel: 'I feel highly embarrassed when you touch my body', 'It makes me extremely annoyed when you kiss me'.

▶ Be clear about what you want to happen now (i.e. that the behaviour should stop and that you want normal and pleasant working relations resumed).

▶ Don't be put off by an attempt to dismiss or trivialise your complaint. If you feel the person may become abusive, you might choose to make your statement in a relatively public place, so that they have to keep a check on what they say and do.

▶ Rather than getting involved in debate or justification, after you've made your statement, you may wish to leave the room.

Many men in the workplace today are very scared that allegations of sexual harassment will be exaggerated or misused. New legislation on unfair dismissal may mean a proven charge of sexual harassment is a more certain and politically correct excuse to get rid of an unwanted employee, as it may be harder to dismiss him for sloppy work or inability to get on with others.

Unfortunately, men's growing concern about sexual harassment charges can stifle their own interdependency and empathy in the workplace.

One female teacher received a phone call at work, informing her that her cousin had just died. About a week later, a friend of hers, a male teacher, was talking to her and he said: 'You know when we were talking last week just after your cousin died, you really looked distraught, like you needed a hug.'

'That would have been the best thing you could have done,' she responded.

He said: 'I don't think I'm allowed to do that now. That's harassment, isn't it?'

The rules aren't clear anymore. A blanket embargo on physical contact limits natural human concern and interdependence. If you're unsure whether touching is appropriate, you may need to be as explicit as, 'You look like you need a hug. Would you like one from me?'. We now need a very refined sensitivity to handle awkward situations and an alertness to what behaviour is invasive and what is genuinely empathic. There are no hard and fast rules. There may be times when a touch or a hug is appropriate, and an arbitrary application of a usually sound rule is uncaring and unnecessary. When in doubt, ask!

## STUMBLING BLOCK 3: ALIENATED IF OTHERS WON'T MAKE REAL CONTACT

**'She's never chats to me. She mustn't like me.'**

One of the yardsticks by which women judge another woman is her emotional responsiveness. They may expect her to divulge a reasonable amount of personal information, enough to make her appear human. They will work more cooperatively with her if they have been able to make this personal, and very feminine, connection.

Positional power may not take a woman leader very far with other women. Unless they feel connected to her, they won't like receiving instructions from her. If they feel alienated because she holds very different values or because she won't engage in personal talk, they can be highly critical.

Most women probably don't expect the same level of contact with a male superior as they'd expect with a female superior.

*Women don't like receiving instructions from a woman with whom they don't have rapport.*

Women make some allowances for men being less interactive. But when surrounded by men using only masculine report-style communication, women are likely to feel stressed and uncomfortable. They may not feel they are being valued as a person, just as an efficient producer of services for the organisation. For most interdependent players, this is not enough for job satisfaction.

*STEPPING STONES*

Interdependent people need to make allowances for a reserved style. More reserved people may not be capable of meeting the interdependent person's social needs, but are probably not deliberately shutting them out. Being aware of how important personal contact is for the highly interdependent player can help reserved people to modify their behaviour a little — and a little is often all that's needed to avoid alienating them. If the reserved person is willing to self-disclose a little more, interdependent people usually respond positively. It's as though they're saying: 'Ah, now I see you. Now I can relate to you.' It can make a big difference to their willingness to cooperate

## STUMBLING BLOCK 4: CREATING 'THEM' AND 'US' SITUATIONS

**'Did you hear what they're plotting against us now.'**

In masculine, autonomy-oriented workplaces, women can find that socialising together to create a deeper connection helps to counter feelings of alienation. Between themselves, they can provide a community of mutual support. But this has its dangers. Women grouped for solidarity against men may also unite their opposition! Louise Crossley considered the issue in her year as station leader at Mawson, Antarctica:

*Women grouped for solidarity against men may also unite their opposition.*

There was only one other woman on the station in the winter that year, and she and I were good friends. We supported each other, but we didn't make a thing out of being the only two women. You have to judge situations like that quite finely — how much to be one of the boys and how much to be separate. I've seen strong feminist cells within a male culture result in major confrontation. It became less resolvable the more tightly the women aligned with each other.

Heavy adversarial approaches can make interdependent people highly uncomfortable and so they will often band together as a group. When they become involved in ongoing conflicts, they can be poisoned by gossiping and can stir each other to greater division. Internal fractures in the group are also likely when these dynamics get out of hand. Petty rivalries and infighting can become particularly bitter.[172]

*STEPPING STONES* .
If you find yourself involved in such struggles, asking yourself these questions might help:

What is at stake here? Are we being competitive? If so, why? Is it:

1. the need for recognition?

2. a cover for feelings of inadequacy?

3. an urge to establish a separate identity?

Or is it:

4. representative of a genuine difference of opinion that needs to be resolved?

Look for solutions to these problems rather than participating in ugly rivalries.

## STUMBLING BLOCK 5: DISADVANTAGED WHEN NEGOTIATING

**'I don't have the gall to put in a bid that high.'**

People who place a high priority on interdependence often perceive themselves to be poor negotiators. They're likely to hate hard bargaining. They dislike holding their cards close to their chest, being infinitely more comfortable with an open, self-disclosing style. They tend to make bids based on what they think the other person will accept. They watch in awe and horror when autonomous players make outrageous bids to shift the other person's goal posts.

Research on differences between men's and women's negotiating styles found that when men were placed in conflict with other men they tended to rely on assertive behaviour, while women in conflict with other women were more likely to rely on compromise.[173]

Both negotiating styles can lead people into negotiating faults. Interdependent people might be pushovers in negotiations. Autonomous people's style may be so tough that other people are alienated. Consider **Figure 54: Common mistakes when negotiating** (page 327).

*STEPPING STONES*

Some general negotiating principles may keep both inter-dependent *and* autonomous players out of hot water:

▸ Don't argue positions, go back to everyone's needs.

▸ Settle only for what's fair.

▸ Ask yourself: 'What's easy for me to give and valuable for them to receive? Likewise, what could they offer me?'

▸ Attack the problem, not the person.

▸ Create a win/win climate by offering concessions in return for concessions.

▸ Lower your need for the deal. Consider and, if necessary, improve your alternatives if this negotiation fails.

▸ Distinguish between two different methods of negotiation:
  • towards agreement; and
  • to my advantage.[174]

In the end, in order to create agreements that stay in place, both methods should produce win/win outcomes. 'Towards agreement' negotiating works best with fairly open communication, such as when dividing up tasks between workmates. The 'to my advantage' style generally works best when bargaining over the price of something or negotiating a financial contract. 'To my advantage' negotiations are usually conducted with very limited disclosure of what you are willing to settle for. When negotiating

| COMMON MISTAKES WHEN NEGOTIATING | |
| Interdependent style | Autonomous style |
|---|---|
| Alienated if relationship-building is not occurring before or during the negotiation | Move into tough bargaining without building a relationship when the other side expects it (*e.g. when dealing with women, with many Asian and middle eastern cultures*) |
| Not alert to power issues, strategies and ambit claims from the other side | Not alert to empathy issues that could cause the negotiation to break down |
| Unable to hold their bottom line and may settle for less than what is fair | Do not adequately research the other person's needs |
| Easily intimidated by a hard negotiator | Attack the person rather than the problem |
| Overly concerned that the other person will withdraw from the negotiation as points are debated | May not think creatively about how to give the other person things that sweeten the deal for them |
| Reveals too much keenness for a deal | Maintain an inflated demand and the other person withdraws from the negotiation |
| Unable to ask for more than they are willing to settle for, even when this is the appropriate strategy | Bargain too hard with work colleagues, friends or family |
| Too readily accepts the other person's stated position | Make deals with not enough concessions for the other party, meaning the deal doesn't hold or doesn't earn them repeat business |

*Figure 54: Common mistakes when negotiating*

business contracts, sometimes a period of seemingly inflexible position statements and bluffing will precede the agreement. I interviewed James, who noted:

> My boss is a woman. I know she finds big negotiations a lot more difficult than I do. She'll often leave that side of things to me, particu-

larly if she's got to negotiate with a man who's started off with a bid a very long way from where she needs to end up. I think men are generally more robust when it comes to negotiating. I mean, it's harder work with guys. You have to give up something before you can conclude with them. With women, it's easier for me to get what I had in mind.

'To my advantage' negotiating is a game, one that many very autonomous people thoroughly enjoy. Many interdependent players are only comfortable with the strategies appropriate to a 'towards agreement' style and find 'to my advantage' negotiating stressful, although it becomes less so with practice.

*Interdependent players may find 'to my advantage' negotiating stressful.*

Some men refuse to take women seriously in negotiations. While we all need to break down this type of prejudice, there will be times when it is wiser to do as James's female boss sometimes does and use a man to represent the woman in the negotiations. One wonders whether Elke in the following example may have received a speedier response to her difficulties if she'd let her partner represent her. But I just love how she handled the problem in the end!

I run my office from a small terrace which I own. My partner Matt and I live upstairs. Next door there is a huge multistorey building being built. It's been going on for almost two years. They breach their building permit every day, sometimes working until eleven o'clock at night. They've dropped huge sheets of plate glass in my back garden, lumps of concrete onto my roof and spots of paint all over our cars.

I believe you can negotiate everything, so I kept plugging away at them. In all our negotiations, they've always apologised, but they treated me like an idiot. I'm sure they thought: 'Just agree with her and she'll go away.' Finally, I issued an injunction against them through the courts. They were horrified and asked for a meeting on site. During the meeting, they only talked to Matt. They didn't even look at me. Matt handled it wonderfully. He said to them: 'Excuse me, Elke is the litigant here, she's the one who has the injunction. Really, what I say doesn't matter very much. I'd negotiate with her if I were you.' But they went on talking right over me. They'd make a suggestion and look at Matt as if to ask: 'Is that all right?'

In the end, I got more assertive than I think I've ever been before in my life. I said to them: 'When you are negotiating with me, you keep turning to Matt. I am sure you don't mean to cause offence by that, but I need to tell you, it's very distracting. It's as though you don't think I'm significant enough to negotiate with. I'm sure you don't really feel like that, so can we just agree that you'll face me while we are negotiating.' I felt so powerful after I'd said that and they finally started paying attention to me. We've since reached an amicable settlement. Hallelujah!

# STUMBLING BLOCK 6: ALIENATION FROM TRUE SELF IN BUREAUCRATIC WORKPLACES

**'They're obsessed with their systems. I just don't fit in.'**

Jacob had worked for a government department that was service-oriented. His strong focus on community concerns and building real and caring relationships with clients had been supported in his work. In a government reshuffle, he was moved to a different department that was closely regulated for bureaucratic efficiency. For example, certain types of transactions with clients were required to take no more than two minutes. Jacob tried to adapt himself to fit the new system, but it was a very uncomfortable match.

'I have to be a lot more controlled. The procedure is "it's all straight business. Don't worry about anything else or think about anyone else. When you walk into someone's office, sit down, get to the task at hand, walk out." It's all done in the shortest possible time. You're not expected to, in fact you're actively discouraged from, taking time to be supportive to clients.'

Several months after I recorded this interview, Jacob told me he had left the department. He had no job to go to. His resignation was an act of commitment to his true self. Every day he'd worked there, his core values of interdependence, human concern and compassion were being violated.

A woman made the following statement, but it might well have been Jacob. It probably would express his sentiments very well.

Trying to cut through everything by looking only at efficiency doesn't allow your creative and relating side to function. If you are doing that day after day, five days a week, it starts to have an impact on you as a person and you start to become someone you are not. You are not being true to yourself by allowing other people to dictate the quality of your behaviour.

I reached a point about three years ago where I realised that we each have a lot of assets that act as our strengths, that we were made different for a reason. We should be valuing that diversity and we shouldn't be hiding it or changing it.

For people whose priority is interdependence, the demand to adapt to an incompatible work style can lead to burnout and deep dissatisfaction.

*STEPPING STONES*

*The demand
on interdependent
players to adapt to
an incompatible work
style can lead to
burnout and deep
dissatisfaction.*

While we all must make some adjustments to fit into the work environment, it is often important to stand up for environments that allow real interaction, care and mutual support. We need to reject work practices that we feel are not designed to take into account our human needs. When we do, we are playing our part in the gentle revolution.

## SUMMARY

| INTERDEPENDENCE: STUMBLING BLOCKS | STEPPING STONES: ESTABLISHING A SELF–IDENTITY SEPARATE FROM OTHERS |
|---|---|
| **1 ► Too dependent on others** | |
| *Excessive reliance on others* | Ask openly for what you want from others, but without demand. or manipulation. Celebrate your own self-reliance. |
| *Excessive helpfulness* | Raise your awareness of motivations such as the need for gratitude and contact. Meet these needs in other ways. Make sure that your own work isn't suffering. |
| *Over-involvement in other people's work processes* | Delegate tasks. Communicate questions and requests on paper more frequently. |
| *Excessive concern about what other people think* | Realise that other people aren't as shocked or judgmental as we suppose. |

| STUMBLING BLOCKS | STEPPING STONES |
|---|---|
| 2 ► Merged attachment to others inhibits personal power | |
| *Negative self-talk* | Replace with positive affirmations and act on them. Are you acting out a child's role? 'Power with' is even more powerful than 'power over'. |
| *Lack of clear boundaries* | Enforce your boundaries with assertiveness and humour. |
| *Sexual harassment* | When considering direct action, don't be too concerned about the harasser's feelings. Name their behaviour clearly and how it affects you. Be clear about what you want to happen. Don't be put off by attempts to trivialise your complaint. Then leave the room rather than debate the issue. |
| 3 ► Alienated if others won't make real contact | Make allowances for a reserved style. Reserved people may get better cooperation if they self-disclose a little more to interdependent people. |
| 4 ► Creating 'them' and 'us' situations | Discourage rivalries outside and within interdependent groups. Resolve genuine differences without gossiping or stirring up trouble. |
| 5 ► Disadvantaged when negotiating | *Useful negotiating principles:*<br>► Don't argue positions, go back to everyone's needs.<br>► Settle only for what's fair.<br>► Ask yourself: 'What's easy for me to give and valuable for them to receive? Likewise, what could they offer me?'<br>► Attack the problem, not the person.<br>► Create a win/win climate by offering concessions in return for concessions.<br>► Lower your need for the deal. Consider and, if necessary, improve your alternatives if this negotiation fails.<br>► Distinguish between two different methods of negotiation:<br>  • towards agreement; and<br>  • to my advantage. |
| 6 ► Alienation from true self in bureaucratic workplaces | It is often important to stand up for workplace environments that allow real human interaction, care and mutual support. |

# 14 AUTONOMY: stumbling blocks & stepping stones

## PREVIEW

### STUMBLING BLOCK

1 ▶ Concern about invasion of autonomous areas

2 ▶ Resentment about taking orders or advice

3 ▶ Inability to include other people in decision-making processes

4 ▶ Hidden dependence

5 ▶ Inability to sustain contact

We seek autonomy to be free, to feel independent and have our own sense of identity. Men have always seen work as their path to achieving autonomy. Women in the workforce today are grasping at the same opportunity. Unfortunately, work does not necessarily deliver autonomy to either sex. Autonomy is more than just a pay packet, though financial independence is a significant milestone on the path. Ultimately, autonomy is the freedom to be ourselves; to be self-reliant, empowered, willing to lead and able to function alone; being prepared to stand up for a different opinion we believe in. On these criteria, many of us have little real autonomy at work at all, and perhaps it is still true that fewer women have achieved it than men. Research conducted by myself and Candy Tymson (reported in Appendix 5, page 405–407) indicates that among executives, women are valuing autonomy more highly than men. This is possibly because for them it is still a more distant and hard-won goal.

*Often we clutch at autonomy by standing against others rather than alongside them.*

Often we clutch at autonomy by standing against others rather than alongside them. Are we seeking autonomy by shutting other people out? Are we rejecting the influence of other decision-makers in our work? Do we see leadership as an all-or-nothing role rather than a flexible function that may rotate within the group? Are we failing to recognise and respect our daily reliance upon other people? Or are we failing to build solid channels of communication? When we succumb to these stumbling blocks, the drive towards autonomy can become a limiting rather than a freeing force in our lives.

## STUMBLING BLOCK 1: CONCERN ABOUT INVASION OF AUTONOMOUS AREAS

'Women? You go to work to get away from them.'

Men's traditional areas of autonomy are being challenged in ways probably never before experienced in history. New patterns of relating to women as equal colleagues are called for, but are not always forthcoming. The changes required often clash with men's traditional attitudes to status, power and competition within the workplace.

The shift in the long-established order of things threatens some men's sense of autonomy when it has been defined by the exclusion of women from certain workplace areas. This occurs both at the top and the bottom of the social ladder. Women are still largely excluded from boardrooms of large companies. The glass ceiling issues discussed in Chapter 8 are relevant here. Women are also liable to face enormous opposition from male colleagues if they are trying to work in areas that have been defined as involving heavy labour. The fact that modern equipment places many of these jobs well within the range of women's strength is often ignored.

Behind this resistance to women entering traditionally male domains of employment are a number of pressing and often unstated concerns. These include:

► social obligation to protect women;

► a new requirement to curb bad language;

► fear that women don't have the skills or strength needed;

► loss of male-dedicated space.

The team of firefighters who'd talked to me about teamwork (see Chapter 12, pages 303–306) also discussed these issues. Their responses to the fears they observe in other platoons apply to many traditionally male domains (particularly those involving heavy manual work) which women are beginning to enter.

### SOCIAL OBLIGATION TO PROTECT WOMEN:

*Helena:* What sort of things are these guys worried about?

*Victor:* They might be thinking: you're fighting a fire and a wall comes down. Instead of having a man in front of you on the hose, it's a woman. What are you going to do? Is it going to be all right for you to drop the hose and run? Are you going to have to get her out first?

*Helena:* How real is this fear?

*Victor:* It's rubbish. If there were a guy there, they'd get him out, too. Sure, they might say 'no way', but that's just bravado. On the job, we're all looking out for each other all the time, and we all take risks for each other. That's just what we do.

*Helena:* Are men really more protective of women than of other men?

*Dawn:* In my previous job in a bank, I was a victim of several armed hold-ups. None of the male employees was more protective of me because I was a woman. In those circumstances, self-preservation prevailed. When it comes down to it, human beings are going to look after their friends, their partners, if they possibly can, no matter whether they are male or female.

> *Human beings look after their friends, their partners, if they possibly can, no matter whether they are male or female.*

### A NEW REQUIREMENT TO CURB BAD LANGUAGE:

*Ernie:* Some men are scared that they won't be able to swear any more.

*Dawn [laughing]:* I got my fingers squashed at a job the other day and I didn't say, 'Oh, dearie me, I've hurt myself'. I really let fly. But I think having women around does tidy up language a bit. I used to be on a different platoon and one of the guys said to me: 'You know, there was a lot more decorum and manners on this shift when you were on, Dawn.'

*Steve:* A firefighter from another team joined us on temporary secondment. We were sitting around chatting over lunch and his language was absolutely disgusting.

Finally, I blurted out: 'Listen, I find that language really offensive. I want you to stop.' This guy couldn't believe that it was me who had the problem. 'If the girl doesn't like it, she can tell me to stop,' he said. 'I don't give a damn whether the girl likes it or not,' I said. '*I* find it offensive. So cut it out!'

*Having women around tidies up bad language. But it's not only women who appreciate the difference.*

**FEAR THAT WOMEN DON'T HAVE THE SKILLS OR STRENGTH NEEDED:**
*Dawn:* The selection testing for male and female firefighters is exactly the same. When you explain that, the men will say, 'Oh, is it?'. They're surprised. They obviously haven't taken that into account. But it's funny, when you go to an actual job with them, you're no different. When you're all dressed in the same uniform and wearing an air set, you don't even know who the person next to you is, let alone what sex they are. You're each doing the job you've been assigned, and that's that.

*Jim:* We don't protect Dawn from the heavy stuff. If you see someone dragging a hose, you always give them a hand. Because of Occupational Health and Safety regulations, you have to have two people to lift it up anyway.

**LOSS OF MALE-DEDICATED SPACE:**
*Mark:* We've had guys come in here, and when they find out we have a woman on the team they say: 'A woman on the shift? Hell, you go to

work to get away from them.' Where do they think they are? Women are half the human race. If you want to think like that you can go and sit on an island and be a hermit.

## STEPPING STONES

Women, albeit still in small numbers, are breaking into previously exclusive male domains. Once a mixed sex team is established, many unfounded fears fall away. Introducing a woman to an all-male team does change the dynamic. These firefighters enjoy and appreciate the different perspectives, skills and values of their mixed sex team compared with male-only teams elsewhere in the Service. They don't find they need to be more protective of the woman on their team than they naturally are of their male workmates. They find having women around does tidy up the extremes of bad language, but a number of the men appreciate the difference.

Occupational Health and Safety standards in Australia today require moderation in manual load lifting. This is minimising the effect of differences in physical strength between men and women. If the feminist movement and the influx of women into previously male areas of work has motivated some of these Health and Safety regulations, it is a liberation for men as much as for women. Good teamwork in manually intensive trades has always required mutual support with heavy tasks.

Until they've actually worked with women on their team, men can take some convincing that they won't be personally disadvantaged by including women.

Restrictions still being imposed on women's full participation are usually based on reasons that don't hold up when put to the test. Many men need to ask themselves if their colleague had been a man, would they have invited him to join in the meeting or social gathering. If the answer is yes, they need to reconsider why they are not including their female colleague. Many situations have much to benefit from including appropriate women.

*Women may need to negotiate their involvement if they're being excluded from important meetings or social events.*

Women need to be alert to the existence of important social events where business matters will be discussed or meetings in which they should be included, but to which they haven't been invited. They will need to negotiate their involvement repeatedly until men's attitudes change.

## STUMBLING BLOCK 2: RESENTMENT ABOUT TAKING ORDERS OR ADVICE

### 'No one's going to tell me what to do.'

*Dawn:* 'Will men give me the authority to lead them? I'm sitting for my station officers exam. There are no women station officers in Australian fire brigades. If I pass and if I get a posting, I'll be in charge of guys old enough to be my father. What are they going to think? I don't know whether I'll have the problem, but it will be very important how I handle the position.'

Many men deeply resent taking orders from women. Their need for autonomy seems to come to the fore when women rather than men may be controlling what they do. Autonomous players are liable to resent anyone who takes away their sense of being free to choose exactly what they do and when.

### *STEPPING STONES*

RECEIVING ORDERS IF YOU'RE AN AUTONOMOUS PLAYER: Being an autonomous player, you have a strong need to be the captain of your destiny. How do you reconcile this with being forced to work low down in an organisational hierarchy where you must carry out instructions from others regarding the tasks you are to perform? How can you take charge of yourself under these circumstances?

One way is to learn to align your own free will with the instruction you have received. Of course, you do ultimately have *some* choice. You could refuse to do the work demanded. However, that will have consequences, probably serious ones. For this reason alone, you can *choose* to do what's asked. But fear of negative consequences isn't usually a very good motivation for an autonomy-driven person. You generally need to find a more immediate reason. The challenge is to rethink the situation so that you can put your whole self behind the task.

*Fear of negative consequences isn't usually a very good motivation for an autonomy-driven person.*

Here are some guidelines you could try whenever you notice your need for independence being triggered by someone else's demands:

1 ► *Change your outlook.* At best, you'll be able to see the intrinsic worth of the instruction once you can lay your

rebelliousness to one side. You may have to search for a valid reason that convinces you it's a good idea. Your aim is to align your actions with your thoughts. When you freely choose to do something, even if someone else has suggested or ordered it, you are the cause of your actions.

Learn to notice when you are reacting with a negative attitude and make a conscious decision to take control of your thoughts by choosing how you respond. For example:

*You're told to sort out the filing system.*
Your immediate reaction may be to feel resentful. Recognise this, then take charge of your response. You may need to turn your thinking around, perhaps by reminding yourself that re-organising will increase your own and other people's efficiency.

*You've been ordered to get an overdue report in by the end of the week — or else!*
Your first reaction may be to feel angry and not to want to do the report at all. Choose your response by reminding yourself that getting the report done by the end of the week will give you a great sense of completion — and you'll be able to enjoy the weekend!

When you freely choose a particular action and are not just submitting because you feel you have to, you can engage your creativity within the scope of your personal authority. Creativity is the zest you can bring to a task when you are truly autonomous. It is blocked when you are mentally rebelling or resenting being told what to do by someone else.

2 ▶ *Look for how you can add extra ingredients.* Find ways to make the task more pleasant. For example:

*The decree has come from above: improve productivity.*
You might choose to brainstorm ideas on how to achieve this with a person whose skills you respect.

*You've been ordered to clean out the storeroom.*
Maybe you could take a personal stereo in to work and listen to music to make the time pass more pleasantly. It might also be a good excuse for wearing more casual clothes to work that day.

Sometimes, knowing that you will give yourself a reward after completing a task is another helpful motivation.

We all find ourselves needing to perform tasks we haven't really chosen. True autonomy comes when we take charge of our response instead of falling victim to negative reactions.

## GIVING ORDERS TO AUTONOMOUS PLAYERS:

### Polish your style so it demonstrates the strengths of autonomy

While autonomous players can do much to take charge of their own responses to orders, as leader we can also be sensitive to their issues of resentment. To have our control over others accepted by the people concerned, we must be seen as worthy of respect. Amanda Sinclair, in *Trials at the Top*, lays down four characteristics that are particularly important to develop if leadership is to be respected. They incorporate qualities natural to the interdependent style, but include many of the positives of true autonomy. Autonomous players are more likely to lay aside reservations about taking orders from those who embody the qualities they admire. She suggests that respected leaders are:

*Autonomous players may lay aside reservations about taking orders from those who embody the qualities they admire.*

► *Strong*, knowing when to be tough and when to be pleasant. They have the determination and the ability to tackle the difficult issues.

► *Smart*, intelligent, very alert to the details, and able to hold their own with senior management.

► *Straight*, asking the difficult questions, unafraid of directness, strongly principled, and clear about what they want to accomplish.

► *Display esprit de corps* (literally 'group spirit') which implies being very committed to the organisation, to humanitarian principles and to a people focus.[175]

### Shift the emphasis away from control

While it's easy to step on an autonomous male's toes if you're a woman giving orders, autonomous players may resent being controlled by anyone, male or female. Often, therefore, it's important to shift the emphasis away from control to prevent the autonomous player moving into rebellion or competition. Here's how Louise Crossley handled the issue when she was station leader in Mawson, Antarctica:

*Many men will resent being controlled by anyone, but particularly a woman.*

Basically, though your title is 'leader', you have no control over people in any absolute sense. The more you try to define what people can do, the more they will flout your authority. I twigged to this fairly early, and so whenever I did get heavy on rules, I explained them in terms of structure and safety, so that each rule clearly had its purpose beyond any arbitrary decree. For example, there were rules for going off the station. You were supposed to sign up beforehand to say where and when you were going, then you had to radio in every evening to say where you were heading the next day.

I was out on a field trip off the station. Anyway, these two lads arrived at the place where I was. They shouldn't have been there. They'd said they were going to a place much closer to base camp.

I tore strips off them, as I knew they hadn't followed the rules. 'Look,' I said, 'if we hadn't been here and you'd got lost on the way, what do you think we could have done? We've got no indication of where you are.'

They didn't like that, and not totally without reason. They're skilled scientists. One of them came back with: 'Who are you to tell me what I can do?' 'Can't you see that this is a safety issue,' I replied. 'It's an interference issue, it seems to me,' the other one said. 'I'm not saying that you don't have the capability to range around the place,' I responded, trying my best to bypass the clash with their autonomy. 'That's not the issue. If anything happens and you've stuck by the rules, ultimately I've got much less trouble finding you, and you've got a greater chance of being found!'

Finally, my message got through. I think they saw that it was about structure, not about my imposing my authority.

### Join in some manual labour to soften resentment

*Autonomous men engaged in heavy manual labour can become very resentful of bosses who never get their hands dirty.*

Autonomous men engaged in heavy manual labour can become very resentful of bosses who never get their hands dirty. They think: 'What right have you got to tell me what to do when you don't even know what it's like to do this job?' Often it's important to pitch in and help. It can be a particularly smart move for women managers.

Louise Crossley reports:

In some situations, it was really important to show that you were willing to hoe in and work with the blokes. Unless you did that, they thought you were 'just a woman'. I could tell they really liked it when I joined in.

**Ask for something to be done in ways that indicate freedom of choice**
When issuing instructions to autonomous players, consider seriously the method suggested by John Gray in his book *Men are from Mars, Women are from Venus*. If your natural requesting style is to present all the reasons and soften the instruction with polite phrases such as, 'If you could possibly ...', or 'Would you mind awfully ...', consider whether the person you're dealing with may in fact find your style manipulative rather than polite, leaving them with no real choice about how they respond. Try saying, 'Would you do X?', taking care to use a non-demanding tone. It may work better. Though your request may sound bald, even rude to your ears, autonomous people (particularly men) may hear it as a more open, less manipulative request to which they can either say yes or no, preserving their autonomy.[176]

*Try saying, 'Would you do X?', taking care to use a non-demanding tone.*

**Recognise which autonomy issues it's smarter not to flatten**
*Dawn:* We did a drill at headquarters, rolling out heaps of hose. Afterwards, the officer in charge ordered all the junior people to tidy it away. I wasn't junior so I walked off. But he called me back, though he knows my rank perfectly well. 'You get in there and help roll it up,' he said to me. I said, 'Oh, I must have misheard you. I thought you said you wanted the juniors to do it.' And he said, 'Yeah, but you probably need the practice.' *Well, he's the boss,* I thought. If that's the way he wants to call it, you just have to go along with it. You're probably being assessed on whether you would obey a command. It would be just what he wanted — a fight with a woman shirking on doing the dirty stuff and disobeying an order! This job is so rank conscious. You have to respect a person's uniform, but you might not respect them as a person.

When people place high value on their independence or status, it may be very difficult to reason them out of their opinions. When a woman is in charge of a man, confrontation and control may be useless. There will be times when managers deem it wiser not to push the issue too far. These times come more frequently with a staff member whose autonomy needs are high. Louise Crossley says:

*There will be times when managers deem it's wiser not to push the issue too far.*

I'm a good leader, I don't muck about, I say what I want done, but I always try to create goals within the context of the group. However, I've found that if you are assertive and a reasonably good leader, it's fine if you're a man, but if you're a woman, you're being pushy. You may even have to compromise on some things you would like to see done, in order to avoid a showdown. If you allow a situation of increasing confrontation to develop, it gets harder and harder for people to back down. Sometimes you just have to accept failure for the greater good of the project.

### Handle tests of your fitness to advise with good grace

*Autonomous people can particularly resent having advice imposed on them.*

Autonomous people need to have a good reason why they're listening to someone's advice. They're likely to resent having it imposed on them. Trusting others to steer their thoughts or labour does not come easily. Expect to be observed for your fitness to instruct or advise, and don't be surprised if you're put to the test with a forceful, even rude challenge.[177]

> *Dawn:* The guys will always try and push you. I've been a teacher of our state volunteer firefighters. I remember one group asking me questions about the pump that were totally irrelevant to what we were discussing. So I rattled off the internal diameters and external diameters of hoses and capacities — we have to know all that stuff. They wanted to know if I knew more than them, I think. It seemed an odd way of having to earn respect.

I've experienced something similar as a workshop trainer. 'Helena, what you're saying is a load of hogwash', one man told me in no uncertain terms. I quivered inside, went into 'red alert' with adrenalin racing, but outwardly I met the attack with a calm and reasoned argument to support my point of view. To my considerable surprise, my critic transformed into a long-term, staunch supporter. Men often handle such challenges in their stride. Some women take offence and read the challenge as a personal put-down. Use these challenges as a valuable opportunity for building alliance:

▶ Focus on dealing with the issue rather than raising a counter-attack. Even if the challenge wasn't intended as a test in the first place, it may become an opportunity to earn respect from an autonomous player.

▶ Control your rising anger.

▶ Don't dodge the issue, but at the same time let the other person save face. Often this can be achieved by validating something the other person is saying. Instead of saying 'but' as you deal with an objection, say 'and' so that you include the objection rather than exclude it.[178] Explore opposing ideas and positions. Or try asking a fairly neutral question; for instance, 'What would it take to make this plan work?'

*Naturally worded questions could be the response that restores everyone's dignity.*

In accepting another person's authority over them, autonomous players must sacrifice a measure of their independence. They'll only do so willingly for leaders they judge worthy.

## STUMBLING BLOCK 3: INABILITY TO INCLUDE OTHER PEOPLE IN DECISION-MAKING PROCESSES

**'I make the plans. You follow them.'**

Have you ever watched someone muddling through a difficult situation which would have been so much easier had they asked someone's opinion on how to proceed? It used to be men who most often behaved like this. Today it's just as likely to be a woman not wanting to admit uncertainty or to give ammunition to her male peers. Some people's need for autonomy is so great it appears as though they've got to reinvent the wheel.

The gentle revolution is being pushed forward by market forces. The highly individualistic entrepreneur rarely fits well within larger organisations geared for the future, though they may remain the backbone of small business.[179] With today's technology enabling the easy exchange of information, and with businesses dealing over greater distances, the scope of most business activities is too widespread to rest in one individual. Moreover, organisational structures are, in general, shrinking. They are not merely downsizing, they are out-sourcing many functions that were once fulfilled in-house. More working relationships are contractual rather than controlling; hierarchies are fewer and flatter, and the arrangement of power is often that of partners with mutual respect for each other's expertise.

An insistence on going it alone can have serious consequences in today's workplace. The complexity of the issues facing modern

*An insistence on going it alone can have serious consequences in the workplace.*

management means that the leader is unlikely to have a full perspective on many issues — from firing a staff member within legal requirements to organising an advertising campaign that will not offend the community. A reluctance to consult others is almost bound to lead to imperfect decision-making and is becoming increasingly unacceptable to other workers. Such leaders fail to distinguish between the functions of leadership and the role of leader. Organisations always need leaders. However, in modern downsized, out-sourced organisations, there will be numerous situations where the function of leadership is best performed by people who are *not* the designated leader.[180]

Old-style leaders with old-style autonomy issues can be extremely unwilling to include other people in decision-making processes. One consultant working with a government department told me about the situation there, describing it as the worst he'd seen in ten years of consulting.

> In a team of about twenty people, all the senior positions were occupied by men and all the junior positions were occupied by women. There was a seemingly insoluble rift between these two groups. Two issues were at stake: communication and career path. All the women complained about the way the men would run a meeting: usually only once a fortnight, with eighteen items on the agenda to be covered in one hour. In that sort of time frame, all they could do was to discuss outcomes. Talking about how you felt was impossible and active listening was never used.
>
> The men were administratively and technically very strong. In terms of communication, however — examining team issues, getting a team together, facilitating dialogue — they were a disaster. They were unable to see the sense in discussing things in order to arrive at shared meaning or to empower others with trust and responsibility.
>
> Complaints had been made and the issues were being officially investigated. The findings showed that there was no career path for women and that the men didn't understand what consultation was. They thought it was a meeting where statements such as, 'These are the things that are happening in the office and this is what we are doing about it', were made. They were unable to facilitate discussion on the equity topic at all because they said it was too emotive.

## Resistance to mediation

**'But I can handle my own problems.'**

Obviously, these leaders in the example above didn't have the skill to solve their own problems. This group needed an external mediator, but they were very resistant to the idea, believing quite inaccurately that a mediator would challenge their autonomy.

### STEPPING STONES: MEDIATION

Many people who've taken pride in their ability to manage on their own have great difficulty accepting that, in cases of intractable conflict, they may need some help. Sometimes their resistance lessens when they learn that mediation is no longer considered an unusual step. Most business telephone directories now list professional mediators. More organisations are training key staff in mediation techniques to enable the formal handling of grievances in-house. Even within the legal profession, lawyers now are likely to see their role not just in active advocacy, but in providing services that settle disputes as cheaply and as early as possible. Often today the requirement of litigation is that you must first have tried mediation. Many business contracts now make provision for mediation in the event of disputes.

*More organisations are training key staff in mediation for grievance handling.*

Sometimes resistance can be overcome by clearly explaining the role of a mediator, which is:

▶ *to support the conflicting parties in designing their own solutions*;

▶ *to be objective*, validating both sides;

▶ *to be supportive*, by providing a non-threatening, resolving environment;

▶ *to be non-judgmental*, discouraging discussions about who was right or wrong;

▶ *to use astute questioning*, rather than advising;

▶ *to use a win/win approach*, working towards wins for both sides.

Using these guidelines, someone with good conflict resolution skills who is respected by both parties and who does not have too much invested in the issues may serve very well as an informal

*Mediations have
the capacity to turn
opponents into
problem-solving
partners.*

mediator. Where the consequences will be widespread or possibly litigious, it may be wiser to call in a professional. While mediation is not always the answer, handled well, it has the capacity to turn opponents into problem-solving partners.[181]

There are a number of problems in mediation that may be difficult to address fully. The weaker party is often easily pressured into giving in or giving more, and may be less skilled in bargaining and defending their rights, especially when these conflict with others' claims.[182]

Skilled mediators will be particularly alert to power issues when mediating for men and women in opposition. Women are often, but not always, less powerful. They frequently have a lower earning capacity, fewer resources and they're less likely to be confronting and assertive of their needs in the presence of a man. While their interdependent style is often at the core of this problem, interdependent focusers are not necessarily the weaker party. But there is a tendency for 'woman', 'weaker party' and 'interdependent player' to correlate.

A good mediator, mindful of these difficulties, can push for a fair agreement. Because of this objectively neutral support, the mediation process may be a more comfortable experience for the interdependent person than an arbitration method.

Mediation makes considerable demands of its participants. Participants have to be able and willing to negotiate, to assert their own interests, to know their own rights. They have to be honest and be prepared to compromise. They need to listen and take into account reasonable requests from the other party.

Benefits that both men and women can look forward to from mediation include:

▶ avoiding further hostility;

▶ restoring and maintaining a workable relationship;

▶ a more creative and well thought-through deal.

## Resistance to team goals

### 'You hog our meetings with your own issues.'

There are situations in which highly autonomous players function most appropriately. However, there are an increasing number of work environments in which excessive autonomy will create problems. The trend in many organisations is towards high involvement based on employee empowerment and team-based structures. Autonomous players may not quite fit. Bill talks about this most honestly:

> I have a lot of difficulty absorbing other people's goals as part of my agenda. I'd rather pursue my own. I tend to get into fairly vigorous discussion about things in meetings, and I think sometimes I'm misunderstood.

Excessive individualism may slow the organisation down and create an internally competitive environment where people use their energy *against* each other, rather than *working together* towards group goals. With an excess of autonomy and competition, people may display grossly inappropriate and aggressive behaviours towards colleagues.

### STEPPING STONES: THE CONSENSUS-BUILDING PROCESS

Changing an individualistic, competitive culture may start with new criteria for promotion, such as membership of a successful team and skill in supporting team effort.

Skills in consensus decision-making may not come naturally to the autonomous player, but they are not too difficult to learn. Incorporating even a few can make dramatic differences to an autonomous style.[183] Johnson and Johnson provide a very workable definition of consensus:

> A collective opinion arrived at by a group of individuals working together under conditions that permit communications to be sufficiently open — and the group climate to be sufficiently supportive — for everyone in the group to feel that he or she has had a fair chance to influence the decision. When a decision is made by consensus, all members understand the decision and are prepared to support it.[184]

Refer to **Figure 55: Dos and don'ts of consensus decision-making** (page 348).[185]

*The trend in many organisations is towards employee empowerment and team-based structures.*

*Skills in consensus decision-making support team effort.*

| DOS AND DON'TS OF CONSENSUS DECISION-MAKING | | |
|---|---|---|
| **Do:** | **Don't:** | **Comments:** |
| Involve those people who will be affected by the decision. | *Don't make every decision by full consensus methods.* | Encourage participation from quieter members, or get everyone to take a turn. If the group agrees, smaller committees might make technical or special interest decisions. |
| To start each item, make a precise statement on what is (and perhaps what is not) to be decided. | *Don't presume you must reach a unanimous decision.* | Consensus may not represent everyone's first choice. Not everyone will be totally satisfied, but they will know that their input has been seriously considered. |
| Present your opinions forthrightly. | *Don't argue blindly for your own opinions.* | Maintain an open mind. |
| Listen carefully. Consider all views. Discuss underlying assumptions, needs and values. | *Don't change your mind just to reach a quick agreement or avoid conflict.* | Emphasise common ground as you hear it emerging in the discussion, so people can see they are moving forward. |
| Seek out differences of opinion. | *Don't be inflexible or unwilling to negotiate.* | Don't oppose objections. Include them in your deliberations. 'AND' not 'BUT'. |
| Give the process time. | *Don't use short cuts to decisions; for example, majority voting [49 per cent of participants may be furious!].* | Accept that you'll probably save the time in the long run through everyone's commitment to plans and solutions. While at times a leader must make the final decision, give as much power as possible to the consensus process. |
| Think creatively. Encourage brainstorming. | *Don't judge ideas too soon.* | Get lots of ideas up on a whiteboard or flip chart. Encourage some outrageous thinking. Something may spark a really creative answer. |
| Design solutions that combine the best of all viewpoints and positions. | *Don't assume that someone must win and someone must lose.* | If a stalemate is reached, look for the next most acceptable alternative. Think of ways to 'expand the pie', to add new ingredients, to trade, to get more information if it would help. |

*Figure 55: Dos and don'ts of consensus decision-making*

# STUMBLING BLOCK 4: HIDDEN DEPENDENCE

'I'm not dependent. Make me a cup of coffee, will you?'

Some men affirm their separateness from others because they believe the alternative is unwelcome dependence. When this is their underlying reason, they have not achieved true autonomy. They are instead caught up in rebellious individualism. Some men are so conditioned to expect subservience from others, some are so used to being nurtured, that they don't realise how often they *are* relying on others anyway — both in the workplace and at home.

The unthinking assignment of menial tasks to women because 'that's what women do' is a common source of deep resentment.

## STEPPING STONES
Very autonomous people can take the service of others for granted. When they are conscious of their interdependency on others, they will respect and recognise their reliance on those who do more routine tasks on their behalf. When other people do things for us, it needs:

*Very autonomous people can take the service of others for granted.*

▶ thanks;

▶ praise;

▶ acknowledgment of the interdependent relationship;

▶ adequate financial reward; and

▶ appropriate opportunities to advance to tasks with greater levels of responsibility.

# STUMBLING BLOCK 5: INABILITY TO SUSTAIN CONTACT

'He never takes a moment to just talk.'

For many autonomous players, too large a dose of interaction takes them beyond their comfort zone. Nathan reported how exhausting he found interdependence. He had an excellent relationship with his girlfriend, but he said:

*A lot of interaction may take autonomous players beyond their comfort zone.*

At the end of a three-week holiday with her, I need a break. Things get too demanding. Whereas I'm sure that she could keep going forever, I need some space. That's why I enjoy my surfing. I'm out there where she's not. Now she's trying to get involved. God help me when she finally does! That's what's good about my job — I come to work two nights a week and it gives me space.

Autonomous players and interdependent players sustain different quantities of contact. This difference is most obvious at times of stress, when the interdependent player will usually attempt to engage with other people, while the autonomous player is likely to withdraw. Sometimes autonomous people will appear to be attending when they are not really listening and at other times they don't even pretend. In sustained periods of stress, it can be all too easy for autonomous people to move into isolation and let important relationships fall into disrepair.

Sometimes stress is not the problem. Maria spoke to me about her own drive for autonomy and its pitfalls:

Because I have my own goals, it can rub people up the wrong way. I guess they feel they're not being acknowledged or considered. People who might want to get closer to me could perhaps feel disappointed or even alienated. Perhaps there are bits of my style that could have the sharp corners smoothed off.

*Disconnection from others may mask insecurity or fear of closeness.*

The very autonomous person may find connection with other people difficult at the best of times. Sometimes it's due to an introverted personality style. Sometimes it masks insecurity or a fear of closeness.

### STEPPING STONES
Allow time when you're not overly stressed to connect on a personal level with others who desire it. It doesn't have to be deep and meaningful, but it does have to be personal so they can build a sense of connection with you. Connection is a two-way process — learning about the other person as well as allowing yourself to be known to them. True autonomy is not incompatible with a degree of reliance on others, or with recognising and fulfilling others' reasonable needs for intimacy and involvement.

▼▼▼

For psychological wellbeing, both autonomous and inter-dependent players need to create a balance between both sets of values and cultivate flexibility in adjusting to circumstances. Both need to develop a strong sense of self and an ability to set clear boundaries. Both need to be able to give and receive support without negative consequences. True autonomy gives you a clear sense of your separate self with a capacity to create real connection with others.

# SUMMARY

| AUTONOMY: STUMBLING BLOCKS | STEPPING STONES: DEVELOP THE CAPACITY TO CREATE REAL CONNECTION WITH OTHERS |
|---|---|
| 1 ► Concern about invasion of autonomous areas | Reconsider how necessary it is to create exclusion based on sex. <br><br> Once a mixed-sex team is established, many unfounded fears fall away. Ask yourself: if your colleague were a man, would you have included him in a meeting or social event that combined business with pleasure? Remember many situations benefit from appropriate women. |
| 2 ► Resentment about taking orders or advice | WHEN YOUR NEED FOR AUTONOMY IS HIGH: Align your own free will with the instruction you've received. Change your outlook so that you can support the order. Add extra ingredients where possible to make the task more pleasant. <br><br> WHEN YOU'RE IN CHARGE OF THOSE WITH HIGH AUTONOMY NEEDS: <br><br> ► Polish your style so it demonstrates the strengths of autonomy. <br><br> ► Shift the emphasis away from control. <br><br> ► Join in some manual labour to soften resentment. <br><br> ► Ask for something to be done in ways that indicate freedom of choice. <br><br> ► Recognise which autonomy issues it's smarter not to flatten. <br><br> ► Handle tests of your fitness to advise with good grace. |

| STUMBLING BLOCKS | STEPPING STONES |
|---|---|
| 3 ▶ Inability to include other people in decision-making processes | Be alert to times when it's wiser to separate the function of leadership from the role of leader. |
| *Resistance to mediation* | MEDIATORS' ROLE: to support the conflicting parties in designing their own solutions, to be objective, supportive, non-judgmental, to use astute questioning and a win/win approach. |
| *Resistance to team goals* | BUILD SKILLS IN CONSENSUS DECISION-MAKING: Involve those who will be affected. To start each item, make a precise statement about what is (and perhaps what is not) to be decided. Present your opinions forthrightly. Listen carefully, consider all views, and discuss underlying assumptions, needs and values. Seek out differences of opinion. Give the process time. Think creatively and encourage brainstorming. Design solutions that combine the best of all viewpoints and positions. |
| 4 ▶ Hidden dependence | When other people do things for us, it needs: thanks; praise; acknowledgment of the interdependent relationship; adequate financial reward; and promotion opportunities. |
| 5 ▶ Inability to sustain contact | When not too stressed, recognise and fulfil others' reasonable needs for intimacy and involvement. |

> True autonomy gives you a clear sense of your separate self with
> a capacity to create real connections with others.

# PART VI

# CREATING CHANGE

## Synopsis — where are we now?

We have discussed in detail the polarisation of four pairs of values important to men and women in the workplace. We've seen how they contribute to, and sometimes are, the primary cause of cross-gender conflict.

A NOTE ON THE WIDER APPLICABILITY OF VALUES COLLISIONS TECHNIQUES: Chapter 15 covers techniques that are effective in a wide range of values clashes. We may catch gender difficulties in this net, but we must be open to a wide range of possibilities. While gender may be the most observable difference between two people, other issues may be at stake. Values may clash because of differences in age, cultural background, ideology, education or life experience. Priorities can shift unexpectedly due to factors such as high stakes for one or both parties, inadequate resources or time constraints, to name just a few.

Relatively little has been written in the field of conflict resolution on handling values clashes. Managers, mediators and trainers may find the following techniques particularly useful — these are sophisticated stepping stones for serious conflict resolution practitioners. If the detail is more than you need to know right now, skip to the Summary on page 384.

# 15 ALTERNATIVES FOR HANDLING VALUES COLLISIONS

### PREVIEW

▶ Challenging values you can't accept

▶ Using cognitive dissonance to encourage reassessment

▶ Changing behaviour

▶ Changing structures

▶ What satisfies the values in this situation? How much? How many?

▶ Dialoguing

The deep anger generated by values conflicts is our fire for change. How do we make sure it is a change for the better? In this chapter, we consider when it is appropriate to:

▶ challenge the other person's value;

▶ modify their behaviour;

▶ bypass differences and focus on deeper affinities.

*If we fail to address the values collision, it is likely to fester and become a serious communication breakdown.*

People's values are not easily brought into question. They have a long history. They are generally unlikely to be open for reconsideration. Yet if we fail to address the values collision, it is likely to fester and become a serious communication breakdown.

I first became aware of the significance of a values clash many years ago.

My husband Malcolm and I took our three young children, then aged five, six and eight, to visit the Pompeii exhibition at the art gallery. The exhibition was very crowded, so my husband took charge of two children and I took charge of one. There was a particularly long queue to look at a display of a number of miniature gold statues. Malcolm joined the end of the queue, holding hands with two of our children, one on either side of him. He stood patiently with them for some ten minutes before it was possible for them to view the glass-cased exhibits. I took one look at the queue and quickly decided to 'forget the gold statues'. My daughter and I skirted the whole bottleneck and moved on to linger over a beautifully constructed model of the city of Pompeii. I could 'sell' this to her as a glorified doll's house village.

We emerged from the exhibition long before Malcolm and the other children. As we waited, I became more and more irritated because I believed he had tested their patience too far. My focus was on their feelings.

'Why did you bother to queue like that?' I asked him when they finally emerged.

'If those statues can lie in the ground for 2000 years, we can wait ten minutes to see them,' he said. He was actions-and-objects focused. 'Wasn't the point of going to the exhibition to see everything in it?' he continued.

'No,' I thought, but said nothing. What looked like a mild difference in style had a major values collision just below the surface. I wanted him to think like I did, but he didn't. His values weren't available for reconsideration and nor were mine. We had reached an impasse with each other and backed off — a little colder, a little more distant for the rest of the afternoon.

Neither of us had the skill at the time to deal with our impasse. I thought then that a successful marriage meant two people 'at one', thinking like each other. I knew nothing about the different values and priorities so often associated with different genders, or that I was unlikely to get him to see it my way. I was lost in a quagmire of gender difference.

In some respects, the workplace is a good place to start learning to deal with values collisions. We care a little less and are therefore less likely to hope for an unrealistic alignment of values. At work we just need a solid relationship based on acceptable behaviours, so we can get on with the job. (Perhaps that's all we really need in an intimate relationship, too!)

*EXERCISE*

In addressing gender-linked issues, we need to be realistic about what is possible and what is unlikely to be achieved. Of course, many of the same issues will arise between people of the same sex, or the usual traffic in cross-gender values will be reversed. For example, a man may be more equality focused and a woman more status-minded. Few people perfectly match their own sex's stereotype. Moreover, the difference between the sexes is one of priorities only. Occasions will arise when the lower priority value thrusts its way onto centre stage.[186]

Browse through **Figure 56: Conflicts triggered by gender-linked values** (pages 357–358). Are you facing a conflict right now? Perhaps it is just at the level of discomfort or incident.[187] Perhaps it is more serious! Mark any issues in the table that seem relevant. Keep them in mind as you read on. Some of the alternatives for dealing with values collisions outlined in the rest of this chapter may give you some clues for resolution.

# CHALLENGING VALUES YOU CAN'T ACCEPT

We often presume that other people's values are the same, or ought to be the same, as our own. Morton Deutsch says:

> It is not the differences in values per se that lead to conflict, but rather the claim that one value should dominate or be applied generally even by those who hold different values.[188]

*Values are our guide to what's right for us.* Problems arise when we use our values to dictate what's right for other people, too.

People often see values as objectively true rather than subjectively chosen. Of course, whether there are any values that are objectively correct rather than communally decided is a question that's troubled philosophers for thousands of years. Killing and stealing are good candidates for such an inquiry. But even these values are rarely held as absolute. Many people condone killing in wartime or killing an attacker if it's the only way to save your own or another person's life. Most of us would look differently upon stealing if it was in order to feed a starving child.

While our general condemnation of killing and stealing is

| CONFLICTS TRIGGERED BY GENDER-LINKED VALUES | | | |
|---|---|---|---|
| Equalisers angered or hurt when: | Others angered or hurt by equalisers who: | Status–watchers angered or hurt when: | Others angered or hurt by status–watchers who: |
| ☐ others engage in power plays<br>☐ others demand blind obedience<br>☐ their skills and abilities are undervalued<br>☐ a situation seems to be extremely unfair | ☐ ignore lines of authority<br>☐ cut down tall poppies<br>☐ bitch about those in authority<br>☐ are uncomfortable about their own use of authority | ☐ they lose face<br>☐ they are not shown due respect<br>☐ others are insubordinate<br>☐ they are cast in subservient roles or relationships | ☐ enforce rigid and cumbersome hierarchies<br>☐ will not admit their errors<br>☐ are patronising<br>☐ value male over female employees |
| Agreers angered or hurt when: | Others angered or hurt by agreers who: | Competers angered or hurt when: | Others angered or hurt by competers who: |
| ☐ others use an adversarial style<br>☐ others refuse to address issues<br>☐ others won't give up entrenched issues<br>☐ others are in bad moods | ☐ don't say what they really think<br>☐ complain when others haven't considered their unspoken needs<br>☐ negotiate badly<br>☐ fail to address important issues | ☐ their successes are not acknowledged<br>☐ others challenge their competitive style<br>☐ there is no opportunity to prove themselves<br>☐ they repeatedly fail when competing | ☐ ignore human, community or ecological responsibility<br>☐ overemphasise the bottom line<br>☐ apply illegal or dubious practices<br>☐ put down or sabotage others |

*Figure 56: Conflicts triggered by gender-linked values*

© Copyright Helena Cornelius, *The Gentle Revolution* (Simon & Schuster, Australia, 1998).
For further information contact: The Conflict Resolution Network, PO Box 1016,
Chatswood NSW 2057, Australia. Tel.: +61 (0)2 9419 8500. Fax: +61 (0)2 9413 1148.
**Figure 56 may be reproduced for non–commercial use if this credit appears.**

| CONFLICTS TRIGGERED BY GENDER-LINKED VALUES (continued) | | | |
|---|---|---|---|
| Feeling focusers angered or hurt when: | Others angered or hurt by feeling focusers who: | Actions-and-objects focusers angered or hurt when: | Others angered or hurt by actions-and-objects focusers who: |
| ☐ people are not considered<br><br>☐ their emotions are ignored or not respected<br><br>☐ logic is used against them or others to manipulate or confuse<br><br>☐ others offer advice when they just want to be heard | ☐ dissolve easily into tears<br><br>☐ cannot be corrected without being offended<br><br>☐ don't seem focused on the job at hand<br><br>☐ can't be firm when it's needed | ☐ their judgment is questioned by others<br><br>☐ their action is blocked by others<br><br>☐ someone else's response is not well thought through<br><br>☐ other people's emotions interfere with their effectiveness | ☐ demand extended working hours (stressful or impossible for those with family care responsibilities)<br><br>☐ exclude process and people from their consideration<br><br>☐ insist on 'being rational' and ignoring feelings<br><br>☐ use excessive technical jargon as a smokescreen |
| Interdependent relaters angered or hurt when: | Others angered or hurt by interdependent relaters who: | Autonomous relaters angered or hurt when: | Others angered or hurt by autonomous relaters who: |
| ☐ others refuse to consult<br><br>☐ the impact of an action on the whole team is not considered<br><br>☐ opportunities to interact with others are withdrawn or are not available<br><br>☐ others don't take on or recognise a responsibility of care | ☐ spend too much time socialising<br><br>☐ schedule apparently unnecessary meetings<br><br>☐ create unwieldy work teams<br><br>☐ are overly concerned about conflicts in the group | ☐ they are forced to rely on others (e.g. in group projects or because of infirmity)<br><br>☐ someone else who has responsibility does not use it well<br><br>☐ they have to accept orders or instructions<br><br>☐ how they work, is too closely supervised | ☐ forget or refuse to consult<br><br>☐ act aloof<br><br>☐ block information flow<br><br>☐ presume women and subservient men are there to 'mop up' after them, completing their work |

*Figure 56: Conflicts triggered by gender-linked values (continued)*

relatively constant, other communally held values change more obviously over time. An authoritarian, controlling managerial style was once good practice. It is not regarded as such any longer. Concern about the environmental impact of trade waste was namby-pamby stuff. Now legislation is beginning to support new community values on environmental responsibility. Values are relative to our current awareness. Yet, once we have a raised awareness to an area of concern, it's hard for us to consider that these new values are not objectively 'correct'. 'You *should* consult', 'You *should* protect the environment', jump easily onto our tongues. We care passionately. We're in danger of conflict with anyone who doesn't see it our way. Values don't lie quietly. They are often the source of conflict. Moral injunctions follow close on the heels of values.

*Moral injunctions follow close on the heels of values.*

While the call to ethics or morality may be just what the situation needs to get people back on track, it must be gauged carefully. It can be extremely irritating and may invoke exactly the opposite result to the one we want. Sometimes the moral high ground looks like arrogance. Many who use it frequently hold very rigid positions. Underneath they may be protecting themselves against a deep fear of uncertainty or against the possibility of personal attack. Sometimes they feel they must stand as a beacon of light in an evil world. Such underlying issues can entrench positions and make resolution extremely difficult. We can get very righteous about gender-linked values, too. Consider the person who cannot abide having their instruction questioned, or who believes all people ought to be open about their feelings.

When communicating your point of view, limit your use of 'oughts', 'shoulds' and 'musts'. Useful alternatives are: 'The way I see it …', or 'What seems important to me to consider is …'.

When someone is expressing values you personally disagree with, you may wish to make it clear that their value is personal to them: 'So do you feel that it's really important to preserve your status in this situation', or 'So you feel a bit of healthy competition is a good thing here?', or 'So you want to keep relationships between staff harmonious?'. You move the emphasis away from moral imperatives and back to statements of legitimate, but personal, opinions.

Sometimes, you will wisely decide you must make a very firm stand for your own values. Christa's boss asked her to fudge some numbers. She refused. His urge to compete had got out of hand and he wanted to make his department's performance appear better than it was. Here's her explanation of her position:

> My values are honesty — you don't tell lies. I'm aware there are consequences when you say 'No' like that to a supervisor. But at least I'll develop a reputation for what I want to have a reputation for.

## USING COGNITIVE DISSONANCE TO ENCOURAGE REASSESSMENT

In dealing with a clash of values where the other person's value is not particularly honourable or suitable, it is sometimes wiser *not* to encourage them to state the value they hold. Let's consider here a psychological theory developed by Leon Festinger — *cognitive dissonance*, the term he used for the inner tension that causes us to alter either values or behaviours.[189] When our values and behaviour clash, we restore their alignment by changing one or the other. If there is a discrepancy between what is publicly declared and what is privately believed, this is usually resolved by the person shifting the *privately* held value to align with the publicly stated one. So be careful. People cement in place values they publicly declare. If someone can be encouraged to state in public a *positive* value, the positive value is more likely to motivate future action, even if at the time they don't really believe it.

Robert B. Cialdini talks about our nearly obsessive desire to be (and to appear) consistent with what we have already done:

> Once we have made a choice or a stand, we will encounter personal and inter-personal pressures to behave consistently with that commitment. Those pressures will cause us to respond in ways that justify our earlier decision.[190]

For example, if Christa says to her boss, 'I'm sure you wouldn't want me to do something that I thought was dishonest', she invites him to agree and thereby publicly state a value that probably does not align with his privately held one. She creates a psychological tension in him that may, over time, help him to shift to greater levels of honesty, or at least reduce his expectations of dishonest practices from his staff.

We often presume that values drive behaviours. However, values have been built by experiences and are changed by experiences, too. Getting people to do something different often impacts on the value. Hugh Mackay says:

> Our experience shapes our attitudes [values] and our attitudes, in turn, shape our subsequent behaviour — pending new experience.[191]

The theory of cognitive dissonance maintains that although values/behaviour modification is a two-way street, the heaviest traffic is in the direction of behaviour driving the revision of values. Thus, if you are able to get people to alter their behaviour, their values are likely to shift gradually, too. This is the hidden strength of all behavioural approaches to handling values collisions.

*If you are able to get people to alter their behaviour, their values are likely to shift gradually, too.*

values ◄━━━━━━━ behaviour

Here's how it might work:

| | |
|---|---|
| **Experience:** | Demands made in childhood by adults to share and 'play nicely'. |
| **Lesson:** | If I want to be liked, I should try always to agree with other people. I should ignore my own needs if it's necessary to maintain harmony. Anything else is selfish. |
| **Value:** | Agreement. |
| **Behaviour:** | I say 'yes' when my boss wants me to work late, although it doesn't suit me. |
| **Experience:** | My boss repeatedly asks me to work late. My social life is in tatters. |
| **Lesson:** | This person will never consider me. I'll have to stand up for myself. |
| **Behaviour:** | I say: 'Enough! No!' |
| **Cognitive dissonance:** | I've said 'no', but my value has been to agree. |

| | |
|---|---|
| **Lesson:** | Standing up for myself felt good. To heck with always being accommodating! |
| **Impact on value:** | I have the right to value myself. How can I do it in an agreement-style way? |

To keep the theory of cognitive dissonance in perspective, it's important to remember that most people maintain a fairly consistent set of values throughout their lives. I believe this applies to the eight gender-linked values discussed in this book. Experience will modify behaviour to some extent and thereby impact on the value and refine it, but in the crisis of conflict people return to their preferred 'conflict corners' that have probably been established since childhood (see page 28).

# CHANGING BEHAVIOUR

Working towards a change in behaviour is an approach that can be used in a wide variety of circumstances. Here's another example:

Deborah was director of a design agency. She negotiated the contracts, oversaw the projects and hired consultants to work according to her general specifications. She had a team of consultants she regularly used. One of them, Michael, preferred working alone, dealing directly with the client. But sometimes he took jobs through Deborah's agency. He was so used to being autonomous that he really resented the commission that Deborah charged for going through her agency. Despite the fact that it was a set percentage known in advance, he grumbled about it frequently to her office staff. She became concerned that these abrasive conversations with Michael were undermining her staff's morale. Moreover, she felt that Michael didn't respect her right to earn an income from jobs he got through her agency. She was about ready to strike him off the books.

The root of the problem was a values collision. Deborah saw herself as providing a much-needed service for all the designers on her books. She enjoyed and fostered the interdependence and community spirit they shared. Michael didn't want to acknowledge that to be fully employed he also needed the agency group and that this came at a cost.

Deborah chose not to challenge the autonomy/interdependence clash, however. She asked instead for a change in his behaviour:

'I really respect how much you want to be an independent operator, and I understand that your issues with the agency fee arise from that, but I must ask you not to discuss this sort of problem with my staff any more. If you have to talk about it, then do so with me. But I must warn you, the fee is not negotiable. That's your cost of getting work through us.'

She requested a *behavioural change he could achieve* and was clear about her bottom line — no reduction in fees.

A request for more appropriate behaviour is often the most appropriate way to handle values collisions without directly discussing the value itself. If we get our intervention right — that is, it appears relevant and achievable — we may also be a catalyst for some values reassessment.

# CHANGING STRUCTURES

The behavioural approach may also be the most effective method for transforming patriarchal workplace cultures that discriminate against women. Legislation and organisational policy may well impact on group-held values over time.

Festinger says: 'Following public compliance there is frequently a subsequent change of private opinion.'[192]

► Laws which punish people for sexual harassment not only act as a deterrent, but by changing the whole context of acceptable and unacceptable behaviour, may shift the values of potential harassers in the long term.

► As people are forced to provide equal opportunity to women in the workplace, they may finally come to believe in it.

An affirmative action policy that dedicates particular positions or a quota of positions to women gives them the chance to demonstrate their competence. Without firm policy on the matter, women with a more feminine style and set of values are often undervalued and denied the opportunity to show what they can do. Their managerial skills are particularly likely to go unrecognised if those skills have been developed in the context of domestic duties. Many men have no concept of the organisational skills it takes to run a household well under the time pressures imposed by part-time or full-time work. Pre-defined places where women can prove their worth in the workplace create career paths for women in spite of male-oriented workplace values.

Such methods, however, are not without cost to male–female relationships in the workplace. Regulating equality can have the effect of stifling frank discussion and may force change before many men are ready for it. While in the long term we can expect the values shift that follows changed behaviour, in the short term a good number of men resent what seems like unfair favouritism and may resist the process. And not without some cause. Affirmative action policies can force a bad or unfair decision concerning promotion. Ultimately its phasing out is the measure of its success, once merit is no longer judged through a patriarchal filter. But backlash in the form of powerful opposition may well occur along the way. The mismatch between enforced behaviour and the values held (cognitive dissonance) is stressful and at times infuriating. Changing the values that underlie the problem is a very uncomfortable process.

Informal discussion and explanations are important processes in the much-needed culture shift. Already, there are many men who abhor values that put women down, discriminate against them or sexually harass them. They are important allies in the education of other men. By virtue of their gender, they may be more credible in challenging outdated patriarchal values than women can ever be. Lobbying for and the implementation of affirmative action policy will and must go on. Women also need the support of other women as they stand up to management for the structural changes that will ultimately shift workplace cultures. They can use women's networks for support, but they shouldn't ignore the large numbers of supportive males.

Structural changes in organisational policies, such as career paths for part-time employees, job sharing and alternative care allowances, have a slow and steady effect on changing workplace cultures and the values that underlie them.[193] Yes, some men will complain about positive discrimination in favour of women, but many of these changes will have to be instituted across the board and will create a more balanced work life for men, too. Organisations can be persuaded to make such changes because they constitute sound business sense. Family-friendly organisations attract the best men and women, reap higher workplace performance from them, and retain trained and experienced personnel through and beyond crises and major life transitions.

## WHAT SATISFIES THE VALUES IN THIS SITUATION? HOW MUCH? HOW MANY?

Issues involving broad groups of people lend themselves to structural solutions, involving organisational policy or government legislation. But a wide range of gender-relevant conflicts cannot be solved by the application of general rules. It is then that all or some of the elements of the *clarify and quantify* approach may be helpful. It's a method of jointly constructing rules tailored to the particular situation.

Clarifying and quantifying values is a technique that works well when the values you will uncover in the other person are themselves acceptable by community standards. Your difficulty is not the value as such, though it may not be your own, but the solution the other person is pushing for.

Ask yourself what you really need changed. If the answer is *behaviour*, rather than the *value* itself, the clarify and quantify approach can be useful. It has two significant advantages:

*Ask yourself what you really need changed.*

▶ You'll both know what you are dealing with. There need be no hidden agendas.

▶ It is often much easier to encourage behavioural changes than values shifts. From our understanding of cognitive dissonance, we can see that in many circumstances, it may be our most effective method of addressing underlying issues.

**Figure 57: Clarifying and quantifying needs, concerns and values** (page 366) presents an overview of the method. Note the letters in brackets refer to examples in the text.

Step 1 ▶ **Unfold the value(s)** behind this conflict. Asking 'Why do you want X?' will often lead you past opposing positions (a) towards underlying values, but you may need a number of attempts to achieve reasonable statements of values.

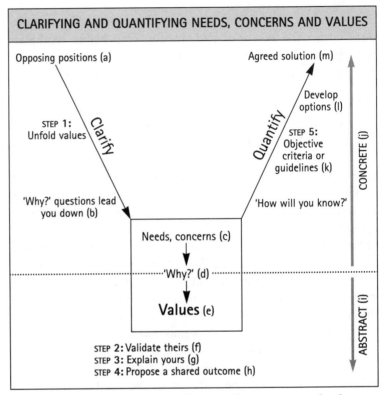

*Figure 57: Clarifying and quantifying needs, concerns and values*

John Haynes makes a useful distinction between *ends* and *means*. He puts forward the following simplified example to explain:

> 'I need a Mercedes.'
> 'Why?'
> 'I need transport and a Mercedes has prestige.'[194]

The Mercedes is the 'means'. Transport and the boost to status offered by a prestige car were the 'ends'.[195] In relation to gender-linked values, you might uncover a sequence like the following:

> 'I need my own office.'
> 'Why?'
> 'I need to be able to concentrate on my work.'

*Means:* An office
*Ends:* (in this case, a value) Focus on actions and objects.

People don't always have uppermost in their minds the values that are driving their behaviour. Sometimes values are completely unconscious and the values that people say they hold contradict their actual behaviour. If the person asking for their own office seems more concerned about getting a nameplate for the door than with making the room operational quickly so that work flow isn't interrupted, you might suspect that status had a major part to play in their request.

It's often hard to move further in resolving conflict until the most relevant values are explored. You'll need some conversational skills to move people, already hot under the collar from the conflict, into a reasonably calm exploration process. 'Why?' style questions lead you down into the deeper motivations behind position statements (b), such as 'I need my own office'. The first time you ask someone why they hold a particular position, they'll often deal only with concrete, substantive needs and concerns (c). They are likely to stay up at the concrete level of the problem where more or less of something will solve their problem (c, j).

'I need my own office.'
'Why?'
'I need more space.'

Values are more abstract. They may be as mild as a preference for a team approach to a complex task, or as core as the demand to be respected.

If a value is of primary concern in a conflict, it may be elicited from your first exploration. That is, the person plunges straight down to the abstract level (e, i).[196] For example, they may say: 'Everyone else at my level has an office except me!' You will probably now suspect you're dealing with a hot-under-the-collar equaliser.

Sometimes you don't have to explore with questions at all. The value is signalled pretty clearly in complaints such as those in **Figure 58: Values issues signals** (page 368).

To get people to explore deeper, the key is to avoid a challenging tone. 'Why?' or 'Why is that?' can work if emotions are not too inflamed, and you sound concerned and genuinely interested (d). 'Why?' alone, thrown up as a demand or complaint, will probably be read as further confrontation and

| VALUES ISSUES SIGNALS | |
|---|---|
| Complaint | Issue |
| That's not fair! | Equality |
| Show some respect! | Status |
| Why do you always have to make such a fuss? | Agreement |
| If you can't stand the heat, get out. | Competition |
| You don't give a damn about how I feel! | Feeling focus |
| Shut up and get on with it! | Actions-and-objects focus |
| We're all in this together! | Interdependence |
| Let me do it myself! Don't tell me what to do! | Autonomy |

*Figure 58: Values issues signals*

produce defensiveness, provoking such answers as, 'Because!', or 'None of your business!', or 'That's just how I want it!'. There are lots of ways to ask 'why?' style questions. You don't even always need to use the 'why?' format. (See **Figure 59: 'Why?' style questions that work**, page 369.)

Once you get to the point where there is no real sense in asking 'why?' any more, you've hit the values level for this problem (e). You might confirm that you've got it right with a question such as, 'Are you concerned about lack of equality here?', or 'You're looking for a fair deal?'. If you get an emphatic *yes*, you'll know you've chosen a way of discussing the value that works for the person you're with. Try to find key words they are comfortable using. When you've found them, you both can acknowledge and talk about their value in their 'shorthand' as you progress in the resolution process.

Don't expect that all the values you'll uncover this way will relate to gender-linked values. Don't expect that it will always be productive to continue your 'why?' questions until you arrive at a values level. Frequently, staying at the level of needs and concerns will do nicely (c, j). For example, if you can't provide the office

> ### 'WHY?' STYLE QUESTIONS THAT WORK
>
> ► Why is that important to you?
> ► What's important to you about that?
> ► What's concerning you about what's happened?
> ► What's the reason behind that?
> ► What is it about that which bothers you?
> ► What could happen if you didn't get that?
> ► What is this an example of?
> ► For what purpose?
> ► What is your intention?

*Figure 59: 'Why?' style questions that work*

they're asking for, you may move on to look for alternative ways you can meet the person's substantive need for more space. You will at times find it very difficult to draw clear distinctions between needs, concerns and values, and often that won't matter. Remain flexible. Take whatever you find and work with it.

> **Mapping the needs, concerns and values of**
> ***all* people who have something at stake may be a valuable**
> **process at this point.**[197]

Step 2 ► Validate their value(s) (f). It only needs a sentence: 'You're after a prestige car? [their shorthand for status] Fair enough', or 'You're worried about how everyone's going to take the news? [their description of their feeling focus] That sounds important'. If someone complains that they don't think they're being treated fairly, a thoughtful, considering head nod may even serve as validation if you really mean it.

It only takes a second to validate another person's perspective, yet conflicts can go on for hours, months or years if you don't. Ignoring this step may well be read as a challenge to the value, and that's a very risky business. But you must really mean your 'Fair enough!' or your 'That sounds important!'. With the conflict between my husband and I at the Pompeii exhibition, it would have made a difference to my afternoon, and probably his too, if I'd said: 'I understand that you don't want to miss any part of the exhibition. You came to see the whole thing', or 'I'm really impressed by your respect for the age of the statues'. But back then, I'd have thought I was selling out my value by acknowledging his.

*Values aren't right or wrong. They just are.*

People identify strongly with their own values. They are often a core part of the individual's personality. He or she will defend them vigorously. Quite honestly, in 95 per cent of situations it's not a smart battle to fight. In our Pompeii exhibition conflict, the value of consideration for the children's limited patience collided with the value of making every effort to succeed fully in the task we had taken on out of respect for the antiquity of the objects. Who was right? You might have an opinion. It will be based on your own priorities. But values aren't right or wrong. *They just are.* The validity of a value is that it is held by someone. Generally, therefore, it need not be questioned. To move safely through Step 2 you'll need to show you respect the other person's value *because they hold it*, not necessarily because it's your own value too or has as high a priority for you.

Well, you might ask, if neither person's value can be questioned and each implies a different solution, what hope is there of resolution? You'll never know till you try.

Step 3 ▶ **Explain your values** (g). In acknowledging the other person's values, don't leave yours out in the cold. You want the same respect for your values as you're giving to theirs.

*And* not *but.*

Don't presume the other person understands the values you find important in the situation. You're probably going to have to clarify them. Don't begin with the word 'but'. Say 'and' instead. Use this language technique regularly to move out of opposition into joint problem-solving. 'You're fed up with her coming late AND she needs the job', 'We need to win the contract AND we can't take risks on cheap, unsafe chemicals.'

So, I could have said to my husband: '... AND I wanted to make sure the visit was a positive experience for the kids. I wanted them

to like it, so they'll be happy to come again.' Don't be afraid to 'sell' your value. For instance: 'It could be the start of a real interest in art and history for them.'

*Encourage reprioritising.* Somewhere, a little lower on their priority list, your value probably exists for the other person, too. Some good advocacy may increase its rating in their eyes. At the very least, you need it to be considered. Here's a selling technique:

► Consider the language and way of speaking used by the other person. It will give you clues to their underlying values.[198]

► Try to match your language to theirs. In the example I refer to next, Joseph is very task-oriented. Cassie, who is arguing with him about who should do the filing, may persuade him better if she explains herself in *task-oriented terms*. 'We need a really efficient routine. AND we also need one that's fair *because that will affect efficiency in the long term, too.*' If you are feeling focused and you present your arguments in a emotion-centred way, this will not impress. 'Filing's so boring' invites 'Well, she can leave!', or 'That's the job'.

▶ Focus on their value. Appeal to that value, but offer a broader perspective. If your concern is teamwork and the other person is motivated by competition, you might try saying: 'If we are really going to compete effectively in the marketplace, we need to pull together as a team.' Another approach is to *explore the consequences of not focusing some attention on those values that you see as particularly important*. 'If we don't come up with a filing routine that's seen as fair, there's likely to be a lot of unnecessary unrest which will certainly affect our output.'

Can't think that fast on your feet? Talk around the issue until you find appealing reasons. Ask yourself out loud: 'I wonder why I prefer this alternative?', or 'Let me think why I favour the solution of getting everyone to do their own filing'. It may be appropriate to ask yourself such questions in front of the other person. If all of us possessed good conflict resolution skills, the other person would probably ask you these questions, instead. However, chances are you will have to be the one to steer the conversation in the direction of resolution. You need to explain your own values and work towards the other person acknowledging them — not *instead of* but *as well as* their own.

You can explain your values, but the other person might not acknowledge them until you've achieved Step 4.

**Step 4 ▶ Propose a shared outcome that you can both agree on (h).** Reframe the conflict into a joint problem to be solved: 'I wonder how, in the future, we could see the whole exhibition AND keep the kids happy?' This is a shift away from positions or conflicting solutions such as, 'Should we or shouldn't we have queued?'.

With a new, *shared outcome*, you're ready to develop some new options. Combining both parties' values into a joint statement is just one way to formulate a shared outcome. Sometimes you can agree on the outcome with a wider perspective.

Let's use Joseph and Cassie's argument about filing to demonstrate further:

Joseph wants everyone to put all letters to be filed in a tray for the office junior to file daily in the communal filing drawers. Cassie wants everyone to file their own correspondence. They are disagreeing on means, but not on ends. By shifting the focus away from their differences for a moment onto their wider perspective — a filing routine that works — they can take some of the heat out of their conflict. Now they're searching for solutions on common ground.

*Shared outcome: a filing routine that works.*

Step 5 ► **Set up objective criteria or guidelines for success** (k). What behaviour in particular would indicate that the value is operating in this situation? How much? How often?

Naming values has taken us down into the abstract level (i).[199] This level may be valuable for understanding, but the search for a solution demands we move back to the concrete (j). A new question such as, 'What would that mean (or imply) in this situation?', may take you back up to the concrete with some extra information and sensitivities. You need to relate a value to the particulars of the situation in order to address it appropriately. You need to know if more or less of something concrete will in fact address the value in question. Values made concrete offer guidelines for solutions.

For an efficient filing method, Joseph's guidelines may include:

► *No more than one week's backlog in filing.*

► *All correspondence from the same person filed in the same place.*

► *Everyone in the office can access all files.*

Cassie has no quarrel with these criteria, but has others she wants added as well: her feeling focus and equality buttons are pressed as filing is a boring job. Cassie's priorities are that:

► *No one person is lumbered with the whole task.*

► *A person who needs the letter again will know exactly where to find it.* She believes that the person who reads the letter the first time is the most likely person to want the correspondence again and should choose how best to file it; for example, under the company name, the individual's name, the country or state.

Cassie's first solution was therefore that everyone does their own filing (l). Joseph definitely doesn't want to do his own. 'It would be totally inefficient for me to file,' he says firmly. His job entails many outside appointments and he has little time to attend to paperwork.

Quantifying Cassie's equity value may lead to a breakthrough. She could ask herself, or Joseph could ask her: 'How many people would need to be involved in the filing to distribute the load more fairly?' To Cassie, the ideal answer initially appears to be that everyone does their own filing. But is that really fair? In this office, the office junior creates almost no filing of her own and Joseph, who reads most of the correspondence that comes in, generates a lot. Setting up the criteria in discussion with each other exposes this problem that Cassie hadn't previously recognised. On consideration, she decides that for a fair load distribution she wants at least three or four people to do filing.

Once Cassie accepts the principle that some, not necessarily all, employees could share the filing load, then the 'who?' and 'how?' questions are reasonable negotiation points.

---

**Sometimes it helps to quantify:**

1 ▶ where you are now;
2 ▶ where you want to be; and then
3 ▶ negotiate on how you will close the gap.

---

For example:

1. *Where you are now:* At the present time in Cassie and Joseph's office the secretary is supposed to do the filing (and does so occasionally). The secretary sometimes co-opts the office junior. That's two people.

2. *Where you want to be:* Cassie wants three or four people to do the filing.

3. *The gap:* Cassie has a gap of at least one person around which to negotiate.

This is a very neat conflict resolution manoeuvre! Here is another way of approaching it. Apply the method to each value that's a sticking point in the conflict.

| DEVELOPING CRITERIA TO GAUGE WHETHER THE VALUE IS SATISFIED | |
|---|---|
| Translate the value into specific behaviours | These behaviours are those relevant to the situation and should be objectively verifiable in order to judge success or failure. |
| Quantify the value | How much or how often is enough for the value to be satisfied here? |

Figure 60: Developing criteria to gauge whether the value is satisfied

John Haynes, international trainer in mediation skills, successfully used the quantifying method to resolve a difficult issue for a divorcing couple about the religious education of their child. As mediator, he asked both parents how many times they each felt the child should attend a religious service in any month. He says: 'The value question was unresolvable. But, once the value was quantified, both sets of needs could be met and an agreement became possible.'[200]

Once you start quantifying values, you need to be clear about your boundaries and your bottom line, and before those cut-off points, the extent of your flexibility. Only one person doing all the filing was below Cassie's bottom line. Working on the criteria and, in particular, on quantifying the values for this situation, moves the conflict from impasse to negotiation. Keep referring back to the shared outcome you agree on (h). In this case, *a filing method that works.* Although all people doing all the filing was Cassie's preferred option at first, as she investigates further, it looks pretty unrealistic in the light of their shared outcome or goal.

You may be well on the way with Step 6 before you formally take it.

Step 6 ► Develop options that support the agreed criteria. Be creative. Don't dismiss any option too soon. Keep the options fluid with, 'Yes, that's a possibility. What else?', or a similar comment. You are looking for a combination of suggestions that will mean all or at least the most important criteria have been met (l).

Again, the language tool of *and* not *but* can keep you both focused on a win/win approach. Sometimes you just cannot support both values simultaneously, but could possibly support each of them sequentially. For example, with my family's excursion to the art gallery, we might have agreed that if we did decide to see each item in the exhibit, we'd also include an ice-cream break for the children and some time in the park afterwards, so that the visit would be fun and not too taxing. We could have clocked time spent on each event as a quantifier for each value. To meet the relevant needs and values, the agreed solution will probably have a number of components (m). One component in the filing solution may be that the reader marks how the person should file that letter.

## DIALOGUING

*Dialoguing relies on people telling their personal stories rather than debating their issues.*

I spoke with Peter Melser, an innovative mediator and facilitator who is part of a group pioneering a new type of resolution process. It arises out of 'narrative' and 'brief' therapy processes and is often called *mediation dialogue*. The method relies on people telling their personal stories rather than debating their issues. The facilitator interferes in the process as little as possible, occasionally directing a turn in the conversation and no more. Peter bases much of his work on that of Sallyann Roth in the United States, who uses the approach for public and community values conflicts. She has conducted dialogues with proponents of the right to abortion and 'right to lifers'.[201] Small groups of Arabs and Israelis have been brave enough to engage in dialoguing in Israel's political tinderbox. Citizen diplomacy efforts in the 1980s used similar methods for tackling the cold war between America and Russia at a grass roots level.

At a time when the Australian community was very divided by an upsurge of anti-Aboriginal sentiment, my own organisation, Conflict Resolution Network, hosted a variation on the dialoguing theme with a very successful reconciliation meeting called 'Woman to Woman'. The process can go deeper with small groups, but I found myself moved to tears of admiration as the personal stories unfolded before some 200 people at the meeting. At the end, I came away saying to myself, 'Nothing really happened, and yet everything happened'. There were no prepared speeches. It was just seven pairs of women — each pair made up of one Caucasian and one Aboriginal. Each couple took their turn on stage, chatting together in a private way in front of a shared microphone, telling stories to each other about how they formed their values, and about their influences and the difficulties they faced in their daily work of reconciliation.

It seemed so strongly a woman's way that I was moved to ask Peter Melser if the process works with men. 'Well, yes it does,' he replied. 'Men do get caught up in the 'rational', impersonal kind of debate that keeps conflict going, but it is quite possible to get them talking more personally. The aim is to help people explore the meanings and experiences behind the beliefs and values that are clashing. When people start to dialogue in this way, more of the complexity and ambiguities start to come through. It's never as clear cut as the sharp debating positions make it seem. People talk about their pain around the issue, their doubts about their stance and their unanswered questions. This shifts the focus from the abstract values or the "wrongs" that are generating the conflict, to the richness of the people themselves. Once they start hearing one another's stories, people view the conflict in a different way. They see that what the other person is saying might be right for that person, even if it's not right for themselves. Through this kind of reflective dialogue they see the person, as well as the conflict, and the conflict seems to matter less.'

*Dialoguing uncovers the complexities and ambiguities in the way values are held.*

Christine James, another mediator/facilitator was present at my meeting with Peter Melser. She commented:

'I'm a great believer in letting the pain be very apparent. We want to solve a problem if it's causing us enough pain. Sometimes it's important to start by focusing on the pain in order to develop a willingness to participate. If you focus people on their values, you can invite all the righteousness they've developed as the conflict has escalated. The facilitator often needs to tone down all that righteousness and bring them face to face with the consequences of their increasing polarisation. Sometimes the

*We want to solve a problem if it's causing us enough pain.*

facilitator will have to raise their awareness of the sensation of symptoms of unresolved conflict. Often it's not until the eleventh hour that people will turn around and say "Gee, I don't want that", and start to take some responsibility for their own contribution to the continuing conflict. As facilitator, I'm trying to create a space where people can enact that choice of cooperation. Even as the process progresses, I'm still likely to keep their awareness of the pain up there on the agenda. I don't want to make them feel better too soon. If you hide the pain, there's very little chance for dis-integration.'

'What's this "dis-integration"?' I asked Christine.

*The facilitator is not the fixer, just the rudder steering the process.*

'There's a moment of dis-integration in the resolution of any entrenched conflict,' she responded. 'You have to dis-integrate before any re-integration can take place in a new shape. If you hide the pain, there's very little chance for dis-integration. It's not up to me as facilitator to fix the problem. That leap is, in fact, most likely to occur at the moment when I feel totally *unable* to fix their problems. It's for the participants to make an emotional shift. When the process reaches that point, the facilitator can reflect back to them by disclosing their own feelings about it: "Well, I'm totally stumped". You're actually encouraging them to give up. What happens then is really interesting. Whatever is positive in them then emerges. In a sense, *they* come to the rescue. Their own leadership emerges. This is totally appropriate. It isn't the facilitator's problem anyway. It's theirs. The facilitator is not the fixer, just the rudder steering the process. In the end the participants should be able to say: "The facilitator didn't really solve it, we did."'

Christine's comments reminded me of Chinese philosopher Lao-tzu's *Tao Te Ching* when he said:

When [the Master's] work is done,
The people say, 'Amazing:
we did it, all by ourselves!'[202]

Christine continued: 'It's very empowering. I've seen that moment of dis-integration happen in a public meeting with several hundred irate people. Suddenly, after all the hoo-hah, we reached a place of thundering silence when the penny finally dropped that they hadn't gathered in order to fight each other. They'd really all come there to solve a problem.'

'Can you get to that place using a dialogue method, Peter?' I asked.

'Yes, you can, but the route seems more subtle. It's certainly not like a formal mediation where both parties have a list of things that you work through methodically with each of them. You may not even come up with brilliant firm alternatives. You don't get a resolution as straightforward as that.

'I think it is always very useful to remind ourselves that when people come into mediation, they have usually made a decision to try to get away from the conflict, to try to break its influence in their lives. Now this makes a really good starting point. I will often start by ignoring the conflict altogether and ask each party: "If this mediation dialogue were successful and it made a real difference to your relationship, what will be different when we finish?" Usually they say things like, "Well, we'll be a lot happier, we'll be smiling with one another", or "We'll accept one another's differences more, and be able to exchange our ideas and know that while it's not what we think, it's okay that they think it", or "We'll be able to combine our ideas creatively and do things that neither of us could do without the other".

'These kinds of statements point to "alternatives" to the conflict story, and it's likely that there is a history to these statements just as there is a history to the conflict. So I might then ask, "Can either/any of you think of any times in the past when it has been like that?". People will usually start coming up with examples. I get everyone to talk about what each of these occasions had been like for them. People compare stories that show their relationship working in ways they want it to. They still recognise the ways they are different from one another, but they listen carefully and relive these earlier events. Putting this history into words builds up its reality.

'You see, getting back to actual occasions when things have been different, and the conflict has not dominated, does several things to help to dislodge the conflict. It gives "air-time" to the parts of people's lives that are separate from the conflict. The stories demonstrate to everyone involved that they are capable of a productive relationship. It reminds them it is a reality they are capable of having. When combined with the strong desire to break the conflict, reliving this experience builds people's belief that they can do it. The stories provide concrete examples of how to get along together without the conflict, and also the principles for managing the relationship better in the future. The important factor is that these are strategies that the people have *already* used — they have worked before and can work again.

'With this information, we can start to reflect on what inner resources people demonstrated that allowed them to work together without the conflict; what they did to enable that kind of constructive relationship to be more dominant than the conflict itself. Then we could move on to discussing what the various parties might do to redevelop that kind of relationship now. People come up with constructive suggestions for changing the relationship. Any agreements that emerge can be written down, but these are usually less important than the change in people's attitude to one another. I might even get all the way through a mediation dialogue without people even talking about the conflict, and sometimes the conflict is completely resolved by the end of it.'

I asked Peter: 'Where else can you go with that kind of dialogue?'

'Well, this kind of beginning also makes a very good place from which to look at the conflict. We can ask, for example: "Now that we see how well you can manage your relationship, can we look at how you get captured by the conflict? What is it that you do that gets you caught up in it?" That is a very useful way to talk about the conflict. In one work-based conflict between two groups (one in marketing and the other in manufacturing), they came up with a whole list of ways that the "conflict" influenced their thinking to keep the conflict going. First, the conflict generated an "us and them" attitude, and they saw one another through gener- alisations and stereotypes. Second, it created win/lose situations in which only one side could have what they wanted. It also created suspicion and mistrust, everyone was looking for "hidden agendas". The "us and them" attitude meant that each group blamed the other whenever anything went wrong. They resented each other for so-called "past injuries" and they misinterpreted others — who were just getting on with their work — as being "secretive" and "shutting the door" on working together. Each saw the other as having all the power and the privileges, and themselves as having none. When they came out with all that, I was amazed. It was like the archetype of conflict; all the things that you see all the time. When they said it, they could see what the conflict was doing to them. Just saying it was breaking the hold the conflict had on them.'

'How do you move people past problems such as these and forward into solutions?' I asked.

'Well, to move them to the next stage, I might pop some "miracle questions" into the conversation, or sometimes I use them to get the ball rolling,' said Peter. 'Steve de Shazer, an American who "solution focused" or "brief" therapy coined these questions to help people see themselves in another way. He asks:

> What if something quite surprising were to happen tonight, if a miracle occurred, and when you wake up tomorrow the conflict has been completely resolved and everything happens just as you'd dreamt — what is the first thing you'd notice about the way your relationships with [whoever] were working? What would people be doing differently? What would communication be like?

'There are a whole series of questions which enable you to draw out specific information that will build up the reality of these alternative stories and will indicate to people their capacity to manage their relationships in ways that are free of the entrenched conflict.

'People usually believe that the only way to resolve conflict is through a rational analysis of the dispute — deciding who's right and wrong, attributing blame, reaching agreement, apologising and starting off again with a clean slate. In my experience, a lot of that kind of talking actually builds the reality of the conflict, rather than defusing it. When we are caught up in *blaming*, we are really seeing the "person" as the problem. That makes the problem very difficult to sort out because, to solve the problem, the person has to change—and that is hard to do. In this different way of talking, we say "the person is not the problem: the problem is the problem". The aim is to separate the problem — the conflict — from the people. When this approach works, the problem *dissolves* rather than *resolves*.

*The person is not the problem: the problem is the problem.*

'There is a lovely example of this. It was a conflict between someone with an actions-and-objects focus, very rational and logical, and someone with a feeling focus who relied more on relationship connection with people. In this case, both people were young women, both from a small developing country, both working in quite technical roles. Because they had so much in common, they were very drawn to one another, but their different points of focus often put them at loggerheads. Their colleagues couldn't understand what was going on and had all sorts of theories about it. Conflict would flare up when the feeling focuser would seek help from the actions-and-objects focuser, who would try to help, but would then be blamed if her solution did not work. The feeling focuser would then persuade other people to blame her, too. It became very complicated very quickly.'

'The two women began the resolution process by trying to examine the events that led to the conflict and that seemed very difficult. The actions-and-objects woman was very rational and logical and seemed "right" all the time. This path led only to humiliating the other woman; it certainly wasn't a way out of the conflict, more a good example of the conflict becoming more entrenched with that sort of rational analysis. It was becoming a long and painful meeting, and the only way out seemed to be to cut off contact, a suggestion made by the actions-and-objects focuser. I moved their discussion to ways of "managing our relation-ship". I asked them what the relationship reminded them of, what it was like. I was seeking a metaphor they could relate to. One said that they were like two sisters and the other said it felt like problems between friends in kindergarten. I asked questions about the connection between the metaphors and their situation. They began talking more appreciatively with one another as they made connections with their different metaphors. They talked about spending more time together and dealing with their issues between themselves rather than bringing other people into it. It seemed to me at the time that the conflict had not been *resolved*; through the process of dialogue, the conflict had *dissolved*. It wasn't the focus any more.'

'Can anybody facilitate a dialoguing process?'

'I think it does take some skill as a facilitator to create the right circumstances for that sort of discussion and to move it forward at the right pace. You do need very good conflict resolution skills yourself. For starters, you must never take sides.[203] As a facilitator, it's more about what you don't do, than what you do. Minimum intervention is the key. *(Refer to the lists of dialoguing questions on page 385.)* Just encourage the personal stories. You're working towards a change in the choice — from choosing the conflict to choosing cooperation.'

▼▼▼▼

Values collisions are particularly likely to occur at times when society's attitudes are in a state of flux. Attitudes to and of women in the workforce are changing with enormous speed. Both men and women struggle with defining new boundaries of acceptable behaviour. Expectations are changing so rapidly, that people often don't know where they stand.

As we absorb what the media, legislation, latest best business practice and colleagues are saying, we are swept away from rigidly defined masculine and feminine stereotypes and values. The new workplace mix of men and women is taking us into uncharted waters. We cannot fall back on prescribed, clear gender roles any longer. Individuals must work out their own personal response to the enormous choice. In this sea of new relationships, conflict resolution skills and techniques for handling values collisions are life rafts. They can give us the courage to tackle the tough issues.

A willingness to resolve conflict, first in yourself and then in the other person, will be the major breakthrough. As soon as you start focusing attention on the conflict resolving or dissolving process, things generally begin to change for the better — and often very rapidly.

> **Energy follows attention**
> **and**
> **energy creates change.**

# SUMMARY

## SIX ALTERNATIVES FOR DEALING WITH VALUES COLLISIONS

1 ► Challenge the other person's values on the grounds of ethics or morality.

2 ► Use the principles of cognitive dissonance to catalyse values reassessment. For example, you may encourage the other person to make a public statement of a value you'd prefer them to run with.

3 ► Bypass the value and aim for behaviour changes that are easier to live with.

4 ► Alter structures by legislating or developing organisational policy that minimises discrimination.

5 ► Clarify the values underlying the conflict and translate them into quantifiable terms, deciding how much or how many of 'what?' will satisfy the values for the situation. (See 'Six steps for the clarify and quantify approach' below.)

6 ► In suitable circumstances, explore the nature of the participants' communication patterns and/or encourage the exchange of stories about personal history, ultimately deepening empathy in order to rebuild the bridges of relationship. (See 'Useful questions for mediation dialogue' and 'Useful questions for dialoguing values', below.)

## SIX STEPS FOR THE CLARIFY AND QUANTIFY APPROACH

1 ► Unfold the other person's values.

2 ► Validate their values.

3 ► Explain your values.

4 ► Formulate a shared outcome that you can both agree on.

5 ► Set up objective criteria for success. Translate values into behaviours and quantify.

6 ► Develop options that support the criteria.

You may not need to move formally through each of these steps. If the resolution process is going well, some parts will happen automatically and some will be implied rather than explicit.

## USEFUL QUESTIONS FOR MEDIATION DIALOGUE[204]

► If this dialogue is successful, what differences will you notice?

► Let's say that this dialogue proves useful to you, how will you know?

► Many people experience dilemmas or uncertainties about their views. I'd like to invite you to share any grey areas, any pockets of uncertainty or any concerns you may have about your views.

► If when you awoke in the morning everything was different and the conflict had disappeared completely, what would be the first thing you would notice? What other things would you notice? What would you notice about the relationship [or other relevant topic]? What would another involved person [or group] notice?

► When was a time when these [positive things noticed in answer to the previous questions] were present [in the relationship]?

► When was the last time that you noticed [the difference]?

► What did you do differently that enabled that to happen?

► How was the relationship different when you first met?

► What suggestions do you have that would meet the various concerns we have heard today?

► What ideas do you have about how we might resolve this issue in a way that meets all the concerns?

► What will you take away from today's meeting that was useful to you?

► What did you hear today that confirmed what you already knew?

► What did you hear that you hadn't heard before?

► What have you done (or not done) to make this conversation go as it has?

## USEFUL QUESTIONS FOR DIALOGUING VALUES

► If this dialogue is successful, what differences will you notice?

► How did you come to have these values?

► Has there been an important experience in your life that made you believe in what you believe?

► Can you tell us about a personal experience?

► Has there been a time when you have had doubts?

► Are there areas of less certainty?

► Are there situations in which you don't apply the value?

# 16 THE UNCONSCIOUS AT WORK FOR CHANGE

## PREVIEW

▶ Wholeness divided

▶ Jung's masculine and feminine archetypes

▶ Archetype/stereotype link

▶ Projection

▶ Integration

▶ Where are we heading?

This final chapter puts male–female conflicts into the broad perspective of human life. If we choose to view our life as a path of growth, we can create meaning and direction for ourselves, and our time at work can hold experiences quite as personally significant as our time spent in intimate relationships or in solitary contemplation. The concepts discussed in this chapter — wholeness, division into polarities, archetypal images and projection — can provide an expanded framework for understanding others and ourselves in a process of emerging consciousness. These concepts also begin to explain some of the apparently very irrational behaviour of men and women when relating to the opposite sex.

## WHOLENESS DIVIDED

The concept of wholeness, or 'One', is the starting place for many religious philosophies. That One is the formless ground with infinite potential to individualise. The individualising begins with a split, a division, the formation of the first polarity — masculine and feminine. Both are needed to create life, the physical universe. The Taoists describe this division as *yin* and *yang*. In Greek mythology, the two forces are depicted as the Mount Olympus couple, Zeus and Hera, as well as a complex tribe of other male and female gods, often divided against each other. In the Old Testament, the split is symbolised by Adam and Eve in the Garden of Eden. Followers of the Jewish Cabbala study the tree of life, which defines the interplay of masculine and feminine principles.

Throughout the centuries, despite differing cultures, philosophies and religions, explorers of deeper thought pondered the issue of gender differences. They saw in this division the fundamental building blocks, not only of the manifest world, but also of our own psyches.

The unmanifest wholeness preceding this masculine/feminine split is seen as the resource from which we as individuals draw out those characteristics that we are emphasising in our lives.

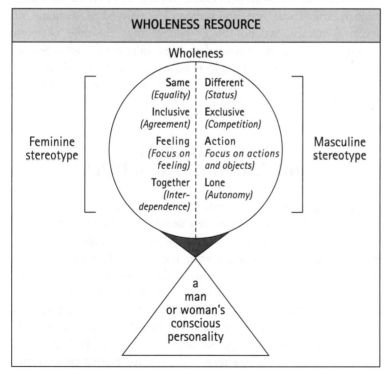

*Figure 61: Wholeness resource*

Of course, the polarities we've discussed in this book by no means cover the full spectrum of what makes each of us individuals. They do describe key forces, evident in the workplace, from which we build our images of masculine and feminine — our stereotypes. **Figure 61: Wholeness resource** (page 387) gives us a useful picture of this. The individual man or woman will draw down qualities from both sides of the split. Many men will favour values from the right and many women will favour those from the left. These values are dynamic forces at the core of the individual's personality.

In medieval times, alchemists used their experiments in making gold to symbolise and also to hide their interior search for personal purification. They believed that both material and spiritual gold would be produced by the perfect conjunction of masculine and feminine elements and energies. They called this the *alchemical wedding* — a fertile union of opposites. Alchemy was frowned on by the Church, but its deeper essence has become, over the centuries, mainstream. Today we are intimately involved in alchemy of spirit. Generally, we no longer believe that the split between masculine and feminine personality styles, values and roles is permanent and unchanging. The split is now only an abstract boundary we can cross at will once we recognise that we have that freedom. We've come a long way very fast in the twentieth century.

## JUNG'S MASCULINE AND FEMININE ARCHETYPES

At the beginning of the century, when developing his theories, psychologist Carl Jung journeyed deeply into many of the great religions. While some psychoanalysts and sociologists reject his work, Jung's thoughts align with the spiritual beliefs of many cultures, past and present. He used the terms *logos* and *eros* to define the masculine and feminine psychological structures he observed in a person's make-up. The man in a traditional western patriarchal society lived out the masculine (logos) principle while suppressing the feminine (eros) side of his psyche. Perhaps as he aged, he would begin to express some of his buried eros nature. The woman, if she'd 'bought' her traditional female role in society, expressed herself through the eros principle. Life events stirred her sleeping logos nature, gradually awakening and giving it some expression in her personality.

Jung formed his concepts in a very different society from the one we face today. Even Jung's enlightened theories were blinkered by rigid gender roles. Feminism this century has made enormous contributions to our thinking. Yet as recently as the 1970s and 1980s, women activists still had to spell out the point. Susan Brownmiller, in *Femininity*, wrote:

> When law and custom deny women the full range of public expression and economic opportunity that men claim for themselves, a woman must place much of her hopes, her dreams, her feminine identity and her social importance in the private sphere of personal relations.[205]

Nancy Chodorow, in *The Reproduction of Mothering*, railed at women's enforced inequality:

> The sexual division of labour and women's responsibility for child care are linked to and generate male dominance ... Women's continued relegation to the domestic ... as an extension of their mothering functions, has ensured they remain less social, less cultural, and also, less powerful than men.[206]

Brownmiller, Chodorow and many others envisioned the changes pregnant in society. Did any of them anticipate the speed or the necessity of masculine/feminine integration that the ordinary person now faces, or the speed with which it happened? It is no longer a task just for the highly conscious person towards the end of their lives. It is being demanded of us on a daily basis. Over the past fifty years, with the dramatic shift in female participation, workplaces have become the new arena for the interplay of Jung's two primordial archetypes, eros and logos. We are in a pressure cooker process of drawing through into consciousness the feminine in men and the masculine in women that in previous generations remained suppressed through rigid gender roles.

*We are drawing through into consciousness the feminine in men and the masculine in women once suppressed by rigid gender roles.*

The integrating process is a tortuous one, to be played out in both the personal and the public arena. It is a bumping, jostling, temper-strewn path to personal and collective growth.

To understand this process better we may need to redraft our diagram. If we say that the triangle in **Figure 61: Wholeness** resource (page 387) represents only that part of the whole we are consciously working with and expressing in our lives, perhaps it is more accurately drawn sitting *within* the wholeness circle. See **Figure 62: Conscious and unconscious fields** (below). We can never really fall out of wholeness. The grey area of the circle stands for that unconscious field of possible awarenesses.

Let's continue a little longer with a Jungian framework, as it can help us to make sense of those types of male–female conflicts that have a rigid stereotyping component. Within the unconscious field, powerful forces which so far we have not integrated into our personality may coalesce as an archetype, a shared image in the unconscious mind of many people that gives rise to myths, fairytales, religious concepts and patterns for developing ourselves and perceiving others. As an archetype rises towards conscious-ness, it pushes up with it our fears, angers and dependencies, forcing them to the surface, too. These cannot be integrated while

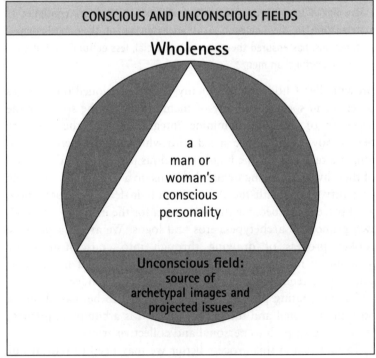

*Figure 62: Conscious and unconscious fields*

they remain in the unconscious field. Reason, life experience and conflict are the purifiers of these unprocessed materials.

We hold in our unconscious mind powerful archetypal images of *masculine* and *feminine*. If these images surface into full consciousness, the unconscious forces that create them can release our potential to express ourselves more fully. But if they are suppressed, they will indicate their presence in myths, dreams and images. When the archetype is denied the clear light of consciousness it throws out a distorted image of itself, like a flickering candle casting shadows on a wall. Often the image borrows from unresolved early family relationships, childhood terrors or adolescent fantasies. A simple workplace conflict may trigger the release of these unprocessed dormant energies from the subconscious.

A man who rigidly denies his own feminine qualities may insist that a women to whom he relates closely, act out his stereotyped image of how a woman 'ought' to be. If she's pretty, she might become fair game for his sexual innuendos or persistent overtures. Her true self is overlaid with an image of 'Wood Nymph' or 'Princess in the Castle', to be wooed, even harassed, in order to prove his manhood. Women are *supposed* to be supportive. There's no perceived duty to give a female work colleague credit for her input into a project. She's just a support person, an aspect of his 'Mother' archetype. A woman asking for an upgrade of her job title or voicing objections to his plans can be seen to have evil designs and therefore must be curbed. She may well trigger his archetype for 'Evil Siren' or 'Witch'. If so, his response to her will seem extreme.

Karen Hornig, noted German psychoanalyst, in *Feminine Psychology*, tackled the longstanding hidden resentment of men towards women.

> This resentment expresses itself, also in our times, in men's distrustful defensive manoeuvres against the threat of women's invasion of their domains.[207]

Her words, though written in the 1960s, are still relevant. Negative childhood images — bad mother, cruel sister or evil witch — can warp adult thinking.

Betty and Theodore Roszak, in *Masculine/Feminine*, acknowledge men's deification of these unconscious figures:

Earth mother, muse, love goddess, siren, nymph, angelic maiden ... in one form or another, all the feminine qualities have been elevated to the highest cultural status ... Granted, such idealisation has been cynically used to thwart women's claim to equality and workaday dignity in a thousand ingenious ways. Mythologising woman has been a standard method of gilding her cage.[208]

# ARCHETYPE/STEREOTYPE LINK

Archetypal images in the unconscious can feed stereotypes and generate inappropriate attitudes and behaviour in both men and women. The more unconscious people are of their own connection to wholeness, the more powerfully the archetypal images will colour their thinking.

*Archetypes are the language of images with which the unconscious mind communicates with consciousness.*

Archetypes are the language of images with which the unconscious mind communicates with consciousness. The unconscious thinks in sweeping categories, gathers present-time people in all their complexity, drops them into a category which may have been formed in childhood and then keeps them pigeonholed there regardless of how badly or how well they fill these roles. This is the archetype/stereotype link — drawing general conclusions about people from particular instances. It is the psyche's defence against complexity. It simplifies the world, removes its ambiguity, tantalises with an offer of clear guidelines for action. Dangerous stuff! In workplaces that reward certainty, stereotyping is a tempting shortcut.

However, when a man categorises a woman into one of his childhood-formed archetypes, he creates for himself a major problem. Her real self is invisible to him. If she fails to perform the role he has unconsciously assigned to her, he may use control, manipulation, anger or even violence (in the workplace it's usually verbal, at home it might be physical) to make her conform. In this lies his only hope of retaining his internal status quo. His behaviour is a measure of his resistance to the upward-to-consciousness rush of energy as the archetype seeks to make itself known and be integrated into awareness.

Archetypes roam through the woman's unconscious, too. Unless she's broken the hold of her unconscious images of men,

she will expect men to conform to them. Men are supposed to be strong. They're supposed to epitomise action, decision, leadership and certainty. A patriarchal boss is measured up against her mythologised childhood picture of her father. If a male colleague is a slow decision-maker, she labels him as indecisive, ineffective. She's not only influenced by idealised parental images, however. Television, radio, how her best friend's husband acts, all make an impression on her stereotypes of men. Beneath her surface 'woman of the world' probably lurks a Cinderella yearning for Prince Charming. Today, Prince Charming is the good-looking male actor in the latest popular film. When the real men in her world fall short of the movie-star image, she may inflict on them her anger or her cold disdain. She may well be on a search, both personally and professionally, for the Sensitive New Age Guy, but when she meets him she misinterprets his tentative style as weakness or his rapport with others as flirtatiousness. In fact, what she is doing is undervaluing the feminine in him — possibly because she has issues with her own femininity that she needs to resolve.

When these unconscious forces stir, not only may she project her archetypal images onto others, she may be moved by them herself. They can provide powerful metaphors or even 'ways of envisioning and thus calling up needed strengths and qualities within ourselves,' says Gloria Steinem.[209] She can become Diana, the huntress of classical mythology always on the hunt for the man who fits the confused, sometimes contradictory images of masculine perfection she holds in her mind's eye.

Her archetypal masculine is not always idealised. Sometimes it is terrifying. The ogre, the beast, the rapist, the powerful king to whom absolute submission is due. If a man's actions, looks or tone of voice links him to any of these archetypes, she has found her enemy — the battle is on. He has hooked the fears, anger, rebelliousness or volatile submission she feels in relation to these negative archetypal images. The workplace can become her Mount Olympus and she is involved in the battle of the gods.

*We need to be very skilled in conflict resolution to hold our own with someone in the grip of their own unresolved issues with men or women.*

We need to be very skilled in conflict resolution to hold our own with someone in the grip of their own unresolved issues with men or women.

## PROJECTION

When archetypal images from the unconscious pigeonhole a person of the opposite sex, the psychological mechanism of *projection* is at work.

> Projection occurs when an unconscious part of ourselves seems to be in the minds of others. We see in the other person and their behaviour our own unconscious thoughts and feelings. It's as if their behaviour is a mirror reflecting for us things about ourselves that we don't acknowledge.[210]

Our reaction to a person or situation gives us a clue to our own projected issue. When strong emotions stir us, chances are that the unconscious is at work. We can ask ourselves: 'Am I *inflamed* or *informed*?' Inflamed feels very different from informed. If we're inflamed about a problem, we're liable to fly off the handle and respond in a way that is out of proportion to the seriousness of the issue. If we're informed about a problem we'll still wish to express anger or dislike, but we won't be so emotionally engaged. We can often get an inkling that we are projecting when bystanders don't seem to be nearly as distressed as we are about the problem.

While we may not be stirred to the extreme of reactions motivated by archetypal images, projection can occur around any value or quality that we deny in ourselves. Power issues between men and women make prime candidates on which to hang projections. Issues of status or equality can become overheated where we have not yet integrated both masculine and feminine values. A woman who suppresses her own competitive drive may envisage those who display that quality as far more cutthroat and self-seeking than they really are. To a man out of touch with his feelings, an emotional woman may appear self-indulgent or ridiculous. A woman embedded in partnership may be deeply hurt by a man's desire for independence and his need to make his own mark.

Our reaction to a situation, behaviour or person may have as much to do with who we are as it does with the external event. If we use conflict wisely, it can support a deeper connection with our own wholeness.

► We can ask ourselves: 'Am I inflamed or informed?' If we recognise that we are inflamed, we know we're likely to have some inner work to do to integrate a suppressed aspect of our own natures.

► If we can steer the conflict to a successful win/win outcome, we will have new information with which to reassess negative judgments about qualities and values in ourselves and in others. 'Well, maybe he's not so bad after all.' 'I guess her way works, too.'

## INTEGRATION

Many men still suppress the feminine in themselves, seeing the development of their masculine side as how it's meant to be. Nevertheless, men's feminine sides are developing, even though they may dismiss this process bubbling along inside of them. Often, the gentle revolution is happening without their noticing. It is slowly having its effects even in very masculine work cultures. Status and hierarchies mean a little less. More and more men today recognise their right to fair pay and conditions. They are supporting new management practices which develop agreement and consensus rather than authoritarian control. They watch with interest the emerging men's movement and the permission it offers men to talk about private feelings, such as their stress in response to outdated social pressures to be the sole provider in their family or to work until they drop. They are changing their ethics as they open up to interdependence with its wider community and global responsibilities. True, they are unlikely to name this the developing of their feminine qualities. 'Feminine' as a name attached to a man still has bad press! It gets mixed up with homosexuality and the need for certainty about sexual identity.

Despite these positive signs, the feminine qualities in men still seem to be more securely trapped in their unconscious than the masculine is in women. Women are generally doing well in integrating the masculine alongside their feminine. They are generally more than ready for situations which challenge them to shoulder the responsibilities that accompany higher status; to test themselves in the pursuit of goals where others are also competing; to focus on action and the mastery of complex material objects in the workplace; to become autonomous individuals who can stand alone in the world. What they often still lack is *opportunity*. This is often denied to them by those men who do not value women's feminine style, because they have not yet integrated their own feminine within.

Simone de Beauvoir, in *The Second Sex*, asked in 1969:

> Is it enough to change laws, institutions, customs, public opinion and the whole social context for men and women to become truly equal?[211]

She believed an inner transformation must occur — a difficult one, as women's relations to the world are constantly modified by the action of others. However:

> Sooner or later they will arrive at complete economic and social equality, which will bring about an inner metamorphosis.[212]

As we move into the new century, that metamorphosis is now in progress. Individuals are empowering themselves by developing both masculine and feminine strengths, no matter what their gender. Where will it lead? June Singer's description tells us what it might look like when we arrive:

> Without a sense of disjunction, the person would become at once tender and firm, flexible and strong, ambiguous and precise, focused in thinking and diffused in awareness, nurturing and guiding, giving and receiving.[213]

Life becomes a fluid dance. There is an integrated flow of energies. The well-balanced person functions comfortably with their masculine qualities or their feminine qualities, depending on the needs of the situation. The result of this fluid dance is not asexuality but *wholeness*. Masculine and feminine are *combined*, not *confused*. A woman doesn't lose her femininity, she adds strength. A man does not lose his masculinity, he becomes more responsive to the people around him. Much of the demand that the opposite-sexed person should behave in some prescribed fashion falls away. The opposite-sexed person no longer has to represent to us the missing part in our own psyche.

## WHERE ARE WE HEADING?

Good managers are good precisely because they embody the wide range of skills, abilities and perspectives that come from both their masculine and feminine sides. As stated in Chapter 1, good managers work in remarkably similar ways, regardless of their gender. If they truly understand the integration they themselves have achieved, they will foster its development in others, creating a climate of respect for the gifts from both the masculine and the feminine, coaching each person's self-empowerment in the development of a broad range of both male and female qualities and skills.

*Good managers work in remarkably similar ways, regardless of their gender.*

Strong currents sweep the tide of human development as we enter the millennium. We need a new expertise to surf the frequently tumultuous seas. We are not just victims of these currents, we are making the waves. We do it when we fight for 'power with' rather than 'power over' relationships; when we stop compromising ourselves by serving outmoded workplace systems; when we give our support to more compatible workplaces or relationships; when we stand up for cooperation, for team, for listening to the wisdom of all members of the group.

There are good questions to ask ourselves on the path towards wholeness. Can we focus on process as much as on goals? Can we make place for intuitive leaps as well as logical analysis? Can we find out our own and others' emotional responses as well as the hard facts? Can we value strategic whole concept planning as well as detailed administration? Can we snap to decisions when appropriate, and tolerate ambiguity or incompletion until life flows through with answers?

We need to become more comfortable with the ebb and flow of masculine and feminine energies within ourselves, and through the changing circumstances of our lives. Ebb and flow are the dynamics of successful living.

Workplace structures of the future ideally will reflect this integration. Such a vision demands change, movement forward. We're unlikely to get there without conflict — conflict handled well, handled with understanding, handled with a win/win approach. If either the masculine or the feminine principle is squashed in our workplaces, we are all less powerful, less whole.

This movement towards the integration of masculine and feminine, both within the individual and within our organisations, is the gentle revolution. It is well under way, and we are all participants.

# APPENDIX 1

## Statistical date of significant findings from 'Men and Women at Work' survey
(Helena Cornelius, 1995–1996)

| Questionnaire statement | Percentage of women | | | Percentage of men | | |
|---|---|---|---|---|---|---|
| | Agree | Disagree | Don't know | Agree | Disagree | Don't know |
| 1 Men and women approach their work differently. | 90.1 | 9.9 | – | 75.1 | 21.6 | 3.3 |
| 2 There is a 'glass ceiling' which prevents women being promoted beyond a certain point. | 82.7 | 11.1 | 6.2 | 46.7 | 45 | 8.3 |
| 3 Women have to be better than men to get adequate recognition. | 91.3 | 6.2 | 2.5 | 71.6 | 28.4 | – |
| 4 Women usually undervalue themselves when they ask for a pay rise. | 86.4 | 6.2 | 7.4 | 40.1 | 41.6 | 18.3 |
| 5 Men usually think it is more important to be respected rather than liked. | 76.5 | 13.6 | 9.9 | 71.7 | 23.3 | 5.0 |
| 6 Women usually think it is more important to be liked rather than respected. | 60.6 | 38.2 | 1.2 | 38.3 | 48.4 | 13.3 |
| 7 I usually do what my boss asks even if I disagree with it. | 37 | 61.8 | 1.2 | 53.4 | 43.3 | 3.3 |
| 8 Women behave differently if men are present. | 77.7 | 19.8 | 2.5 | 58.3 | 28.4 | 13.3 |
| 9 Women prefer to reach agreements with other people rather than telling them what to do. | 85.2 | 12.3 | 2.5 | 53.3 | 40.0 | 6.7 |
| 10 I would rather compromise than create an argument. | 64.2 | 35.8 | – | 45.0 | 55.0 | – |

| Questionnaire statement | Percentage of women | | | Percentage of men | | |
|---|---|---|---|---|---|---|
| | Agree | Disagree | Don't know | Agree | Disagree | Don't know |
| 11  Women usually try to prevent problems while men solve them once they have occurred. | 70.4 | 18.5 | 11.1 | 30.0 | 55.0 | 15.0 |
| 12  Men like to talk about their achievements more than women do. | 76.5 | 21.0 | 2.5 | 68.3 | 26.7 | 5 |
| 13  I don't like to hear others boast about their work. | 56.8 | 40.7 | 2.5 | 66.6 | 31.7 | 1.7 |
| 14  Men usually put their jobs before their families. | 59.3 | 28.4 | 11.1 | 58.4 | 38.3 | 3.3 |
| 15  Women usually put their families before their jobs. | 75.3 | 18.5 | 6.2 | 58.3 | 35.0 | 6.7 |
| 16  I find it stressful to work with someone I dislike. | 82.8 | 16 | 1.2 | 71.6 | 28.4 | – |
| 17  Women are more likely than men to praise someone's work. | 69.1 | 18.5 | 12.4 | 41.7 | 41.6 | 16.7 |
| 18  Men prefer working independently. | 48.2 | 37.0 | 14.8 | 43.4 | 53.3 | 3.3 |
| 19  I am the main financial provider for my household. | 47.0 | 48.1 | 4.9 | 83.3 | 16.7 | – |

*Figure 63: Questionnaire — percentage responses*
*Sample size: 81 women, 60 men.*

# APPENDIX 2

## Other relevant gender-linked values research

The model of gender-linked values, outlined in Chapter 2 and developed in the rest of this book, is corroborated in some research studies. Two such studies are presented here.

### COLINS AND CHIPPENDALE

Because we are dealing with societal stereotypes, these splits between masculine and feminine styles are widely observed and discussed. Gender literature frequently alludes to them.

Colins and Chippendale believe: 'Over the years we all unconsciously take on board a set of assumptions concerning what life's all about.' They have done considerable research on 125 values by direct self-assessment and concluded that some of the values they tested are definitely gender-linked. Colins and Chippendale write:

> Women have a 'ready-aim-fire' strategy while men have a 'ready-fire-aim' strategy. How do we deduce this from the value priorities? Well, [generally] women have values like Sharing/Listening/Trust, Intimacy, Knowledge/ Discovery/Insight and Rights/Respect ahead of Decision/Initiation. This means they place a higher priority on gathering information and finding out what people want before taking action (Decision/Initiation). Men [generally] have Decision/Initiation as their highest priority value and values such as Sharing/Listening/Trust, Knowledge/Discovery/Insight and Intimacy are a lower priority. This means the majority of men will prefer to make snap decisions and act on them and deal with the consequences later.[214]

In order to develop an easy-to-understand model, I have used value categories. Many of Colins and Chippendale's values can be included under my category headings. Alphabetically listed here are those gender-linked values proposed by Colins and Chippendale which relate to my model.[215] Colins and Chippendale considered a value gender-linked if they found it had a higher priority for 10 per cent or more women than men, or men than women.

### MYERS-BRIGGS

Although there is no direct correlation between my typology and the widely used psychometric test the Myers-Briggs Type Indicator, Myers and Briggs' research results offer some further corroboration. They found that two-thirds of male high school students tested fell into their Thinking category. Only one-third of them fell into the contrasting Feeling category. With high school girls, these percentages were reversed.[216]

Values research is still in its infancy. Moreover, the ground is constantly shifting beneath our feet as society makes its transition to full acceptance of women and feminine-style values in the workplace.

| VALUES WITH A HIGHER PRIORITY FOR WOMEN | |
|---|---|
| Colins and Chippendale | Parallels in Cornelius |
| Care/nurture | Feeling focus |
| Community/personalist | Interdependence |
| Community/supportive | Interdependence |
| Expressiveness/freedom/joy | Feeling focus |
| Health/healing/harmony | Agreement |
| Human dignity | Equality |
| Integration/wholeness | Feeling focus |
| Search, meaning, hope | Feeling focus |

| VALUES WITH A HIGHER PRIORITY FOR MEN | |
|---|---|
| Colins and Chippendale | Parallels in Cornelius |
| Achievement/success | Actions-and-objects focus |
| Administration/control | Status |
| Collaboration/subsidiarity | Status |
| Competition | Competition |
| Criteria/rationality | Actions-and-objects focus |
| Duty/obligation | Status |
| Faith/risk/vision | Competition |
| Hierarchy/priority/order | Status |
| Obedience/duty | Status |
| Ownership | Status |
| Technology/science | Actions-and-objects focus |

*Figure 64: Colins and Chippendale comparisons*

# APPENDIX 3

## Values-driven language

| EQUALITY | STATUS |
|---|---|
| That's fair/not fair. | Do it because I say so. |
| That is/isn't even-handed. | Show me some respect. |
| Let's compromise. | Don't tell me what to do. |
| What's the win/win solution here? | Winning's what counts. |
| They're 'up' themselves. | Now that's someone I can respect. |
| They're not better than me. | Who are you to ... (questioning authority) |

*Figure 65: Language driven by equality and status values*

| AGREEMENT | COMPETITION |
|---|---|
| Don't rock the boat. | All's fair in love and war, and this is war. |
| Let's just smooth things over. | Don't let 'em get away with it. |
| Let sleeping dogs lie. | You've got to accept the rough with the smooth. |
| Let's compromise. | Let's make a killing. |
| I don't want to make a fuss. | If you're not going forwards, you're going backwards. |
| I don't have the stomach for the fight. | They've got guts/ no guts. |

*Figure 66: Language driven by agreement and competition values*

| FEELING FOCUS | ACTIONS-AND-OBJECTS FOCUS |
|---|---|
| How do you feel? | What do you think? |
| I'm too upset to concentrate. | Get on with the job! |
| But that's how I feel! | It's stupid to be upset. |
| The systems here treat you like a number. | It's results that count. |
| I was so disappointed/ anxious./I love it./What fun! (A wide range of emotions is openly acknowledged.) | I was furious. I've had it!/That's alright./Okay. (Angry emotions are the only ones talked about. Positive emotions are played down.) |
| You need to consider how people feel. | I was uncomfortable./It gives me a headache. (Feelings are described as body sensations.) |

*Figure 67: Language driven by feeling- and actions-and-objects focus values*

| INTERDEPENDENCE | AUTONOMY |
|---|---|
| What do you think we should do? | I don't have to listen to your ideas. |
| Don't shut me out! (from ideas/thinking/decisions) | Stand on your own two feet. |
| We have to consider what other people say. | If you don't look out for yourself, nobody else will. |
| I'm not with you yet. Can we talk about it some more before we move on? | Every man for himself. |
| If we're in it together, we need to do it together. | If you want a job done well, do it by yourself. |
| This is a mutual decision. It's not yours to make alone. | Get off my back. |

*Figure 68: Language driven by interdependence and autonomy values*

# APPENDIX 4

## Strategies to enhance gender equality

Listed below are a number of strategies that maximise the talents and skills of women and men and enhance gender equity. (See also Chapter 15, Alternatives for handling values collisions, pages 354–385.) A number of these strategies have been extracted from a yearly publication by the Affirmative Action Agency, *Good Ideas*, 1995–1996, (Australia: Commonwealth of Australia, 1996).

▶ Acting or relief positions to be equitably distributed between men and women in the organisation.

▶ Rotate jobs and assignments to develop promotional eligibility. Rotating executive assistant positions that are designated for women can be a particularly effective strategy. For a period of perhaps three months, a promising woman at a lower level of the organisation shadows a senior manager, offering support services.

▶ Flexible working arrangements such as part-time work, working from home, adjustable work hours and job sharing. Job-sharing has so far proved particularly useful to women, though some older men are beginning to find it frees them to broaden the scope of their activities once financial security is assured. It costs the organisation very little and gives two good heads for roughly the price of one. Working from home is another option that is becoming increasingly viable, and some organisations set up central pools of equipment for employees to borrow when working from home.

▶ Career paths for part-time employees. Part-time employees, particularly women with family responsibilities, are often viewed as uncommitted employees and therefore given menial or traditionally female tasks, such as repetitive clerical duties. However, they may indeed be just as committed and competent as any full-time employee. The creation of part-time senior positions is often viable and economically sound. The nature of work is changing. In the future, more and more people are likely to opt for part-time work. Smart organisations are already planning for this.

▶ Permanent versus casual work contracts. In many employment situations, this distinction can be important. Apart from the legal protection a permanent contract provides against uncompensated retrenchment. The status of permanency is often necessary for promotion.

▶ Initiatives for child and family care responsibilities. A family leave policy that accommodates: school vacations; caring for sick children (e.g. a child care referral service); alternative care allowances for staff with family care responsibilities (e.g. a child or elder family member with a disability), paid when attending out of the workplace courses, conferences or meetings out of work hours.

▶ Provision for twelve months' unpaid leave, such as maternity/paternity leave or sabbaticals, with appropriate 'keeping in touch' strategies. Where contact policies are effective, the organisation benefits by a proven higher return to work percentage.

▶ Explicit sexual harassment workplace policies and education sessions to raise awareness. Both men and women benefit from formal grievance procedures in the organisation.

▶ Job and equipment redesign to reduce heavy lifting in manual work. Ergonomic assessments can identify areas that unnecessarily disadvantage women, and suggest strategies to make women's employment possible in non-traditional positions.

▶ Management sanction of women's networks and mentoring programs.

▶ Equitable distribution between men and women of training opportunities that promote career development.

# APPENDIX 5

## Summary of findings on 'Gender values
## quiz' survey responses
*(Helena Cornelius and Candy Tymson, December 1997)*

*SAMPLE*

| | | |
|---|---|---|
| Size | 168 men, 168 women | |
| Age | 24.12% | under 36 years |
| | 36.01% | 36–45 years |
| | 30.94% | 46–55 years |
| | 8.93% | over 55 years |
| Company | 40.77% | large company |
| | 44.35% | small to medium company |
| | 9.82% | government department |
| | 5.06% | other (mostly industry associations and charities) |
| Position | 39.87% | managing director |
| | 24.12% | senior manager |
| | 25.59% | middle management |
| | 7.44% | staff |
| | 2.98% | other |

*RESULTS*

| *Feminine style values* | *Masculine style values* |
|---|---|
| **Equality** | **Status** |
| Male 7.81 | Male 10.70 |
| Female 7.98 | Female 11.42 |
| **Agreement** | **Competition** |
| Male 10.55 | Male 8.60 |
| Female 10.77 | Female 8.36 |
| **Feeling** | **Actions and objects** |
| Male 10.13 | Male 10.62 |
| Female 10.13 | Female 10.41 |
| **Interdependence** | **Autonomy** |
| Male 10.61 | Male 7.99 |
| Female 11.02 | Female 8.73 |
| **Grand total feminine values** | **Grand total masculine values** |
| Male 39.10 | Male 37.95 |
| Female 39.72 | Female 38.88 |

*Mean standard deviation was 2.52 for each value and 6.40 for grand totals.*

Note: the results above are the subtotals from the quiz scoring sheet, not percentages.

## INTERPRETATION

The questionnaire focuses on eight values that operate in pairs. Equality, agreement, feeling and interdependence represent the 'feminine style' and are paired with status, competition, actions-and-objects focus and autonomy, which represent the 'masculine style'.

When not under pressure, most people's scores indicate that they hold both values in each pair, though the strength with which they hold each value will give them an individual profile.

As the original purpose of the questionnaire was to focus on management in Australia, the sample could be considered atypical for the general population. Ninety-five per cent of respondents worked in privately owned companies and 90 per cent were middle to senior management. Forty per cent of the respondents worked for large companies. Because they took the time to fill out the questionnaire, the people sampled demonstrated their interest in gender issues. The results confirm that, for this group, their self-reported behaviour showed little difference between the men and the women.

Women reported marginally higher scores on status and autonomy values than their male peers, pushing their grand total for masculine values slightly above men's. This raises two questions: Do these scores reflect the type of women who will achieve managerial status or do they reflect circumstances that push women to draw heavily on their masculine values in order to reach or maintain their management position?

It is interesting to note that the mean scores for equality, competition and autonomy for both men and women were lower than for the other values in the questionnaire. Approximately 80 per cent of scores in this sample rated 10 or less. Scores of 11 or more were registered by only about 20 per cent of the sample. Mean scores on individual questions indicate that, on the whole, these managers are: in favour of consultation processes; no longer believe that motivating people by having them prove they are better than others is particularly helpful; are relatively unconcerned about issuing orders or disciplining staff.

For all other values, approximately 80 per cent of respondents scored 13 or less. A score of 14 or more was needed to place them in the top scoring 20 per cent. Given the rating scale used, this would suggest that the respondents in general closely align with the values of agreement, feeling, interdependence, status and actions-and-objects focus, insofar as these are tested by this questionnaire.[217]

## FURTHER RESEARCH

Areas for further research include looking at a sample that is representative of the working population as a whole and comparing responses of non-managerial with managerial staff. It would also be valuable to develop a research tool that measures men's and women's stereotyped images of gender characteristics. As this questionnaire uses a self-reporting method, it would be interesting to compare results with a scale that measured behaviour as reported by others.

Another area for investigation is to measure the strength of these eight values when people are in conflict situations. I believe that when a particular value is called into question during a conflict, people tend to polarise and move to opposing extremities. The hypothesis would be that during conflict, particularly when an individual is in opposition to someone of the opposite sex, more men align closely with values from the stereotypically masculine style and more women with values from the feminine.

# ENDNOTES

CHAPTER **1**

[1] Elizabeth Grosz, *Jacques Lacan*, Allen & Unwin, Australia, 1990, p. 20.

[2] Margaret Mead, *Sex and Temperament,* 2nd edn, William Morrow, U.S.A., 1935, 1950.

[3] Dorothy Dinnerstein, *The Rocking of the Cradle and the Ruling of the World*, Harper & Row, U.S.A., 1976, pp. 9–10.

[4] See C. de Lacoste-Utamsing & R. L. Holloway, 'Sex differences in the fetal human corpus callosum', *Human Neurobiology*, no. 5, 1986, pp. 93–96, referenced in Anne Moir & David Jessel, *Brainsex*, Mandarin, U.K., 1989, p. 47.

[5] Moir & Jessel, p. 15.

[6] Filigrees of dendrites have now been observed in the process of growing new connections in response to learning demands. See the video series *The Brain*, hosted by David Suzuki, NHK Creative & Discovery Productions, 1994.

[7] Carl Sagan & Ann Druyan, *Shadows of Forgotten Ancestors*, Random House, Australia, 1992, p. 217.

CHAPTER **2**

[8] With thanks to Catherine Huntington and Shirley Heilemann.

[9] All figures have been rounded to the nearest whole number. See pp. 399–400, for statistical data.

[10] The average weekly earnings, excluding overtime, of Australian women employed full time was 86 per cent of men's earnings in a similar situation. Source: *The Australian Women's Yearbook 1995*, Commonwealth of Australia, 1995, pp. 138–139.

[11] Many women purposely don't put pictures of their family on their desk at work in order to minimise this stereotyped thinking. If a man has a picture of his family on his desk, it is perceived quite differently. It's often regarded as a positive quality that he acknowledges them in his work life.

[12] Dr Greg Tillett, *Conflict Resolution HPP 260* (Independent Learning Package), Centre for Conflict Resolution, Macquarie University, Sydney, 1990, p. 3.7.8.

[13] Hugh Mackay, *Why Don't People Listen?*, William Morrow, Australia, 1994, p. 215. For further discussions on cognitive dissonance, see Chapter 15.

[14] See Appendix 5, pp. 405–406, for mean scores on a sample of largely middle to upper management.

[15] Roger Fisher & Scott Brown, *Getting Together*, Houghton Mifflin, U.S.A., 1988, pp. 154–155.

[16] Fisher & Brown, p. 155.

[17] Janette Blainey, Kim Davis & Brynnie Goodwill, *Valuing Diversity*, Working Together, Australia, 1995, p. 35.

[18] Blainey, Davis & Goodwill, p. 35.

[19] See Chapters 3 and 4.

[20] See Chapters 3 and 5.

[21] See Chapters 6 and 7.

[22] See Chapters 6 and 8.

[23] See Chapters 9 and 10.

[24] See Chapters 9 and 11.

[25] See Chapters 12 and 13.

[26] See Chapters 12 and 14.

## CHAPTER 3

[27] See 'Language' in Preface, p. vii.

[28] See also 'Find the good purpose', in Helena Cornelius, Shoshana Faire & Sonya Hall, *Conflict Resolution Trainers' Manual: Eight Sessions*, Edition 4, Conflict Resolution Network, 1993, p. 3.9.

[29] Janet Chafetz, *Sex and Advantage*, J. J. Rowman & Alanheld, U.S.A., 1984. Quoted in Ken Wilber, *Sex, Ecology, Spirituality: The Spirit of Evolution*, Shambhala Publications, U.S.A., 1995, p. 383.

[30] Chafetz, p. 383.

[31] From 'Flexible work practices in the National Park and Wildlife Service', a paper delivered by Vicki Lee at the Women in Utilities Conference, Sydney Water, 28 June 1996.

[32] Anthony Robbins, *Unlimited Power*, Simon & Schuster, U.S.A., 1986, pp. 20–21.

[33] Steve Biddulph, *Manhood*, Finch, Australia, 1994, p. 142.

[34] Anne Moir & David Jessel, *Brainsex*, Mandarin, U.K., 1989, p. 81.

[35] Abraham Maslow, *Motivation and Personality*, Harper & Row, U.S.A., 1970.

[36] Source: Joseph A. DeVito, *Human Communication*, Harper & Row, U.S.A., 1985, p. 389. Based on Abraham Maslow, *Motivation and Personality*, Harper & Row, U.S.A., 1970.

[37] K. Townsend & W. McLennan, *Australian Women's Yearbook 1995*, AGPS, Australia, 1995, p. 118.

[38] Sally Helgesen, *The Female Advantage*, Currency & Doubleday, U.S.A., 1990, p. 255.

[39] See Chapter 7, '"I" statements', p. 176–180.

[40] See Appendix 1, Question 3: 'Women have to be better than men to get adequate recognition'. Men appeared less aware of this problem for women. Only seven out of ten agreed.

[41] 'Women do better than men on tests of verbal ability', Moir & Jessel, p. 17. They believe the reason for this is because the female brain is organised to respond more sensitively to all stimuli, but particularly auditory input.

[42]

| POWERBASE PREFERENCES | |
|---|---|
| EQUALITY: | STATUS: |
| Valued relationship | Position |
| Expertise | Reward/punishment |
| Persuasiveness | Persuasiveness |
| ▶ verbal (for one-on-one with peers) | ▶ verbal skills (particularly in meetings) |
| | ▶ charisma |

*Figure 69: Powerbase preferences*

[43] Source: Adapted from Fiona Hollier, Kerrie Murray & Helena Cornelius, *Conflict Resolution Trainers Manual: 12 Skills*, Conflict Resolution Network, Australia, 1993, p. 5.5.

[44] See Chapter 7, '"I" statements', pp. 176–180.

[45] See Chapter 4, p. 84.

## CHAPTER 4

[46] See Chapter 3.

[47] For more on inclusion, openness and control, see Will Schutz, *The Truth Option*, Ten Speed Press, U.S.A., 1984.

[48] Deborah Tannen, *Talking from 9 to 5*, Virago Press, U.K., 1994, p. 35.

[49] Tannen, pp. 44–51.

[50] See also Chapter 6, 'Not apologising or apologising after confrontation', p. 161.

[51] John Gray, *Men, Women and Relationships*, Hodder Headline, Australia, 1995, pp. 27–28.

[52] Tannen, pp. 54–57.

[53] Susie Orbach & Luise Eichenbaum, *Between Women*, Arrow Books, U.K., 1987, p. 92.

[54] See Appendix 1.

[55] Robert Wright, *The Moral Animal*, Abacus, U.S.A., 1994, pp. 239–242.

[56] Wright, pp. 245–246.

## CHAPTER 5

[57] Will Schutz, *The Truth Option*, Ten Speed Press, U.S.A., 1984, pp. 211–230.

[58] Daniel Goleman, *Emotional Intelligence*, Bloomsbury, U.K., 1996, p.139.

[59] Developed by Christine James, director of Conflict Resolution Network Mediation Services, and adapted from Fiona Hollier, Kerrie Murray & Helena Cornelius, *Conflict Resolution Trainers' Manual: 12 Skills*, Conflict Resolution Network, Australia, 1993. This method uses: (i) an active listening approach (for more on active listening, see Chapter 8, 'Stumbling block 4: Poor listening skills', pp. 211–214); and (ii) the 'I' statement method (for an outline on this method, see Chapter 7, '"I" statements', pp. 176–180).

[60] Sam Keen, *Fire in the Belly*, Bantam, U.S.A., 1991, p. 208.

[61] See Figure 50, 'Controlling explosions', p. 274.

[62] See Chapter 7, '"I" statements', pp. 176–180.

[63] See also p. 274, 'Stepping stones', paragraph 2.

[64] Andrew Floyer Acland, *A Sudden Outbreak of Common Sense*, Hutchison, U.K., 1990, p. 56.

[65] See also: Chapter 15, 'Changing structures', pp. 363–365; and Appendix 4, p. 404 for structural changes that can minimise inequalities in the workplace.

## CHAPTER 6

[66] I have chosen to coin the term 'competer' rather than use the word 'competitor', in order to create a parallel linguistic structure with 'agreer'.

[67] Baden Eunson, *Dealing with Conflict,* John Wiley & Sons, Australia, 1997, p. 121.

[68] Roger Lewin, 'All for one, one for all', *New Scientist,* 14 Dec. 1996.

[69] See also: 'What is the good intention' in Chapter 3, p. 46, Chapter 9, p. 229 and Chapter 12, p. 297; and 'Find the good purpose' in Helena Cornelius, Shoshana Faire & Sonya Hall, *Conflict Resolution Trainers' Manual: Eight Sessions*, Edition 4, Conflict Resolution Network, Australia, 1993, p.3.9.

[70] See Chapter 16, 'Projection', pp. 394–395. See also Helena Cornelius & Shoshana Faire, *Everyone Can Win*, Simon & Schuster, Australia, 1989, 'Willingness to resolve', pp. 104–116.

[71] Deborah Tannen, *You Just Don't Understand*, William Morrow & Co., U.S.A., 1990, p. 245–246.

[72] Tannen, *You Just Don't Understand*, p. 247–279.

[73] See also Chapter 9, 'Body language', p. 232.

[74] See Appendix 3.

[75] Eunson, pp. 117–119. Here he tables an extensive list of differences between males and females that researchers measured. Those which relate to gender differences in agreement and competition priorities are included in *The Gentle Revolution*, Chapter 6.

[76] B. W. Eakins & R. G. Eakins, *Sex Differences in Human Communication*, Houghton-Mifflin, U.S.A., 1976. Their research indicates that women use more disclaimers, qualifiers and hesitation than men. This research was confirmed by L. R. Smeltzer & K. W. Watson, 'Gender differences in verbal communication during negotiations', *Communication Research Reports*, no. 3, 1986, pp. 74–79.

[77] See Chapter 6, 'Report- or rapport-talk', p. 163.

[78] Harriet Goldhor Lerner, *The Dance of Anger*, Harper & Row, U.S.A., 1985, p. 96.

[79] Goldhor Lerner, p. 96.

[80] See Chapter 9.

[81] See also Chapter 4, 'Too many apologies', p. 84.

[82] L. R. Smeltzer & K. W. Watson, 'Gender differences in verbal communication during negotiations', *Communication Research Reports*, vol. 3, 1986, pp. 74–79.

[83] Tannen, *You Just Don't Understand*, pp. 74–95, in particular p. 77; and Tannen, *Talking from 9 to 5*, Virago Press, U.K., 1994, p. 71.

[84] P. Cozby, 'Self-disclosure: a literature review', *Psychological Bulletin*, no. 79, 1973, pp. 73–91. Cozby's review of research indicates that women usually find self-disclosure more socially acceptable than men do. See also J. H. Berg & V. J. Derlega, 'Themes in the study of self-disclosure', in *Self-disclosure: Theory, Research, and Therapy*, V. J. Derlega & J. H. Berg (eds), Plenum, U.S.A., 1987, pp. 117–130.

[85] See p. 57 and endnote 34. Also, K. E. Moyer, 'The physiology of aggression and the implications for aggression control' in *The Control of Aggression and Violence*, J. L. Singer (ed.), Academic Press, U.S.A., 1971, pp. 61–92. See also D. McGuiness (ed.), *Dominance, Aggression and War*, Paragon House, U.S.A., 1987.

[86] Tessa Souter, 'Girls will be boys', *HQ*, July/August 1995, p. 106. There are also reports of long-term effects of abnormally high dosages of female hormones on male foetuses. Diabetic mothers, with low levels of natural female hormones, had taken the synthetic female hormone diethylstilbestrol to avert spontaneous abortion — a common complication of their disease. Anne Moir and David Jessel report some evidence that boys born to these mothers grew up unusually shy and unassertive. They also quote the work of psychologist Dr June Reinisch, who says that we are all 'flavoured by our prenatal chemical development' and that low prenatal testosterone levels correlate with 'boys who were less aggressive and assertive, less athletic … [and] more willing than their peers to cooperate and sacrifice their own individualism to the will of the group'. Moir and Jessel conclude: 'What matters is the degree to which our embryonic brains are exposed to male hormone. The less they get, the more the natural, feminine mindset will survive.' Anne Moir & David Jessel, *Brainsex*, Mandarin, U.K., 1989, pp. 31–36.

See also J. M. Reinisch, 'Effects of prenatal hormone exposure on physical and psychological development in humans and animals: with a note on the state of the field', in *Hormones and Behaviour*, E. J. Sachar (ed.), Raven Press, U.S.A., 1996, pp. 69–94.

[87] See also Thomas F. Crum, *The Magic of Conflict*, Simon & Schuster, U.S.A., 1987, for an approach to conflict drawn from the martial art of Aikido. Thomas Crum uses the concept of 'flow' to describe a method for redirecting opposing energies in conflict.

[88] See also Figure 50, 'Controlling explosions', p. 274.

[89] See also Crum, pp.111–129.

## CHAPTER 7

[90] There are a number of excellent books on assertiveness, some specifically for women. For example, see Stanlee Phelps & Nancy Austin, *The Assertive Woman*, Impact, U.S.A., 1975.

For more on 'I' statements in the format explored here, see Helena Cornelius & Shoshana Faire, *Everyone Can Win*, Simon & Schuster, U.S.A., 1989, pp. 60–67, and Fiona Hollier, Kerrie Murray & Helena Cornelius, *Conflict Resolution Trainers' Manual: 12 Skills*, Conflict Resolution Network, Australia, 1993, pp. 4.1–4.15.

[91] The conflict resolution approach chosen correlates with gender differences. Munro, DiSalvo, Lewis & Borzi report that gender was found by a number of researchers to influence an individual's choice of style in a conflict situation. Men were reported 'to be more verbally aggressive … to compete more and compromise less … to emphasise dominance more and reflect less concern for relational outcomes … to confront more and avoid less.' Craig Munro, Vincent S. Di Salvo, James J. Lewis & Mark G. Borzi, 'Conflict behaviours of difficult subordinates: interactive effect of gender', *The Southern Communication Journal*, vol. 56, Fall, 1990, p. 13.

[92] See also Cornelius & Faire, pp. 130–149.

[93] See Figure 26, 'Handling a verbal attack', p. 115.

[94] C. W. Kennedy & C. T. Camden, 'Interruptions and nonverbal gender differences', *Journal of Nonverbal Behaviour*, no. 8, 1983, pp. 91–108.

[95] K. Townsend & W. Mohennan, *Australian Women's Yearbook 1995*, AGPS, Australia, 1995, p. 130.

[96] Amanda Sinclair, *Trials at the Top*, The Australian Centre, University of Melbourne, Australia, 1994, p. 5.

[97] David Karpin (ed.), *Enterprising Nation*, Industry Taskforce on Leadership and Management Skills, AGPS, Australia, 1995. *The Affirmative Action Act 1986* (Australian federal legislation) seeks to correct discriminatory practices. The Act is implemented through the Affirmative Action Agency in Australia, which does splendid ongoing work on structural change in organisations.

[98] L. Lippman, *The Aim is Understanding: Educational Techniques for a Multi-Cultural Society*, Australia & New Zealand Book Co., 1997, p. 2.

CHAPTER **8**

[99] Source: K. Townsend & W. McLennan, *Australian Women's Yearbook 1995*, AGPS, Australia, 1995, p. 130.

'Women continue to be under represented at all levels of management, with the greatest under representation occurring at the most senior management levels: Across all private sector industries, women represent 11 per cent of the most senior managers (Tier 1), 14 per cent of Tier 2 managers and 28 per cent of Tier 3 managers.' *Annual Report 1995–96*, Affirmative Action Agency, p. 19, based on surveys of Australian organisations with 100 or more employees.

[100] Charles Handy, *Beyond Certainty*, Arrow Books, U.K., 1996, p. 213.

[101] Eva Cox, *Leading Women*, Random House, Australia, 1996.

[102] Alex Kennedy, 'Ms Guv', *The Qantas Club* magazine, Dec./Jan. 1997.

[103] Australian Bureau of Statistics.

[104] Andrew Kakabadse & Charles Margerison, 'The female chief executive: an analysis of career progress and development needs', *Journal of Managerial Psychology*, vol. 2, no. 2, 1987, pp. 17–25.

[105] See Figure 37, 'Collaborative negotiation skills', p. 186.

[106] Amanda Sinclair, *Trials at the Top*, The Australian Centre, University of Melbourne, Australia, 1994, pp. 27–28. See also Chapter 4, 'Stumbling block 1: Being too modest', pp. 75–86.

[107] 'Research by Whitleson and others has proven that women have a comparatively larger, thicker and heavier corpus callosum, the connecting nerve fibres between the left and right hemisphere … Kimura

says, 'taken altogether, the evidence suggests that men's and women's brains are organised along different lines from very early in life'. Eric Jensen, *The Learning Brain*, Turning Point for Teachers, U.S.A., 1994, pp. 291–293.

'This more rapid, inter-hemispheric transit time means that many females can move ideas back and forth faster than the average male can.' Ned Herrman, *The Creative Brain*, The Ned Herrman Group, U.S.A., 1988, p. 36. Men engage more readily in what has become known as 'right' brain intuitive functions. I use inverted commas here because left and right hemispheres are not proven to be the exclusive spatial location of these different thinking functions. However, the brain undoubtedly has two very different methods of processing information.

[108] See Hermann, *The Creative Brain*.

[109] Other useful words to describe whole system awareness include open or closed systems, dynamics, movement, flow, cohesion and blockages. For an excellent description of burnout in pattern-making, systems thinking terminology see William L. White, *Incest in the Organisational Family*, Lighthouse Training Institute, U.S.A., 1986.

[110] Claire Burton, *The Promise and the Price*, Allen & Unwin, Australia, 1991, p. xi.

[111] See also Chapter 7, 'The win/win approach', pp. 183–187.

[112] See Figure 26, 'Handling a verbal attack', p. 115.

[113] Pat Heim & Susan Golant, *Smashing the Glass Ceiling*, Fireside, U.S.A., 1993, p. 48.

[114] Alastair Rylatt, *Learning Unlimited*, Business & Professional Publishing, U.S.A., 1994, p. 242.

CHAPTER 9

[115] See comment in endnote 118.

[116] Eunson says that men tend to 'talk about things and activities such as cars, sports, jobs and mechanical things', whereas women are more likely to want to 'talk about people, relationships, clothes, diets, feelings and children'. He also suggests that 'they use more psychological or emotional verbs such as "I feel", "I love", "I hope" (e.g. "I feel so sad").' Baden Eunson, *Dealing with Conflict*, John Wiley & Sons, Australia, 1997, pp. 119–120.

[117] Ken Wilber, *Sex, Ecology, Spirituality: The Spirit of Evolution*, Shambhala Publications, U.S.A., 1995.

[118] For ease of reading, I frequently shorten the way I refer to a person focused in the world of actions and objects to actions person, or actions focuser. I presume you will remember that their focus will also be on things. I prefer the use of the plural actions as there is less implication that the person is necessarily hyped up for activity. Those who are focused in the domain of actions and objects may or may not be driven by busyness and activity.

Despite the lack of symmetry, I use the singular feeling rather than feelings. I prefer to use feelings as a synonym for emotions. The inner focus of feeling that I am referring to in this book includes our sensitivity to more than just emotions. It may, for instance, include sensitivities to aesthetics, intuitions and consciousness. I often refer to people who place a high priority on the realm of feeling as feeling focusers.

[119] This is the principle of projection. See Chapter 16, ' Projection', pp. 394–395.

[120] A review of findings about gender and emotion appears in Leslie R. Brody & Judith A. Hall, 'Gender and emotion', *Handbook of Emotions*, Michael Lewis & Jeannette Haviland (eds), Guilford Press, U.S.A., 1993.

[121] See Chapter 6, 'Non-responsive or responsive to facial expressions', p. 155.

[122] See also Chapter 11, 'Stumbling block 3: Focus too open', pp. 257–260; Chapter 12, 'Stumbling

block 3: Contracted awareness under stress', pp. 281–283; and Chapter 13, 'Stumbling block 2: Merged attachment to others inhibits personal power', pp. 317–323.

[123] John Gray, *Men, Women and Relationships*, Hodder Headline, Australia, 1995, p. 65–66.

[124] See Figure 59, '"Why?" style questions that work', p. 369.

[125] John Haynes & Stephanie Charlesworth, *The Fundamentals of Family Mediation*, Federation Press, Australia, 1996, p. 203.

[126] See Figure 45, 'Katrina and Kevin's map', p. 239.

[127] For more detailed explanations of the mapping process, see Helena Cornelius & Shoshana Faire, *Everyone Can Win*, Simon & Schuster, Australia, 1989, pp. 117–129, and Fiona Hollier, Kerrie Murray & Helena Cornelius, *Conflict Resolution Trainers' Manual: 12 Skills*, Conflict Resolution Network, Australia, 1993, pp. 8.1–8.12.

[128] See Chapter 9, pp. 236–237, and Figure 59, '"Why?" style questions that work', p. 369.

## CHAPTER 10

[129] Daniel Goleman, *Emotional Intelligence*, Bloomsbury, U.K., 1996, p. 3–4.

[130] Goleman, p. 3–4.

[131] See Chapter 9, 'Mapping', pp. 233–240.

[132] Rosemary Howell, director of Strategic Action, introduced me to the decision tree developed by Liz Gray of Harvard School of Negotiation. My thanks to both people for many of the concepts in these two tables.

[133] See also Chapter 8, 'Whole system awareness', pp. 203–205.

[134] If people open up to you, particularly if you encourage them to do so, you would do well to respect their privacy and confidence religiously. This will keep you out of hot water and ensure you are trusted.

[135] Deborah Tannen makes this distinction. See her book, *You Just Don't Understand*, William Morrow & Co., U.S.A., 1989, pp. 110–120.

[136] For more on energetic approaches to mastering feelings see Julie Henderson, *The Lover Within*, Station Hill Press, U.S.A., 1987.

[137] My thanks to Christine James, director of Conflict Resolution Network Mediation Services, for this table.

[138] See also Chapter 4, 'Stumbling block 3: Continued resentment', pp. 91–93.

[139] John Welwood, *Journey of the Heart*, HarperCollins, U.S.A., 1990, p. 107.

## CHAPTER 11

[140] Anne Moir & David Jessel, *Brainsex*, Mandarin, U.K., 1989, pp. 58–59.

[141] Reported in *Brain Mind Bulletin*, vol. 20, no. 11, Aug. 1995, pp. 1, 8.

[142] Jutta Townes, 'Training the emotions', *Management*, Australian Institute of Management, Sept. 1996, p. 24.

[143] See Chapter 5, 'Shaming', p. 111–115.

[144] A field of counselling called *bio-energetics*, or *bio-dynamics*, focuses on this body–mind approach. An excellent starting text on the subject is Ken Dychtwald, *Bodymind*, Jove, U.S.A., 1977.

[145] For more on managing emotions, see Cornelius & Faire, pp. 87–103, and Fiona Hollier, Kerrie Murray & Helena Cornelius, *Conflict Resolution Trainers' Manual: 12 Skills*, Conflict Resolution Network, Australia, 1993, pp. 6.1–6.10.

[146] See Helena Cornelius & Shoshana Faire, *Everyone Can Win*, Simon & Schuster, Australia, 1989, pp. 60–67. See also Chapter 7, '"I" statements', pp. 176–180.

[147] See also Chapter 16, 'Projection', pp. 394–395.

[148] See Figure 26, 'Handling a verbal attack', p. 115, and Chapter 8, 'Poor listening skills', pp. 211–214.

[149] Clare Colins & Paul Chippendale, *New Wisdom II*, Acorn Publications, Australia, 1995, pp. 40–41. See also Appendix 2.

[150] See also comments in Chapter 3, 'A long history of suppressing women's self-esteem and self-actualisation needs', pp. 59–63.

## CHAPTER 12

[151] Susie Orbach & Luise Eichenbaum, *Between Women*, Arrow Books, U.S.A., 1987, p. 10.

[152] See also Chapter 13, 'Stumbling block 2: Merged attachment to others inhibits personal power', pp. 317–323.

[153] Orbach & Eichenbaum, p. 154.

[154] Nancy J. Chodorow, *Feminism and Psychoanalytic Theory*, Polity Press, U.S.A., 1989, p.110.

[155] Daniel J. Levinson, *The Seasons of a Man's Life*, Ballantine Books, U.S.A., 1978, pp. 91–93.

[156] For a report on research findings on this subject, see Priscilla Roberts and Peter M. Newton, 'Levinsonian studies of women's adult development', *Psychology and Ageing*, vol. 2, no. 2, 1987, pp. 154–163.

[157] Roberts & Newton, p. 163.

[158] See Chapter 6, 'Report- or rapport-talk', p. 163.

[159] People may hold similar values but disagree about how you exercise that value in the particular situation. These differing standards produce conflicting outcomes, making a win/win result difficult, but not impossible, to achieve.

For more on men's and women's differing ethical structures, see Adrienne Mendell, *How Men Think*, Ballantine Books, U.S.A., 1996, pp. 25, 155. See also Charles Hampden-Turner, 'The structure of entrapment: dilemmas standing in the way of women managers and strategies to resolve these', *The Deeper News*, vol. 5, no. 1, Jan. 1994.

[160] David Karpin (ed.), *Enterprising Nation*, Volume 2, Industry Taskforce on Leadership and Management Skills, AGPS, Australia, 1995, p. 1258.

[161] Craig Schindler & Gary Lapid, *The Great Turning*, Bear, U.S.A., 1989, Chapter 12 and p. 210.

[162] Charlotte Waterlow, *The Hinge of History*, One World Trust, U.K., 1995, p. 233.

[163] For more on the conflict between professional and feminine identity, see Leonie V. Still, *Where to from Here? The Managerial Woman in Transition*, Business & Professional Publishing, Australia, 1993.

[164] See Gordon F. Shea, *Mentoring*, Crisp Publications, U.S.A., 1992, for an excellent guide to the mentoring process.

## CHAPTER 13

[165] Two particularly helpful books on codependency are: Pia Mellody, *Facing Codependence*, HarperCollins, U.S.A., 1989, and Melody Beattie, *Codependent No More*, 2nd edn, Hazelden Foundation, U.S.A., 1992.

[166] This discussion on personal power expands the discussion of interpersonal power bases in Chapter 3, 'How power is exercised', pp. 65–69.

[167] For a detailed exploration of these conflicting processes, see Susie Orbach & Luise Eichenbaum, *Between Women*, Arrow Books, U.K., 1987.

[168] Anthony Robbins, *Unlimited Power*, Simon & Schuster, U.S.A., 1986, pp. 20–21.

[169] See Figure 19, 'Manipulation or influence', p. 70. See also Figure 23, '"Power over" — demand behaviour', p. 106, and Figure 24, '"Power with" — an alternative to demand behaviour', p. 107.

[170] For an outline of dysfunctional boundaries issues see Pia Melody, pp. 11–21.

[171] Carrie Herbert, *Sexual Harassment in Schools*, David Fulton Publishers, U.K., 1992, pp. 71–72.

[172] For a helpful discussion on women and competition, see Orbach & Eichenbaum, pp. 101–115.

[173] Papa and Natalle found men conflicting with other men will use little bargaining and women conflicting with other women will use a lot of bargaining, i.e. conversations to establish the nature of the compromise needed. Research results indicated that gender composition of the dyad [male/male or male/female or female/female] had a significant effect on the selection of the method of influence. Male/male dyads used assertiveness and reason consistently over time, while female/female dyads shifted from high levels of assertiveness and reason early in the negotiation to bargaining as the negotiation progressed. Male/female dyads used reason and bargaining throughout their interactions. See M. J. Papa & E. J. Natalle, 'Gender, strategy, selection and discussion satisfaction in interpersonal conflict', *Western Journal of Speech Communication*, no. 53, 1989.

[174] Bill Scott, *The Skills of Negotiating*, Management Skills Library, U.S.A., 1981, distinguishes between 'towards agreement' and 'to our advantage' styles of negotiating. Another important text on negotiating strategy is Roger Fisher, *Getting to YES: Negotiating Agreement Without Giving In*, Century Business, U.K., 1981.

### CHAPTER 14

[175] Amanda Sinclair, *Trials at the Top*, The Australian Centre, University of Melbourne, Australia, 1994.

[176] See John Gray, *Men are from Mars, Women are from Venus*, HarperCollins, U.K., 1992, pp. 248–252.

[177] See also Chapter 5, 'Rejection of unproven authority', pp. 130–132.

[178] See Chapter 15, 'Step 3', pp. 370–371.

[179] Charles Hampden-Turner, 'The structure of entrapment: dilemmas standing in the way of women managers and strategies to resolve these', *The Deeper News*, vol. 5, no. 1, 1995.

[180] This distinction is well put by Bruce Kokopeli and George Lakey in *Leadership for Change: Towards a Feminist Model*, New Society, U.S.A., 1984.

[181] For an introduction to the skills of mediation, see Helena Cornelius & Shoshana Faire, *Everyone Can Win*, Simon & Schuster, Australia, 1989, pp. 150–164. For professional study, there are many texts, including Andrew Floyer Acland, *A Sudden Outbreak of Common Sense*, Hutchison, U.K., 1990; John M. Haynes & Stephanie Charlesworth, *The Fundamentals of Family Mediation*, Federation Press, Australia, 1996; Christopher W. Moore, *The Mediation Process*, Jossey-Bass, U.S.A., 1986.

[182] Mediators' strategies that can minimise the impact of power imbalances may include discussing issues privately, before formal mediation; initial statements made to the mediator rather than to each other; mediation ground rules that give each person equal rights to speak and prevent the use of interruptions or intimidation tactics; provision for the parties to have a supporter; the mediator's rewording of emotive statements into neutral language; and probing questions to draw out the real issues and the possible solutions. In some circumstances the mediator might keep the parties separate for some or all of the process, with the mediator shuttling between them.

While the mediator uses these methods to minimise the impact of a power imbalance, unless the mediator is astute, those less able to assert themselves may have difficulty in getting a totally just agreement and those who have more power may perhaps be less than completely honest and open.

See John Crawley, *Mediation UK: Training Manual in Community Mediation Skills*, Mediation UK, U.K., 1995, pp. 203–222.

[183] For a comprehensive guide to consensus decision-making, see Michel Avery et al., *Building United Judgment*, The Center for Conflict Resolution, U.S.A., 1981.

[184] David W. Johnson & Frank P. Johnson, *Joining Together: Group Theory and Group Skills*, Prentice-Hall, U.S.A., 1987, p. 102.

[185] Source: Johnson & Johnson, p. 103, and Kerrie Murray, director of Conflict Resolution Network Consulting Group. See also Figure 21, 'Control in consensus decision-making', p. 82.

## CHAPTER 15

[186] See Chapter 2, pp. 29–31, for a more detailed discussion of these considerations.

[187] See Figure 35, 'Levels of conflict', p. 181.

[188] Morton Deutsch, *Resolution of Conflict*, Yale University, U.S.A., 1993, p. 16.

[189] Leon Festinger, *A Theory of Cognitive Dissonance*, Tavistock Publications, U.S.A., 1959.

[190] Robert B. Cialdini, *Influence: How and Why People Agree to Things*, Quill, U.S.A., 1984, p. 66.

[191] Hugh Mackay, *Why Don't People Listen?*, Pan Macmillan, Australia, 1994, p. 214.

[192] Festinger, p. 22.

[193] See Appendix 4 for more strategies to enhance gender equity.

[193] John Haynes & Stephanie Charlesworth, *The Fundamentals of Family Mediation*, The Federation Press, Australia, 1996, p. 202.

[195] Other conflict resolution theorists have used different terminology for the same distinction. You may prefer one of the following:

| COMPARISONS IN CONFLICT RESOLUTION TECHNOLOGY | |
|---|---|
| John Haynes | means ◀▶ ends |
| Roger Fisher & William Ury | positions ◀▶ interests |
| Greg Tillett | expectations or demands ◀▶ needs |
| Henena Cornelius & Shoshana Faire | solutions ◀▶ needs and concerns |

*Figure 70: Comparisons of conflict resolution terminology*

[196] 'Down' here is somewhat arbitrary. Neurolinguistic programming (NLP) practitioners, in describing a hierarchy of ideas, place the abstract level at the *top* of the hierarchy and specific details at the *bottom*. I prefer to think of the movement of communication into the abstract as 'going down below the surface', diving into deeper layers of self and then returning to the concrete here and now to solve the problem. NLP practitioners describe the process of exposing values as chunking *up* or grouping to take in the big picture by asking questions about particular situations: 'What is this an example of?', 'For what purpose…?', 'What is your intention…?'. These are particularly useful questions for getting to values. The process of movement from the concrete to the abstract and back again could also be

seen as circular or even spiralling, as it may occur a number of times before the problem is successfully resolved. Source: Tad James, Monika Gaede.

[197] See also Chapter 9, 'Mapping', pp. 233–240, and Figure 57, 'Clarifying and quantifying needs, concerns and values', p. 366.

Note: The letters in brackets in Figure 57 refer to examples in the text that will help you incorporate values into the mapping method. See also Helena Cornelius & Shoshana Faire, *Everyone Can Win*, Simon & Schuster, Australia, 1989, Chapter 8, pp. 117–129.

[198] See Appendix 3.

[199] See the horizontal dotted line in Figure 57, 'Clarifying and quantifying needs, concerns and values', p. 366.

Note: The letters in brackets in Figure 55 refer to examples in the text.

[200] Haynes & Charlesworth, *The Fundamentals of Family Mediation*, p. 200.

[201] Carol Becker et al., 'From stuck debate to new conversation on controversial issues: a report from the public conversations project', in *Cultural Resistance: Challenging Beliefs About Men, Women and Therapy*, Kathy Weingarten (ed.), *Journal of Feminist Family Therapy*, vol. 1/2, no. 7, The Haworth Press Inc, U.S.A., 1995.

[202] Stephen Mitchell (trans.), *Tao Te Ching*, Harper & Row, U.S.A., 1988, p. 17.

[203] For an introduction to the skills of mediating and facilitating, see Cornelius & Faire, pp. 150–164.

[204] Many thanks to Peter Melzer for contributing this list of questions to the book.

CHAPTER **16**

[205] Susan Brownmiller, *Femininity*, Hamish Hamilton Ltd, U.K., 1984, p. 28.

[206] Nancy Chodorow, *The Reproduction of Mothering*, University of California Press, U.K., 1978, p. 214.

[207] Karen Hornig, *Feminine Psychology*, Norton, U.S.A., 1967, p. 113.

[208] Betsy Roszak & Theodore Roszak, *Masculine/Feminine*, HarperCollins, U.S.A., 1969, p. 99.

[209] Gloria Steinem in the foreword to Jean Shimoda Bolen, *The Goddess in Everywoman*, Harper & Row, U.S.A., 1984, p. xi.

[210] Fiona Hollier, Kerrie Murray & Helena Cornelius, *Conflict Resolution Trainers' Manual: 12 Skills*, Conflict Resolution Network, Australia, 1993 p. 7.5.

[211] Simone de Beauvoir, *The Second Sex*, Knopf, U.S.A., 1953, quoted in Betsy Roszak & Theodore Roszak, *Masculine/Feminine*, p. 150.

[212] Simone de Beauvoir, pp. 154–155.

[213] June Singer, *Androgyny*, Sigo Press, U.S.A., 1976, p. 200.

APPENDICES

[214] Clare Colins & Paul Chippendale, *New Wisdom II*, Acorn, Australia, 1995, pp. 40–41.

[215] Colins & Chippendale, pp. 42–43.

[216] Isabel Myers Briggs, *Gifts Differing*, Consulting Psychologists Press, U.S.A., 1980, pp. 34–35.

[217] Some refinements were made to the Gender values quiz, pp. 21–25 following our findings in this survey.

# BIBLIOGRAPHY

Aburdene, P. & Naisbitt, J., *Megatrends for Women*, Random House, U.K., 1993. Future directions for women.

Acland, A. F., *A Sudden Outbreak of Common Sense*, Hutchison, U.K., 1990. One of my favourite books on mediation. It's now out of print, but much of the content is published under a new title:

Acland, A. F., *Resolving Disputes Without Going to Court*, Random House, U.K., 1995.

Affirmative Action Agency, *Annual Report 1995–1996*, Commonwealth of Australia, 1996. An overview of the position of women in Australia and initiatives to overcome problems.

Affirmative Action Agency, *Good Ideas 1995–1996*, Commonwealth of Australia, 1996. Gender equity initiatives which are being successfully implemented.

Andrews, P. H., 'Gender differences in persuasive communication and attribution of success and failure', *Human Communication Research*, vol. 13, no. 3, 1987.

Australian Federation of Business and Professional Women Inc., *Why Women Should Play Snakes & Ladders: The Enterprise Bargaining Game*, K. Tully (ed.), Ambassador Press, Australia, 1994.

Avery, M. et al., *Building United Judgment*, The Center for Conflict Resolution, U.S.A., 1981. A comprehensive guide to consensus decision-making.

Beattie, M., *Codependent No More*, Hazelden, U.S.A., 1992. A bestselling primer on taking care of your own needs in relationships.

Beauvoir, S. de, *The Second Sex*, Knopf, U.S.A., 1953. Originally published in French in 1949, de Beauvoir was an early writer on feminine gender issues.

Belenky, M. F., Clinchy, B. M., Goldberger, N. R., *Women's Ways of Knowing: The Development of Self, Voice and Mind*, Basic Books, U.S.A., 1969.

Berryman-Fink, C. & Brunner, C. C., 'The effects of sex of source and target on interpersonal conflict management styles', *The Southern Speech Communication Journal*, no. 53, Fall, 1987.

Biddulph, S., *Manhood*, Finch, Australia, 1994. Sound and reasonable perspectives on the current men's movement.

Blainey, J., Davis, K. & Goodwill, B., *Valuing Diversity*, Working Together, Australia, 1995.

Bolen, M. D. & Shimoda, J., *The Goddess in Everywoman*, Harper & Row, U.S.A., 1984.

Borisoff, D. & Victor, D. A., 'Conflict management: a communication skills approach', *Communication Monographs*, no. 47, 1980.

Borisoff, D., & Victor, D. A., *Conflict Management and Communication Skills Approach*, Prentice Hall, U.S.A., 1989.

Brody, L. R. & Hall, J. A., 'Gender and emotion', in Lewis, M. & Haviland, J. (eds), *Handbook of Emotions*, Guilford Press, U.S.A., 1993.

Brownmiller, S., *Femininity*, Hamish Hamilton Ltd, U.K., 1984.

Burggraf, C. S. & Sillars, A. L., 'A critical examination of sex differences in marital communication', *Communication Research*, vol. 54, Sept. 1987.

Burrell, N. A., Donohue, W. A. & Allen, M., 'Gender-based perceptual biases in mediation', *Communication Research*, vol. 15, no. 4, 1988.

Burton, C., *The Promise and the Price*, Allen & Unwin, Australia, 1991. Explores the relationship between gender and power in organisations and EEO in Australia.

Canary, D. J., Cunningham, E. M. & Cody, M. J., 'Goal types, gender, and locus of control in managing interpersonal conflict', *Communication Research*, vol. 15, no. 4, 1988.

Chafetz, J., Sex and Advantage, Rowman & Alanheld, U.S.A., 1984. Quoted in Ken Wilber, *Sex, Ecology, Spirituality: The Spirit of Evolution*, Shambhala Publications, U.S.A., 1995.

Chater, K. & Gaster, R., *The Equality Myth*, Allen & Unwin, Australia, 1995. Draws modern communication theory into the area of gender relationships.

Chodorow, N. J., *Feminism and Psychoanalytic Theory*, Polity Press, U.K. 1989. An authoritative feminist work.

Cialdini, R. B., *Influence: How and Why People Agree to Things*, Quill, U.S.A., 1984. Principles of effective persuasion — what makes people say yes and what makes them say no.

Colins, C. & Chippendale, P., *New Wisdom II*, Acorn Publications, Australia, 1995. Discusses values and the role they play in personal and organisational life.

Connell, R. W., *Masculinities*, Allen & Unwin, Australia, 1995. Issues facing men in modern society.

Conrad, C., 'Communication in conflict: style–strategy relationships', *Communication Monographs*, vol. 58, 1991.

Cornelius, H. & Faire, S., *Everyone Can Win*, Simon & Schuster, Australia, 1989. The conflict resolution twelve skills approach of the Conflict Resolution Network is clearly outlined and provides an expansion of the conflict resolution concepts in *The Gentle Revolution*.

Cox, E., *Leading Women*, Random House, Australia, 1996. The potential and limitations in women's character, as women become agents for societal change in a masculine-oriented environment.

Crawley, J., *Mediation U.K.: Training Manual in Community Mediation Skills*, Mediation U.K., U.K., 1995. One of the most comprehensive resources available for learning and teaching mediation skills.

Crum, T. F., *The Magic of Conflict*, Simon & Schuster, U.S.A., 1987. The Aiki approach to conflict, which uses the concept of flow for redirecting the energies of conflict situations.

Deutsch, M., *Resolution of Conflict*, Yale University, U.S.A., 1993. Conflict resolution theory.

Dinnerstein, D., *The Rocking of the Cradle and the Ruling of the World*, Harper & Row, U.S.A., 1976. An authoritative feminist work.

Duff, C. S., *When Women Work Together*, WomenWorks Inc., U.S.A., 1993. Getting along with female co-workers, understanding their comfort zones and overcoming the pitfalls.

Duxbury, E. L. & Higgins, C. A., 'Gender differences in work-family conflict', *Journal of Applied Psychology*, vol. 76, no. 1, 1991.

Dychtwald, K., *Bodymind*, Jove, U.S.A., 1977. Through body–mind awareness you can learn how the physical body mirrors mental states.

Eunson, B., *Dealing with Conflict*, John Wiley & Sons, Australia, 1997. Full of useful graphs and tables, Eunson brings together research and theories from a wide variety of disciplines.

Fisher, R. & Ury, W., *Getting to YES: Negotiating Agreement Without Giving In*, Century Business, U.K., 1981. An excellent text on negotiating for mutual agreement.

Fisher, R. & Brown, S., *Getting Together*, Houghton Mifflin, U.S.A., 1988. Communication skills.

Friedan, B., *The Second Stage*, Summit Books, U.S.A., 1981. The struggle to reconcile new-won freedom in the workplace with needs for love, children, family and home.

Garner, H., *The First Stone*, Pan Macmillan, Australia, 1995. The story of a sexual harassment allegation and its affect on the offender.

Goleman, D., *Emotional Intelligence*, Bloomsbury, U.K., 1996. Claims the key to a successful life is not just IQ, but also self-awareness, impulse control, persistence, self-motivation, empathy and social deftness.

Gray, J., *Men are from Mars, Women are from Venus*, HarperCollins, U.K., 1992. A useful and much-quoted reference on differences between men and women in communication patterns in family life.

Gray, J., *Men, Women and Relationships*, Hodder Headline, Australia, 1995. The effect of gender differences on intimate relationships.

Grosz, E., *Jacques Lacan*, Allen & Unwin, Australia, 1990. Useful introduction to feminist thought.

Hampden-Turner, C., 'The structure of entrapment: dilemmas standing in the way of women managers and strategies to resolve these', *The Deeper News*, Global Business Network Publication, vol. 5, no. 1, 1994. The thesis is that corporations need gender diversity to prosper.

Handy, C., *Beyond Certainty*, Arrow Books, U.K., 1996. Highly respected business futurist.

Handy, C., *The Empty Raincoat*, Arrow Books, U.K., 1995. An outstanding analysis of the paradoxes facing the individual and society in creating balanced lives that serve the community.

Haynes, J. M. & Charlesworth, S., *The Fundamentals of Family Mediation*, Federation Press, Australia, 1996. A very helpful text on mediation.

Heim, P. & Golant, S., *Smashing the Glass Ceiling*, Fireside, U.S.A., 1993.

Helgesen, S., *The Female Advantage*, Doubleday/Currency, U.S.A., 1990. Examines how women lead differently from men and views these differences as strengths not weaknesses.

Henderson, J., *The Lover Within*, Station Hill Press, U.S.A., 1987. This book is about understanding ourselves as energy and contains exercises for improving our energy relationships to the world.

Herbert, C., *Sexual Harassment in Schools*, David Fulton Publishers, U.K., 1992. A handbook on how to recognise and deal with issues of sexual harassment.

Herrman, N., *The Creative Brain*, The Ned Herrman Group, U.S.A., 1988. Provides thought-provoking insights into how brain dominance affects behaviour.

Hollier, F., Murray, K. & Cornelius, H., *Conflict Resolution Trainers' Manual: 12 Skills*, Conflict Resolution Network, Australia, 1993. The twelve skills approach to teaching conflict resolution.

Hornig, K., *Feminine Psychology*, Norton, U.S.A., 1967. Seminal feminist text.

Jensen, E., *The Learning Brain*, Turning Point for Teachers, U.S.A., 1994. Research findings on the structural and processing differences between male and female brains.

Johnson, D. W. & Johnson, F. P., *Joining Together: Group Theory and Group Skills*, Prentice-Hall, U.S.A., 1987.

Julius Matthews, J., *Good and Mad Women*, Allen & Unwin, Australia, 1984. An exposition on the historical change that has taken place in the definitions of femininity.

Jung, C. J., 'The Syzygy: Anima and Animus', in *The Collected Works of C. J. Jung*, Vol. IX II, Routledge Kegan Paul, U.K., 1959.

Karpin, D. (ed.), *Enterprising Nation*, Industry Taskforce on Leadership and Management Skills, AGPS, Australia, 1995. In-depth analysis of Australian workplace practices and trends.

Kaufman Hall, V., *Women Transforming the Workplace*, University of Western Sydney, Australia, 1995. Doctoral thesis on twelve women's experiences using archetypes.

Koberg, C. S. & Chusmir, L. H., 'Relationship between sex role conflict and work-related variables: gender and hierarchical differences', *The Journal of Social Psychology*, vol. 129, no. 6, 1989.

Kokopeli, B. & Lakey, G., *Leadership for Change: Towards a Feminist Model*, New Society Publishers, U.S.A., 1984. Uses a feminist perspective to analyse and share leadership functions.

Lerner, H. G., *The Dance of Anger*, Harper & Row, U.S.A., 1985. Shows women how to turn anger into a constructive force for reshaping their lives.

Levinson, D. J., *The Seasons of a Man's Life*, Ballantine Books, U.S.A., 1978. Describes specific periods of and transitions in men's lives and the developmental tasks of each stage of life.

Lewin, R., 'All for one, one for all', *New Scientist*, 14 Dec. 1996. Explains superorganisms.

Mackay, H., *Why Don't People Listen?*, William Morrow, Australia, 1994. Communication issues.

Marshall, J., 'Viewing organisational communication from a feminist perspective: a critique and some offerings', in *Communication Yearbook 16*, S. A. Deetz (ed.), Sage Publications, U.S.A., 1993.

McKinney, D. H. & Donaghy, W. C., 'Dyad gender structure, uncertainty reduction, and self-disclosure during initial interaction', *Interpersonal Communication: Evolving Interpersonal Relationships*, Kalbfleisch, P. J. (ed.), Lawrence Erlbaum Associates, U.S.A., 1993.

Mead, M., *Male and Female: A Study of the Sexes in a Changing World*, Penguin, U.S.A., 1950. A sociological study of the interdependence of male and female roles in primitive and modern societies.

Mead, M., *Sex and Temperament*, 2nd edn, William Morrow, U.S.A., 1950. Indicates how culture imposes patterns of behaviour on men and women.

Melody, P., *Facing Codependence*, HarperCollins, U.S.A., 1989. Traces the origins of codependence to childhood abuse and offers an effective path to recovery.

Mendell, A., *How Men Think: The Seven Essential Rules for Making it in a Man's World*, Ballantine Books, U.S.A., 1996. Good advice for women making it in a male-dominated working culture.

Mesch, D. J. & Dalton, D. R., 'Gender context in resolution of American workplace conflicts', *The Journal of Social Psychology*, vol. 129, no. 5, 1989.

Mills, A. J. & Chiaramonte, P., 'Organisation as gendered communication act', *Canadian Journal of Communication*, vol. 16, 1991.

Mitchell, S. (trans.), *Tao Te Ching*, Harper & Row, U.S.A., 1988. Chinese Taoist philosophy.

Moir, A. & Jessel, D., *Brainsex*, Mandarin, U.K., 1989. Research of the differences between male and female skills, behaviours and brain function.

Moore, C. W., *The Mediation Process*, Jossey-Bass, U.S.A., 1986. An authoritative text on mediation.

Moore, J. H., *But What About Men?*, Ashgrove Press, U.K., 1989. Discusses men's potential redundancy in future societies of liberated women if they fail to redefine themselves.

Munro, C., Di Salvo, V. S., Lewis, J. J. & Borzi, M. G., 'Conflict behaviours of difficult subordinates: interactive effect of gender', *The Southern Communication Journal*, no. 56, Fall, 1990.

Natalle, E. J., 'Gender and communication theory', *Communication Education*, no. 40, 1991.

Nobel, V., *Mother Peace*, Harper & Row, U.S.A., 1958. Mythological stereotypes of women.

Orbach, S. & Eichenbaum, L., *Between Women*, Arrow Books, U.K., 1987. What women won't say to each other in relationships and what goes wrong because they don't.

Papa, M. J. & Natalle, E. J., 'Gender, strategy selection and discussion satisfaction in interpersonal conflict', *Western Journal of Speech Communication*, no. 53, 1989.

Phelps, S. & Austin, N., *The Assertive Woman*, Impact, U.S.A., 1975. An excellent guide to assertiveness, relating its instruction to the problems women face in work and personal life.

Pinkola Estes, C., *Women Who Run With the Wolves*, Random House, U.K., 1992. A revaluing of women's intuitive wisdom, instinctive self-confidence and wildness.

Roberts, P. & Newton, P. M., 'Levinsonian studies of women's adult development', *Psychology and Ageing*, vol. 2, no. 2, 1987. A report on research findings on the subject of women's career goals.

Rosenthal, D. B. & Hautaluoma, J., 'Effects of importance of issues, gender and power of contenders on conflict management style', *The Journal of Social Psychology*, vol. 128, no. 5, 1988.

Roszak, B. & Roszak, T., *Masculine/Feminine*, HarperCollins, U.S.A., 1969.

Rylatt, A., *Learning Unlimited*, Business & Professional Publishing, Australia, 1994. Requirements for an organisation committed to learning and promoting mentoring and coaching.

Sagan, C. & Druyan, A., *Shadows of Forgotten Ancestors*, Random House, Australia, 1992. The evolution of animal behaviour and its relationship to the human species.

Schindler, C. & Lapid, G., *The Great Turning*, Bear, U.S.A., 1989. Visions of a 'great turning' in the way people and nations manage conflicts.

Schockley-Zalabak, P. S. & Morley, D. D., 'Sex differences in conflict style preferences', *Communication Research Reports*, vol. 1, no. 1, 1984.

Schutz, W., *The Truth Option*, Ten Speed Press, U.S.A., 1984. Common workplace relationship issues. Excellent sections on inclusion, openness and control are relevant for consensus decision-making.

Scott, B., *The Skills of Negotiating*, Management Skills Library, U.S.A., 1981. Makes the distinction between 'towards agreement' and 'to our advantage' styles of negotiating.

Shea, G. F., *Mentoring*, Crisp Publications, U.S.A., 1992. An excellent guide to the mentoring process.

Sinclair, A., *Trials at the Top*, The Australian Centre, University of Melbourne, Australia, 1994. Executive officers talk about men, women and the Australian culture.

Singer, J., *Androgyny: The Opposites Within*, Sigo Press, U.S.A., 1989. An outstanding analysis of psychic wholeness and the integration of masculine and feminine into the personality.

Smelzer, L. R. & Watson, K. W., 'Gender differences in verbal communication during negotiations', *Communication Research Reports*, vol. 3, 1986.

Souter, T., 'Girls will be boys', *HQ*, Jul./Aug. 1995. Reports on the effects of intake of artificial male hormones by lesbian women.

Spender, D., *The Writing or the Sex*, Permagon Press, Australia, 1989. Looks at masculine bias in written communication.

Stewart, L. P. & Ting-Toomey, S., *Communication, Gender and Sex Roles in Diverse Interaction Contexts*, Ablex Publishing Corporation, U.S.A., 1987.

Still, L. V., *Where to from Here? The Managerial Woman in Transition*, Business & Professional Publishing, Australia, 1993. Current status of women managers and their quest for identity.

Tannen, D., *Talking from 9 to 5*, Virago Press, U.K., 1994. Gender communication differences in the workplace; a 'this is how it is' rather than a 'how to' guide.

Tannen, D., *You Just Don't Understand*, William Morrow & Co., U.S.A., 1990. Gender communication differences.

Townes, J., 'Training the emotions', *Management*, Australian Institute of Management, Sept. 1996. The importance of well-handled emotions in the workplace.

Townsend, K. & McLennan, W., *Australian Women's Yearbook 1995*, AGPS, Australia, 1995. Statistics on women's position across a broad range of areas.

Welwood, J., *Journey of the Heart*, HarperCollins, U.K., 1990. A wonderful book on intimate male–female relationships.

White, W. L., *Incest in the Organisational Family*, Lighthouse Training Institute, U.S.A., 1986. Analysis of burnout in systems terminology.

Wilber, K., *Sex, Ecology, Spirituality: The Spirit of Evolution*, Shambhala Publications, U.S.A., 1995. A scholarly, in-depth philosophical analysis of life and the evolutionary process.

Wood, W., 'Meta-analytic review of sex differences in group performance', *Psychological Bulletin*, vol. 102, no. 1, 1987.

# ACKNOWLEDGMENTS

This book surveyed the thoughts and insights of people from a wide cross-section of employment fields. There are an enormous number of contributors to thank for their input. First, thank you to the 550 people who responded to my 'Men and Women at Work' survey and the later 'Gender Values' quiz. Many others also gave their time with enormous generosity for interviews, feedback and a whole heap of other support, both personal and practical. Thank you to everyone and particularly to:

Alan Bassal, Integra, for inviting me to join him in piloting this material in organisations.

Peter Becke, university and TAFE lecturer in English, for advice on academic presentation.

Claire Boone, for her enormous support in the final stages of the editing process.

Susan Brehm, training consultant, for her insights into workplace issues.

Michelle Brenner, mediator, for her insights into Asian cultures.

Jenny Brice, organisation development manager, CSR Timber, for her model of the roles in which men cast women colleagues to make sense of the relationship.

Stella Cornelius, co-director of Conflict Resolution Network, for emotional, conceptual and editorial support every step of the way through the two and a half year project.

Deborah Cornelius, journalist, for composing four of the quizzes in the book and for editorial advice.

Louise Crossley, for her fascinating anecdotes from her time as Mawson station leader in Antarctica.

Mike Davies, management consultant, for his feedback on men's fears of harassment allegations.

Professor Ed Davis, Macquarie University, for support in distributing the 'Men and Women at work' survey.

Marie de Lepervanche, for her clear perspectives on feminist thought.

Brigitta Doyle, senior editor at Simon & Schuster, for copy editing and her unfailing humour and consideration of my needs.

Shoshana Faire, Conflict Resolution Network Professional Facilitators, for ongoing conceptual support and relevant anecdotes.

Monica Gaede, counsellor and consultant, for insights into values research and NLP parallels.

Robyn Gaspari, Conflict Resolution Network Community Based Projects, for distributing questionnaires and for references on values and ethics.

Walter Gaspari, Conflict Resolution Network Community Based Projects, for leading me gently through the woods of government statistical surveys on the workplace.

Patricia Gaut, author and writing teacher, for inspiring my writing process.

Anne Gillespie, for insights into glass ceiling issues in upper management.

Lesley Gillett, consultant, for steering me through written material in the field of language differences.

Glebe Unit, NSW Fire Brigade, for stories and insights into women joining traditionally male work teams.

Gill Goater, consultant, for pointing me to useful literature and for ongoing support of the writing process.

Patricia Harris, Attorney's General's Department, for her insights into grievance handling procedures.

Catherine Heilemann, for support in distributing surveys and questionnaires, and insights into workplace issues.

Shirley Heilemann, my research assistant, for meticulous and generous support and knowledgeable discussion throughout the first year of the project.

Jill Hickson, literary agent, for her trust in me, her advice and her support for the project.

Fiona Hollier, consultant, for her profound editorial comments that inspired me to try a little harder.

Rosemary Howell, Strategic Action, for training perspectives on gender issues.

Catherine Huntington, Huntington Research, for generously sharing her professional expertise to develop questionnaires and present statistical findings.

Christine James, Conflict Resolution Network Mediation Services, for ongoing conceptual support and creative elaborations of emerging ideas, and for being there when the going was rough.

Joseph Loewy, for conceptual input on masculine perspectives and his contributions to the front cover.

Rhonda Macken, musician and author, for invaluable feedback on early drafts.

Sandy May, consultant, for editorial comments and leading a brainstorming session with twenty-five readers of the first draft.

Dawn Maynard, NSW Fire Brigade for her perspectives on being a female firefighter in a traditionally and still largely male realm, and for allowing me into her workplace for an inside view.

Dr. Peter Melser, Change Works, for his groundbreaking contributions on dialogue as an approach to the resolution of values conflicts.

Susan Morris-Yates, when commissioning editor at Simon & Schuster, for conceiving the book.

Judy Mullins, consultant, for good, juicy chats on gender problems and her positive outlook on future societies.

John Murray, company secretary, for sharing his experience of male–female differences and relating it to the matrix presented here.

Kerrie Murray, Conflict Resolution Network Consulting Group, for her concepts on a behavioural approach to the resolution of values conflicts.

Nerida Pierce for her experience in large organisations and the gender mis-communications that can occur there.

Kate Ramsay, And Consulting, for her inspirational approach to coaching Australian women leaders.

Angela Rossmanith, author, for her contributions to the development of the eight gender-related values and feedback on the first draft.

Alastair Rylatt, Excel Human Resource Development, for his advice on the book's structure, and his depth of understanding of differential brain functions.

Shirley Saunders, University of Technology, Sydney for her help with relevant research in the area of gender differences in communication and distribution of questionnaires.

Lynne Segal, when commissioning editor at Simon & Schuster, for editing advice from her wealth of experience and her warm and positive encouragement through the hard times that face any writer.

Jane Sieber, for support on the technology of computer wizardry.

Courtney Taylor, for her perspectives on working in an all-male area.

Jim Taylor, SE Qld Electricity Board, for support in piloting the questionnaire to 'blokes'.

Kerry Turnbull, designer, for her perspectives on discrimination faced by young women in the workplace.

Malcolm Turnbull, for perspectives on gender issues in government employment from a male point of view, and a stunning and detailed critique of the first draft from a man's perspective.

Martin Turnbull, Conflict Resolution Network, for editorial input and his perspectives on younger men's issues.

Candy Tymson, Tymson Communications, for fine-tuning the 'Gender Values' quiz, piloting it in her Gender Games workshops and to her extensive mailing list and organising responses for statistical analysis.

Stuart Walker, company secretary, for examples of gender conflicts amongst fellow professionals.

Julie Wells, training consultant and counsellor, for her astute observations on differences between men and women working as a team.

Maggie Wildblood, human resources consultant, for her insights into gender issues dealt with by HR officers.

Sharon Wilson, for her enthusiastic and insightful debate of the issues raised in developing the concepts.

Robyn Woolley, TAFE NSW, who highlighted issues for women TAFE students.

Thank you, too, to the many friends who, whenever they heard a good gender story, remembered me and passed it on, and to the friends who offered references, book loans, gifts of books, pamphlets, articles and contacts. Reassured by the broad perspective they brought to my writing, I did my best to distil from their wealth of material the structure and content of this book. At the time of writing, my office is still a right proper mess, but each piece of paper these wonderful people generated held a gem. I only wish I'd had space for them all.

Correspondence with Helena Cornelius
or any of the above contacts can be addressed to:

**The Conflict Resolution Network**
PO Box 1016   Chatswood   NSW 2057   Australia

# LIST OF FIGURES

# INDEX

LIBRARY
ST. LOUIS COMMUNITY COLLEGE
AT FLORISSANT VALLEY